D0402863

Return to Armageddon

*The United States
and the Nuclear Arms Race,* 1981-1999

RONALD E. POWASKI

OXFORD
UNIVERSITY PRESS

2000

OXFORD

UNIVERSITY PRESS

Oxford   New York

Athens   Auckland   Bangkok   Bogotá   Buenos Aires   Calcutta
Cape Town   Chennai   Dar es Salaam   Delhi   Florence   Hong Kong   Istanbul
Karachi   Kuala Lumpur   Madrid   Melbourne   Mexico City   Mumbai
Nairobi   Paris   São Paulo   Singapore   Taipei   Tokyo   Toronto   Warsaw

and associated companies in
Berlin   Ibadan

Copyright © 2000 by Ronald E. Powaski

Published by Oxford University Press, Inc.
198 Madison Avenue, New York, New York 10016

Oxford is a registered trademark of Oxford University Press

All rights reserved. No part of this publication may be reproduced,
stored in a retrieval system, or transmitted, in any form or by any means,
electronic, mechanical, photocopying, recording, or otherwise,
without the prior permission of Oxford University Press.

Library of Congress Cataloging-in-Publication Data
Powaski, Ronald E.
Return to Armageddon: the United States and the nuclear arms race, 1981-
1999/
Ronald E. Powaski.
p. cm.
Includes bibliographical references and index.
ISBN 0-19-510382-3
1. United States—Military policy. 2. Arms race—History—20th century.
3. Nuclear Weapons. I. Title.
UA23.P624 1999
327.1'747—dc21   99-19999

Book design by Adam B. Bohannon

9 8 7 6 5 4 3 2 1
Printed in the United States of America
on acid-free paper

To
Daniel Weidenthal, M.D.
and William Reinhart, M.D.

Contents

Preface

When I began writing this book in 1995, I was optimistic that the nuclear arms race was winding down. The Cold War was over. Eight years had passed since the administration of President Ronald Reagan had concluded the Intermediate-range Nuclear Forces (INF) Treaty, which eliminated, for the first time, a whole class of nuclear weapons. By 1993, Reagan's successor, George Bush, had completed the negotiation of two Strategic Arms Reduction Treaties (START I and START II), which together would bring about massive reductions in the strategic nuclear arsenals of the two former adversaries. In START II, the two sides would lower their total nuclear warheads to between 3,800 and 4,250 warheads by the year 2000, and to between 3,000 and 3,500 warheads by the year 2003. The accord would reduce the number of strategic weapons held by both sides to a quarter of the amount they had deployed in 1990, and to the lowest levels since 1969.

In 1995, a new administration had been in office for two years, that of William Jefferson Clinton, which was openly committed not only to reversing the "vertical" proliferation of U.S. and Russian nuclear weapons through the START process, but also to halting the "horizontal" spread of nuclear weapons to the nonweapon states of the world. During that year, the Clinton administration was instrumental in gaining the indefinite extension of the Nuclear Nonproliferation Treaty (NPT). This agreement requires nonweapon state parties to refrain from acquiring nuclear weapons. During the following year, the Clinton administration also played a major role in negotiating a comprehensive test ban treaty (CTBT). This agreement requires its parties to refrain from conducting nuclear weapons tests, which, many believe, is a major deterrent to the development of nuclear weapons.

Unfortunately, as the new millennium approaches, I have become less optimistic that humanity can avert some form of nuclear catastrophe, and thus the title of this book: *Return to Armageddon*. Continued U.S.-Russian cooperation on nuclear matters can no longer be assured for a variety of reasons, not the least of which is NATO's decision to expand its membership by including three states—Poland, Hungary, and the Czech Republic—that were all once members of the Soviet-dominated Warsaw Pact. NATO's expansion is partly responsible for the failure of the Russian parliament to ratify the START II Treaty. The inability of the Clinton administration to maintain a common policy with Russia toward Iraq is another reason for thinking that U.S.-Russian nuclear cooperation can no longer be taken for granted.

To make matters worse, the CTBT is stuck in the U.S. Senate's Foreign Relations Committee because its chairman, Senator Jesse Helms, and other Republicans believe the treaty cripples the ability of the United States to maintain an effective nuclear deterrent and hinders the U.S. effort to build an antiballistic missile (ABM) defense system.

Perhaps even more ominously, efforts to halt the horizontal proliferation of nuclear weapons may have been dealt a major blow by nuclear weapon tests conducted by India and Pakistan in May 1998. Not only did their action weaken the effort to gain "universal" participation in the NPT and the CTBT, but it also threatens to encourage other states—like Iran, to mention only one—to develop nuclear weapons. And, again, there is the ongoing problem of preventing Iraq from developing—and using—weapons of mass destruction, including nuclear weapons.

If this were not enough to frighten the most stouthearted, there is also the possibility that nuclear weapons or materials will be smuggled out of Russia and find their way into the hands of terrorists willing to threaten an American city with destruction unless their demands are met.

What this study attempts to do is present the history of the U.S. effort to diminish the nuclear threat facing the world during the Reagan, Bush, and

Clinton administrations. It also attempts to assess each administration's progress in moving toward that goal. In so doing, it explains why nuclear weapons remain a major threat to the continued existence of civilization, despite the progress that has been made in reducing their importance.

As its title indicates, this study is a sequel to my earlier work on the subject, *March to Armageddon: The United States and the Nuclear Arms Race, 1939–1986*. As in that study, I am indebted to countless other scholars whose work I have attempted to incorporate in my synthesis. I have tried to recognize my debt to them in the endnotes and in the suggested readings list at the end of the book. In gaining access to recent scholarship, I am particularly grateful for the always friendly assistance provided by the staff of the Global Age Resource Center, including its director, Joanne M. Lewis, and staff members Heidi Makela, Peggy J. Wertheim, and Vicki Zoldessy. I also thank Karen Thornton, of Case Western Reserve University's Kelvin Smith Library, for helping me procure hard-to-find documents.

This study would not have been possible without the research assistance, encouragement, wise counsel, and infinite patience of my wife, Jo Ann. It certainly would not have been completed without medical intervention by two caring and highly skilled eye surgeons (who, coincidentally, also like to read history books), Dr. Daniel Weidenthal and Dr. William Reinhart, to whom this work is gratefully dedicated.

:: Return to Armageddon ::

Introduction
The Nuclear Arms Race, 1939–1981

World War II and the Cold War

American participation in a nuclear arms race began as a direct result of a letter sent to President Franklin D. Roosevelt in August 1939 by eminent physicist Albert Einstein. In it, Einstein warned the president that the Nazis were preparing to develop nuclear weapons. Roosevelt responded by initiating action that ultimately led, in August 1942, to the establishment of the Manhattan Project, the U.S. program to develop the atomic bomb.

The fact that the Germans were unable to build nuclear weapons before they were defeated in World War II did not bring the Manhattan Project to an end. Instead, Roosevelt had decided in September 1944 that the atomic bomb, if it were successfully developed, would be used against Japan, which continued to fight after Germany had surrendered.

The moral problem of using the atomic bomb against civilian targets like Hiroshima and Nagasaki apparently did not bother Roosevelt or his successor, Harry S. Truman. World War II had helped to anesthetize American moral sensibilities concerning the killing of civilians. In fact, more people were killed by the firebombing of Tokyo in one night than died in either Hiroshima or Nagasaki. Moreover, Truman and many others argued afterward that use of the atomic bombs saved the lives of hundreds of thousands of U.S. soldiers by precluding the planned invasion of Japan. It is also true, however, that no significant effort was made to seek a negotiated termination of the war before the bombs were used.

Besides saving American lives, there was another reason for dropping the atomic bomb on Japan—U.S. leaders hoped it would counter the threat to Western Europe that was posed by the Soviet Union. In the wake of the collapse of the German and Japanese empires, and even before their demise, U.S. and Soviet interests collided in areas in which these wartime allies attempted to establish their preeminent influence—in Europe, the Middle East, and the Far East.

What made conflicting U.S. and Soviet interests impossible to reconcile, and the subsequent nuclear arms race between the two countries inevitable, was the depth of the ideological chasm between them. Most Americans considered Soviet communism repugnant, particularly as it was personalized during the brutal dictatorship of Josef Stalin. These feelings, however, were repressed during the war against the common enemy. But as the euphoria of victory began to wane and it became obvious that the Soviets had no intention of leaving Eastern Europe, Americans were led to believe, by President Harry S. Truman and his advisers, that the containment of Soviet communist expansion must be the primary requirement of U.S. security. In rapid order followed the Truman Doctrine, which provided military and economic aid to Greece and Turkey, the Marshall Plan, the U.S. program to rebuild the war-ravaged economies of Europe, and, two years later, the creation of the North Atlantic Alliance, which committed the United States to the defense of Western Europe.

To Stalin and his accomplices, on the other hand, the U.S. desire to contain the Soviet Union was only a ruse to disguise the capitalist desire to dominate the world's resources and to use them to destroy the international communist movement. The need to insulate the Soviet Union from capitalist subversion and aggression, in part, prompted Stalin to insist that the Soviet Union must have a permanent security buffer composed of friendly states in Eastern Europe. To counter the U.S. containment policy, Stalin rejected the participation by the Soviet Union and its Eastern Europe satellites states in the Marshall Plan. To counter the U.S. nuclear monopoly, he also spurred the Soviet effort to build an atomic bomb.

Nuclear Deterrence

For a variety of reasons, nuclear weapons became the main instrument of the U.S. effort to contain Soviet expansionism. In the wake of the rapid demobilization of America's conventional armed forces after World War II, the nation's political and military leaders considered nuclear weapons the only feasible deterrent to the massive conventional forces of the Soviet Union. Compared to maintaining large conventional forces, which the American people were not inclined to support during peacetime, nuclear weapons were inexpensive to construct and deploy. More importantly, they were the ultimate instruments of destruction. And, until the Soviets developed nuclear weapons, they could not be countered in kind.

Shortly after the explosion of the first Soviet nuclear device in August 1949, Truman approved the development of the hydrogen (fusion) bomb, which was successfully tested in 1953. But the Soviets only followed suit, exploding their first hydrogen device during the following year. During the 1950s, when the Soviets began to produce a substantial number of nuclear weapons, and the means to deliver them on U.S. targets, nuclear weapons became even more important to the United States. They not only became the primary means of deterring a Soviet nuclear attack on the U.S. homeland, they also came to be regarded as a way of countering a wide variety of lesser communist military challenges. The United States made nuclear threats during the offshore islands crisis with China in the 1950s, during the Berlin crises of 1948 and 1961, during the Cuban missile crisis in 1962, and during the Arab-Israeli War of 1973.

Considering the deep distrust that developed between Stalin and Truman, it is understandable why serious negotiations to end (or at least control) the nuclear arms race did not begin until after the Soviet dictator's death (in 1953). Yet not much progress occurred toward that end until after the Cuban missile crisis of 1962—the closest approach to nuclear war that occurred during the entire Cold War. In the following year, President John F. Kennedy and Soviet leader Nikita S. Khrushchev negotiated the Limited Test Ban Treaty, which prohibited the testing of nuclear weapons in the atmosphere, in outer space, or beneath the surface of the seas.

America's willingness to engage in nuclear diplomacy with the Soviets was to a large extent made possible by the overwhelming nuclear superiority the United States possessed until well into the 1970s. With the exception of intercontinental ballistic missiles (ICBMs) and antiballistic missile (ABM) systems, the United States led the Soviet Union in developing and deploying every major strategic nuclear weapon system. U.S. nuclear superiority was not only deemed essential to national security, it was also considered a vital compotent of national prestige. To many (if not most) Americans, nuclear superiority was the clearest manifestation of their country's status as the world's preeminent power.

Not surprisingly, the Soviets felt compelled to play nuclear "catch-up" with their more technologically advanced adversary. And, in time, the Soviets succeeded in matching virtually every major U.S. nuclear weapon. Paradoxically, however, the ultimate and inevitable result of this so-called action-reaction cycle was an increase in U.S., as well as Soviet, insecurity. The more nuclear weapons the U.S. targeted on the Soviet Union, the more nuclear weapons the Soviets aimed at the United States.

Although both sides gave lip service to the prospect that the development of additional nuclear weapons would increase the likelihood that they would be used, whether by accident or miscalculation, neither side was capable of breaking its continued reliance on them. In the United States, new "counter-force" doctrines (which emphasized the destruction of enemy military installations rather than cities) were developed in an attempt to explain the paradox of why more nuclear weapons were needed than could possibly be used. With the Soviets achieving rough nuclear parity in the late 1960s, U.S. military experts feared that a Soviet first strike would leave the United States with too few strategic weapons to react effectively against the Soviet Union. To retaliate with insufficient forces would be suicidal, they argued, for U.S. cities would then be exposed to retaliation from the enemy's second and third strikes. To preclude that possibility, counterforce proponents argued, the United States required not only more nuclear weapons but also more accurate systems to ensure that the Soviet Union would not escape devastating U.S. retaliation if it attacked first.

The Military-Industrial Complex
The birth of the nuclear age coincided with a development that was unique in the history of the United States, what President Dwight D. Eisenhower called a "conjunction of an immense military establishment and a large arms industry."[1] This so-called military-industrial complex contributed much to maintaining the momentum of the nuclear arms race. The military component of the complex wanted more nuclear weapons because they were considered necessary for deterrence and, if need be, defense. But in arriving at that assessment, military planners usually relied on worst-case scenarios of Soviet capabilities rather than more prudent estimates of what the Soviets were likely to do.

Nuclear weapons were also important as "yard markers" in the intraservice competition for defense appropriations. In the 1940s and 1950s, the armed services competed for the role of America's primary strategic deterrent force. Even though the air force won that contest, the army and navy were placated with nuclear weapon systems of their own. In the sixties and seventies, the air force lobbied vigorously for what would become the B-1 bomber and the MX ICBM, fearing that without them the navy's ballistic missile submarines would make that service the preeminent strategic deterrent force. Ultimately, both the navy and the air force received the strategic nuclear weapons they desired, and the United States built more nuclear weapons than it needed.

Yet the armed services were not the only ones to benefit from the nuclear arms race. Defense contractors, scientists, universities, labor unions, and politicians all prospered. The nuclear arms race meant large contracts for companies doing business with the Defense Department and jobs for favored congressional districts. For many universities, grants for conducting nuclear research were tantamount to receiving generous federally financed endowments.

No doubt, most scientists who engaged in nuclear weapons work concluded that the United States had no alternative but to stay ahead of the Soviet Union in the nuclear arms race. On the other hand, some scientists believed that they had a moral responsibility to use their knowledge and prestige to halt the nuclear arms race. In fact, the first proposals for negotiated nuclear arms control agreements were made by nuclear scientists— Niels Bohr, Leo Szilard, and James Franck. But theirs was a frustrating and sometimes dangerous struggle. The fate of J. Robert Oppenheimer, the "father" of the U.S. atomic bomb, is the most prominent and extreme example of the penalties a scientist could incur by resisting the thrust of the nuclear arms race. Oppenheimer was publicly disgraced (by being denied a security clearance), primarily because he opposed the idea of developing the hydrogen bomb.

To arouse congressional and public support for increased defense spending, the military, defense contractors, and scientists more than once made exaggerated estimates of Soviet capabilities. The result was a series of "gap" scares that were produced by their incorrect assertions that the Soviet Union possessed an overwhelming lead over the United States in the development and deployment of key nuclear weapon systems. The bomber gap of the mid-1950s was followed by other alleged, and false, gaps: the missile gap in the late 1950s, the ABM gap of the late 1960s, and a missile throw weight (payload capacity) gap during the 1970s. In its effort to gain congressional appropriations, the military-industrial complex was assisted by more than a few politicians who believed that nuclear buildups were not only necessary to counter alleged Soviet leads, but that they were also politically advantageous to themselves and to their party.

Unfortunately, most Americans proved susceptible to the scare tactics employed to obtain their support for the nuclear arms race. To the general public, each augmentation of Soviet military power, whether real or not, had to be met first by increased defense spending and only later (if ever), by arms control negotiations. This rationale was effective; it explains the strong public support for Kennedy's nuclear buildup intended to "close" the nonexistent missile gap.

The media, at least until the late 1960s, generally supported the military-industrial complex's quest for larger defense appropriations. It was only late in that decade—as a result of the Vietnam War, the ABM debate, and the beginning of the Strategic Arms Limitations Talks (SALT)—that the news media began to give nuclear weapons more critical coverage. Yet when Americans were confronted with the horrible prospect of a nuclear Armageddon, most seemed to engage in a form of psychic denial: they refused to think about the effects of a nuclear war in the hope that what they did not know would not hurt them. When Americans were compelled to think about the topic, they were easily overwhelmed by its complexity. Accordingly, it is not surprising that they were more than willing to defer to the judgment of the nuclear "experts," which, in turn, made most Americans passive enablers of the military-industrial complex.

Moreover, from the beginning of the Manhattan Project until the late 1960s, when public and congressional support for the U.S. containment strategy began to break down as a result of its failure in the Vietnam War, Congress rarely challenged the nuclear strategy fashioned by the executive branch. In fact, the Manhattan Project and the hydrogen bomb program were initiated without the knowledge of most members of the legislative branch. The secrecy surrounding both projects, in turn, did much to preclude the possibility of congressional, as well as public, debate on the wisdom of developing these weapons.

As a result of congressional and public acquiescence (or more accurately ignorance), the power to produce and, if necessary, use nuclear weapons was assumed by the executive branch and, ironically and frighteningly, by presidents who, for the most part, had little personal expertise in military or diplomatic affairs, let alone nuclear strategy. With but one significant exception—Dwight D. Eisenhower—America's Cold War presidents lacked the military knowledge necessary to make, and stick with, a realistic assessment of the Soviet threat. As a result, one president after another accepted worst-case scenarios as valid bases of U.S. deterrence strategy, and then used them to garner congressional support for nuclear weapon programs.

The Failure of Nuclear Arms Control

Although Cold War presidents did their part to augment the power of the U.S. nuclear arsenal, all of them felt compelled to attempt to end, or at least to control, the nuclear arms race. Growing public pressure to relieve, or at least diminish, the doomsday threat was partly responsible. And so too were America's European allies, who, in the event of war with the Soviet Union, were destined to be the first to be struck by Soviet nuclear weapons.

But the various nuclear arms control negotiations in which the United States and the Soviet Union engaged between the late 1940s and the 1980s had only limited success. The SALT I agreements of 1972 placed a ceiling on strategic launch vehicles—ICBMS, SLBMS (submarine-launched ballistic missiles), and bombers. The ABM Treaty in the same year placed major restrictions on the development and deployment of antiballistic missile systems. In addition, the Nuclear Nonproliferation Treaty (NPT), which went into effect in 1970, did much to curb the acquisition of nuclear weapons by nonweapon states.

But as the 1980s arrived, the end of the nuclear arms race appeared nowhere in sight. Jimmy Carter left the White House in 1981 with none of his initial nuclear arms reduction goals achieved. The SALT II Treaty, which he had negotiated with the Soviets and which called for the first significant strategic arms reductions in the history of the Cold War, was in limbo, due largely to Carter's decision to withdraw the treaty from the Senate's consideration as a consequence of the Soviet invasion of Afghanistan in 1979. Also sidetracked by the Soviet Afghan adventure was the long effort to conclude a comprehensive nuclear test ban treaty. More ominously, the Soviet invasion of Afghanistan prompted Carter to adopt a nuclear strategy that placed even more emphasis than before on a counterforce strategy and, with it, the perceived need to develop more nuclear weapons.

Given the ideological and national rivalry that characterized Soviet-American relations, in addition to the fear that was generated by the ongoing threat of nuclear preemption or retaliation, the climate of trust that is the prerequisite of successful negotiations on arms control rarely and only superficially existed during the Cold War. In fact, both sides attempted to derive as much advantage from nuclear arms talks as they had from their own nuclear weapon programs. Indeed, the objective of arms control talks was usually to place as many limits as possible on the other side's deployments and as few as possible on one's own.

In addition, the U.S. negotiating posture was almost always based on the assumption that the Soviets would not restrict their own nuclear weapon programs without first being confronted with the threat, or reality, of new U.S. nuclear weapon deployments. In other words, according to this rationale, it was necessary to build new nuclear weapons in order to ultimately reduce them. As a result, rather than attempt to persuade the Soviets to restrain their nuclear programs by engaging in a policy of U.S. nuclear restraint, one administration after another attempted to intimidate the Soviets with new nuclear weapon programs.

As another consequence of the prevailing build-them-to-reduce-them rationale, it proved to be extremely difficult to limit by treaty the deployment of weapon systems developed for bargaining—or for intimidation—purposes. One example of this was the U.S. decision to develop multiple independently retargetable reentry vehicles (MIRVs) in the late 1960s, supposedly to counter the development of a potentially large Soviet ABM system. Placing limitations on MIRV deployments proved impossible in SALT I and difficult in SALT II. Not surprisingly, the Soviets responded by MIRVing their own missiles, thereby not only making a Soviet first strike much more of a threat to the United States, but also creating another major obstacle in the nuclear arms reduction talks.

The dearth of U.S. trust for political solutions, as well as preference for technical solutions to the nuclear arms race, was another obstacle in the way of concluding agreements with the Soviet Union. This was demonstrated, for one example, in the unsuccessful effort to conclude a comprehensive test ban agreement in the late 1950s and early 1960s. Despite overwhelming political reasons for ending the nuclear arms race at that time, when the Soviet nuclear arsenal was vastly inferior to that of the United States, the inability to resolve technical issues, such as the number of annual inspections, effectively derailed the CTBT for almost forty years. Moreover, as technological developments continued and nuclear weapons became more sophisticated, nuclear arms control agreements also became more difficult to complete.

The asymmetrical relationship between U.S. and Soviet strategic arsenals that developed during the 1960s was another factor that complicated the nuclear arms talks. The U.S. side refused to accept the Soviet argument that they needed more ICBMS, SLBMS, and throw-weight to compensate for the superior accuracy and numbers of U.S. nuclear warheads. However, the Soviets refused to acknowledge the threat to U.S. land-based missiles that would be posed once the Soviet Union combined its superiority in missile throw weight with substantial numbers of MIRVed missiles it planned to deploy. Even after recognizing the validity of these asymmetrical threats, both sides were reluctant to admit that they nevertheless possessed effective retaliatory capacity, no matter how potentially effective their opponent's first-strike forces became. Admitting this, it appeared, would have taken much of the force out of the argument that each required additional nuclear weapons.

In addition, the presence of U.S. and Soviet intermediate-range nuclear forces on and around the Eurasian landmass, and the existence of independent nuclear forces in Western Europe and in China, also complicated the nuclear arms talks. Because these nuclear forces were either independent of U.S. control or were nonstrategic in nature, the United States insisted that they should not be counted in the superpower strategic-nuclear equation. But the Soviets insisted that any nuclear weapon capable of striking Soviet territory was "strategic" and therefore must be included in a strategic arms agreement.

The willingness of U.S. presidents to make nuclear arms control talks one more arena of Soviet-American military competition also complicated the task of maintaining public and congressional support for particular agreements. Jimmy Carter, for example, failed to win strong support for the SALT II Treaty, not only because the treaty was too complex for most Americans to understand, but also because it was insufficiently restrictive to attract much needed liberal support. On the other hand, the treaty's opponents were not only well organized and financed but also had a more effective strategy than Carter's. Rather than attack the value of arms control agreements directly and thereby incur the public's wrath, they simply stated that they wanted a better agreement than the one negotiated by the president. But in so doing, they undermined public and congressional support for the existing treaty without offering anything remotely negotiable in its place.

The advantages the opponents of arms control enjoyed during the Cold War were compounded by the ease with which arms control agreements could be blocked in the U.S. political system. The Joint Chiefs of Staff possessed a virtual veto over arms control proposals. Without Pentagon support, it was politically impossible to gain the affirmative vote of two-thirds of the Senate's

membership that is required as a part of the ratification process. In an attempt
to ensure Pentagon support for arms control measures, some presidents were
willing to promise to develop and deploy new weapon systems they knew were
militarily unnecessary. John Kennedy, for example, had to promise to back a
vigorous program of underground nuclear testing in order to get the Pentagon's support for the Limited Test Ban Treaty. Jimmy Carter approved the
deployment of the MX ICBM, the Pershing II intermediate-range ballistic missile (IRBM), and the Tomahawk cruise missile in order to gain Pentagon support for the SALT II Treaty.

The Soviet Role

In many respects, the factors that drove the nuclear arms race in the United
States were mirrored in the Soviet Union. Soviet civilian leaders had to contend with pressure from their military services to build nuclear weapons.
And the secrecy that surrounded the U.S. nuclear weapon programs was
even more pervasive in the Soviet Union. Moreover, Soviet leaders—Nikita
Khrushchev was a classic example—were not adverse to engaging in nuclear
diplomacy with the United States from a position—greatly exaggerated
though it then was—of excessive military strength.

Of course, Soviet domestic and foreign policies also made it difficult to
obtain the degree of trust from Americans that is a prerequisite of successful
negotiations. Americans found it easy to sympathize with the victims of
Soviet oppression, both in the Soviet Union and in its satellite states. Soviet
aggression—in Hungary, Czechoslovakia, Afghanistan, and elsewhere—
undermined U.S. congressional and public support for superpower arms
control agreements at crucial points in the negotiations. Perhaps it was asking too much of the Soviets to surrender more limited interests for the sake
of concluding agreements to curb the nuclear arms race. But it was obviously
asking too much of Americans to ignore Soviet aggressive actions. As a
result, one U.S. administration after another linked nuclear arms talks to
Soviet behavior on other issues—with adverse effects to both the talks and
the unrelated issues.

The Growing Threat of Horizontal Nuclear Proliferation

The inability of the superpowers to effectively curb the growth of their own
nuclear arsenals during the Cold War set a bad example for nonweapon
states contemplating the acquisition of nuclear weapons. Nor was the international effort, initiated with President Eisenhower's Atoms-for-Peace Plan

in 1954, able to dissuade every nonweapon state from acquiring nuclear weapons by offering them ostensibly peaceful nuclear technology and materials. In 1974 India tested a "peaceful" nuclear device that it had constructed largely with Western civilian technology and materiel received under the Atoms-for-Peace program. In addition to the six countries with nuclear weapon arsenals or proven capacity by 1974—the United States, the Soviet Union, China, Great Britain, France, and India—other states (among them Israel, South Africa, and Pakistan) had acquired or were in the process of acquiring the capability to produce nuclear weapons.

As India proved, it was extremely difficult, if not impossible, to prevent the military application of nuclear technology and materials designed for purely civilian purposes. With the seeming inability of the superpowers to end the nuclear arms race and halt the acquisition of nuclear weapons by the nonweapon states, it became possible to envision a world filled with nuclear weapons, with increased opportunities for nuclear accidents and nuclear terrorism, and a deterrent relationship so complicated by the emergence of a multiplicity of nuclear weapon states that deterrence itself might become impossible and a superpower nuclear war inevitable. Indeed, the dawn of the 1980s would bring to the White House a president who not only thought a nuclear Armageddon was prophecized in the Bible but whose policies during his first term almost made a nuclear Armageddon inevitable. That president was Ronald Reagan.

1

The Reagan Nuclear Buildup

Ronald Reagan and the New Cold War

In January 1981 Ronald Reagan, like the overwhelming majority of his Cold War predecessors, entered the White House with almost no background in national security affairs. Before entering the political arena in the early 1960s and then serving as governor of California from 1966 to 1974, he had been in movies and television. His only military experience consisted of making training and documentary films during World War II. Reagan's knowledge of communism and the Soviet Union was also limited. It was based almost entirely on personal experience rather than study. In the late 1940s, as president of the Screen Actors Guild, he fought what he believed was a communist effort to take over the motion picture industry. The experience made him deeply suspicious of communism and the Soviet Union, in particular. In 1983 he called the Soviet Union "the focus of evil in the modern world."[1]

Not surprisingly, Reagan had little use for Soviet-American détente. He called it "a one-way street" that profited only the Soviet Union. The economic concessions that his predecessors had been prepared to grant the Soviets, Reagan charged, would have propped up an inefficient economic system, an oppressive political structure, and a menacing military establishment. Yet Reagan centered his antidétente attack on the SALT (Strategic Arms Limitation Talks) II Treaty, which he called a "flawed" agreement. Rather than encourage Soviet restraint and reciprocity, he argued, SALT II had "allowed the Soviet Union to double their nuclear capacity," giving the Soviets "a definite margin of superiority" over the United States. If nuclear arms talks with the Soviets were going to take place, Reagan insisted, they must redress this alleged imbalance; the Soviets would have to make major reductions in their nuclear forces, particularly their ICBM arsenal. As a result, he warmly accepted the suggestion that SALT be renamed START (Strategic Arms Reduction Talks).[2]

However, Reagan did not believe the Soviets would agree to reduce their nuclear weapon arsenal until the United States demonstrated its willingness to match them weapon for weapon. "I intended," he recalled in his memoir "to let the Soviets know that we were going to spend what it took to stay ahead of them in the arms race." The Pentagon did what it could to satisfy Reagan's goal. It envisioned a total expenditure of $2.7 trillion on defense from 1982 through 1989, with a projected military budget of nearly $450 billion for fiscal year 1989 alone. In the end, the administration would request over $430 billion less than it had initially projected, and Congress would eventually cut nearly $150 billion from that amount. Nevertheless, the Reagan administration undertook the largest military buildup in peacetime history, one that exceeded military spending during two wars, the Korean and Vietnamese conflicts.[3]

The Reagan Nuclear Buildup

Lacking substantive knowledge about national security affairs, Reagan relied on his advisers to a much greater extent than most other Cold War presidents. Most of his national security advisers were members of the Committee on the Present Danger, the nucleus of conservative opposition to the SALT II Treaty. By the end of 1981, thirty-two of the committee's 182 members had received key positions in the administration, including Paul H. Nitze, the committee's chairman, who became the chief negotiator in the intermediate-range nuclear force (INF) Talks, Richard Allen, Reagan's first national security adviser, and U.S. Arms Control and Disarmament Agency (ACDA) director Eugene V. Rostow.

The nuclear strategy formulated by Reagan's advisers built on the nuclear doctrine of his predecessor, Jimmy Carter. In July 1980 Carter issued presidential directive (PD) 59, which called for the United States to develop an enhanced "counterforce" capability—one designed to destroy "hardened," or reinforced with concrete, ICBM silos. The Carter nuclear strategy was based on the mutual assured destruction (MAD) doctrine that had governed U.S. deterrent strategy since the early 1960s. MAD called for the United States to ride out a Soviet nuclear first-strike attack and still have sufficient forces remaining to deliver a devastating retaliatory attack on the Soviet Union.[4]

To the Committee on the Present Danger, however, MAD offered no credible deterrent to Soviet aggression, primarily because it made no provision for the failure of deterrence short of suicide by retaliation. What the committee feared most was the possibility that a Soviet first strike aimed solely at U.S. military installations would be so devastating that the United States would have too few strategic forces remaining to retaliate effectively against the Soviet homeland. To retaliate with insufficient forces would be suicidal, they insisted, because America's cities would then be exposed to retaliation from the enemy's second and third strikes. Faced with the prospect of being forced to accept the destruction of U.S. military installations, in order to avoid the destruction of America's cities through an expansion of the war, the Committee on the Present Danger believed that any president would suffer a paralysis of will that would lead to U.S. capitulation to Soviet nuclear blackmail. To counter the possibility that the Soviets might attack only U.S. military installations and hold U.S. cities hostage to Soviet nuclear blackmail, Reagan's advisers insisted that the United States must enhance its capability to attack only counterforce targets in the Soviet Union. But they did not want U.S. nuclear forces limited only to a retaliatory role. If America's vital interests were threatened, they argued, the United States must be prepared to initiate and "prevail" in a nuclear conflict.

The Reagan nuclear strategy was outlined in a national security decision directive (NSDD-13) that was leaked to the *New York Times* in 1982. It called for the United States to have the capability to wage a "protracted nuclear war" involving repeated, carefully designed, limited nuclear strikes against Soviet targets, interspersed with pauses to allow for diplomatic activity. It also advocated "nuclear decapitation" of the Soviet political and military leadership and destruction of its communication lines.[5]

To meet these requirements, the administration planned to spend approximately $180 billion on nuclear weapons between 1981 and 1986. Included in the program were 100 MX ICBMs, 100 B-1 bombers, 400 air-launched cruise missiles, 3,000 sea-launched cruise missiles, and 15 Trident submarines with 360 Trident I SLBMs. Funds also were appropriated for the development of the Stealth bomber, designated the B-2, and for accelerated development of the Trident II missile, designated the D-5, which would have the capability to destroy "hardened" Soviet ICBM silos. Of particular interest to administration planners were high-tech weapons, an area in which they believed the Soviets would have a difficult time competing. Included in this category were spaced-based antisatellite weapons (ASAT), which the administration hoped to have operational by 1987. In addition, the administration intended to give U.S. command, control, communications, and intelligence systems (c3I) the capability to wage and survive a nuclear exchange.[6]

In addition to modernizing strategic forces, the Reagan administration embarked on a program to update tactical nuclear weapons. By 1988, 400 nuclear-armed, sea-launched cruise missiles were to be deployed on attack submarines and surface ships. F-4 Phantom attack planes in the Marine Ground Task Force that were not certified for delivering nuclear weapons would be replaced by F-18 Hornets that were. Nonnuclear 105 mm howitzers would be replaced by the dual-capable 155 mm gun, almost doubling the size of the U.S. nuclear artillery arsenal. In addition, army and marine 8-inch howitzers would be equipped to fire a neutron warhead, a weapon whose deployment, but not development, Carter had rejected in 1978.

To provide nuclear warheads for these systems, the Reagan administration significantly expanded the U.S. nuclear stockpile. Spending on production of nuclear materials for warheads increased by 190 percent in constant dollars during President Reagan's first term, with a further 10 percent real increase slated for the first years of the second term.[7]

The Soviets reacted with shock and anger to the bellicose words and actions of the new U.S. administration. Yet the Soviet leadership clearly was reluctant to engage in an expensive arms race with the United States. Accordingly, they pledged to do their utmost to revive détente and particularly the effort to reduce nuclear armaments. Politburo member Konstantin Chernenko said that the Soviet Union was "prepared to engage in businesslike and detailed negotiations, which must take account of the interests of both sides." However, some Soviet military leaders, in particular Marshal Nikolai Ogarkov, were upset by the political leadership's unwillingness to undertake new military programs to match the U.S. buildup. When Ogarkov continued to object, he was sacked.[8]

The Nuclear War Scare
The Reagan nuclear buildup, his failure to make arms control talks the major priority of his first term, and his harsh rhetoric toward the Soviet Union did

much to fan fear of a nuclear war. An NBC/Associated Press survey in mid-December 1981 found that 76 percent of the American people believed that nuclear war was "likely" within a few years, an increase from 57 percent the preceding August. One defense expert after another warned that a nuclear war was inevitable if not imminent. "Never in my thirty-five years of public service," George Kennan, the "father" of the containment strategy, stated, "have I been more afraid of nuclear war."[9]

The media fanned the nuclear war scare. In November 1983, a made-for-television movie, *The Day After*, depicted the destruction of Lawrence, Kansas, following a nuclear exchange between the United States and the Soviet Union. It created such a nationwide stir that George Shultz, who succeeded Alexander Haig as secretary of state in July 1982, felt compelled to appear on television immediately after the program in an attempt to assure the American people that the Reagan administration was doing everything possible to prevent the kind of nuclear holocaust depicted in the movie.

Ironically (considering the massive nuclear buildup his administration had initiated), even Reagan was affected by the nuclear war scare. After privately screening *The Day After*, he recorded in his diary that the movie had left him "greatly depressed" and determined "to do all we can . . . to see that there is never a nuclear war." Underpinning Reagan's abhorrence of nuclear weapons was his fascination with the biblical story of Armageddon, in which a plague destroys a large army from the east. Reagan believed this plague would be a nuclear war, citing its description of "the eyes burning from the head and the hair falling from the body and so forth." Much to the dismay of the president's political advisers, who feared that the public expression of such sentiments would jeopardize the administration's nuclear buildup, Reagan repeatedly expressed his fear that world conditions were right for Armageddon to happen.[10]

The Nuclear Freeze

The public fear of nuclear war gave an enormous boost to the so-called nuclear freeze movement. Instead of arguing about numbers of delivery systems, as the superpowers had done in the Strategic Arms Limitation Talks (SALT), nuclear freeze advocates believed that the numbers should be left where they were until an agreement reducing the number of deployed nuclear weapons could be implemented. The freeze proposal had two major advantages that made it attractive to the antinuclear movement. First, unlike previous arms control proposals, it was simple and direct. Second, it was explicitly bilateral; both sides would have to freeze their nuclear weapon programs.

Antinuclear groups soon adopted the freeze idea. In May 1982 a nationwide "Ground Zero" education week on nuclear war prompted thousands in every state to sign petitions calling for an immediate halt to the testing, production, and deployment of nuclear weapons, followed by major reductions in weapons stockpiles. A month later, between a half and three quarters of a million people jammed Central Park in New York to support an end to the nuclear arms race.

The freeze idea soon proved to be very popular with the American people. A May 1981 Gallup poll showed 72 percent of those polled supported a mutual freeze. Although support for the freeze cut across racial, religious, regional, income, and party affiliation, it was strongest among the younger, more affluent, and better educated. Paradoxically, however, most of the public still favored getting tough with the Soviets and spending more on defense. Nevertheless, a substantial majority also feared the consequences of a nuclear arms race and wanted arms control agreements. But even support for more military spending faded quickly. In 1981 more than 51 percent thought too little was being spent on defense, whereas 15 percent said the amount was too high. By November 1982, 16 percent said too little was being allocated to defense, whereas 41 percent said the amount was too high.[11]

The political impact of the freeze issue was evident in more than public opinion polls. By mid-1982, over four hundred town meetings, more than two hundred city councils, and nine state legislatures had passed freeze resolutions. In the congressional election in November of that year, freeze referenda passed in eight states (including California) and the District of Columbia, losing only in Arizona. And out of an estimated 30 percent of the U.S. electorate that had the opportunity to vote on the freeze, about 60 percent cast their ballots in the affirmative. Although few House and Senate outcomes could be directly attributed to the power of the freeze, the issue pervaded many campaigns. Pro-freeze candidates fared well in the elections as Democrats picked up twenty-six seats in the House of Representatives.[12]

Recognizing a popular issue when they saw one, politicians quickly jumped on the freeze band wagon. In 1982 a nuclear freeze resolution, jointly sponsored by Senators Edward Kennedy (D-Mass.) and Mark Hatfield (R-Oreg.), as well as seventeen other senators and 122 representatives, called upon the superpowers to negotiate an agreement halting the testing, production, and further deployment of nuclear arms as a prelude to a treaty providing for mutual and verifiable reduction of strategic nuclear weapons. Freeze advocates argued that the superpowers had more than enough explosive power in their nuclear arsenals, with the combined equivalent of 6,000 pounds of TNT for every man, woman, and child on the planet.[13]

During 1982 many churches officially endorsed the nuclear weapons freeze proposal through their respective hierarchies. In 1983 the Roman Catholic bishops issued a pastoral letter in which they asserted that it is categorically immoral to use nuclear weapons against civilian populations, even in retaliatory strikes. They also rejected counterforce targeting, claiming that the use of even the most limited and accurate weapons would most likely escalate into all-out war. They pointed out that the U.S. counterforce targeting plan included sixty "military" targets in the city of Moscow alone and 40,000 nationwide. The arms race, they charged, "robs the poor and the vulnerable."[14]

The growing public support for a nuclear freeze stunned the White House, since it threatened to erode support for the administration's nuclear buildup. The Congress, which had given overwhelming approval to the administration's military program in 1981, began to question the wisdom of spending so much money on defense. With its nuclear buildup threatened, the Reagan administration counterattacked the freeze proposal vigorously. The president took advantage of that fact; although the American people genuinely feared a nuclear war, they apparently feared the Soviets even more. Playing on this fear, Reagan called the freeze "a very dangerous fraud" that "would prevent the essential and long-overdue modernization of U.S. and allied defenses and would leave our aging forces increasingly vulnerable." Moreover, he warned, a nuclear freeze "would remove any incentive for the Soviets to negotiate seriously." Reagan called freeze proponents a group of "honest and sincere people" who were being manipulated by "some who want the weakening of America," a charge a subsequent FBI investigation could find nothing to substantiate.[15]

To save his nuclear arms programs in Congress, Reagan adroitly backed an emasculated nuclear freeze resolution that was introduced in the House by Representative William Broomfield (R-Mich.). It called for a nuclear weapon freeze at "equal and substantially reduced levels." In effect, this meant that a freeze could only occur after the Soviets had agreed to massive reductions in the size of their nuclear arsenal. Although passage of the Broomfield resolution did not satisfy most freeze advocates, it did help to impress upon the administration the need to begin arms talks with the Soviets.

A False START

In a speech delivered at Eureka College on May 9, 1982, Reagan finally—after almost sixteen months in office—unveiled his administration's START proposal. He also announced that the first round of the talks would begin in Geneva, Switzerland on June 29, 1982. The administration's slowness in getting START going created the impression—which was hard to refute—that it was more interested in deploying additional nuclear weapons than it was in negotiating their elimination. The administration clearly wanted to reverse the so-called margin of superiority the Soviets allegedly enjoyed over the United States in nuclear weapons before moving onto START. By 1982, the administration could argue that the U.S. nuclear buildup was sufficiently under way to safely allow START to begin.[16]

Strobe Talbott, a journalist (and later an assistant secretary of state in the Clinton administration), argued that the delay in the opening of START was also a result of Reagan's inability to give meaningful direction to the U.S. START delegation. During deliberations on the administration's initial negotiating position, Talbott wrote that the president was "a detached, sometimes befuddled character. There was ample evidence that he frequently did not understand basic aspects of the nuclear weapon issue and of policies promulgated in his name." As a result, "many of his decisions were compromises jerry-rigged from competing options favored by the different agencies."[17]

Alexander Haig, Reagan's first secretary of state, inadvertently supported Talbott's assessment of the president's knowledge of nuclear issues. In the administration's first START proposal, Haig recalled, "the President decided to give each supplicant half the baby." It contained a State Department plan for gradual reductions and the Pentagon's demand for major reductions in the throw weight (payload capacity) of Soviet ICBMs. The result, Haig believed, was a "flawed START position."[18]

The "flawed" START proposal that Haig referred to called on each side to reduce ICBMs and SLBMs to an equal level of 850 missiles over a five- to ten-year period. The size of the proposed reductions was roughly one-half the then-current U.S. level of about 1,700 delivery vehicles, but almost two-thirds of the total Soviet force of roughly 2,350 launchers. Of the 850 launchers, no more than 210 could be "medium" missiles, like the MX and the Soviet ss-19, and no more than 110 could be "heavy" missiles, such as the Soviet ss-18. In addition, the total number of warheads on strategic missiles would be cut to about 5,000. Of that number, no more than 2,500 could be on ICBMs. Yet limits on bombers and cruise missiles were excluded from this first stage of START, since they were a category of weapons in which the United States enjoyed superiority over the Soviet Union. In a second phase of the talks, the administration would try to equalize missile throw weight at a ceiling of about 4 million pounds. Since total U.S. throw weight was then about 4.2 million pounds and the Soviet Union's was about 11.2 million pounds, the Soviet Union clearly would have to make a much larger reduction. In one of the few concessions that the administration was prepared to offer, it stated that it would discuss bomber reductions and cruise missile limits in the second stage of the talks.[19]

Not surprisingly, the Soviets rejected Reagan's Eureka proposal. Acceptance would have required Moscow to scrap about 1,500 strategic missiles, compared to about 850 for the United States. To get down to the ceiling of 2,500 ICBM warheads, the Soviets would have had to dismantle all 308 of their ten-warhead ss-18 heavy missiles and roughly 100 of their six-warhead ss-19s or their four-warhead ss-17s. It would have left them with about 400 MIRved ICBMs, compared to their then current level of 818. The United States could have met the proposed combined ICBM-SLBM ceiling of 5,000 warheads by dismantling 500 older single-warhead ICBMs and roughly 130 MIRved Poseidon SLBM launchers. In addition, by not including bombers in the first phase of the reductions, the proposal was more advantageous to the U.S. side, since U.S. bombers carried about 3,000 nuclear weapons compared to less than 300 carried by those of the Soviet Union. Excluding cruise missiles in the proposal protected another area of U.S. technological superiority. Finally, and very importantly, the arms control constraints called for in the president's proposal would not have had much effect on the administration's strategic force modernization program. The United States would have remained free to deploy the B-1, the MX, Trident II, as well as cruise and Pershing II missiles.

Rejecting Reagan's plan, Brezhnev countered with a proposal for a nuclear freeze that would have applied both to the numbers of weapons and to the modernization of existing weapons. Later, the Soviets tabled a proposal that would have preserved the structure of SALT II, but also would have somewhat reduced launcher ceilings and subceilings. It was probably very similar to what the Soviets would have offered in SALT III, had the SALT II Treaty been ratified. The Soviet offer called for reduction to a level of 1,800 strategic nuclear delivery vehicles. It also called for specified limits on the total number of nuclear weapons, including cruise missiles and other bomber armament, and modest reductions in the SALT II MIRV sublimits.[20]

Needless to say, the Soviet proposal was unacceptable to the Reagan administration. A nuclear freeze would have left the Soviet ICBM advantage in tact, the administration argued, while preventing the introduction of any new U.S. nuclear weapon systems. The Soviet proposal also would have used launchers as the principal counting units rather than missile warheads, which was favored by the Americans. In addition, the Soviet proposal would have permitted trade-offs between bombers and ballistic missiles, instead of concentrating exclusively on missiles. Furthermore, it contained no provision for the limitation of ballistic missile throw weight, thereby maintaining the Soviet advantage in that category. Moreover, although the Soviet proposal would have prohibited all long-range cruise missile deployments, it would have permitted cruise missile development, testing, and production, thereby allowing the Soviets to catch up to the Americans in cruise missile technology. Finally, the entire Soviet proposal was contingent on U.S. willingness to cancel deployment of its Pershing II and Tomahawk missiles in Europe, which the Soviets considered "strategic" because they could reach targets in the Soviet Union. In effect, the Soviets explicitly linked progress in START to their goals in the INF talks, thereby ensuring that the deployment of the new U.S. missiles in Europe would jeopardize both negotiations.[21]

The Zero Option
The deployment of new U.S. nuclear weapons was opposed by many Western Europeans as well as the Soviets. Two weeks after the administration entered office, defense secretary Caspar Weinberger stated—without authorization—that the United States was going to deploy enhanced radiation (neutron) weapons in Western Europe and would "probably want to make use of" them in the event of war. Weinberger's statement provoked a hostile reaction in Europe. Many feared that the use of neutron weapons would lower the nuclear "fire break" that separated conventional and nuclear weapons and would make a nuclear war on their continent more likely. Reagan reinforced their concern when, in impromptu remarks in October 1981, he seemed to say that it would be possible to limit a nuclear war to Europe. In response to public pressure, the West German government announced that it would not permit the deployment of neutron weapons on its soil. The Rea-

gan administration reacted by announcing that the neutron warheads would not be deployed in Europe but rather would be stored in the United States.[22]

Yet an even more controversial issue than the so-called neutron bomb was the administration's decision to go ahead with the planned deployment of 572 Pershing II IRBMs and Tomahawk cruise missiles in Western Europe, an action that had been approved by NATO in 1979. Like the Carter administration, which had supported deployment of the new weapons, Reagan believed that stationing these missiles in Western Europe was necessary, not only to counter the stationing in Eastern Europe of Soviet ss-20 intermediate-range missiles but also to reinforce the U.S. capability to wage a protracted nuclear war on the continent.

However, many West Europeans feared that, like the neutron bomb, the deployment of the U.S. Pershing and Tomahawk missiles in their countries would increase the risk of nuclear war. And they suspected, quite correctly, that the Reagan administration was more interested in deploying the Pershing IIs than it was in removing the Soviet ss-20s. Hard-liners in the administration insisted that the deployments must not be derailed by hostile European opinion, which they believed was being fanned by the Soviets to prevent the deployment of U.S. missiles. Nevertheless, with the growing European hostility to the U.S., INF was responsible for the increasing pressure from the NATO allies to pursue the other track of the dual-track approach approved in 1979, that is, conducting negotiations with the Soviets for the purpose of eliminating intermediate-range nuclear missiles.

Assistant Secretary of Defense Richard Perle offered a solution to the dilemma that the administration eventually adopted. If negotiations were to be conducted, Pearl recommended that they should aim at eliminating all U.S. and Soviet INF. Privately, Perle believed this so-called zero option was unlikely to be accepted by the Soviets. This would enable the U.S. missile deployments to go ahead as planned, while creating the impression that the Soviet Union was the chief obstacle to the elimination of nuclear weapons in Europe. The zero option appealed to Reagan not only because it appeared fair but because it would be easy for the public to understand.[23]

Not surprisingly, the Soviets rejected the zero option when it was submitted to them at the end of November 1981. They pointed out that, although the proposal would require both sides to eliminate their INF, it would have left unaffected other NATO theater nuclear weapons deployed in Western Europe, including 108 Pershing I medium-range missiles as well as U.S. dual-capable fighters. The Soviet counterproposal called for an immediate freeze on long-range INF deployments, followed by a two-thirds reduction in their numbers by 1990. It was quickly rejected by the United States and its NATO allies, not only because it would have maintained the Soviet superiority in IRBMS but also because it included British and French systems in the U.S. total. The proposal was rejected by NATO.[24]

Both sides displayed more flexibility in 1982 and 1983. Yuri Andropov, who succeeded Leonid Brezhnev as Soviet leader after the latter died in 1982, offered to reduce the number of Soviet SS-20s that were aimed at Western Europe from 243 to 162, a figure that matched the combined total of British and French ballistic missiles. He also proposed to redeploy the remaining SS-20s at sites about seven hundred miles farther east, on the far side of the Ural Mountains. But the Soviet proposal was rejected by the Reagan administration, arguing that the mobile SS-20s stationed beyond the Urals could be moved back to positions in the western part of the Soviet Union in the event of a crisis. Moreover, the proposal would have precluded the deployment of any Pershing II and Tomahawk missiles, which were designed to counter the SS-20s. Nevertheless, the administration was under considerable pressure from the allies to pursue both aspects of the dual-track plan, that is, negotiations to reduce INF on the continent as well as deployment of the Pershing II and Tomahawk missiles. The allies did not consider the zero option a serious proposal.[25]

In an attempt to break the stalemate in the INF talks, Paul Nitze, head of the U.S. Geneva delegation, offered his Soviet counterpart, Yuli Kvitsinsky, a compromise proposal while they took a break from the talks and walked together in the woods surrounding the city. Nitze proposed a package that would limit both sides to seventy-five missile launchers, eliminate Pershing II deployments, and restrict SS-20s in Asia in return for a ceiling of 150 on nuclear-capable aircraft. However, Richard Perle bitterly opposed Nitze's plan and worked tirelessly to discredit it. Although the Joint Chiefs of Staff did not overtly repudiate Nitze's proposal, they had misgivings about giving up the Pershing II, whose deployment they believed was necessary to strengthen nuclear deterrence in Europe. The ban on Pershing IIs also was opposed by the president, who felt that the slow-flying U.S. Tomahawk cruise missiles alone were not an adequate counter to the Soviet SS-20. As a result, the Nitze "walk-in-the-woods" proposal was rejected by the administration.[26]

It was not until March 30, 1983, that Reagan finally gave into allied pressure and modified the zero option. In its place he offered an "interim agreement," which would have permitted the deployment of equal numbers of U.S. and Soviet INF warheads "on a global basis" at the "lowest possible levels." But the Soviets rejected the new U.S. offer. They insisted that French and British forces must be included in the limitations, and they rejected the concept of global ceilings because it would have included Soviet missiles deployed in eastern Asia.[27]

Stalemate

Reagan's inability to achieve either an INF agreement or a START treaty during his first term was undoubtedly exacerbated by a crisis in U.S.-Soviet relations that occurred on September 1, 1983. On that day, a Soviet air force jet shot down a South Korean civilian airliner, Korean Air Lines flight 007, which had flown into Soviet airspace over the Sea of Okhotsk, a heavily militarized region north of Japan. All 269 passengers, including a member of the U.S. Congress, were killed.

The Soviets claimed the plane was on a spying mission for the United States, a charge the administration vigorously denied. In all probability, however, the crew of KAL-007 had set the plane's automatic pilot system incorrectly, allowing it to stray more than 300 miles into Soviet airspace. In addition, the Soviets may have mistaken the civilian plane for a U.S. military aircraft, for earlier that evening a U.S. intelligence plane had briefly crossed KAL-007's flight path as it neared Soviet airspace. Although the Soviet aircraft fired warning shots at the South Korean plane, the crew of KAL-007 probably did not see them, as the shots were fired from below the aircraft just as it was climbing to a higher altitude. The Soviet pilot also violated rules of engagement by not visually identifying the plane before launching an attack. Nevertheless, President Reagan reacted strongly to the incident, calling it an act of barbarism. He charged that the Soviets had known the KAL-007 was a civilian jet at the time they shot it down, thus underscoring, he said, "the refusal of the Soviet Union to abide by normal standards of civilized behavior." Privately, however, administration officials admitted the incident was more a result of human error than Soviet barbarism.[28]

The Soviets, needless to say, regarded the exceptionally hostile U.S. reaction as further proof that the Reagan administration was more interested in confrontation than détente. In fact, Richard Perle and much of the National Security Council (NSC) staff pushed for shutting down INF negotiations in the wake of the KAL-007 incident. But Reagan refused. For him, the tragedy demonstrated that a nuclear war could start from human miscalculation.

Rather than cancel INF talks, the president decided that he must play a stronger personal role in "eliminating" nuclear weapons. Yet he refused to alter the U.S. negotiating position in the INF talks, reaffirming the zero option and the continuation of the Pershing II missile deployments in Germany.[29]

The U.S. proposal, which was restated by the president in a speech at the United Nations on September 26, 1983, was bluntly rejected by Soviet foreign minister Andrei Gromyko. However, on October 26, shortly before the first U.S. cruise missiles were scheduled to arrive in Britain, Andropov again altered the Soviet position. He proposed to reduce Soviet SS-20 deployments in Europe to 140—a figure that was reduced further to 120 in November— and to halt further SS-20 deployments in the Far East. In exchange, he demanded the cancellation of the Pershing II and Tomahawk deployments and a freeze on the level of British and French nuclear forces. By this time, however, the administration wanted to avoid doing anything that would delay the deployment of the first U.S. missiles. Consequently, it rejected the Soviet offer.[30]

On November 23, one day after the West German Bundestag voted to reaffirm support for the NATO missile deployments, the Soviets responded by walking out of the Geneva talks. They also announced that they were increasing the number of SS-20s deployed in Eastern Europe, accelerating the deployment of Soviet tactical weapons in that region and stationing more Soviet missile-launching submarines off the coasts of the United States. "By trying to lessen our security," Kvitsinsky concluded, "the United States has lessened its own security."[31]

Other Nuclear Arms Control Actions
At the end of May 1982, President Reagan announced an arms control decision that was somewhat surprising, considering his past opposition to the SALT II Treaty. He stated that his administration would abide by the unratified agreement as long as the Soviets did. Although Reagan had condemned the SALT II Treaty, more knowledgeable voices, including those of Secretary of State Haig and the Joint Chiefs of Staff, persuaded him that the United States would be worse off without the unratified treaty. They pointed out that the treaty placed more restrictions on Soviet nuclear activities than it did on those of the United States. Without the SALT II restraints, the Joint Chiefs argued, the Soviets could add many more warheads to their existing military forces than the United States.[32]

Although Reagan gave the arms controllers a major concession, in abiding by the unratified SALT II Treaty, he also killed a major arms control effort. On July 20, 1982, it was announced that he had decided to set aside the long effort to negotiate a comprehensive ban on nuclear testing. The ostensible reason for the decision was the administration's allegation that existing verification measures were inadequate to detect Soviet cheating. However, administration critics charged that the real reason behind the decision was that a test ban treaty would have prevented the testing of nuclear warheads for new U.S. weapon systems.[33]

Later, it was revealed that in 1982 Reagan had signed a national security directive (NSDD-51) that tacitly authorized the United States to resume clandestine nuclear tests, a long-standing practice that had been abandoned during the last year of the Carter administration and replaced by a policy of publicly announcing tests. In another directive issued in 1985, NSDD-173, Reagan also authorized the United States to violate treaties concerning nuclear weapons, including agreements limiting nuclear tests, when those violations were "proportionate U.S. responses" to alleged treaty violations by the Soviet Union. The agreements included the Limited Test Ban Treaty of 1963, as well as two unratified nuclear arms agreements—the Nuclear Threshold Test Ban Treaty and the Peaceful Nuclear Explosion Treaty, which had been observed previously by the United States.[34]

The administration also upset arms controllers by taking actions that they believed would further the proliferation of nuclear weapons. In spite of the president's announced intention to urge all supplier nations to apply comprehensive safeguards to all nuclear sales, the administration approved the sale of U.S. nuclear equipment and materiel to India, Argentina, China, and South Africa. The Nuclear Nonproliferation Act of 1978 required all recipients of U.S. nuclear fuel to subscribe fully, in all their nuclear facilities, to the safeguard system of the International Atomic Energy Agency (IAEA). Yet these states had refused to open all their nuclear facilities to international safeguard inspections. In addition, they refused to ratify the Nuclear Nonproliferation Treaty (NPT), which barred nonweapon signatory states from acquiring or developing nuclear weapons. These states either had exploded a nuclear device or were strongly suspected of developing the means to do so.[35]

In spite of the suspicion that the Chinese were believed to be helping the Pakistanis develop weapon-grade uranium, the Reagan administration permitted U.S. companies to sell technology needed to build highly sophisticated "turn-key" nuclear power plants to the Chinese. In return for this assistance, China permitted the Americans to station sophisticated monitoring devices in its Sinkiang province to monitor Soviet nuclear and missile tests. The U.S. side agreed to share the information collected by those devices with Chinese military intelligence. Clearly, the administration was more than willing to play the "China card" against the Soviets by providing the Chinese with nuclear assistance. Reagan also seemed to be doing all he could to implement his prepresidential position that the United States should not interfere with countries attempting to acquire the means to produce nuclear weapons. In January 1980 he said, "I just don't think it's any of our business."[36]

Better than MAD: The Strategic Defense Initiative

The widespread belief that Reagan was more interested in building new weapons than dismantling existing systems was reinforced by his March 1983 announcement that the United States would undertake a five-year, $26 billion program for research and development of a nationwide, ballistic-missile defense system (NMD). The program was called the Strategic Defense Initiative (SDI), although the media quickly dubbed it "Star Wars."

In a nationwide television address on March 23, Reagan posed this question to the American people: "What if free people could live secure in the knowledge that their security did not rest upon the threat of instant retaliation to deter a Soviet attack, that we could intercept and destroy strategic ballistic missiles before they reached our soil or that of our allies?" Reagan called "upon the scientific community, . . . those who gave us nuclear weapons, to turn their great talents now to the cause of mankind and world peace," in order to give the United States "the means of rendering these nuclear weapons impotent and obsolete."[37]

Reagan's decision to proceed with SDI was formed in part by his recollection of his visit in late July 1979 to the headquarters of the North American Air Defense Command (NORAD), deep inside Cheyenne Mountain in Colorado. He asked NORAD commander, General James Hill, what could be done if an incoming missile were detected. Nothing, the general responded. "We can't stop it." Reagan was shocked. The United States had no means of defending itself against a Soviet missile attack, except the threat of destroying the Soviet Union in retaliation, a step that would have risked an all-out nuclear holocaust. To Reagan, SDI made much more sense than continued reliance on mutual assured destruction. "It was the craziest thing I ever heard of," he said of MAD. He likened this to "two westerners standing in a saloon aiming their guns at each other's head—permanently."[38]

However, many, if not most, of Reagan's advisers believed that MAD had been responsible for preventing World War III. George Shultz told Reagan that nuclear weapons could not be "uninvented," but he conceded that he had made "no real impact on the President with this line of reasoning." Although Reagan admitted that MAD had kept the peace for more than three decades, Shultz recalled, the president "believed that it also had created a condition of perpetual fear and despair." SDI, on the other hand, Reagan insisted, would "free the world from the threat of nuclear war" by "rendering nuclear weapons impotent and obsolete."[39]

Reagan's confidence in SDI was reinforced in part by retired air force Lieutenant General Daniel O. Graham, who believed that SDI would not only protect the United States against enemy missiles but would also "severely tax, perhaps to the point of disruption, the already strained Soviet technological and industrial resources." Graham's "High Frontier" proposal embodied a space-based ABM employing kinetic "kill" vehicles, that is, projectiles designed to destroy Soviet warheads by colliding with them in space well before they could reach the United States. At the very least, argued Edward Teller, the "father" of the U.S. hydrogen bomb, the program would force the Soviets to increase their military expenditures beyond what they could reasonably afford. If it did that alone, Teller stated, "we would have accomplished something." If it worked, it might allow the United States to achieve victory over the Soviet Union once and for all, not through war, but by neutralizing the Soviets' ability to threaten war.[40]

At first the Pentagon had little use for the High Frontier proposal. A report prepared by the air force, the army, and private industry and released March 31, 1982 concluded that the High Frontier "concept, as proposed" was "not technically feasible" and that the proposal should "not be funded as proposed, nor modified and funded." As a result, defense secretary Weinberger wrote General Graham that "we are unwilling to commit this nation to a course which calls for growing into a capability that does not currently exist." Richard DeLauer, Pentagon chief of research and development, stated that an ABM program would be "a multiple of Apollo programs" and that Congress would be "staggered at the cost."[41]

Reagan was not deterred. On February 11, 1983, he asked the Joint Chiefs of Staff, "Is it possible . . . to develop a weapon that could perhaps take out, as they left their silos, those nuclear missiles?" He later recalled that "when they did not look aghast at the idea and said yes, they believed that such a thing offered a possibility and should be researched, I said 'Go.'" However, the

Joint Chiefs did nothing to implement Reagan's order before he delivered his SDI speech to the nation on March 23. In fact, they were shocked when the president told the American people that he was going ahead with the project. They had only meant to suggest that research on strategic defenses should get more consideration and funding, not that a crash program to develop it should begin.[42]

Nevertheless, a number of key Reagan aides—attorney general Edwin Meese III, Martin Anderson, White House adviser on economic and domestic matters, national security adviser Richard Allen, and his successor, William Clark—pushed SDI. They used the rather contradictory advice of two ad hoc commissions to support the program. One panel, headed by James Fletcher, studied the technological feasibility of strategic defense, while another panel, headed by Fred Hoffman, studied the strategic implications of defense. Although the Fletcher and Hoffman studies did not provide a ringing endorsement of either the strategic wisdom or the technological feasibility of a comprehensive ABM, the Pentagon used the joint findings to bolster its case for SDI.[43]

Political considerations were also important in Reagan's decision to proceed with SDI. One was the nuclear freeze movement. It had almost persuaded the House to pass a freeze resolution in August 1982. It also had figured prominently in the 1982 congressional elections. More important to the Reagan administration, the freeze movement had prompted Congress to paralyze the MX program, the centerpiece of the strategic modernization program. "Reagan knew it was time to go, politically speaking," Martin Anderson recalled. "He was settled in his job, his respect at home and abroad was growing, and his power as a sitting president about to run for reelection was nearing its peak."[44]

In the view of historian Daniel Wirls, an important motive for the Star Wars speech was "to provide the administration with a positive initiative in the realm of strategic and defense policy at a time when it was losing the public relations battle in that area." Reagan wanted something positive to say following the negative press he had received for his March 8 speech characterizing the Soviet Union as the "focus of evil in the modern world." More importantly, SDI also gave Reagan a means to counter the nuclear freeze movement, which sought to preserve massive retaliation as a deterrent strategy. Reagan argued that "making nuclear weapons impotent and obsolete was preferable to freezing the U. S. into a position of strategic inferiority."[45]

In addition, Reagan claimed that SDI would also provide the leverage needed to bring the Soviets back to the negotiating table. Subsequently, however, he rejected the suggestion that SDI should be a bargaining chip that could be traded away for Soviet arms control concessions. Reagan obviously expected SDI to be deployed. For him, in the opinion of historian Kerry Hunter, SDI was more than just a program; it came to symbolize the very essence of his presidency. In the end, Reagan would not abandon his dream of a "nuclear-free world."[46]

Total Protection

The ballistic missile defense system that Reagan had in mind was much more ambitious than the "Safeguard" ABM system proposed and built by the administration of Richard Nixon in the 1970s. Safeguard had been designed to provide only a "point" defense of "hard" targets, such as missile silos and command bunkers. But according to Caspar Weinberger, who quickly got on board the SDI bandwagon, the defensive system the president was talking about was not designed to offer only partial protection. "What we want to try to get," he said, "is a . . . defense that is thoroughly reliable and total." In other words, SDI would be designed to protect soft targets such as cities as well as hard targets.[47]

Reagan acknowledged that the achievement of his goal for SDI would be no small accomplishment. An effective nationwide defense would have to intercept and destroy virtually all the 10,000 or so nuclear warheads that the Soviets were capable of committing to a major strategic attack. But to Reagan, even an imperfect SDI made a lot more sense than MAD, whose implementation he—as well as many others—admitted would have been suicidal. Moreover, Reagan's vision of SDI was similar to Kennedy's vision of putting humans on the moon. It was a challenge that U.S. technology and ingenuity could not fail to meet. Reflecting this optimism, Lieutenant General James Abrahamson, director of the Strategic Defensive Initiative Organization (SDIO), told Congress in 1984 that "we indeed can produce miracles."[48]

Many did not think so. The critics of SDI asserted that the Soviets could easily take a number of relatively inexpensive countermeasures that would render the system ineffective. They could simply increase the number of their deployed ballistic missiles, load some of them with duds, and overwhelm the U.S. defensive system. For every ruble the Soviets might spend on such relatively inexpensive countermeasures, the United States would have to spend millions of dollars on devices that could differentiate between real warheads and duds. Richard DeLauer, Pentagon chief of research and development stated, "There's no way an enemy can't overwhelm your defenses if he wants to badly enough." Even some SDI supporters did not believe it could offer total protection. General Abrahamson himself envisioned a much more limited role for SDI, one that would destroy enough Soviet ballistic missiles to create doubt in their minds that a first strike would be successful. In this way, SDI's primary role would be one of strengthening deterrence, not protecting the entire United States.[49]

What bothered SDI's critics most, however, was not what they believed to be its dubious effectiveness and vulnerability, but rather its great potential to destabilize the nuclear balance. Because of technical problems and other uncertainties involved, SDI would be much more effective against a small and disorganized retaliatory attack than it would be in defeating a massive and well organized first strike. In fact, the critics feared that a fully deployed SDI would make a Soviet first strike inevitable. The Soviets would be tempted to strike first in order to have the greatest number of operational missiles rather than await a U.S. first strike and then have to retaliate with fewer missiles, many of which might be destroyed by SDI.

Even Reagan recognized the advantage SDI would give the United States. He admitted to Soviet journalists that "if someone was developing such a defensive system, and going to couple it with their own nuclear weapons, offensive weapons, yes, that could put them in a position where they might be more likely to dare a first strike." But he quickly added, "I don't think anyone in the world can honestly believe that the United States is interested in such a thing or would ever put itself in such a position." SDI, he said, was "an innocent technology that threatens no one." This was a contention the Soviets did not accept. Nor did the Soviets take seriously Reagan's promise to share SDI technology with them. To the Soviets, Reagan's offer seemed an implicit admission that unilateral U.S. deployment of strategic defenses would be destabilizing.[50]

SDI's critics also feared that the program would trigger a dangerous escalation of the nuclear arms race in a theater, space, in which it had been prohibited by existing U.S.-Soviet treaties, including the Limited Test Ban Treaty of 1963, the Outer Space Treaty of 1967, and the ABM Treaty of 1972. The ABM Treaty included a provision requiring the parties "not to develop, test, or deploy ABM systems or components that are sea-based, air-based, space-based, or mobile land-based." SDI, its critics argued, would not only abrogate the ABM Treaty, it would also result in the removal of all constraints on offensive missiles. Critics found it impossible to believe that the Soviets would reduce their ballistic missile force while the United States was building a ballistic missile defense system. In other words, the critics charged, SDI would be incompatible with arms control.[51]

Sharing this concern, Shultz urged Reagan to "say that our research would be consistent with the ABM Treaty and that we would continue to rely on existing strategic doctrine and the existing structure of our alliances." Shultz also warned the president that SDI "can be destabilizing as to what the Soviets do and how they respond. They will assume that we have a major scientific breakthrough. I don't know the implications of that." Shultz, and other less Russophobic members of the administration, like Paul Nitze and national security adviser Robert McFarlane, saw SDI as a potential bargaining chip in START. They supported the idea of a "grand compromise," in which the Soviets would be persuaded to make major reductions in the size and power of their ICBM arsenal in exchange for a U.S. promise to restrict the development and deployment of SDI. However, advocates of this grand compromise idea had to tread lightly toward this goal, for the deployment of SDI was more important to the president than the conclusion of a START agreement. And this remained true for the balance of his presidency.[52]

Almost as significant as Reagan's attachment to SDI was the newfound enthusiasm for the program exhibited by Weinberger and Perle, both of whom initially had opposed the program. (Perle once had called the idea of a nationwide ballistic defense system "the product of millions of American teenagers putting quarters into video machines.") But both Perle and Weinberger gradually came to see SDI as a way not only to scuttle the ABM Treaty, but START as well. Neither had much use for arms reduction, believing that security was found in more, rather than less, nuclear weapons. In this respect, they differed significantly from Reagan, who had a genuine abhorrence for nuclear weapons. Yet because of Reagan's determination to eliminate nuclear weapons, they, like Shultz, Nitze, and McFarlane, had to tread softly on START, for fear of raising the president's ire. Rather than attack START directly, they championed the early deployment of SDI in the hope that it would discourage the Soviets from making the deep cuts in their nuclear arsenal that a START treaty would require.[53]

In spite of the objections of SDI's critics, Reagan pushed ahead with the program. Between 1983 and 1989, almost $17 billion was spent on SDI research. And the general public reacted favorably. By December 1985, one poll showed that 61 percent of those who were aware of SDI favored it. Moreover, a consistent but shrinking majority favored continued development throughout the remainder of Reagan's presidency. And although Reagan's SDI speech took the military services by surprise, their initial reluctance was overcome rather quickly. By 1987, SDI research and development represented nearly 10 percent of total military spending. Each service wanted a large piece of that "pie."[54]

They were not alone. The aerospace, computer, and electronics industries also wanted access to SDI funding. As Wolfgang Demisch, an analyst for First Boston Bank, argued, "SDI is the future of the defense industry. No competitive high-tech company can afford not to be a part of SDI." By April 1987, the Strategic Defense Initiative Organization had made over 3,300 contracts worth $10.9 billion. Lockheed, Boeing, TRW, and Rockwell received the largest contracts. Lockeed alone received $1.4 billion in SDI-related contracts. And even though smaller firms received smaller contracts, they often represented the largest share of their defense contracting. In addition, fifteen federally funded research and development centers received 14 percent of the total SDI dollar amounts. The top three were the Lawrence Livermore, Los Alamos, and Sandia national weapon laboratories. Major universities received 60 percent of the total SDI dollars; eighteen universities received contracts averaging $1 million. In addition, all hoped to get a share of the $75 billion to $1 trillion in government expenditures that full-scale SDI deployment might entail. SDI clearly could have been the largest military bonanza in history.[55]

The Scowcroft Report: Saving the MX and START

While SDI was being launched in 1983, START languished. The Congress, dissatisfied with the lack of progress, increasingly criticized the administration's military buildup. A key target was the MX ICBM, which the administration had euphemistically renamed "Peacekeeper." The easiest aspect of the MX to criticize was the administration's apparent inability to decide where to deploy the missile once it was developed. In 1979 President Carter had approved a plan to deploy the MX on a mobile launcher-vehicle that would move along a roadway to one of twenty-three concrete shelters built at intervals of one mile. All 200 missiles and their mobile launchers would require the construction of 4,600 widely spaced concrete shelters and 10,000 miles of roadway in Nevada and Utah at an estimated cost of $33 billion. However, the governors of those states told a House subcommittee that the Carter deployment plan would forever destroy for their residents "a chosen way of life."[56]

Liberals, on the other hand, concentrated their attack on the MX's potential as a first-strike weapon. With ten highly accurate warheads per missile, 200 MX missiles could destroy a large portion of the Soviet Union's land-based ICBMs, which constituted 70 percent of Soviet deterrent forces. As a result, the MX, they argued, would destabilize the strategic balance by encouraging the Soviets, during an acute confrontation with the United States, to launch their ICBMs first, before they could be destroyed by the MX warheads.[57]

In an attempt to find an alternative to the Carter deployment plan, Reagan resorted to the first of many presidential commissions. In 1981 he formed the Townes Commission, a bipartisan panel of mostly technical experts headed by Nobel laureate physicist Charles Townes. The Townes Commission recommended several basing plans, including airborne deployment, deep underground basing, and closely spaced basing. Congress specifically rejected airborne deployment, the administration's preference, so, as an interim solution, Reagan opted to put a few dozen of the MX missiles in hardened existing silos. Congress responded by refusing to fund additional MX missiles until the administration could produce a more acceptable basing scheme.[58]

In November 1982, after considering some thirty basing options, the administration unveiled its plan for closely spaced basing, called "Dense Pack." The plan called for building fixed launch sites for 100 MX ICBMs, each of which would be deployed 1,800 feet apart in columns fourteen miles long at Warren Air Force Base, near Cheyenne, Wyoming. The administration argued that packing MX launch sites closely together would render some of the MX missiles invulnerable to a Soviet attack. They asserted that the detonation of the first Soviet warheads would commit "fratricide," that is, destroy or disable subsequent incoming Soviet warheads, thereby ensuring that some of the MX missiles would survive. Neither the Joint Chiefs of Staff nor the Congress bought this reasoning. On December 7, 1982, the House of Representatives showed its displeasure with the Dense Pack plan by voting 245 to 176 to eliminate the $988 million from the defense budget that was requested by the administration to begin procurement of one hundred MX missiles.[59]

In January 1983, Reagan responded to Congressional rejection of Dense Pack by establishing another presidential commission to "review the purpose, character, size, and composition of the strategic forces of the United States." It was chaired by retired air force Lieutenant General Brent Scowcroft, a former aide to Henry Kissinger and national security adviser for President Gerald Ford (and later President George Bush). Its members also included

Alexander Haig, William Perry (undersecretary of defense under Carter and secretary of defense under Clinton), and Richard Helms (Nixon's CIA director). Among the senior counselors were former secretary of state Henry Kissinger and former secretaries of defense Harold Brown and Melvin Laird.

Even though no opponents of the MX sat on the Scowcroft Commission, its report, which was completed on April 6, 1983, only partially met the administration's objectives. It recommended the deployment of 100 MX missiles in existing Minuteman silos. But it also closed the administration's alleged window of vulnerability by stating that, as a whole, U.S. nuclear forces would survive a Soviet first strike and retain the capability to devastate the Soviet Union in retaliation. The Scowcroft Report also recommended the construction of a force of small, mobile, single-warhead ICBMs, dubbed "Midgetman," as a better, long-term alternative to the MX. Unlike the MX, the Midgetman would neither threaten nor invite a first-strike. The Scowcroft Report also suggested that the administration should work harder to achieve a strategic arms agreement, particularly one that would decrease the ratio of warheads to launchers on both sides. Such a move would diminish the incentive for either side to strike first, and thereby enhance nuclear stability. Despite misgivings with some parts of the report, Reagan endorsed it on April 19, 1983.[60]

The Congress, however, did not buy the entire Scowcroft plan. It appropriated funds for only 50 missiles, instead of the 100 recommended by the Scowcroft Commission. Moreover, several members from each chamber warned the White House that their continued support for the MX would depend on a serious effort by the administration to conclude nuclear arms reduction agreements with the Soviets.[61]

It was this consideration that helped push Reagan toward reconsidering the idea of negotiations with the Soviets. On June 14, 1983, the president ordered the incorporation of the nuclear strategy recommended by the Scowcroft Commission into the START negotiating position. The directive marked a small shift in the balance of power within the Reagan administration on nuclear arms control issues. Earlier presidential orders had often been decisively influenced by Richard Perle and other hard-liners who held that no acceptable arms control agreement could be reached with the Soviets. But, urged on by George Shultz and Paul Nitze, Reagan signed a directive on October 4, 1983 which reaffirmed the flexible approach in START favored by the Scowcroft Commission. For the first time during the Reagan administration, this directive conceded that there might be "trade-offs"—in a word, some concessions by both sides—as a means of making progress in stabilizing the arms race in strategic nuclear weapons.[62]

However, the death of Yuri Andropov in November 1983 (from kidney failure) and the imminent deployment in Western Europe of the first U.S. Tomahawk cruise missile contributed to the breakdown of START as well as the INF talks. On December 8, 1983, shortly after the collapse of the INF talks, the START talks adjourned with no announced date for their resumption.

2

The Reagan About-Face

A number of developments in late 1983 helped break the stalemate in the nuclear arms reduction talks. Perhaps the most important was Ronald Reagan's increasing concern that his nuclear policies might trigger a nuclear war. Historian Beth Fischer believes that a number of events came together in the fall of 1983 that repeatedly forced Reagan to confront his fears about nuclear annihilation. Reagan's reaction to these events, she contends, was primarily responsible for the change in his administration's policy toward the Soviet Union. The first was the KAL 007 disaster in September 1983. It brought home to Reagan the possibility that human error could produce a nuclear holocaust. "If . . . the Soviet pilots simply mistook the airliner for a military plane," he asked, "what kind of imagination did it take to think of a Soviet military man with his finger close to a nuclear button making an even more tragic mistake?"[1]

The second incident that left a deep impression on Reagan, according to Fischer, was his previewing of the TV movie *The Day After* in early October 1983. That vivid dramatization of nuclear annihilation left him, he recorded, "greatly depressed." *The Day After* was effective, Fischer explains, because "it spoke to his fears about a nuclear Armageddon; it was narrative in style; and, like most of Reagan's own stories, it focused on the lives of ordinary Americans." The movie helped to make the threat of nuclear war a highly salient issue for Reagan.[2]

Still another experience reinforced Reagan's fear of a nuclear Armageddon. Toward the end of October 1983, he participated in a Pentagon briefing on the U.S. nuclear war plan, called the Single Integrated Operational Plan (siop). Although the Pentagon had routinely briefed previous presidents on U.S. nuclear war plans, Reagan had repeatedly refused to attend such meetings. He was too disturbed by the thought of having to rehearse for a nuclear war to participate. However, he finally agreed, reluctantly, that his involvement in the war game was a necessity. During the siop briefing, Weinberger and Chairman of the Joint Chiefs of Staff John Vessey explained that the U.S. was targeting over fifty thousand sites in the Soviet Union, only half of which were military targets. The rest were economic and industrial locations, with high concentrations of civilians. In addition, Reagan was informed that if a nuclear exchange took place, Washington, if not the entire country, would probably be destroyed. Weinberger recounted that the President found the briefing a terribly disturbing experience. Afterwards, Reagan considered the briefing a replay of *The Day After*.[3]

Able Archer 83

Late in 1983, and again in early 1984, Reagan was exposed to still another, even more frightening nuclear war scare. He was advised by cia Director William Casey that a nato exercise, Able Archer 83, which was conducted in November 1983 and had simulated procedures for the release of nuclear weapons by nato, had alarmed the Soviet intelligence agency, the kgb, and presumably the Kremlin leadership as well. In his memoir, Reagan admitted that he was surprised to have learned that the Soviet leaders were genuinely afraid of a U.S. nuclear attack.

Along with Reagan, the Soviet leadership had become increasingly concerned that a nuclear war was imminent. Historically, Soviet leaders had considered the possibility that a "madman" would become the president of the United States and unleash a nuclear attack on the Soviet Union. Reagan, they feared, might be that madman. Since 1981 the president had used increasingly threatening rhetoric against the Soviet Union, initiated a large-scale military buildup to give the United States an ability to wage protracted nuclear war, and then adopted a nuclear war strategy that placed greater emphasis on targeting the Soviet leadership. The Soviets felt especially threatened by the Strategic Defense Initiative because they feared it might diminish the effectiveness of the Soviet Union's retaliatory capability, thereby tempting the United States to launch a first strike. Adding to the Soviet fear of an imminent U.S. first strike was the willingness of the Reagan administration to use military force. In the sixteen months before Able Archer 83, Reagan had sent military forces to Lebanon and Central America and had mounted a military show of force against Libya. On October 25, 1983, only one week before Able Archer 83 began, the United States invaded the Caribbean island nation of Grenada—for the purpose of ousting communist "thugs."

As early as May 1981, while still director of the KGB, Yuri Andropov had concluded that the United States was preparing a nuclear attack on the Soviet Union. Detecting preparations for it, he informed KGB operatives that this must be the agency's top priority. After having spent two and a half years searching for evidence of an impending U.S. nuclear attack, Soviet intelligence agencies believed Able Archer 83 might be it. During the exercise, NATO forces appeared to be on a higher alert status than was customary during allied war games. Consequently, on November 5 Moscow sent messages to its KGB residencies across Europe emphasizing the need for heightened surveillance.

What intensified Soviet concern was the erroneous report, made by two different groups of KGB agents monitoring U.S. military bases in Germany, that U.S. troops had been placed on alert. Moscow immediately sent out flash telegrams from November 8–9 to KGB agents in Western Europe, warning them that American military bases were on a state of increased alert. Moscow warned that Able Archer 83 might be camouflaging Western preparations for a nuclear strike on the Soviet Union.

At this point, the Soviet leadership faced a critical decision. If Soviet intelligence determined that a nuclear strike against the Soviet Union was imminent, Soviet "launch-on-attack" strategy called for Moscow to launch its missiles first, before they could be destroyed by incoming U.S. and NATO missiles. Accordingly, Moscow responded to Able Archer 83 by upgrading the alert status of twelve of its nuclear-capable fighter aircraft and by ordering Soviet forces in East Germany and Poland to prepare for a retaliatory nuclear strike. But obviously the Soviet leadership did not launch a preemptive nuclear strike against the West. They had decided to wait until the West's missiles were launched before launching their own. As a result, Able

Archer 83 ended on November 11 without triggering a nuclear war. Neverthe-less, historian Christopher Andrew called it "the most dangerous moment that the world has lived through since the Cuban Missile Crisis."

Weinberger, as well as Shultz and McFarlane, downplayed Able Archer 83's impact on the Soviets, but Reagan responded with "genuine anxiety" to the news of Soviet panic. Upon learning that Moscow had readied its nuclear-capable aircraft, McFarlane recalled, the president interpreted Soviet behavior as the beginning of an inadvertent nuclear exchange. It seemed to confirm his fear that a nuclear war could result from miscalcula-tion and wipe out humanity in the process. Within one week after the con-clusion of Able Archer 83, the president established a small group within the National Security Planning Group to chart a course toward improved dia-logue with the Soviet Union. "Reagan," Beth Fischer writes, "took the reins and began to redirect U.S. Soviet policy."[4]

Although Reagan was ultimately responsible for reversing the adminis-tration's Soviet policy, Secretary of State George Shultz, supported by the president's wife, Nancy, also helped pushed him in that direction. Although a member of the Committee on the Present Danger, Shultz demonstrated a much more realistic attitude toward the strategic nuclear balance than the hard-liners in the administration. Although he recognized that ideology cer-tainly played a role in Soviet policy, he also believed that national interests usually took precedence in Soviet calculations. Shultz concurred with the hard-liners that détente had allowed the Soviet Union to grow stronger at the West's expense and that a military buildup was therefore necessary, but he also believed that the buildup should be accompanied by efforts to reduce tension in the superpower relationship, if only to reduce the risk of a nuclear war. Believing that the superpowers possessed a rough balance of nuclear forces, Shultz felt that both sides could safely reduce the size of their nuclear arsenals and that arms reduction, therefore, should be the emphasis of the U.S.-Soviet dialogue.[5]

On February 12, Shultz and his wife were invited to the White House for dinner by Nancy Reagan. In the course of the evening, Shultz told the presi-dent that he recognized how difficult it was for him to move forward in dealing with either China or the Soviet Union. The president realized, Shultz recalled, "that he was in a sense blocked by his own White House staff, by the Defense Department, by Bill Casey in the CIA, and by his own past rhetoric." But, Shultz added, "now that we were talking in this family setting, I could see that Ronald Reagan was much more willing to move forward in relations with these two Communist nations—even travel to them—than I had earlier believed." Shultz asked the president, "What would you think about my bringing [Soviet Ambassador Anatoly] Dobrynin over to the White House for a private chat?" Reagan responded, "Great." But he cautioned Shultz that the meeting would have to be kept secret. "I don't intend to engage in a detailed exchange with Dobrynin," Reagan said, "but I do intend to tell him that if Andropov is willing to do business, so am I."[6]

As expected, Shultz's initiative encountered stone-wall opposition from administration hard-liners. "It was apparent to me," Shultz recalled, "that [National Security adviser] Bill Clark and others at the White House were uneasy about how the President would perform. They didn't trust him to act on his own." Moreover, Clark and others on the National Security Council (NSC) staff were opposed to "détenteniks" within the administration—meaning primarily Shultz. Reagan informed him, however, that he wanted to get more involved with the administration's Soviet policy and, therefore, intended to meet with Dobrynin. Rather than the brief meeting with Dobrynin that Shultz had expected, Reagan talked with the Soviet ambassador for almost two hours. The gist of the president's message was, "If you are ready to move forward, so are we." Shultz was elated: "The efforts of the staff at the NSC to keep him out were beginning to break down." Moreover, he recalled, "The President was personally engaged. I felt this could be a turning point with the Soviets." It was.[7]

In his effort to open up a dialogue with the Soviets, Shultz found another ally in Robert "Bud" McFarlane, who succeeded William Clark as national security adviser in October 1983. Like the secretary of state, McFarlane agreed that the United States should rebuild its military capabilities, but he also felt that the president should leave behind a more enduring legacy than just a military buildup. Reagan should seek to negotiate treaties and agreements with the Soviets that would endure after he left office. Toward this end, McFarlane felt the administration should soften its rhetoric and begin to pursue personal contacts on a broad range of issues. He also emphasized the utility of summit meetings in reducing tensions between the superpowers and, like Shultz, advocated a more flexible position on arms control.[8]

The Rapprochement Begins
On January 16, 1984, Reagan delivered the address that announced the administration's new approach to the Kremlin. In sharp contrast to previous

remarks on the Soviet Union, he played down the ideological differences between the two superpowers and spoke at length about their "common interests," foremost of which was the desire for peace. Reducing the risk of war—and especially nuclear war—is priority number one, he declared. He called for a new U.S.-Soviet dialogue and suggested that it should concentrate on three broad areas: (1) the reduction and eventual elimination of force in regional conflicts; (2) the reduction of nuclear arsenals; (3) the creation of a better working relationship "marked by greater cooperation and understanding."[9]

The Soviets, however, initially dismissed Reagan's speech as election-year rhetoric. But Reagan persisted. He decided to communicate directly with Andropov's successor, Konstantin Chernenko. He wrote him a letter designed to allay the "genuine fears" of "some people in the Soviet Union" that the United States was planning a nuclear attack. In June, Reagan repeated his earlier strong desire to have a summit conference with Chernenko. He also softened the preconditions he had set earlier for a summit. It was no longer tied to the Soviet Union's international behavior, the consent of the NATO allies, or to a specific agenda. Now the aim was simply mutual understanding.[10]

The new Soviet leadership slowly came around to Reagan's "new thinking." They began to realize that they had gained nothing from walking out of the INF talks and that Reagan might be more willing to compromise on his zero option before the election than after. Consequently, in late June 1984 the Soviets agreed to resume arms negotiations with the United States. What particularly interested them was an agreement that would prevent the deployment of U.S. space-based weapons. Soviet Ambassador Dobrynin proposed a September meeting with Shultz that would be designed to "prevent the militarization of outer space" by banning testing or deployment of antisatellite and other weapons in space.[11]

After the Soviets publicized the proposal, the United States quickly agreed to meet in Vienna during that month to discuss "verifiable and effective limits" on antisatellite weapons. But the Americans tied talks on ASAT to Soviet willingness to resume the INF and START, which the Soviets considered a rejection of their ASAT talks proposal. That autumn he also arranged a private tête-à-tête with Foreign Minister Gromyko in order to "make it clear that we have no hostile intentions toward his country." In short, the administration's remarks were aimed at the Soviets much more than at American voters.[12]

The Election of 1984

To be sure, politics also played a role in the transformation of Reagan's Soviet policy. Reagan fully appreciated that his administration's lack of progress in the nuclear arms talks gave the Democrats a potent issue in the coming presidential election. "If the Democrats have any chance to win," one Republican strategist commented in 1984, "they have to reinforce the doubts about Reagan as a world leader, as a peacekeeper."[13]

Democratic presidential nominee Walter Mondale attempted to do just that. Mondale, who had served as vice president under President Carter, said that "four years of Ronald Reagan has made this world more dangerous. Four more years will take us closer to the brink." Mondale promised that he would begin nuclear arms control talks with the Soviets six months after his inauguration. During that interval, he said, he would initiate a unilateral freeze on the deployment of new U.S. nuclear weapons as a first step toward achieving a meaningful arms reduction agreement. Mondale also attacked SDI and called for a ban on antisatellite weapons (ASAT).[14]

Mondale's pressure on Reagan was augmented by the Congress. On June 12, 1984, the Senate refused to appropriate additional money for ASAT development unless the president certified that he was "endeavoring in good faith to negotiate the strictest possible limitations on anti-satellite weapons." Eight days later, that body passed a nonbinding amendment, by a vote of 77 to 22, calling for the president to attempt to gain ratification of two unratified, partial test-ban treaties—the Threshold Test Ban Treaty (TTBT) and the Peaceful Nuclear Explosions Treaty (PNET)—and to resume negotiations for a comprehensive test ban agreement. But the Reagan administration charged that the Soviet Union had violated the TTBT 150-kiloton threshold on underground nuclear tests.[15]

The Soviets added to the congressional pressure. To prove that they were not cheating, they agreed to a joint verification experiment, in which scientists from the two sides would conduct very intrusive, and costly, on-site measurements of actual tests at the Nevada and Semipalatinsk test sites. The results apparently confirmed that there was no basis for the administration's charges. On June 29 the Soviets proposed that the two sides begin talks in Geneva on September 19, only five weeks before the presidential election, on ways to ban the militarization of outer space. Until such a ban could be negotiated, they suggested a joint moratorium on all ASAT and ABM tests.[16]

Six weeks before the election, in a speech before the U.N. General Assembly on September 24, 1984, Reagan proposed the establishment of a new U.S.-Soviet negotiating "framework." He suggested combining the various arms control talks under one "umbrella," which, he promised, would make it difficult for a stalemate in one part of the negotiations to disrupt progress in the others. Reagan's ability to defuse the antinuclear weapons movement by pressing the Soviets to return to the negotiating table was a major contributing factor in his landslide election victory in November.[17]

The Geneva Talks Begin

On November 7, 1984—the day after the election—Reagan sent another letter to Chernenko, asking him to resume the nuclear arms reduction talks. Faced with Reagan for another four years, the Soviets expressed interest in his offer for "umbrella" talks. They obviously were intent on doing all they could, even to the point of agreeing to resume talks on strategic weapons and INF, to halt the threat of a nuclear arms race in space. As a result, on November 22 it was announced that Shultz would meet with Soviet foreign minister Gromyko in Geneva on January 7–8, 1985, to negotiate an agenda on limiting nuclear arms. The meeting between Shultz and Gromyko resulted in a formula for the scope of the planned talks, which would be called the Nuclear and Space Talks (NST). They would consist of three sets of negotiations. One would deal with strategic offensive reductions (START), another with intermediate-range missile forces (INF), and a third with strategic defense- and space-based weapons (DST, or Defense and Space Talks).[18]

Although Reagan resumed nuclear arms negotiations with the Soviets, he ruled out U.S. concessions on SDI. Moreover, he signed a national security directive in January 1985 stating that the United States must maintain an arsenal that would allow it to conduct a nuclear war with the Soviet Union, "with the reasonable assurance of success"—a departure from the administration's public rhetoric of the same period, which had emphasized that nuclear war "cannot be won and must not be fought."[19]

Little progress was made during the first two rounds of the new talks, which began in March 1985 and ended in July. Although there were sharp differences between the two sides on several issues, the main obstacle was SDI. The Reagan administration again proposed major reductions in strategic and intermediate-range nuclear weapons but refused to discuss limitations on ballistic missile defenses. Without them, the Soviets refused to make any reductions in offensive strategic and theater weapons. Still, upon Chernenko's death on March 10, Reagan issued a summit invitation to the new Soviet leader, Mikhail Gorbachev. "The stakes were too high," Reagan remarked, "for us not to try to find a common ground where we could meet and reduce the risk of Armageddon."[20]

"New Thinking" in the Soviet Leadership
Fortunately, the new Soviet leader was just as willing as the U.S. president to reduce the number of nuclear weapons. Intelligent, articulate, and relatively young (54), Mikhail Gorbachev was a stunning contrast to his unimaginative and heavy-handed predecessors. He had been raised to the pinnacle of the Soviet power structure from relative obscurity because of the "old guard's" inability to solve a number of critical and, as subsequent events would demonstrate, fatal problems inherent in the Soviet system.

The most significant problem was the Soviet economy, which could no longer produce or absorb the technological innovations—particularly in the field of computers—that were the basis of economic expansion in the advanced industrial countries. As a result, the gap between Soviet economic output and that of the leading industrial countries widened in the 1980s, for the first time in postwar history. The growing Soviet military establishment also placed enormous stress on the Soviet economy. During the Brezhnev period, when defense spending in Western and Eastern Europe averaged between 2 and 5 percent and in the United States about 6-7 percent of Gross National Product (GNP), the defense share of Soviet GNP rose from 12-14 percent in 1965 to 15-17 percent in 1985. (Some sources, which used different estimates of Soviet GNP, put the total as high as 25 percent, which was an enormous burden on the industrial sector.)[21]

Not surprisingly, Gorbachev saw arms reduction as the key element in improving the Soviet image in the West. An end to the arms race would reduce Soviet defense expenditures and make possible badly needed Western economic assistance to the Soviet Union. With respect to European nuclear weapons, Gorbachev's new thinking attached more importance to eliminating U.S. IRBMs in Europe than in achieving a favorable balance of nuclear forces, as Brezhnev and Andropov had sought to do. Not only were the new U.S. missiles a threat to the Soviet homeland, they were a major obstacle to improved relations in Europe. Consequently, in April 1985, only one month after taking office, Gorbachev seized the initiative in arms control by announcing a six-month moratorium on the deployment of Soviet INF as well as the testing of nuclear weapons; he called for similar moratoria by the United States. However, with only one hundred Pershing IIs and Tomahawks deployed by that time, compared to over four hundred deployed

Soviet ss-20s, the Reagan administration was in no mood to reciprocate.[22]

Nevertheless, Gorbachev kept the pressure on the Reagan administration. On June 12 he expressed his readiness to begin joint U.S.-Soviet calibration tests that could verify a ban on virtually all nuclear weapon tests down to a one-kiloton yield. On August 6 the Soviets unilaterally halted all nuclear test explosions until the end of the year (a moratorium that was extended repeatedly) in an attempt to initiate a resumption of the talks on a comprehensive test ban treaty. Gorbachev invited the United States to join the Soviet test moratorium. But the administration rejected the invitation, since the United States was testing new nuclear weapons and did not want to terminate the tests. When Gorbachev, in a letter to Reagan on December 5, committed the Soviet Union to accept on-site inspections as part of any CTBT, the United States replied that a comprehensive test ban was "a long-term objective."[23]

Other actions by Gorbachev reflected his desire to ameliorate long-standing elements of the superpower confrontation. In the fall, Soviet ballistic missile submarine patrols off the U.S. coasts were discontinued. And, for the first time in a decade, there was no Soviet naval visit to the Caribbean (which set a new pattern). Overall, Soviet naval activity around the world declined. By altering the bases of Soviet defense strategy, as well as the ideological foundation of Soviet foreign policy, Gorbachev in effect was declaring that he was prepared to end the Cold War. Reagan was more than willing to oblige. In late July 1985, Paul Nitze met with Shevardnadze to hammer out the terms for a November summit in Geneva between Reagan and Gorbachev.[24]

Reinterpreting the ABM Treaty

On September 30, 1985, over a month before the Geneva summit occurred, the Soviet delegation tabled a proposal to cut nuclear weapons by 50 percent. The Soviet offer called for a combined ceiling of 6,000 warheads and bombs. Of these, no more than 3,600 could be on land-based ICBMs. The proposal also offered to freeze the number of Soviet three-warhead ss-20s at 243 in return for a limit of 120 U.S. single-warhead missiles on French and British missiles; that would bring both sides to an equal warhead total of 729. Apparently, Moscow wanted the limits to apply to cruise missiles only, in an attempt to ban the Pershing IIs.

However, the Soviets made clear that they would not accept radical reductions in their strategic nuclear arsenal unless the United States accepted "a total ban on space-strike weapons." Gorbachev also said the ban must "embrace every phase of the inception of this new class of arms," including research. However, he also said that "fundamental science" would be permitted; that only "out-of-laboratory" work should be banned. This apparently altered an earlier Soviet proposal for a ban on all research on "space-strike arms." The Soviets also proposed an antisatellite weapon ban as a first step toward a complete ban on space-strike arms.[25]

However, Reagan had no intention of banning SDI research, in or out of the laboratory. On September 17 he stated categorically that he would not curtail SDI in exchange for Soviet reductions in offensive missiles. And although the administration had stated that SDI research would be conducted in full compliance with the ABM Treaty, an unnamed White House "senior official"—McFarlane—in a background briefing two days later, claimed that the Soviet "arms buildup" put "very much in question" the value of the ABM Treaty and said that "it might be necessary" to modify the treaty in the future. A few weeks later, Weinberger was characteristically more blunt: he said that the United States should consider breaking the ABM Treaty.[26]

However, Shultz pointed out to Reagan that withdrawing from the ABM Treaty would produce a major political battle with the Senate, which would uphold the sanctity of treaties it had approved. In addition, U.S. abrogation of the treaty would have a serious negative impact on U.S. relations with the Soviet Union, including almost certainly an end to the arms control process. Such a consequence would cause an uproar in NATO, which desired a deepening of détente, not its termination. In other words, unilateral U.S. abrogation of the ABM Treaty was politically impossible for the Reagan administration. On the other hand, amending the ABM Treaty to permit SDI research and development would require the concurrence not only of the Soviet Union but also the Senate, and neither was likely to concur.[27]

As a result, the administration decided to reinterpret the treaty in order to permit continued research and eventual development of SDI. That task was assigned to State Department counsel Abraham Sofaer, whom New York governor Mario Cuomo called "a great New York lawyer. If they tell him, 'Make it legal, Abe,' he'll make it legal." In attempting to do so, Sofaer argued that the ABM Treaty should be interpreted in the context of its entire negotiating record, rather than just the terms of the treaty itself. The result, the so-called broad interpretation, held that the parties of the ABM Treaty were allowed to develop and test ABM systems and components that are sea based, air based, or space based but are not permitted to deploy them. The new interpretation, Sofaer asserted, would permit "experiments" (rather than tests) on subcomponents (rather than components) of the SDI. By comparison, the traditional, strict interpretation allowed no more than fundamental laboratory research.[28]

Although the negotiating record was classified, Raymond Garthoff, who was a member of the U.S. delegation to the ABM Treaty negotiations, argued that the broad interpretation was flawed because the method by which it was reviewed was flawed. According to Garthoff, Sofaer's review of the ABM Treaty negotiating record lasted only two and a half weeks. During this time, he and his three assistants were unable to locate all the relevant negotiating history and did not adequately review known records on subsequent practice. Unlike the negotiating record, however, the ratification record was largely unclassified, and it soon became apparent that Sofaer's study of the issue had omitted, or misrepresented, a number of key statements. Sofaer was forced to withdraw his claim that this record supported the broad interpretation, blaming his ratification studies on "young lawyers" on his staff. For Garthoff, Sofaer's misleading account of the ratification record was not an isolated incident.[29]

Nevertheless, on October 6 McFarlane announced that the administration would adopt the new, broad interpretation of the ABM Treaty. His announcement triggered an uproar on Capitol Hill and in NATO. Senator Sam Nunn, the ranking Democrat on the Senate Armed Services Committee, and House Foreign Affairs Committee chairman Dante Fascell threatened congressional retaliation against the administration's defense program if it ignored a treaty passed by the Senate. NATO allies, for their part, feared that the new interpretation—about which they were not consulted—would undermine the ABM Treaty at a time when they were trying to revive the arms control process. Both Prime Minister Margaret Thatcher of Great Britain and Chancellor Helmut Kohl of West Germany promptly wrote to President Reagan questioning the administration's action.[30]

The Soviet reaction was swift and angry. Marshall Sergei Akhromeyev called the "nonrestrictive" U.S. interpretation "deliberate deceit," which "distorted the essence of the treaty [by] trying to substantiate the lawfulness of experiments" that are prohibited. The Soviets accused the Reagan administration of looking for a way to withdraw from the ABM Treaty. If this were not true, they "expected" the United States to "take practical actions to ensure strict fulfillment of the ABM treaty, including renunciation of preparations to deploy a large-scale ABM system."[31]

Although George Shultz publicly supported Sofaer's interpretation of the treaty, he was upset by "the outrageous way this matter had been handled procedurally." There is no indication that McFarlane had even discussed the matter with the president before he spoke publicly about it, Shultz complained. This, he asserted, was "irresponsible." Moreover, Shultz argued, SDI was a research program that was permitted under the traditional interpretation of the ABM Treaty and, therefore, there was no need to rile up the allies and Congress by a "premature" announcement of the broad interpretation.[32]

Shultz's stance on the ABM Treaty was attacked by Weinberger. In a meeting between the two men and the president on October 11, the transcript of which was leaked to the press, Shultz reportedly said, "It's hard to say what the Soviets would do" if the broad interpretation were adopted by the administration. Weinberger responded, "We shouldn't debate with the Soviets what can and can't be prohibited." Reagan sided with Weinberger. "Why don't we just go ahead [with SDI] on the assumption that this is what we're doing and it's right. . . . Don't ask the Soviets. Tell 'em." Not only Shultz, but Admiral William J. Crowe, chairman of the Joint Chiefs of Staff, strongly objected to this approach.[33]

In an attempt to sidestep the mushrooming controversy between his two most important national security advisers, Reagan accepted a compromise position by which the United States would, for the moment, continue to respect the narrow interpretation of the ABM Treaty while reserving the option to adopt the broad interpretation at a later date. Although the compromise temporarily quieted the firestorm caused by the broad interpretation, it did not settle the issue of the ABM Treaty interpretation. Although the administration could argue, as it did, that the treaty did not prohibit research on, and testing of, SDI components, it was quite clear to most in the know that the treaty barred their development and deployment. Even SDIO Director General Abrahamson admitted as much. "There clearly will come a time," he said, "when we enter the development phase, and the development phase will require [so] much more direct testing, that we will have to have a modified treaty in some way in order to proceed . . ."[34]

Nevertheless, the administration's broad interpretation, even though not adopted, threatened to undermine the ABM Treaty as well as START. By affirming the validity of the broad interpretation, the administration had asserted its right to change, unilaterally if necessary, the terms of the ABM Treaty. The administration could hardly deny the Soviets the right to do so as well. Further, the Soviets had stated repeatedly that they would not accept deep reductions in offensive weapons while the United States argued that it was free to develop spaced-based defensive weapons. Compliance with the traditional, strict interpretation of the ABM Treaty, the Soviets insisted, was a prerequisite for reductions in strategic offensive arms.

Since Weinberger and Perle were aware that this was the Soviet position, it can only be concluded that scuttling both the ABM Treaty and START was their ultimate objective. Realizing this, Shultz, with the support of McFarlane and White House chief of staff Donald Regan, persuaded the president to keep Weinberger in Washington during the Geneva summit. Piqued by his exclusion and concerned that Shultz would persuade Reagan to "give away the store" at Geneva, Weinberger sent a letter to the president that strongly urged him not to agree to any limitation of SDI at the summit. The letter was intentionally leaked to the press the very day Reagan arrived in Geneva. Speaking anonymously as a senior White House official, McFarlane told the press that Weinberger's letter was clearly an attempt to prevent any agreement that could even peripherally curb SDI.[35]

Soviet Cheating

Ironically, while the Reagan administration was attempting to circumvent the ABM Treaty, it accused the Soviet Union of repeatedly violating not only that agreement but also various other arms control agreements. Among alleged Soviet violations, one that was later substantiated, was the so-called large phased-array radar (LPAR) installation near the village of Abalakova, about one hundred forty miles north of the Siberian city of Krasnoyarsk. The Krasnoyarsk installation, the administration charged, constituted a violation of the ABM Treaty, which bars construction of radar stations and other equipment, except at national borders, that could enhance a country's defense against incoming missiles or serve as an early warning system for an ABM system.[36]

Even though the U.S. Joint Chiefs of Staff concluded that the East-West nuclear balance of forces would not be affected by the Krasnoyarsk project, the National Security Council concluded that its "political consequences were vast," as Shultz put it. An unnumbered national security decision directive that was issued on February 1, 1985, contended that the alleged Soviet violations demonstrated not only their intention to disregard U.S.-Soviet arms treaties in general, but a specific plan to build an antimissile battle-management network designed to protect the entire Soviet Union. If the administration could prove these charges, hard-liners argued, it would effectively preclude the need to reach any new agreements with the Soviets. The

alleged Soviet violations were employed subsequently by administration officials as a reason to continue U.S. underground nuclear testing, increase
spending on chemical and biological warfare programs, develop and deploy
controversial weapon systems (such as the MX missile and the B-I bomber),
abandon the limits of the SALT II Treaty in late 1986, and justify the broad
reinterpretation of the ABM Treaty.[37]

The Soviets responded to U.S. accusations regarding the Krasnoyarsk
radar by asserting that it was being built for space tracking and verification
purposes only and was therefore exempt from the ABM Treaty's geographical
restrictions on early warning radars. Ironically, the provision in Agreed
Statement F of the ABM Treaty, which exempts space-tracking radars from
these restrictions, was reportedly inserted at the insistence of the United
States, which wanted to keep open the option of developing and deploying
large phased-array radars for tracking satellites. They also questioned two
large phased-array radars that were being constructed by the United States at
Thule, Greenland, and Fylingdales Moor, England. Both involved the
replacement of old electronically steered, early-warning radars by new LPARS.
But since the two new radars were not on the periphery of U.S. territory facing outward, the Soviets charged that they were violations of the treaty.

In response, the United States claimed that the radars were not violations
because the sites already existed at the time the ABM Treaty was signed.
Moreover, the radars were being modernized, an activity not prohibited by
the treaty. When added to President Reagan's strong commitment to the
Strategic Defense Initiative, however, the U.S. radars gave the Soviets plenty
of reason for concern. But instead of resolving conflicting interpretations
concerning these radars in the Standing Consultative Commission (SCC),
which was created by the ABM Treaty to settle U.S.-Soviet disputes over
treaty compliance, the Reagan administration took its case directly to the
Congress and the public.[38]

The Geneva Summit, November 1985
Shortly before the Geneva summit, Shultz met with Gorbachev. He again
complained about the Krasnoyarsk radar. He also told the Soviet leader that
the assumptions on which the ABM and SALT I treaties were made "haven't
held up." He explained that, under these agreements, the number of strategic
offensive forces had increased and not diminished. Although the ABM Treaty
permitted each country to maintain one ABM site, the United States abandoned its only site in 1975, whereas the Soviets continued to maintain one

around Moscow. Gorbachev responded by asserting that the real threat to the ABM Treaty was the administration's broad interpretation, not the Krasnoyarsk radar. He told Shultz: "You only invented this [broad] interpretation of the ABM Treaty . . . because you wanted to get out of the ABM restrictions." He then said the Soviet Union would accept 50 percent reductions in the number of nuclear warheads if the United States promised to abide by the strict interpretation of the ABM Treaty. But he also warned Shultz that if the Reagan administration pursued "superiority through your SDI . . . we will let you bankrupt yourselves. But also we will not reduce our offensive missiles; we will engage in a buildup that will break your shield."[39]

Gorbachev also told Shultz that he hoped that the Geneva meeting, scheduled for November 19-20, would not simply be a "get-acquainted meeting," which it indeed turned out to be. At the summit, Reagan submitted a proposal to Gorbachev that called for a 50 percent reduction in strategic armaments. It called for a ceiling of between 1,250 and 1,450 ICBMs and SLBMs for each side. In addition, each side would be allowed a combined limit of 4,500 ICBM and SLBM warheads. Of this number, only 3,000 could be placed on ICBMs. The administration proposal also offered to limit bombers to 350, instead of the 400 figure it previously had favored. The offer also proposed to reduce cruise missiles to 1,500, instead of the 4,000 proposed earlier. But the administration again insisted that the total throw weight of both sides must be reduced by 50 percent. In addition, the administration called for a ban on mobile ICBMs in an attempt to force the Soviets to scrap their new SS-24 and SS-25 ICBMs. Yet this also would require the United States to give up the Midgetman mobile ICBM. Finally, the administration proposed to limit long-range INF to 140 missiles for each side but to exclude those of Britain and France.[40]

However, the U.S. reduction proposal was tied to Soviet acceptance of SDI. The president outlined his goal of moving deterrence toward greater reliance on defense and away from the threat of nuclear retaliation, but he assured the Soviet leader that the U.S. research program would remain consistent with the ABM Treaty. The U.S. proposal also sought a Soviet commitment to jointly explore a cooperative transition from mutual assured destruction to mutual defenses. To improve "predictability" in strategic defenses, the U.S. proposal also called for an "open laboratories" initiative, in which both sides would share information and reciprocal laboratory visits on strategic defense. Reagan also attempted to persuade the Soviet leader to modify his opposition toward space-based defenses with an impassioned argument about how much better the world would be if both nations could defend themselves against nuclear missiles. He expressed his abhorrence at having to rely on the ability to "wipe each other out" as the means of keeping the peace. "We must do better, and we can," he said. After what seemed like an interminable time, Shultz recalled, Gorbachev replied, "Mr. President, I don't agree with you, but I can see that you really mean what you say." But he still rejected the U.S. proposal, saying that it "would allow the U.S. to forge ahead with sdi."[41]

Although the two sides were unable to achieve a meeting of the minds on sdi at Geneva, they did agree, in a joint statement, "that nuclear war cannot be won and must never be fought." Moreover, they emphasized the importance of preventing any war between the United States and the Soviet Union, whether nuclear or conventional. They also agreed that the two sides "will not seek to achieve military superiority." Gorbachev also accepted Reagan's invitation to visit the United States, and the president accepted Gorbachev's recommendation that they plan a follow-up summit in Moscow.[42]

After his return to the United States, Reagan told a joint session of Congress that he had called for a "fresh start" and added that he believed one had been made. "We understand each other better and that's a key to peace. . . . We remain far apart on a number of issues, as had to be expected," but "we're ready and eager for step-by-step progress." Although hard-liners were uneasy and unhappy about launching a new dialogue with the Soviet Union, the American press reflected the unanimous view that Reagan had "won" the summit encounter with Gorbachev.[43]

Summit Interlude

If Reagan "won" the Geneva summit, neither Congress nor Gorbachev eased the pressure on him to engage in meaningful arms reduction talks. On December 19, 1985, shortly after the United States conducted an antisatellite weapon test, Congress banned further asat testing, as long as the Soviet Union continued its unilateral moratorium on such tests. In March 1986 House Speaker Thomas "Tip" O'Neill (D-Mass.) urged a halt to underground testing of nuclear weapons. Gorbachev, for his part, expressed his willingness to accept on-site inspection of nuclear test ranges in order to verify a nuclear test moratorium. But the Reagan administration was not interested.[44]

Realizing that the nuclear arms talks were again going nowhere, Gorbachev was free to make a grandiose proposal without fearing that the

United States would accept it. On January 15, 1986, he proposed a broad timetable for the elimination of all nuclear weapons by the end of the century. But he repeated his stand that "such a reduction is possible only if the USSR and the U.S. mutually renounce the development, testing, and deployment of space-strike weapons." Reagan welcomed the Soviet proposal and then, ignoring it, offered a counterproposal of his own. In essence, the new offer was a restatement of the zero option of 1981, except that it called for the elimination of intermediate-range missiles in Europe and Asia over a three-year period. In the first year, intermediate-range missiles in Europe would be cut to 140 for each side, while the Soviets would be obliged to make proportional reductions in their ss-20 force based in Asia. In the second year, the remaining intermediate-range missiles would be cut in half and, in the third year, they would be totally eliminated. Gorbachev responded by calling Reagan's counterproposal inadequate.[45]

Reagan put additional pressure on the Soviet Union. On May 27, 1986, he stated flatly that, in the light of the alleged violations of the SALT II Treaty by the Soviets, and partly because the treaty, even if ratified, would have expired in 1985, the United States would no longer abide by it. (Until then, the United States had stayed within the treaty's limits by withdrawing old nuclear weapons systems as new ones were deployed.) However, Reagan hedged somewhat by stating that he might reconsider his decision if the Soviets reversed their pattern of violations. Gorbachev responded by stating that Reagan's decision raised "the legitimate question of whether Washington really wants a new [summit] meeting." In late 1986 the administration decided to deploy air-launched cruise missiles on B-52s, a step that would put the United States over SALT II's limits.[46]

Although the United States abandoned the SALT II limits, both sides continued to pursue a START agreement. On June 11 the Soviets tabled a new START proposal, contingent upon "nonwithdrawal from the Antiballistic Missile Treaty for at least 15 years, and restricting SDI work to laboratory research, that is, the threshold already actually reached by the U.S." The administration responded to the new Soviet proposal on July 25, in a letter from Reagan to Gorbachev, which was subsequently described in the president's September 22 address to the U.N. General Assembly. Reagan proposed that "first, both sides would agree to confine themselves through 1991 to research, development, and testing, which is permitted by the ABM Treaty, to determine whether advanced systems of strategic defense are technically feasible. Second . . . if, after 1991, either side should decide to deploy such a system, that side would be obliged to offer a plan for sharing the benefits of strategic defense and for eliminating offensive ballistic missiles. And this plan would be negotiated over a two-year period. Third, if the two sides can't agree after two years of negotiation, either side would be free to deploy an advanced strategic defensive system after giving six months' notice to the other." The president also proposed that the United States and the Soviet Union discuss "elimination of ballistic missiles"—a phrase that would come back to haunt him during the summit at Reykjavik, Iceland, later that year.[47]

Thus, by the summer of 1986, both sides had agreed on the concept of a period of several years during which neither would withdraw from the ABM Treaty, although they disagreed on virtually everything else, including what would be permitted during the period, how long it would last, and what would happen afterward.

The Reykjavik Summit, October 1986

On September 19, 1986, Gorbachev sent a letter to Reagan in which he suggested a preliminary summit meeting that would attempt to break the logjam in the Geneva talks. Reagan accepted, and the meeting was scheduled to take place in Reykjavik, Iceland, from October 11-12. Given the immensely favorable publicity the president had received as a result of the Geneva summit the previous November, Reagan hoped that the Reykjavik meeting would have beneficial effects on Republican fortunes in the congressional elections only a month later. A summit would also serve to keep the Democratic-controlled Congress in line. Arguing that he did not want his hands "tied" at Reykjavik, Reagan persuaded the Democratic leadership of the House to withdraw two of their key resolutions on arms control. One mandated continued U.S. compliance with the SALT II Treaty. The other called for a one-year moratorium on nuclear testing. The House leadership dropped the resolutions in exchange for Reagan's promise to work for an agreement with the Soviets that would restrict nuclear testing.[48]

Although billed as a preparatory meeting, Gorbachev arrived in Reykjavik with detailed proposals that turned the meeting into a full-scale summit. The Soviet leader offered a START proposal that again called for deep, 50 percent reductions in strategic nuclear weapons. He proposed that, over a five-year period, the number of warheads carried by ballistic missiles and air-launched cruise missiles (ALCMs) should be lowered to 6,000 and the number of long-range missiles and bombers to 1,600. (At the time of the Reykjavik summit, the Soviet Union had 2,500 missiles and bombers, and the United

States about 2,100.) The Soviets also dropped their earlier demand for a common limit on missile warheads and bombs. They proposed instead that each bomber with multiple bombs and short-range attack missiles should count as one weapon under the 6,000 ceiling, and each bomber with ALCMS as well as bombs and short-range missiles would count as two weapons under the total ceiling. The Soviets also agreed to exclude sea-launched cruise missiles from the 6,000 ceiling.[49]

However, neither side could agree about what would transpire in the second year of the proposed ten-year agreement. Reagan suggested that both sides eliminate all offensive ballistic missiles, in effect leaving each with only cruise missiles and bombers to constitute their strategic deterrent forces. Gorbachev, however, favored the elimination of all long-range nuclear weapons, including bombers and cruise missiles. Surprisingly, considering that Reagan had not consulted his allies, whose defense rested heavily on nuclear weapons, he responded positively to Gorbachev's proposal. He then went one step further and called for the abolition of all ballistic missiles within ten years. Gorbachev "saw and raised" the ante: He proposed eliminating all strategic nuclear weapons in the ten-year period. Reagan agreed, saying he would be ready to eliminate all nuclear weapons in ten years; Gorbachev agreed at once.[50]

The second area of agreement at Reykjavik concerned INF. Both sides accepted a global limit of 100 INF warheads, with the Soviet deployments restricted to Asia and America's constrained to the United States. Thus both sides agreed to implement Reagan's original zero option; they would withdraw all their intermediate-range missiles from Europe. (By October 1986 the Soviets had deployed 513 warheads on 171 ss-20 missiles in Asia and 810 warheads on 270 ss-20s in Europe. The United States had deployed 108 Pershing II IRBMS and 160 Tomahawk GLCMS, for a total of 268 warheads.) Reagan and Gorbachev also agreed on verification steps and on freezing shorter-range missiles pending further negotiations.[51]

Nuclear testing was a third subject on which agreement was reached at Reykjavik. Gorbachev accepted Reagan's proposal for a phased reduction of nuclear testing, starting with the verification of existing treaties and working toward an ultimate cessation of tests. The president, however, refused to say what types of limits on testing he favored, but two types were under consideration within the administration. One would gradually lower the number of nuclear tests permitted each year, whereas another would gradually reduce the limit on the size of explosions below the threshold of 150 kilotons.[52]

However, as in the Geneva summit the preceding November, the Iceland meeting fell apart over SDI. Late in the last day of the summit, Gorbachev announced that all the concessions that he had made were contingent on U.S. adherence to a strict interpretation of the ABM Treaty, which banned the development and deployment of space-based ABMs. Gorbachev insisted that there be no testing and development of ABMs and that research be confined to the laboratory. The Soviet interpretation, Reagan said, was designed to kill SDI. He expressed his administration's willingness to abide by the ABM Treaty, but only for an additional ten years, provided research, development, and testing in accordance with the broad interpretation could continue. During that period, both sides would eliminate all their offensive ballistic missiles and would then be free to deploy defensive systems. Reagan's proposal would have permitted the United States to continue to develop SDI while eliminating Soviet as well as American offensive missiles. Reagan also promised that if SDI worked, the United States would share its fruits with the Soviet Union. But Gorbachev expressed doubt that the United State would share SDI technology, considering that at the time the administration was denying the Soviet Union oil-drilling technology. He argued that, since neither side would have nuclear weapons, there would be no need for defensive systems. As a result, the Reykjavik summit ended in disagreement, with each side blaming the other for its collapse.[53]

Nevertheless, there are some "what-ifs" in connection with the Reykjavik summit. Shultz recounted in his memoir that as the summit was about to collapse over the issue of restricting the testing of space-based ABMs to "the laboratory," Reagan slipped a note to him asking, "Am I wrong?" Shultz reports that he looked at him and whispered back, "No, you are right." Analyst Raymond Garthoff suggests that Reagan may only have been seeking confirmation of his no-yield position on SDI. But, Garthoff wondered, what would have happened if Shultz had said, "You could propose no testing of weapons in space, and no research and testing of space systems except as allowed by the ABM Treaty?" Or, what if Gorbachev's Politburo-cleared position had been framed that way? Perhaps an agreement could have been reached on that basis at Reykjavik.[54]

Along the same line, Senator Sam Nunn, the Democratic chairman of the Armed Services Committee, wondered why the president let pass an opportunity for major reductions in the number of Soviet nuclear weapons in order to preserve SDI, which the senator considered at best only a technological "possibility." But Nunn also quipped, "if the Soviets took us up" on Reagan's proposal to eliminate all ballistic missiles, "every general in the Army and the Air Force, and probably some admirals, too, would have had a heart attack."[55]

Nunn was closer to the truth than he may have realized. The Joint Chiefs of Staff, as well as the military and political leaders of NATO, were stunned by Reagan's apparent willingness to abandon, without any advance consultation with them, nuclear weapons, the core of the alliance's flexible response deterrence strategy. Some of the allies were also upset by Reagan's willingness to eliminate all INF missiles in Europe, after declaring, in presummit consultation with them, the U.S. intention to retain a level of 100 INF. But the allies were reluctant to appear opposed to progress in arms reductions and therefore did not protest too loudly or long. Fortunately, from their point of view, the Reykjavik agreement to eliminate offensive nuclear weapons fell apart on the ABM Treaty issue. Nevertheless, in the eyes of the allies, Reagan's credibility as a stalwart of alliance defense was severely shaken by the Reykjavik summit.[56]

Reagan's unwillingness to trade away SDI at the Iceland summit laid to rest the argument that it was pursued primarily for arms control purposes. Had he been willing to abandon SDI, an agreement could have produced a vastly reduced nuclear arsenal. In doing what he did, Reagan demonstrated the truth of what he had been saying all along: SDI was not negotiable. Reykjavik also demonstrated the high expectations he had for SDI. "I told Gorbachev," Reagan recalled, "that SDI was a reason to hope, not to fear, that the advance of technology, which originally gave us ballistic missiles, may soon be able to make them obsolete. . . . I could no more negotiate on SDI than I could barter with your future."[57]

Reagan tried to put on the best possible face after the summit's failure. Two days after it ended, he said, "Believe me, the significance of that meeting at Reykjavik is not that we didn't sign agreements in the end; the significance is that we got as close as we did. The progress that we made would've been inconceivable just a few month ago." But Gorbachev was deeply upset by his inability to shake Reagan's continued adherence to SDI. He charged that the president was "being held captive by the [military-industrial] complex" and hence was "not free to take such a decision."[58]

Gorbachev's assessment of Reagan, however, was off the mark. The president genuinely wanted to shift U.S. strategy from nuclear retaliation to nuclear defense. Nevertheless, like Reagan, Gorbachev had an interest in not letting the Reykjavik summit appear a total failure. Not only was his own reputation as a negotiator at stake, he also could not forget the economic necessity of reducing the size of the Soviet military establishment. And he needed détente with the West in order to make possible Western economic assistance to the Soviet Union. Accordingly, members of the Soviet Geneva delegation said that Gorbachev was impressed by Reagan's readiness to agree to zero INF missiles in Europe and even to entertain the idea of eliminating all nuclear weapons.[59]

Scaling Back SDI

When Reagan terminated the Reykjavik meeting without an agreement, administration hard-liners, led by Caspar Weinberger, could barely conceal their relief. However, they couched their feelings with praise for the president's ability to avoid being "trapped" by Gorbachev. Still, hard-liners were alarmed by the closeness of Reagan's approach to an agreement at Reykjavik. Accordingly, after the summit, they lost little time in deciding that the only way to prevent the president from making concessions on SDI was to push for early deployment of the system. Proponents of early deployment also believed that changing SDI from a research to a construction program would result in greater pressure for high spending levels, particularly from states and congressional districts, like Colorado, in which components of the program would be produced. Attorney General Meese captured the essence of this sentiment by arguing for an early deployment of SDI "so it will be in place and not tampered with by future administrations." Meese fully understood Reagan's importance to SDI. Without him, the program did not stand much of a chance.[60]

There were a number of other reasons for pushing the early deployment of SDI. Ironically, one was related to a number of technical problems that proved more difficult to solve then originally anticipated. They included acquiring the capability to discriminate real missiles from decoys, writing the computer software that would coordinate the entire system, launching the components into space (a problem aggravated by the tragic explosion of the *Challenger* shuttle in January 1986), protecting the components against attack once they were in orbit, and bringing costs down to an affordable level. These and other problems, combined with repeated congressional cuts in SDI appropriations, forced the administration to conclude that no substantial missile defense could be fully deployed before the turn of the century, an estimate that itself was highly optimistic.

As a result, the administration began to argue for early deployment of a limited system, called Phase 1. It included space-based interceptors, designed to attack Soviet missiles just after launch, during their boost and postboost phases, and ground-based Exoatmospheric Reentry Vehicle Interceptor System (ERIS) missiles, designed to shoot down Soviet warheads during mid-course flight in space. These would be combined with space- and ground-based sensors to detect and track Soviet missiles, and a battle-management system to tie the defense together. SDI's original goal was also scaled down. Instead of the total, nationwide coverage established as a goal by Reagan in 1983, Phase 1 called for a defense that could stop at least 30 percent of a limited "first-wave" Soviet attack using as many as 5,000 warheads. This would still allow over 3,300 Soviet warheads to detonate on U.S. soil, even if Phase 1 worked as advertised.

However, a report issued in June 1988 by Congress's Office of Technology Assessment (OTA) raised serious doubts about Phase 1's ability to achieve its more limited goals. The report concluded that the command software problem was so severe that "there would be a significant probability that the first (and presumably only) time the ballistic missile defense system were used in a real war, it would suffer a catastrophic failure." The report also concluded that survivability was the number one piece of "missing technology" for the Phase 1 system, arguing that the possibility of "attack by ground-based lasers and ASATs in peacetime is particularly disturbing." It suggested that the Soviet Union could deploy additional ICBMs more cheaply than the United States could deploy additional spaced-based interceptors to defend against them. And even SDIO acknowledged that faster-burning missiles could release their warheads before they could be intercepted.[61]

Even more disturbing, the OTA report argued that deployment of missile defenses could ignite a new arms race in space. It stated that "if the Soviet Union had ballistic missile defenses comparable to the United States, the net effect of trying to defend land-based missiles against a Soviet strike would be to *reduce* the U.S. ability to carry out planned retaliatory missions." Although the survivability of the land-based missiles would be improved, both they and sea-based missiles would then have to penetrate Soviet defenses. The result "could be to weaken, not strengthen, deterrence."[62]

The astronomical cost of Phase 1 was another major concern. Representative Jack Brooks (D-Tex.), chairman of the Government Operations Committee, noted in a May 2, 1988 memo that the amount of research funding required to begin making "informed technical decisions" on whether to proceed to full-scale engineering development of a missile defense system had grown from $26 billion to $57.5 billion. SDIO estimated that full deployment of Phase 1 would cost $75-150 billion, not counting such important expenses as operations and maintenance. Critics argued that for a system whose goals were such a far cry from Reagan's original dream of a nationwide ABM, phase 1 was very expensive. The House of Representatives agreed. On May 4, 1988, by a vote of 244 to 174, it passed an amendment that would prevent SDIO from spending more than 40 percent of its budget on development of a partial Phase 1 defense. This marked the first time Congress had provided a binding budgetary ceiling on the SDI program, rather than simply a limit on the overall dollars that could be spent.[63]

The Joint Chiefs of Staff also "expressed concern" with the "big bite [SDI] would take out of the strategic budget," in the words of Joint Chief of Staff vice chairman General Robert Herres. In June 1988, SDIO director General Abrahamson was told that the projected costs of the Phase 1 system were simply too high and that the amount of money SDIO was planning on spending over the next few years was not going to be appropriated. As a result, SDIO went back to the drawing board, and by October of that year it redesigned virtually every aspect of the system, thereby cutting its projected cost by $46 billion, nearly half of the initial estimate.[64]

Just as Meese and others had feared, SDI's momentum was declining as Reagan's presidency waned. Some bemoaned the fact that SDI's future was so tightly tied to his vision. In the opinion of J. D. Crouch, national security assistant to SDI advocate Senator Malcolm Wallop (R-Wyo.), that vision was not realistic enough to win the long-term commitment that SDI required. Such a commitment, he believed, would have required a greater effort by Reagan to begin the deployment of a limited SDI system. But Reagan did not really want a limited SDI; he wanted one that would defend the entire nation. Neither SDI version was deployed before he left the White House in January 1989.[65]

Early Deployment and the ABM Treaty

Administration hard-liners also pushed for early SDI deployment to force abrogation of the ABM Treaty. They hoped to do this by mandating testing in space and deployment of space-based systems, both prohibited by the treaty. A decision for early deployment of SDI would also force the hands of those in the administration—particularly George Shultz—who had attempted to avoid open opposition to SDI (and the president) by supporting continued research on—but not deployment of—the system. In December 1986 Weinberger and Abrahamson won Reagan's support for a series of new SDI tests in space that most outside observers agreed would violate the ABM Treaty. Two months later, on February 3, 1987, Weinberger sought an immediate presidential decision to begin the deployment of SDI.

Predictably, Shultz led the battle against early SDI deployment. He pointed out that, at Reykjavik, the president had offered to refrain from deployment (though not necessarily from testing in space) for a period of ten years. The Weinberger proposal ran counter to this offer. Max Kampelman, the chief arms control negotiator in Geneva, reiterated that the U.S. Reykjavik proposal was still on the table. Moreover, Shultz and his assistant, Paul Nitze, argued that the new SDI tests were technologically unnecessary and politically provocative, though not illegal per se. They were able to convince the president to consult with NATO and with Congress before authorizing any new tests. Reagan promised to adhere to the restrictive interpretation but said he was legally justified in moving to the broad interpretation when desirable. On February 8, Shultz announced that a decision on early deployment could not be made for at least another two years; although the administration was considering conducting new SDI tests under the broad interpretation of the ABM Treaty, it would not do so without consulting the allies or Congress.[66]

Shultz also tried to get the Soviets to give the United States more leeway on SDI testing. In a meeting with Shevardnadze in Moscow on April 13-15, 1987, the secretary of state proposed that the United States and the Soviet Union "commit through 1994" (rather than for ten years as discussed at Reykjavik) "not to withdraw from the Antiballistic Missile Treaty." He also proposed that "after 1994, either side could deploy defensive systems of its choosing, unless mutually agreed otherwise." The U.S. proposal was contingent on implementation of a START agreement. Shultz also elaborated on an earlier U.S. "open laboratories" proposal by urging that "the United States and the Soviet Union carry out reciprocal briefings on their respective strategic defense efforts and visits to associated research facilities" and that both powers establish "mutually agreed procedures for reciprocal observation of strategic defense testing."[67]

Shevardnadze rejected Shultz's proposal. Later, on July 29, the Soviet Union tabled a draft treaty on "measures to strengthen the ABM Treaty regime and prevent an arms race in space," calling for a ten-year nonwithdrawal period, during which work on space-based ABMs would be confined to "research within laboratories on Earth." The Soviet draft treaty included a list of several ABM-related technologies to be barred from space testing by mutual agreement, including lasers and rockets capable of shooting down ballistic missiles. After the accord went into effect, the two sides would discuss ASAT and space-to-ground weapons. Violation of the agreement would release the other side from any strategic arms reductions agreement. The Soviet Union clarified what "laboratory" research it was prepared to allow in the SDI program: "research work on the ground, in institutes, at proving grounds, and at plants." The Soviets also proposed that both sides meet to define "the list of devices which would not be allowed to be put into space in the course of this research."[68]

In another meeting, in Washington from September 15-17, Shultz and Shevardnadze made little progress on ABM-related issues. The Soviet foreign minister emphasized the ABM Treaty rather than attacking SDI per se. Shevardnadze proposed that the sides agree either "to strictly abide by the ABM Treaty as it was signed and ratified in 1972" or to adopt a list of "devices not to be put into space and thresholds for associated critical parameters," making clear that ABM-related space testing below those parameters would be allowed. The Soviets tabled a proposed list of "the parameters and characteristics of such devices," but the United States rejected this "parametric" approach. Shevardnadze warned that "this question [of the ABM Treaty], which we believe is the root question of Soviet-U.S. relations, has to be moved forward in the period remaining before the meeting of the ministers, so that they could prepare productive agreements for approval at the summit."[69]

From October 22-23, Shultz and Shevardnadze met again, in Moscow, to discuss final details of an INF Treaty and to set a date for a summit in Washington. They again made no progress on ABM-related issues. Gorbachev warned Shultz that he would not be "comfortable" going to Washington with so little progress on the ABM/SDI issue. Although balking on a summit, Gorbachev informed Shultz that "the Soviet Union would unilaterally introduce a one-year moratorium on all work which had been done" on the Krasnoyarsk large phased-array radar, long considered a violation of the ABM Treaty by the Reagan administration. Gorbachev called for a similar moratorium on construction of the U.S. radar installation at Fylingdales Moor in Britain.[70]

In a surprising reversal of Soviet foot-dragging with respect to a summit, however, on October 30 Shevardnadze agreed that a Washington summit to sign the INF Treaty would begin on December 7, 1987, with another summit to occur "in the first half of 1988." But Shevardnadze continued to emphasize the ABM Treaty and the concepts of stability and predictability, rather than SDI, saying, "We are not speaking about SDI. . . . SDI is not our program." Shevardnadze emphasized that "the important thing is that the ABM Treaty should be observed. . . . This is the foundation for strategic stability during the 50 percent reductions of strategic offensive weapons."[71]

Meanwhile, administration officials appeared on television arguing in favor of a broad interpretation of the ABM treaty that would permit the testing of Phase 1 SDI components. But their lobbying effort ran into vigorous congressional opposition, as Shultz had predicted it would. In mid-March, 1987 Senator Sam Nunn and a large bipartisan group of senators publicly rejected the broad interpretation of the ABM Treaty. Nunn threatened a showdown with the administration if it altered a ratified treaty. He sent a strongly worded letter to the president warning that such action would provoke "a constitutional confrontation of profound dimensions." Nunn's staff also completed a series of three studies of the administration's reinterpretation of the ABM Treaty, which concluded that Sofaer's legal analyses justifying the broader view were all in "serious error." He then joined with Senator Carl Levin (D-Mich.) in sponsoring an amendment to the defense authorization bill barring any SDI testing beyond the bounds of the traditional interpretation of the ABM Treaty. After a bitter partisan battle and a prolonged Republican filibuster, a modified version of the Nunn-Levin language was approved in late 1987. Similar language was approved with far less controversy in subsequent years.[72]

The general issue of the Senate's treaty-making power took on increasing importance as the INF Treaty neared completion. After a prolonged and sometimes rancorous debate, the Senate overwhelmingly approved a condition for accepting the INF Treaty. Fashioned principally by Senator Joseph R. Biden, Jr. (D-Del.), this "Biden Condition" reaffirmed the constitutional principle that treaties must be interpreted on the basis of the understanding shared by the Senate and the executive branch at the time of ratification, unless the executive branch received specific congressional approval for a change in interpretation. In effect, the passage of the Biden Condition made clear that the traditional interpretation of the ABM Treaty was the law of the land and therefore that the broad interpretation was illegal under the Constitution of the United States. Reagan averted a confrontation with the Congress, and possible defeat of the INF Treaty, by agreeing to abide by the strict interpretation of the ABM Treaty. Testing under Reagan never breached the traditional interpretation of the treaty. Nevertheless, the refusal to sacrifice (or even compromise on) SDI at the arms control table, and the willingness to test and strain congressional tolerance on the ABM treaty, demonstrated the strength of the administration's commitment to SDI.[73]

Reagan's retreat from the broad interpretation of the ABM Treaty was a contributing factor in the departure of key SDI supporters from the administration, most important of whom were Caspar Weinberger and his deputy, Richard Perle. Throughout 1987 Weinberger had remained opposed to the more conciliatory approach that Reagan had adopted toward the Soviets, but when he realized he was having no effect on that policy, he resigned late in the year.

Another development that contributed to the decline of hard-liner influence in the waning months of Reagan's presidency was the public revelation of the Iran-Contra affair. In November 1986 the public learned that the administration had approved and facilitated the sale of U.S. arms to Iran and that some of the proceeds from that sale had been illegally diverted to administration-backed Nicaraguan rebels, the Contras, who were fighting the Sandinista government. Discredited by the Iran-Contra affair, and blamed for the mushrooming national debt that had reached over $3 trillion, right-wing members of the Reagan administration lost much of their influence. The more pragmatic Frank Carlucci, who replaced Weinberger as secretary of defense, continued the purge of hard-liners in the Pentagon by firing Frank Gaffney, Richard Perle's chosen successor. Another hard-liner, Kenneth Adelman, the director of the Arms Control and Disarmament Agency, resigned. As a result, pragmatists now controlled the administration's Soviet policy without significant internal opposition.[74]

INF Finale

These changes on the U.S. side were complemented by a transformation in the Soviet attitude toward SDI. Although the Soviets continued to express apprehension about military spin-offs from SDI, and about the dangerous impact of deploying space-based weapons, they began to consider SDI a potential drain on the U.S. economy whose cost would most likely prohibit large-scale development and deployment. Thus, for the Soviets, the prospect for maintaining strategic stability by preserving the ABM Treaty was much better than before, and Gorbachev felt he could safely concentrate on concluding the INF Treaty. In February 1987 the Soviet leader said that the stakes were too high to "waste more time on trying to outplay one another" in traditional arms control diplomacy. On February 28 he proposed the elimination of all Soviet and U.S. intermediate-range forces (INF) in Europe, with no strings attached, either to SDI, or even to British and French intermediate-range forces. In effect, Gorbachev had capitulated to Reagan's attempts to implement the zero option without tying it to an ABM agreement. Reagan, hardly daring to believe the good news, reacted ecstatically. However, he did not credit the change in Soviet policy to Gorbachev's new thinking but rather to the administration's policy of "peace through strength."[75]

Still, one last major obstacle to an INF agreement remained. West German Chancellor Helmut Kohl insisted that short-range, tactical-nuclear missiles (below 500 kilometers) must also be included in the treaty. Theater nuclear forces in Europe were divided into three categories: intermediate-range (1,000 to 5,500 kilometers), short-range (500 to 1,000 kilometers), and tactical (less than 500 kilometers). The zero option, or first zero, involved intermediate-range missiles: Soviet SS-4s, SS-5s, and SS-20s, U.S. Pershing IIs, as well as ground-launched cruise missiles (GLCMs) on both sides. The second zero encompassed short-range missiles, the Soviet SS-12/22s and SS-23s, and the Pershing Is of the United States. Kohl was particularly concerned about the three-hundred-kilometer-range Soviet Scuds that were aimed at West Germany. In response, the Soviets demanded that all short-range nuclear warheads be included in the treaty, specifically those deployed on seventy-two aging Pershing I-A missiles stationed in West Germany. Kohl objected to the Soviet proposal, not only because he believed the missiles were necessary to counter Soviet superiority in conventional forces but also because the Pershing I-As were owned by the Federal Republic, and therefore, he argued, could not be included in a superpower agreement.[76]

On July 23 Gorbachev again took the initiative to break this impasse. He proposed a global, double zero, eliminating all INF and SRINF in Asia (and America) as well as in Europe. Although not directly affecting the German Pershing I-As, the Soviet proposal added momentum for a general ban on all such missiles. Kohl was subjected to enormous international and domestic pressure to give up the Pershing I-As, since they were the last major obstacle to an agreement that would eliminate all Soviet INF. Even Reagan added to that pressure by writing the chancellor a private letter in which he said the West German concession would contribute to the cause of disarmament. As a result, on August 26 Kohl announced Germany's willingness to destroy its Pershing I-As, but only after U.S. and Soviet INF and SRINF (short-range intermediate nuclear forces) missiles were eliminated.[77]

After several remaining issues were cleared up, an INF treaty was finally initialed by Shultz and Shevardnaze at Geneva on November 24. Two weeks later, on December 8, it was signed by Reagan and Gorbachev in a Washington summit.

The INF Treaty

The INF Treaty was a historic arms control measure. For the first time, the United States and the Soviet Union had not only agreed to reduce their nuclear arsenals but also to eliminate an entire category of nuclear weapons. The INF Treaty banned all land-based missiles with a range of 1,000-5,500 kilometers as well as short-range intermediate nuclear forces, land-based missiles with a 500-1,000 kilometer range. In signing the treaty, the United States committed itself to dismantling 429 Pershing II and Tomahawk missiles already deployed, and an additional 430 missiles that were not deployed. The Soviet Union agreed to eliminate 857 deployed missiles and an additional 895 in storage, a total of 1,752 missiles. Altogether, the treaty committed the United States to dismantle just under 1,000 warheads and the Soviet Union over 3,000. Although the missiles were to be destroyed at specified sites, the treaty permitted the nuclear material in their warheads to be reprocessed for other purposes. A decisive factor in the U.S. decision to sign the INF Treaty was Soviet acceptance of a comprehensive verification program, including—for the first time in the history of nuclear arms agreements—on-site inspection. The two sides agreed to verify the initial totals of missiles to be destroyed, a quota of spot checks to verify the treaty's implementation, inspection measures to confirm the removal of missiles from bases, and procedures to oversee the destruction of missiles at agreed sites.[78]

The last obstacle to a vote on the resolution of ratification by the Senate was the demand by the Democratic leadership that the administration accept the so-called Biden Condition. Even Republican senators accepted that condition after Democrats agreed to compromise language offered by Senator William Cohen (R-Maine). It stated: "If, subsequent to ratification of the Treaty, a question arises as to the interpretation of a provision of the Treaty on which no common understanding was reached . . . that provision shall be interpreted in accordance with applicable United States law." The compromise condition passed by a vote of 72 to 27 on May 26. The next day, after the administration said it would abide by the Biden-Cohen condition, the Senate approved ratification of the INF Treaty by a vote of 93 to 5. The vote marked the first arms control treaty approved for ratification by the Senate since the 1972 ABM Treaty. The treaty was ratified by the Supreme Soviet on

May 29, 1988, one day before Reagan's arrival in Moscow for his final summit as president. The signing of the INF Treaty brought to an end one of most divisive issues in the alliance's forty-year history.[79]

Reagan certainly deserves a great deal of credit for the successful conclusion of the INF talks. Encouraged by Shultz and by Mrs. Reagan to secure his place in history as a man of peace, and terrified by the prospect of a nuclear war, Reagan displayed courage and perseverance in sweeping aside the opposition of the hard-liners in his administration who saw the zero option as only a propaganda ploy and wanted the United States to retain some INF systems, even if greatly reduced in quantity. However, some observers, such as Strobe Talbott, viewed the successful conclusion of the INF Treaty as an example of an administration that had succeeded in spite of itself. According to Talbott, "INF was doomed to success," despite the best efforts of administration hard-liners to defeat it. Talbott argued that the public's desire for U.S.-Soviet conciliation made the conclusion of the INF Treaty a political necessity for Reagan, particularly after congressional hearings publicized the Iran-Contra affair and strengthened the impression of some that the president's hold on national security affairs was not too tight. Although this assessment is accurate as far as it goes, it does not go far enough. Talbott did not put sufficient emphasis on Reagan's genuine interest in doing away with nuclear weapons, a realization that shocked the hard-liners when they were forced to accept it.[80]

Nevertheless, the lion's share of the credit for the treaty's completion should be given to Gorbachev, not Reagan, since the Soviet leader made most of the concessions that were necessary to make it possible. Without Gorbachev's willingness to accede to even the most stringent of U.S. demands, the effort to complete the INF Treaty might well have languished into the Bush administration. Instead, Gorbachev accepted Reagan's zero option, even though it required the elimination of far more Soviet missiles than U.S. missiles. He also accepted Reagan's demand that the limitations of the INF Treaty be global in scope, thereby giving up IRBMs in the Far East, where the United States and its allies had none. Gorbachev also dropped his predecessors' insistence on including British and French nuclear forces in the agreement, a demand the United States refused to accept. In addition, the Soviet leader accepted the inclusion of shorter-range nuclear systems, another category of weapons in which the Soviets had to make asymmetrical reductions. Finally, and most surprisingly, Gorbachev reversed long-standing Soviet objections to intrusive forms of verification and agreed to the most complicated inspection regime that had ever been accepted by the superpowers.

An Unfinished START

Despite the sluggish pace of START, compared to the accelerated pace of the INF negotiations, Reagan and Gorbachev did make some progress on strategic force reductions during the Washington summit in December 1987. They accepted, within a ceiling of 6,000 strategic warheads, a subceiling of 4,900 warheads on ballistic missiles. The Soviets also agreed to cut in half the number of their heavy ICBMs—to 154, which would be permitted to carry no more than 1,540 warheads—and accepted a 50 percent reduction in the throw weight capacity of the remaining Soviet ICBMs and SLBMs. The Soviets, however, refused to accept a ceiling of 3,300 warheads on land-based missiles until the United States agreed to the same numerical ceiling on SLBM warheads, a condition Reagan rejected. The United States, for its part, accepted the inclusion of nuclear-armed sea-launched cruise missiles (SLCMs) in the agreement. And both sides agreed to incorporate into the final text intensive verification provisions based on those contained in the INF Treaty. [81]

However, despite a shared political incentive to accentuate the positive, neither Reagan nor Gorbachev could report much progress in START after the Washington summit. Neither the shuttle diplomacy of Shultz and Shevardnadze nor the efforts of the Geneva negotiators made much headway in concluding the remaining issues. The key obstacle to the completion of an agreement remained SDI. On November 16 Reagan again declared, "SDI is not a bargaining chip. . . . We will research it; we will develop it; and when it is ready, we will deploy it." Nevertheless, the president was compelled to sign a defense authorization bill that contained congressionally mandated provisions requiring U.S. compliance with the traditional interpretation, at least through October 1, 1988. [82]

Realizing that both superpowers were marking time on the SDI issue, Gorbachev admitted in a November 30 interview that "the Soviet Union is doing all that the United States is doing . . . we are engaged in research, basic research, which relates to those aspects which are covered by the SDI." But Gorbachev insisted that the Soviet Union would not deploy a nationwide ballistic missile defense and called upon the United States to make the same promise. Moreover, he again linked a START agreement to "strict observance" of the ABM Treaty but added that he would "let America indulge in [SDI] research" to the degree that it did "not run counter to the ABM Treaty."[83]

Gorbachev's latest concession was the basis for a formula that attempted to circumvent the ABM problem and thereby permit START to proceed. The formula, which was drafted during the Washington summit, called for the two leaders to instruct their delegations in Geneva to "work out" an agreement that would commit each side to observe the ABM Treaty, as signed in 1972, while permitting them to conduct research, development, and testing "as required." The proposed agreement also would bind each side not to withdraw from the ABM Treaty for a specified period of time. But the agreed statement also maintained that each side would be "free to decide its course of action" should either deploy ABMs in space. Reagan, mistakenly, thought that the formula "resolved" the dispute over ABM research. He announced that "we have agreed that we are going forward with whatever is necessary in the research and development [of SDI] without any regard to an interpretation of ABM." But the Soviets subsequently and emphatically stated that what they had meant was that they would take necessary countermeasures—including their own ABM deployments—if the United States violated the ABM Treaty by going ahead with the deployment of space-based SDI components. In effect, the whole ABM issue was simply put off again.[84]

Gorbachev was undoubtedly more disappointed by the inability to make progress on strategic defenses and space weapons than was Reagan. Although the president had been compelled to sign legislation under which Congress mandated continued application of the traditional strict interpretation of the ABM Treaty (as well as cutting the SDI budgetary request by one-third), he still refused to make any such commitment to Gorbachev. Instead, in early 1988, the U.S. delegation in Geneva tabled a draft treaty calling for research, development, and testing of advanced defenses based on the broad interpretation of the ABM Treaty, and again the Soviets rejected the broad interpretation. The United States also asserted its right to withdraw from the treaty after a specified period of time, but the Soviets argued that article 15 of the treaty did not permit withdrawal as a consequence of the successful development of an effective strategic defensive program. As a result of the superpowers' inability to resolve this imbroglio, a START agreement proved impossible to conclude before Reagan left office in 1989.[85]

In spite of the stalemate in START, both sides did take steps to reduce the risk of a nuclear war resulting from an accident, misinterpretation, or miscalculation. On September 15, 1988, Shultz and Shevardnaze signed an agreement to establish nuclear risk reduction centers in Washington and Moscow. Shortly before Reagan left office, another agreement was reached that provided for the advance notification of ICBM test launchings and for joint experimentation on monitoring underground nuclear test limitations.[86]

Dealing with Horizontal Nuclear Weapons Proliferation: South Asia

While the superpowers were preoccupied with the vertical proliferation of nuclear weapons (the ongoing development and deployment of nuclear weapons by the nuclear weapon states), the threat of uncontrolled horizontal proliferation (the acquisition of nuclear weapons by nonweapon states) increased during the Reagan years. By the 1980s, several states were suspected of having acquired the capability to build nuclear weapons or having built them. One was India. In 1974 the Indians exploded a nuclear device, which they insisted was solely for peaceful purposes. Nevertheless, nuclear experts realized that nuclear explosives developed for peaceful purposes could easily have military application.

The Indian nuclear test made a mockery of the international effort to control the horizontal proliferation of nuclear weapons. Technically, the Indian government broke no law, treaty, or agreement in exploding a nuclear device. India was not a party to the Nuclear Nonproliferation Treaty, which prohibited its signatories from building or acquiring nuclear weapons. India was, and still is, a member of the International Atomic Energy Agency (IAEA), which monitors nuclear activities, but membership in that organization does not require a member state to fully implement IAEA safeguards, and India did not. Moreover, the IAEA statute does not cover peaceful nuclear explosions, which the Indians claimed was the nature of their nuclear test.

Nor did the Indians violate any bilateral agreements with the United States or Canada. Both countries provided India with nuclear technology and materials without first insisting that India ratify the NPT and agree to abide by all the nuclear restrictions of the IAEA. The Indian nuclear device contained plutonium that was obtained from a nuclear reactor provided by Canada in 1956. The heavy water (deuterium) that the reactor employed was provided by the United States. In effect, India demonstrated that it was far easier for a state that was not a party to the NPT to acquire the means to build nuclear weapons than it was for states that had agreed to abide by the provisions of that agreement.

The United States had quickly appreciated the danger of the "peaceful" Indian test. If other states followed the Indian example, the risks of a nuclear accident, unauthorized use of a nuclear weapon, or even a preemptive nuclear strike would increase dramatically. Indeed, any multiplication of nuclear powers could make the maintenance of a stable deterrence relationship between the United States and the Soviet Union virtually impossible. With a multiplicity of nuclear states, a nuclear strike could come from any quarter.

To discourage the horizontal proliferation of nuclear weapons, the United States had strengthened its own controls over the export of nuclear materials and technology. In 1976 Congress passed an amendment to the Foreign Assistance Act that was drafted by Senator Stuart Symington (D-Mo.). It prohibited U.S. aid to nonnuclear-weapon states that deliver or receive uranium enrichment equipment or technology unless the recipient placed all of its nuclear installations under IAEA safeguards. Another measure, the Nonproliferation Act of 1978, required all recipients of U.S. nuclear fuel to subscribe fully to the IAEA safeguard system. Recipient countries also had to guarantee that U.S. exports would be used strictly for peaceful purposes, that they would place transferred U.S. equipment and materials under IAEA safeguards, and that they would maintain adequate physical security over imports and nuclear materials produced through their use. Recipient countries also would have to obtain prior U.S. consent to retransfer U.S.-origin technology or materials and to reprocess or enrich U.S.-origin materials or materials produced in U.S.-supplied facilities.

The United States was also instrumental in creating the so-called London Nuclear Suppliers Club, a loose association of major states (Britain, France, Australia, Canada, West Germany, and the Soviet Union) supplying nuclear technology, equipment, and materials to other states. Members of the Suppliers Club promised to prevent the inadvertent transfer of nuclear weapons manufacturing potential and to discourage free market competitiveness in the sale of nuclear technology.

India's capacity to produce nuclear weapons prompted the Pakistanis, who had suffered a crushing defeat in a 1971 war with India, to acquire that capacity, too. Using technology illicitly acquired from Western Europe, the Pakistanis built an unsafeguarded enrichment facility that they used to begin producing weapons-grade nuclear material in 1986, making Pakistan a de facto nuclear power. As with India, the United States was also instrumental in helping the Pakistanis develop nuclear weapons. Since the mid-1950s, Pakistan had been linked with the United States in two regional containment alliances and a bilateral pact that pledged the United States to help Pakistan resist communist aggression. Because of its strategic location and friendly stance, Pakistan had been a major beneficiary of U.S. military aid. The Carter administration did attempt, at least initially, to curb Pakistan's attempt to build nuclear weapons by cutting off U.S. aid in 1979. However, the Soviet invasion of Afghanistan that year greatly decreased the U.S. desire to crack down on Pakistan's nuclear development program; Pakistan had become an essential component of the U.S. effort to support and supply the Afghan resistance forces. As a result, the aid cutoff was reversed six months after it began, an action that ushered in nearly a decade of unprecedented bilateral cooperation and netted Pakistan billions of dollars in military and economic assistance.

Although the Reagan administration was concerned about the danger of a nuclear arms race in South Asia, Pakistan's role in helping the Afghan rebels caused it to look the other way with respect to the Pakistani nuclear program. Instead of trying to punish the Pakistanis, the Reagan administration tried to get them to refrain from acquiring a nuclear-weapon producing capability. To this end, in 1981 the administration persuaded Congress to waive the application of the Symington Amendment on Pakistan and to approve a six-year, $3.2 billion package of economic and military assistance to the Pakistanis. Although Congress approved the administration's request and also reaffirmed a 1959 U.S.-Pakistan mutual security agreement (for defense against the Soviet Union, not India), it also warned that acquisition or detonation of a nuclear weapon by Pakistan would have grave consequences for U.S.-Pakistani relations. Moreover, an amendment drafted by Senator John Glenn (D-Ohio) to the Foreign Assistance Act for that year required a cutoff of U.S. economic or military aid to any nonnuclear-weapon state that received, or detonated, a nuclear explosive device. It also required that the same penalty be applied to any state that transferred a nuclear explosive to a nonnuclear-weapon state.[87]

Nevertheless, during the period when the Symington Amendment was suspended, between 1981 and 1984, Pakistan completed its enrichment plant. President Reagan responded by seeking assurances from the Pakistanis that they would not enrich uranium to more than 5 percent, a level not usable for nuclear weapons. (To be usable for nuclear weapons, uranium must be upgraded, or "enriched," to increase the concentration of desirable uranium atoms from 0.7 percent, the naturally occurring concentration, to 93 percent.) Pakistan agreed to this limit but apparently surpassed it in late 1985 or early 1986, producing some weapon-grade, highly enriched uranium. The Reagan administration, however, still wanted a friendly Pakistan that would continue to facilitate U.S. assistance to the Afghan resistance movement. Consequently, it did not want to crack down on the Pakistani nuclear development program by terminating U.S. economic and military assistance. In fact, in 1986 the administration offered Pakistan a second six-year aid package totaling $4.02 billion. To persuade Congress to approve it, the administration held talks with the Pakistanis in August 1987 seeking "concrete evidence of Pakistani nuclear restraint." But the initiative was unavailing. By the summer of 1987, Pakistan was believed to have produced enough nuclear-weapons material at its enrichment facility for one or possibly two nuclear explosives.[88]

In response to growing evidence of the Pakistani effort to achieve a nuclear explosive capability, Congress took action that the administration was unwilling to initiate. In 1985 Senator Larry Pressler introduced, and the Congress passed, legislation providing that the president must certify to Congress that Pakistan did not possess a nuclear explosive device before he would be permitted to supply economic aid or military sales to Pakistan. He also had to certify that the proposed U.S. aid package would reduce significantly the risk that Pakistan could possess such a device. Reagan provided the required certifications, arguing that Pakistan did not technically "possess a nuclear explosive device." Nevertheless, by the end of Reagan's administration, there was little doubt that Pakistan could assemble and deploy several nuclear weapons.[89]

The Nuclear Threat in the Middle East

Although the United States made halfhearted, and ultimately ineffective, efforts to prevent a nuclear arms race in South Asia, it did next to nothing to deter Israel from acquiring nuclear weapons. During Reagan's presidency it was obvious that Israel enjoyed a regional nuclear monopoly. Any doubt about this was erased in late 1986, when a former Israeli nuclear technician, Mordechai Vanunu, revealed a number of significant details about the Israeli nuclear arsenal, including its size: sixty to one hundred devices. The veracity of Vanunu's revelation appeared to have been certified by the long prison term he was given by the Israeli government. Adding to Israel's nuclear power was its ability to deploy advanced ballistic missile delivery systems, a capability that was convincingly demonstrated by its September 1988 launch of *Offeq* (Horizon), its first space satellite. In fact, the U.S. government stated that if the rocket used to orbit the satellite—a three-stage launcher known as the Shavit-2—was adapted as a ballistic missile, it would have a range of 3,000 miles. Israel is believed to have developed its first nuclear-capable missiles in the 1960s and deployed the so-called Jericho-2 missile—

which is designed to carry a nuclear warhead four hundred miles—during the early 1980s. Israel, however, has refused to confirm any of these reports. In addition, Israel was developing an antitactical-ballistic-missile system, the Arrow, with U.S. assistance. Until the Arrow could be deployed, however, the Israelis intended to rely on a three-pronged response: civil defense measures, the planned destruction of enemy missiles preemptively, when possible, and deterrence based on a not too ambiguous threat of nuclear deterrence.

With respect to the latter, defense minister Yitzhak Rabin made the following statement in July 1988: "One of Israel's fears is that the Arab world and its leaders will mistakenly believe that the lack of an international response to the use of rockets and gas [in the Iran-Iraq War] affords them a legitimization of sorts to employ them. . . . If, heaven forbid, they dare to employ these means, the response will be one hundred times stronger." Although the word "nuclear" was never used in Israel's warnings, there can be little doubt that its ability to "hit back many times over" was intended as an important revision of the country's traditional stance that it "will not be the first to introduce nuclear weapons into the Middle East."[90]

Although the United States embargoed the export of nuclear materials to Israel in 1980, there is no evidence that the embargo affected Israel's decision to build a nuclear arsenal. Quite to the contrary, the embargo probably was instrumental in persuading the Israelis to begin producing their own nuclear weapons rather than relying on the United States to provide them. Nor did the United States try to reverse, or even slow, the development of Israel's nuclear stockpile. Instead, U.S. policy appears to have been based on a tacit understanding that the Israeli program would remain undeclared and that Israel would not engage in nuclear testing. In addition, by helping Israel to maintain its superiority in conventional forces, promoting regional peace initiatives, and pursuing traditional nonproliferation efforts to prevent the spread of nuclear arms to other states in the region, Washington tried to reduce the possibility of Israel's nuclear weapons ever being used. Needless to say, the Arab states did not consider this an equitable counterproliferation policy.

It is safe to say that Iraq's president, Saddam Hussein, did not think it was fair. But Hussein also believed it was necessary for the Arabs, and Iraq in particular, to have nuclear weapons to counter Israel's. And with Western assistance, Iraq pushed very close to acquiring a nuclear capability shortly before the 1991 Persian Gulf War. In 1976 the Iraqis purchased from France a large (40 megawatt) research reactor capable of producing significant quantities of

plutonium and, from Italy, three hot cells in which small quantities of plutonium could be separated from irradiated fuel. Iraq also began to negotiate for
a large heavy-water power reactor that could produce large amounts of plutonium, and a reprocessing facility.

In 1980 the Iraqis took two steps which suggested their intent to acquire
nuclear capability. First, they purchased large amounts of natural uranium on
the open market that could be used in the heavy-water power reactor. Second, they contracted with a West German firm to purchase depleted-ura-
nium fuel pins that could be irradiated in the research reactor to produce
plutonium. The Iraqis developed an elaborate plan of camouflage, concealment, and deception to assure secrecy for their nuclear weapons development
program. Israel reacted to developments in Iraq by bombing Iraq's French-
supplied Osiraq research reactor in June 1981, shortly before the reactor was
due to start up. The attack set back the Iraqi nuclear program, but it did not
stop it.[91]

The Iraqis repeatedly assured the international community that their
nuclear activities had solely civilian purposes. Iraq ratified the NPT in 1969
and in 1972 signed a safeguards agreement with the IAEA. Nevertheless, without technically violating either of these agreements, the Iraqis were capable
of putting into place every element of a nuclear weapons program, including
production facilities. Moreover, after Saddam Hussein had completed these
preparations and was ready to produce the weapons, he then could have
invoked the NPT clause that allows a signatory to withdraw from the treaty
after giving ninety days notice by declaring that "extraordinary events,
related to the subject matter of this Treaty, have jeopardized" its "supreme
interests." Even the restrictions of the Nuclear Suppliers Group did not prevent Iraq from buying the components it needed to produce nuclear
weapons. Indeed, neither the United States nor the international community
did anything meaningful to halt Iraq's nuclear weapons program until the
Persian Gulf War in 1991.[92]

The Missile Technology Control Regime

One major counterproliferation initiative that the Reagan administration
did undertake was an effort to halt the spread of ballistic missiles. Between
1983 and 1987, the United States worked with its partners in the Group of
Seven Industrial Nations (G-7) to develop missile export controls. The result,
in April 1987, was the formation of the Missile Technology Control Regime
(MTCR), an informal arrangement consisting of guidelines to constrain the

transfer of equipment or technology that would provide, or help a country build, missiles capable of delivering a 500 kilogram (1,100 pound) warhead to a range of 300 kilometers (186 miles) or more. These distances were designed primarily with the Middle East in mind. However, the Arab states did not fail to notice that the administration's effort to prevent the proliferation of ballistic missiles in the region was compromised from the first by continued U.S. cooperation with Israel in developing its Arrow missile. Although both the United States and Israel argued that the Arrow was a defensive missile, the Arabs realized that the U.S. technological assistance received by Israel could be useful in developing offensive missile systems as well. Nor was the MTCR completely successful in shutting down the transfer of ballistic missiles in other areas of the world. It did not, for example, prevent Saudi Arabia from importing the CSS-2 ballistic missile from China. Nor did it prevent India from successfully testing its Prithvi and Agni ballistic missiles, or Pakistan from testing an indigenously built rocket.[93]

Clearly, there were (and still are) weaknesses in the MTCR. For one, the MTCR was specifically designed to control the transfer of equipment and technology that could contribute to *nuclear-capable* missiles, which can and has been interpreted to mean that a country that does not have nuclear warheads is a suitable recipient for missile technology. In this way, the Chinese export of its CSS-2 missile to Saudi Arabia was not a violation of the MTCR guidelines because there was, and is, no evidence to suggest that Saudi Arabia has obtained or is trying to obtain nuclear warheads. Moreover, missiles with a military capability could be transferred to a recipient country that ostensibly would use them to launch space satellites. It took the United States some eighteen months to get France and the other G-7 countries to accept fully the notion that controlling space launch technology was necessary to have effective controls on ballistic missile technology.[94]

The Quest for a Comprehensive Test Ban

Despite the Reagan administration's halfhearted efforts to halt the horizontal proliferation of nuclear weapons, it refused to accept what many regarded as the most effective way of doing so, a comprehensive nuclear test ban treaty (CTBT).

Reagan was subjected to increasing pressure to conclude such an agreement during his second term. On January 15, 1986, Gorbachev extended the Soviet unilateral nuclear test moratorium that he had initiated the previous April for an additional three months, to March 31. Superseding that deadline, on March 13 the Soviet Union announced it would extend its nuclear test moratorium until the United States performed another test. Adding to the Soviet pressure, on February 26 the House of Representatives passed a resolution urging Reagan to negotiate a CTBT. On August 7 the Senate called on the president to seek its advice and consent to ratify of the Threshold Test Ban Treaty and the Peaceful Nuclear Explosions Treaty and urged him to resume CTBT negotiations. The next day, the House passed an amendment to the fiscal 1987 defense authorization bill prohibiting funds for nuclear tests with an explosive yield greater than one kiloton for a period of one year, provided that the Soviet Union agreed to the same testing limit and accepted in-country seismic monitoring acceptable to the Reagan administration. Gorbachev responded on August 18 by extending its unilateral test moratorium to January 1, 1987.

Yet the Reagan administration, determined to test nuclear warheads for new and existing weapon systems, refused to succumb to the pressure. Instead of a CTBT, and in return for Congress's dropping the one-kiloton test limit legislation passed by the House, on October 10 Reagan offered to request the advice and consent of the Senate on ratifying the Threshold Test Ban Treaty and the Peaceful Nuclear Explosions Treaty—but only after verification measures that were mutually acceptable to the United States and the Soviet Union were established. The administration insisted that the current seismic methods of verification were inadequate to determine Soviet compliance with the TTBT's 150 kiloton limit on underground nuclear tests. Once the treaties had been ratified, Reagan pledged to "propose that the United States and the Soviet Union immediately engage in negotiations on ways to implement a step-by-step program . . . limiting and ultimately ending nuclear testing." A House-Senate conference committee responded by dropping the one-kiloton limit. Although the Congress eased the pressure on Reagan to negotiate a CTBT, Gorbachev increased it. On October 12, at the end of the Reykjavik summit, he asked Reagan to begin negotiations to establish limitations on the permitted yield and number of nuclear explosions in order to move toward a CTBT. He even linked, albeit briefly, progress on strategic arms reductions, intermediate-range nuclear forces, missile defenses, and testing in a single package. Yet Reagan still refused to proceed on a CTBT. Consequently, on December 18 the Soviet Union again announced it would end its unilateral testing moratorium with the first U.S. test of 1987. On February 26, 1987, after a U.S. test on February 3, the Soviet Union ended its almost two-year-long moratorium on nuclear testing.[95]

Prompted by the continuing delay on a CTBT, both the Congress and the Soviets turned their emphasis to the verification procedures that might make possible ratification of the TTBT, the PNET, and eventually a CTBT. On May 19, 1987, the House of Representatives again passed an amendment to a defense authorization bill prohibiting funds for nuclear explosions with a yield greater than one kiloton, as long as the Soviet Union adhered to the same limit and agreed to accept in-country seismic monitoring that the administration judged acceptable. On June 9, at the Conference on Disarmament in Geneva, the Soviet Union presented new proposals for an international body to monitor a nuclear test ban, and indicated its willingness to open test sites to mandatory inspection. As a result, on September 17 both sides agreed to initiate "stage-by-stage" nuclear testing negotiations by December 1. The talks were to focus on drafting verification protocols to the unratified TTBT and PNET, pursuing intermediate nuclear testing limitations, and proceeding to the ultimate goal of a CTBT. Prompted by this agreement, on September 24 the Senate, by a 62 to 35 vote, rejected a Kennedy-Hatfield nuclear testing amendment, which would have stopped tests with yields greater than one kiloton for two years if the Soviet Union adhered to this yield limit and agreed to in-country seismic monitoring approved by the administration.[96]

The Nuclear Test Talks began in Geneva on November 9, 1987. But they soon focused exclusively on TTBT and PNET verification issues, rather than the broader agenda originally announced in the September agreement. The administration proposed protocols to the TTBT and PNET that would incorporate more advanced—and intrusive—means of verification.

The administration's preferred method was a "hydrodynamic" system called CORRTEX (Continuous Reflectometry for Radius versus Time Experiments). This system employed a cable attached to an electronic unit that is lowered into the "emplacement" hole containing the nuclear device, or into a separately drilled "satellite" hole parallel to the emplacement shaft. When a nuclear device is detonated, the resulting shock wave travels outward and progressively crushes the cable, producing a fast-moving short circuit. The larger the explosion, the faster the shock wave travels. Its movement is recorded by the electronic unit on the surface as a function of time. Using this data, a computer can calculate the yield of the explosion. The CORRTEX method of measuring explosive yields is completely different from seismic methods, which measure ground motions caused by the elastic waves that propagate around and through the earth after an underground explosion or earthquake. Whereas seismic sensors can measure yields at great distances from the explosion, CORRTEX can work only at very short ranges—a few tens of meters at most.[97]

At the December 1987 Washington summit, the two superpowers agreed to conduct a joint verification experiment (JVE) to demonstrate the operation of the CORRTEX system (as well as a similar Soviet system) and evaluate its applicability as a routine means of nuclear test verification in the future. Administration officials hoped the JVE would convince the Soviet Union to accept the protocols. On August 17, 1988, as part of the JVE, the Soviet Union monitored a U.S. underground nuclear test in Nevada; on September 14, the United States monitored a Soviet test in Semipalatinsk. Yet the Reagan administration still resisted a CTBT. As a result, on April 28, 1988, for the third year in a row, the House passed an amendment to a defense authorization bill that would have halted all tests above a one-kiloton yield if the Soviet Union adhered to the same limit and permitted in-country seismic monitoring acceptable to the administration. However, the amendment was again dropped in conference. Later that year, on August 5, the twenty-fifth anniversary of the signing of the Limited Test Ban Treaty (LTBT), which banned all but underground tests, six nonnuclear weapon signatories proposed a conference to amend the LTBT to make it comprehensive. This effort would continue into the administration of Reagan's successor, George Bush.[98]

3
Bush and START I

A New Soviet Policy?

George Bush, Ronald Reagan's successor, approached the Soviet Union with extreme caution for most of his first year in office. He believed that his predecessor had been too quick to respond to Gorbachev's initiatives and that insufficient thought had been given to them. The hasty Reykjavik summit in October 1986, during which Reagan offered to eliminate all nuclear weapons (without consulting America's NATO allies in advance) was, for Bush, a classic example of the kind of diplomacy he wanted to avoid. Moreover, there was concern that Gorbachev might be tricking the West into saving the Soviet system. Brent Scowcroft, Bush's national security adviser, warned that Gorbachev's "peace offensive" might be a calculated strategy to lure the West into letting down its guard while the Soviet Union rebuilt its power for a new global offensive. Accordingly, Bush decided the he would not respond to Gorbachev's peace initiatives until the new administration could review America's grand strategy.[1]

The results of that review, which took four months to complete, were announced by the president on May 12. Bush declared that "now it is time to move beyond containment . . . our objective is to welcome the Soviet Union back into the world order." However, he warned that "in an era of extraordinary change, we have an obligation to temper optimism—and I am optimistic—with prudence." Bush said that the Soviets would have to prove with deeds the sincerity of their promises to change their system and behavior and specifically by reducing Soviet forces "to less threatening levels" than those previously announced by Gorbachev. As an incentive for the Soviets, Bush offered to revive the Open Skies Plan, first proposed by President Dwight Eisenhower in 1955. It called for reciprocal aerial reconnaissance of Soviet and U.S. territory. Bush also offered the Soviet Union an unspecified "broader economic relationship" with the United States, including most-favored-nation trading status. Bush also implied that the United States was now committed to the success of *perestroika*, Gorbachev's reform program.[2]

More than a few observers, however, were disappointed that the new administration's strategic review offered little in the way of new policy initiatives toward the Soviet Union. Observers on both sides of the Atlantic regarded Bush's "new" Soviet policy as excessively cautious. French president François Mitterrand and West German chancellor Helmut Kohl, for example, pressured Bush to be less rigid toward the Soviet leader.[3]

Gorbachev added to that pressure by proposing, as a follow up to the INF Treaty, an agreement to remove short-range nuclear forces (SNF) from the European theater. But Bush initially rejected that idea, which his defense secretary, Richard Cheney, described as a "dangerous trap" that would strip NATO of its nuclear deterrent capability. Gorbachev also announced in mid-May that the Soviet Union would unilaterally eliminate five hundred nuclear warheads from its European arsenal. He also proposed more generous cuts in conventional weapons.[4]

By then, Bush realized that Gorbachev was making the United States look like the primary obstacle to ending the Cold War. Privately, he complained to Scowcroft that he was "sick and tired of getting beat up day after day for having no vision and letting Gorbachev run the show." In an attempt to dispel that impression, the president unveiled his own plan to reduce military forces in Europe at a NATO summit in Brussels at the end of May. He proposed 15 percent cuts in NATO and Warsaw Pact conventional forces, and 20 percent reductions in total U.S. and Soviet military personnel in Europe. He also announced that he was postponing a decision to proceed with the modernization of nuclear armed Lance short-range missiles, which were deployed by the United States in West Germany. He also expressed his willingness to participate in SNF talks with the Soviet Union, but only after an agreement to reduce conventional forces on the conflict was concluded. Bush's initiatives represented the beginning of the end to his cautious approach to the Soviet Union.[5]

The Bush Defense Policy

Even before the administration's strategic review was completed, defense secretary Cheney presented an amended two-year defense budget indicating how the administration's military policy would proceed. On April 25, 1989, he announced that the budget for fiscal year 1990 would total $295.6 billion— $10 billion less than President Reagan's last budget request three months earlier. In addition, the five-year defense plan would be cut by approximately $65 billion for fiscal years 1990-1994. Despite the "very painful" cuts Cheney said this would require, he indicated that the new administration intended to pursue the essence of the Reagan strategic doctrine.

With respect to offensive strategic nuclear weapons, the administration decided to maintain the U.S. nuclear "triad" of ICBMs, SLBMs, and bombers. Regarding ICBMs, the administration announced that it intended to deploy both a rail-based, multiple-warhead MX missile system by 1992 as well as a force of single-warhead Midgetman ICBMs by 1997. Despite criticism that the rail-based MX was vulnerable to surprise attack, the administration announced that it would remove all fifty of the then deployed MX missiles from their stationary silos and redeploy them on trains located at military bases in the western United States. Cheney explained that this decision was the "low-cost" option, that is, "the cheapest way to get mobility built into our land-based ICBM force." In addition, he announced that "at least 250, and maybe 500" Midgetman ICBMs would be deployed.[6]

With respect to the second leg of the nuclear triad, submarine-launched ballistic missiles, the Bush administration left unchanged the Reagan budget for the Trident submarine. In so doing, Cheney rejected navy officials' advice to reduce the Trident construction program by two boats. The administration also planned to purchase sixty-three additional D-5 missiles for the Tridents in fiscal year 1990 and fifty-two missiles in fiscal 1991.

Finally, with respect to the third leg of the nuclear triad, long-range bombers, the administration postponed a decision to procure the B-2, or Stealth, bomber for a year. The complexity and cost of the technology, Cheney informed Congress, required more time before a production decision could be made.[7]

There was also a significant change in the U.S. nuclear targeting doctrine, the Single Integrated Operational Plan. As the Cold War wound down, U.S. planners began to consider, for the first time, that the traditional role of U.S. nuclear weapons—countering the Soviet "threat"—might disappear. General Lee Butler, the head of the Strategic Command, said, "As early as October 1989, we abandoned global war with the Soviet Union as the principle planning and programming paradigm for the U.S. armed forces." The Pentagon responded by reducing the number of targets in the Soviet Union from 10,000 to around 2,500. But this still left many more weapons than targets.[8]

To justify maintaining existing stockpiles of both strategic and nonstrategic nuclear weapons, administration planners began to shift their attention to "a new series of threats" in the Third World. In June 1990 Cheney announced that deterring the use by an enemy of weapons of mass destruction, which he said was spreading around the world, was sufficient reason for maintaining the size of the U.S. nuclear arsenal. On June 1, General Butler said that "our focus now is not just the former Soviet Union, but any potentially hostile country that has or is seeking weapons of mass destruction."[9]

Brilliant Pebbles

There was also a change in the official attitude toward strategic nuclear defense. During the 1988 presidential campaign, Bush was not as enthusiastic about the Strategic Defense Initiative as his predecessor had been. On January 26, 1989, John G. Tower, who had been Bush's first nominee for secretary of defense, openly attacked Reagan's vision of SDI as "unrealistic." He explained: "To begin with, I don't believe that we can devise an umbrella that can protect the entire American population from nuclear incineration." Even though Tower's nomination was rejected by the Senate for other reasons, his views on SDI were considered prophetic.[10]

Cheney, who did get the job as secretary of defense, also thought that Reagan's SDI had been "oversold." He envisioned a much more limited role for SDI, one designed to strengthen deterrence by reducing the effectiveness of any Soviet first strike. He also cautioned that SDI funding had to be balanced with other strategic needs. Accordingly, the new administration's fiscal 1990 budget request for SDI was cut from $5.6 billion to $4.8 billion. Deprived of Reagan's intense enthusiasm, SDI became just another military program. Nevertheless, administration officials asserted in public that their intentions toward SDI were the same as Reagan's: continued research and eventual deployment of a system to protect the United States against a ballistic missile attack.[11]

In Phase 1 of the Bush version of SDI, the United States would place in earth orbit approximately 10,000 ICBM interceptors, called Brilliant Pebbles. The system was first proposed to Reagan in 1987 by Lawrence Livermore Laboratory physicist Lowell Wood, with the support of Edward Teller, the "father" of the U.S. hydrogen bomb and a long-time advocate of nuclear weapons development. The "pebbles" were designed to intercept ballistic missiles in the first minutes of flight, before they could release their multiple warheads and decoys. The system would include missiles capable of boosting the interceptors to near ICBM velocities, sophisticated sensors to independently detect and track Soviet missiles, a high-speed computer capable of identifying Soviet missiles by type, judging which missile to shoot at, predicting its trajectory, and plotting a flight-path for interception, and "several redundant communications channels" to allow human commanders on the ground to give the order to attack.[12]

General James Abrahamson, director of Reagan's Strategic Defense Initiative Organization, estimated that the Brilliant Pebbles system would cost less than $10 billion for research, development, production, and deployment, with another $15 billion necessary for a fleet of high-altitude warning satellites and command and control systems, making the total cost of the program $25 billion, far less than the $69 billion estimated for the Reagan Phase 1 deployment plan. Abrahamson predicted that Brilliant Pebbles could intercept 30 percent of a first-wave Soviet missile attack, and it could be deployed in five years.

Critics immediately charged that Abrahamson's estimate was unrealistic. To stay within his $10 billion ceiling, each space-based rocket would have to cost many times less than the cheapest satellite then in the air force inventory, that is, the nearly $50 million Navstar system. Lieutenant General George Monahan, Abrahamson's successor as director of SDIO, said he did not know any way to gain the level of performance predicted by General Abrahamson for only $25 billion. The General Accounting Office, Congress's nonpartisan investigative agency, also argued that Abrahamson's cost estimates were unduly optimistic. It stated that they referred only to a very partial "first phase" defense that even the SDIO had long acknowledged could be overwhelmed quickly by Soviet countermeasures.[13]

The critics also pointed out that deployment of Bush's paired-down SDI still would violate the ABM Treaty, which prohibits the deployment of space-based ABM components, like Brilliant Pebbles. Cheney acknowledged as much when he said, "If we reach the point where I think we have the capability to deploy SDI—and I fully expect we'll be able to do that some day—and that deployment were inconsistent with the ABM Treaty, then I would advocate the abrogation of the treaty, and that we should move forward and deploy those defenses."[14]

The Jackson Hole Meeting, September 1989: The ABM Treaty
When the nuclear and space talks resumed, after a long hiatus, in Geneva, Switzerland, on June 19, 1989, the U.S. delegation continued to adhere to the broad interpretation of the ABM Treaty. It also sought a START agreement to, as U.S. chief delegate Richard Burt put it, "preserve our options to deploy advanced defenses." The Soviet position also remained unchanged, with the Soviets arguing that the preservation of the ABM Treaty was critical to Soviet acceptance of offensive force reductions. As a result, no progress was made in this eleventh round of the talks, which ended on August 7.[15]

To get the stalled talks going again, the Soviets once again took the initiative. In September, Soviet foreign minister Eduard Shevardnadze met secretary of state James Baker III at the latter's ranch near Jackson's Hole, Wyoming. Baker had served as Reagan's White House chief of staff and secretary of the Treasury, but had little experience with foreign relations. Nevertheless, he was a pragmatist who quickly appreciated the great opportunities that Gorbachev's "new thinking" offered the West. "We want *perestroika* to succeed," he said, "because *perestroika* promises Soviet actions more advantageous to our interests. Our task is to search more creatively for those points of mutual U.S.-Soviet advantage that may be possible." Baker was among the first in the administration to support a more positive approach to the Soviet Union.[16]

At Jackson Hole, Shevardnadze made an apparent major concession to the United States by dropping the Soviet demand for agreed limits on the U.S. SDI program as a prerequisite to completing START. Since late 1985, the Soviet demand for collateral limits on space-based weapons had thwarted final agreement on a START pact. The Soviet Union, Shevardnadze said, is "ready to sign and ratify the START treaty even if, by the time it is completed, an agreement on the ABM problem will not yet have been reached." However, he added the caveat "that both sides would continue to comply with the ABM Treaty as signed in 1972." In reality, the Soviet position on the ABM Treaty remained unchanged. They continued to insist that both countries must abide by the 1972 treaty "as signed"—a phrase the Soviets employed to argue that the treaty bans any tests of space-based ABM weapons.[17]

In a more substantial concession to the United States, Shevardnadze agreed to drop the Soviet demand for a "nonwithdrawal commitment" in the ABM Treaty. But he also called for an explicit provision in the START agreement permitting either side to withdraw if the other side violated or withdrew from the ABM Treaty. He suggested that the Soviet Union's "supreme interests" might be jeopardized if offensive forces were reduced in the absence of the ABM Treaty's limits on missile defenses. Although Baker did not accept Shevardnadze's demand for an explicit START provision linking the agreement to continued ABM compliance, he acknowledged that "there is a provision in the START treaty that would permit withdrawal upon a national interest determination."[18]

In the twelfth round of the nuclear and space talks, which began on September 28, the United States tabled a new draft defense and space treaty that dropped the concept of an agreed period of nonwithdrawal from the ABM Treaty, as accepted by Baker and Shevardnadze at Jackson Hole. The new treaty draft would preserve the ABM Treaty's existing withdrawal options, allowing either side to withdraw on six months' notice, if its supreme interests were threatened, or immediately, if the other party committed a material breach of the accord. However, the Soviets rejected a U.S. proposal that would have permitted either side to make a specific proposal for a cooperative framework for ABM deployments and allow deployments to begin six months after announcing its intent to do so, and if three years of discussion about such cooperative deployments did not reach agreement. The new U.S. draft also contained previous proposals to permit testing under the broad interpretation, allowing up to fifteen ABM weapon test satellites simultaneously in space and placing no limits on either the testing or deployment of space-based ABM sensors. These proposals were also unacceptable to the Soviets, who regarded them as American devices to undermine the strict interpretation of the ABM Treaty.

Although rejecting the broad view of the ABM Treaty, the Soviets suggested a number of "predictability" measures that the United States would eventually accept. The two sides agreed to make annual data exchanges on the planned development, testing, deployment, modernization, and replacement of ABM systems and components. They also approved annual meetings of experts to review the data exchanges and to consider permitting the mutual observation of ABM-related testing. The United States had proposed that such briefings on planned activities and visits should extend in selected cases back to the research stage, that is, even before development began. At

Jackson Hole, U.S. negotiators invited Soviet technical experts to examine two SDI facilities. The Soviets accepted the invitation, but they resisted the U.S. proposal to extend predictability measures to research projects. Since research is not limited by the traditional interpretation of the ABM Treaty, the Soviets did not consider it necessary to extend the predictability measures to cover research projects.[19]

The new Soviet concessions on SDI were prompted by their realization that, at least since 1987, the problem of SDI testing had become a less ominous issue for them. In that year, Congress had mandated continued U.S. observance of the earlier, more restrictive interpretation of the ABM Treaty. Although the Bush administration stood by the broad interpretation in principle, it did not press ahead with any SDI tests that would have violated the strict interpretation of the ABM Treaty.

In still another surprising concession by the Soviet side, Shevardnadze told Baker that the Soviet Union would dismantle the giant phased-array radar at Krasnoyarsk in Siberia, which the United States had long charged was a violation of the ABM Treaty. But the Soviets also repeated their earlier complaints about U.S. radars at Thule, Greenland, and Fylingdales Moor in Britain. The ABM Treaty, the Soviets argued, barred such radars outside U.S. or Soviet territory. But the United States repeated its earlier response to this Soviet complaint by arguing that the two radars were treaty compliant since they replaced older, much less powerful radars that were "grandfathered in" under the pact. However, in the joint communiqué released at the end of the Jackson Hole meeting, the United States "promised to consider" the Soviet concerns "in consultation with its allies." Previously, U.S. officials had simply rejected Soviet concerns about these two radars.[20]

START at Jackson Hole

In still another bid to get the stalled talks moving at the Jackson Hole meeting, the Soviets also announced that they were "delinking" from START the issue of limiting nuclear-armed, sea-launched cruise missiles (SLCMs). The new Soviet offer proposed that limits on SLCMs be agreed upon separately from START, or as part of an overall agreement on naval arms. Nevertheless, Soviet officials indicated that even though limitations on nuclear SLCMs need not be recorded in the treaty, they must be agreed to before START was completed. One Soviet official mentioned, as a precedent for such an agreement, the statement on the Backfire bomber that accompanied the 1979 SALT II Treaty. Shevardnadze also proposed a technique to verify a limit on nuclear sea-launched cruise missiles. But, like the Reagan administration, the Bush team insisted that limits on the number of nuclear SLCMs were impossible to verify, since nuclear and conventional armed versions of the same missile look alike and because their relatively small size made them easy to conceal.[21]

Yet the two sides did endorse, in principle, an earlier U.S. proposal stating that before a START treaty was signed, the parties should conduct, on a trial basis, some of the verification procedures envisioned in the pact. Earlier, during the previous June, the United States had proposed verification "experiments," including an effort to verify the number of warheads on particular multiwarhead missiles and an effort to "tag" missiles as they came off the assembly line to simplify detection of prohibited production. Baker and Shevardnadze also signed an agreement requiring each side to give the other two weeks' notice prior to training exercises involving more than a certain number of long-range bombers.[22]

In a move that had been widely expected, Baker announced that the United States no longer would insist that START ban mobile ICBMs. But the new U.S. stance was contingent on congressional funding for mobile missiles, which the Soviets had already deployed. The Soviets, for their part, proposed a technique to verify a limit on the number of mobile ICBMs. And they agreed to exempt from START up to 100 long-range bombers earmarked for nonnuclear missions. The two sides also agreed that, in START, the unit of account for missiles would be defined in terms of "deployed missiles and their associated launchers" rather than the SALT approach of "operational launchers and their associated missiles."[23]

Nuclear Weapon Test Bans
At Jackson Hole, Baker and Shevardnadze also discussed two nuclear arms control treaties that had been signed in the mid-1970s but never ratified. The first, the 1974 Threshold Test Ban Treaty (TTBT), would limit the size of nuclear weapon tests to no larger than the equivalent of 150,000 tons (150 kilotons) of TNT. The second, the Peaceful Nuclear Explosions Treaty (PNET), signed in 1976, would prevent circumvention of the TTBT by also limiting to 150 kilotons nuclear explosions for "peaceful" purposes, such as using nuclear explosions for large-scale earth-moving projects. The Reagan administration had refused to seek Senate approval of the treaties unless procedures to verify the treaties were made more rigorous. It insisted that all test explosions be monitored by a procedure called CORRTEX, which would have required a measuring device at the blast site. The Soviet government—and

many U.S. critics of the Reagan position—contended that adherence to the 150-kiloton limit could be monitored by seismic instruments hundreds of miles from the test sites.[24]

At Jackson Hole, Baker and Shevardnadze signed an agreement providing that each country could use whichever of the two measurement techniques it desired—CORRTEX or seismic instrumentation—to monitor the other's tests. Moreover, they agreed that either side could monitor two explosions annually for five years, and one test annually thereafter, to calibrate the CORRTEX devices. On June 1, 1990, at a Washington summit, Bush and Gorbachev signed the verification protocols, thereby clearing the way for the ratification of the two treaties. The U.S. Senate approved the treaties and their protocols by a vote of 98 to 0 on September 25, 1990. The Supreme Soviet did so as well on October 9, by a vote of 347 to 0.[25]

However, Bush refused to accept a comprehensive test ban treaty, which most arms control advocates considered the ultimate solution to the nuclear proliferation problem. Without the ability to test new nuclear weapons, the proponents of the CTBT argued, the military would be unlikely to deploy them. However, to ease Defense Department fears that the TTBT and the PNET were the prelude to an eventual CTBT, the Bush administration announced that, before resuming negotiations for a CTBT, there would be a "pause" of indefinite duration to see how well the new on-site verification procedures worked. Critics considered Bush's action an abrogation of President Reagan's early pledge to proceed "immediately," upon ratification of the a TTBT, to negotiations directed at further "limiting and ultimately ending nuclear testing." They charged that Bush's action seriously undercut the international effort to curb the proliferation of nuclear weapons. They pointed out that one of the provisions of the Nuclear Nonproliferation Treaty called for a CTBT as a prerequisite to ending the nuclear arms race and halting the spread of nuclear weapons to nonweapon states. Moreover, the NPT's original twenty-five-year mandate was about to run out, in 1995, requiring a vote by member states to keep it in effect.[26]

The administration's call for indefinite extension of the NPT produced considerable criticism from a number of Third World states, led by India, which called on the declared nuclear powers to terminate all nuclear testing and to provide evidence of intentions to eliminate their nuclear weapons stockpiles, in accordance with article 6 of the treaty, before they agreed to extend the treaty indefinitely. The United States, the critics asserted, was not only jeopardizing the effort to extend the NPT but was also setting a bad example for would-be nuclear powers by refusing to negotiate a CTBT.[27]

Pressure on the Bush administration to accept a CTBT increased as time passed. On April 6, 1989, one-third of the signatories of the Limited Test Ban Treaty (LTBT) requested a conference to change that agreement into a CTBT. On May 11, 23 senators and 142 representatives urged Bush to adopt a step-by-step program for phasing out all nuclear test explosions by 1995. A week later, French president François Mitterand announced that if the United States, Great Britain, and the Soviet Union stopped nuclear testing, France would "follow suit." On October 19, 1989, the Soviet Union began an undeclared test pause that would last just over a year. The following month, Senators Claiborne Pell (D-R.I.) and Mark Hatfield (R-Oreg.) introduced a resolution supporting the LTBT conference to create a comprehensive test ban.[28]

In spite of this pressure, on January 9, 1990, Bush approved a policy statement which declared that the administration "has not identified any further limitations on nuclear testing . . . that would be in the U.S. national security interest." It also stated that no new testing negotiations would be undertaken until after a "period of implementation" of the TTBT and PNET verification protocols. It also stated that the administration viewed a CTBT as a "long-term objective," possible only "when we do not need to depend on nuclear deterrence." The following month, the Energy Department reported that ten more years of testing would be needed in order to determine whether the U.S. deterrent could be maintained if additional test limitations beyond those in the TTBT were implemented.[29]

Finally, at Jackson Hole, Baker and Shevardnadze discussed arrangements for a Bush-Gorbachev summit, which would be held in Washington in the spring of 1990. However, Bush decided not to wait that long to see the Soviet leader. On October 31 the White House announced that the president and Gorbachev would have an "informal meeting" off the coast of Malta on December 2–3, 1989.[30]

The Revolution of 1989

The momentous events that were occurring in Eastern Europe in 1989 served as a backdrop for the Malta summit, as one Soviet satellite after another threw off, or was in the processing of throwing off, its communist systems. In Poland, General Wojtech Jaruzelski, who had imposed martial law in Poland in 1981, had become Polish president and had allowed free parliamentary elections, which took place in June 1989. To the surprise of Jaruzelski and many others, the opposition Solidarity Party won control of both houses of the Polish parliament and, as a result, named the new prime minister, the first to head a noncommunist government in Eastern Europe since 1948. In Hungary, the communist government and newly created opposition parties agreed to conduct a free election in March 1990. The result was the creation of a noncommunist government under the leadership of Jozsef Antall.

East Germany's transition to a free society, however, was more tumultuous. Demonstrations and a general strike rocked that country. In an attempt to restore order, as well as halt the exodus of East Germans to the West through Hungary, on November 9, 1989, the East German government opened the Berlin Wall. Hundreds of thousands of East Germans immediately poured into West Berlin. Nevertheless, demonstrations continued, compelling the communist regime, on December 1, 1989, to promise free elections, which were scheduled for April 1990. East Germany's first noncommunist government was consequently formed under the leadership of Lothar de Mazière, who favored the rapid reunification of the two Germanys. As a major step in that direction, de Mazière negotiated an agreement with West German chancellor Helmut Kohl, providing for the economic merger of the two Germanys on July 2, 1990.

While East Germany was throwing off communism, so too was Czechoslovakia. On December 10 a new cabinet took office, with noncommunists in the majority. On December 29 hard-line President Gustav Husak was replaced by the dissident leader Vaclav Havel, and communists were ousted from the Czechoslovak government as a result of a June 1990 election. Bulgaria was also affected by events in other Soviet satellites. On November 9, 1989, the day the Berlin Wall was opened, Bulgaria's communist politburo removed Todor Zhivkov, who had been the party's leader since 1961, and replaced him with reform communists who were able to hold on to power for more than a year before finally being overtaken by democratic forces. The transition from communism in Romania, however, was far bloodier than in any other satellite state. In December 1989 thousands of Romanians demonstrated against Nicolae Ceausescu, the longtime and much hated Romanian president. Sensing that he was losing control, Ceausescu and his wife attempted to flee the country, but they were captured before they could do so and summarily executed by the army on December 25. By the end of 1989, communism in Eastern Europe was finished.[31]

The Malta Summit, December 1989

The Bush-Gorbachev summit in Malta convened alternately on U.S. and Soviet warships that were rocked by a severe storm while they were anchored off that small island state in the Mediterranean Sea, not far from the coast of North Africa. The president again promised Gorbachev that he would move "beyond containment" and help bring the Soviet Union into the world economic structure. Gorbachev was clearly pleased by Bush's economic concessions and relieved that Bush did not make excessive demands for Soviet concessions in Eastern Europe. Not surprisingly, some historians have called the Malta summit the symbolic end of the Cold War.

With respect to START, the most important result of the Malta summit was Bush's strong affirmation of the framework worked out by Baker and Shevardnadze at Jackson Hole. The president promised to seek completion of a START agreement in time for the Washington summit, which was scheduled for the following June. However, a number of issues had to be resolved before that goal was achieved.

One concerned sea-launched cruise missiles (SLCMs). At Malta, Gorbachev pressed Bush to include limits on SLCMs in the START package, but he got nowhere with the Americans, who again argued that such restrictions were unverifiable. Gorbachev also pushed for negotiations restricting naval forces and in particular focused on the presence of numerous U.S. naval bases and aircraft carrier task forces in the waters around the Soviet Union. Since deep reductions were occurring in strategic nuclear arms and ground forces in Europe, Gorbachev said that "the time had come when we should begin discussing naval forces." Bush also responded negatively to this proposal, arguing that conventional naval forces were not within the realm of START. Gorbachev then proposed the elimination of all tactical nuclear arms at sea. This too was unacceptable to the Americans, who did not want Soviet inspectors on U.S. warships.[32]

The two sides also disagreed with respect to restricting air-launched cruise missiles (ALCMs) that were deployed on heavy bombers. The Soviets wanted ALCMs with a range of more than 600 kilometers counted as one warhead under the START limits. On-site inspection would verify how many ALCMs a bomber actually carried. The United States, however, wanted to count only ALCMs with a range greater than 1,500 kilometers. The Americans also wanted each bomber to be counted as having ten ALCMs, a move that would have eliminated any need for on-site inspection. Another critical issue that remained unresolved at Malta was how many ALCMs and heavy bombers the United States would be permitted to have.

Bush and Gorbachev were also unable to resolve the problem of how to ban the encryption of telemetry, that is, the engineering data that is broadcast from missiles during flight tests. Since the Soviet Union reportedly launched operational missiles without broadcasting telemetry, the United States called for mandatory broadcasting of all telemetric data during ballistic missile flights. This also would have included U.S. missiles, like the Minuteman II, that did not broadcast fully during flight. However, the United States was unwilling to include cruise missiles in the encryption ban, a move the Soviet side had demanded.

The two sides also disagreed on the question of which nondeployed missiles should be subject to START's numerical constraints. The U.S. position called for inventory control and numerical restraints on all mobile ICBMs, heavy ICBMs, and modern silo-based systems. (This would have covered the Soviet SS-25, SS-18, and the mobile and silo-based version of the SS-24.) The Soviet side, on the other hand, indicated that nondeployed, mobile ICBMs could be limited but that nondeployed silo-based systems should be excluded from numerical limits. They also offered to prohibit locating extra or stored missiles near silos.[33]

The February 1990 Ministerial Meeting

During a February 1990 meeting in Moscow, Baker and Shevardnadze attempted to untie the knots in START. They agreed that sea-launched cruise missiles "would be dealt with by parallel, politically-binding declarations for the duration of the START treaty." According to the U.S. interpretation of this agreement, the two sides would initially declare the maximum number of SLCMs they planned to deploy for the first five years of the treaty. In each of the following years, a maximum number would be declared for the next succeeding year beyond the original five-year period. Such rolling declarations would not commit the parties to establish overall ceilings at the outset, and either side could periodically revise its original declared total.

But a number of SLCM issues still remained unresolved. The Soviets maintained that the START limits should include conventionally armed SLCMs, whereas the United States argued that these weapons should be exempted. The two sides also continued to disagree about the accountable range of SLCMs and the feasibility of establishing a regime that would effectively verify limits on SLCM deployments.

Baker and Shevardnadze did resolve another problem in their February 1990 meeting: the ALCM counting method. Each U.S. bomber that was equipped to carry ALCMs would count as having ten warheads but would be permitted to carry as many as twenty, whereas each Soviet bomber equipped to carry ALCMs would count as only eight and would be permitted to carry no more than twelve. Because of this asymmetry, the Soviet Union would be allowed to have more ALCM-carrying bombers than the United States. Following the February meeting, Viktor Karpov, a senior Soviet arms control official, stated that the two sides had "agreed that the Soviet Union could have 40 percent more aircraft than the United States." He added, "according to calculations by the Americans themselves, within the framework of these limitations, they could have approximately 110 aircraft with cruise missiles, while we would have 150." However, the two sides continued to disagree on range limits for ALCMs. The Soviets reiterated their original proposal that all ALCMs with a range of over 600 kilometers should be covered by START while the United States lowered its February proposal from the early range of 1,500 kilometers to 800 kilometers.[34]

The February ministerial meeting also failed to resolve a dispute over the details of a provision permitting the conversion of strategic heavy bombers to a conventional role. The United States had proposed that a number of existing heavy bombers be converted to a conventional-only capability and exempted from the 1,600 limit on strategic nuclear delivery vehicles (SNDVs). The Soviet Union made its acceptance of this proposal contingent on U.S. acceptance of the Soviet position on ALCM range. The United States also proposed that 115 aircraft be exempted from the 1,600 SNDV limit, whereas the Soviet Union argued that no more than 100 should be exempted.[35]

Spring 1990 Stalemate
The United States tried to break the START stalemate in March 1990, proposing a ban on land-based missiles carrying multiple warheads. The U.S. proposal, presented to the Soviets as an informal suggestion, was designed to take place in two steps. The first would ban mobile, land-based missiles with more than one warhead. This step, which could be taken as a part of START, would prevent the United States from deploying ten-warhead MX missiles on rail cars. It also would force Moscow to remove its ten-warhead SS-24 missiles from railroad launchers and put them in stationary silos. The second step of the U.S. plan called for the elimination of all land-based missiles with multiple warheads at some unspecified date. The U.S. proposal, analysts

believed, was largely motivated by the reluctance of Congress to fund the rail-based mode for the MX missile. In addition, influential members of Congress, including Senator Sam Nunn, the Georgia Democrat who headed the Armed Services Committee, had urged the administration to propose a ban on mobile land-based missiles with multiple warheads.

Gorbachev replied that the U.S. proposal was too limited because it excluded sea-based ballistic missiles. He was particularly concerned about U.S. plans to deploy new, highly accurate D-5 ballistic missiles on U.S. Trident submarines. Each D-5 missile was designed to carry eight warheads. But the United States had repeatedly rebuffed Soviet suggestions that it sharply curtail its force of submarine missiles, on which it deployed most of its ballistic missile warheads. The Soviets, by contrast, had deployed most of their ballistic warheads on land-based missiles.[36]

The failure to narrow these differences during additional Baker-Shevardnadze talks in Washington in April surprised administration officials. They were under the impression that the tougher position taken by the Soviet delegation reflected the growing influence of the Soviet military over Gorbachev in response to worsening problems within the Soviet Union, including an attempt by Lithuania to declare its independence, the weakening of the Soviet economy, and the possibility of a split between reformers and hard-liners at the scheduled full Congress of the Soviet Communist Party in July. However, during talks with Baker in Moscow in early May, Gorbachev appeared to be firmly in charge of the Soviet government.[37]

Despite the lack of progress in START, however, the date for the next Bush-Gorbachev summit in Washington was moved up from late June to May 30-June 3, 1990, apparently to accommodate Gorbachev's busy schedule. However, the earlier summit date gave the United States and the Soviet Union less time than previously anticipated to resolve the major remaining issues. In order to address these problems, the two sides agreed to schedule another Baker-Shevardnadze meeting in the Soviet Union from May 16-19.[38]

The Moscow Ministerial Meeting, May 1990

Baker and Shevardnadze were finally able to break the START logjam during their Moscow meeting, shortly before the scheduled Bush-Gorbachev summit in Washington. After four days of talks, Baker and Shevardnadze announced that they had resolved two major obstacles to a strategic arms reduction treaty that would make possible a 30 percent reduction in the size of their respective nuclear arsenals.

One of those obstacles was the air-launched cruise missile. Baker and Shevardnadze agreed that all existing ALCMs with a range over 600 kilometers, except for the U.S. conventionally armed Tacit Rainbow missile, would be considered START accountable. Future nonnuclear ALCMs with a range over 600 kilometers would not be considered START accountable if they were distinguishable from long-range nuclear ALCMs. There would be no restrictions on deploying externally distinguishable, nonnuclear, long-range ALCMs on aircraft not limited by the START treaty.

The two sides also agreed to place a limit on the number of bombers equipped with ALCMs that could be "discounted," or counted at less than their full complement of ALCMs. They agreed that current and future U.S. heavy bombers could be equipped with no more than twenty long-range nuclear ALCMs. Existing and future Soviet heavy bombers could be equipped with no more than twelve long-range nuclear ALCMs. The first 150 U.S. ALCM-carrying bombers would be counted as having ten ALCMs each, and the first 210 Soviet ALCM-carrying bombers would be counted as having eight ALCMs each. After these respective limits were reached, each ALCM-carrying bomber would be counted as having the number of weapons for which it is actually equipped. However, at this time, it seemed unlikely that either side would decide to deploy enough bombers with ALCMs to even come close to those ceilings. If either side had chosen to do so, it would have been forced to make even larger cuts in its arsenal of ballistic missile warheads than START required to reach the limit of 4,900.

Baker and Shevardnadze also agreed that nuclear sea-launched cruise missiles (SLCMs) would be dealt with outside the START treaty, with each side making "politically binding" declarations concerning the number of nuclear SLCMs with a range over 600 kilometers that it planned to deploy. The declared number of SLCMs would not exceed 880 for the duration of the START treaty. (This limit would not have had much practical effect on the United States, since the navy had stated that it planned to deploy no more than 758 nuclear SLCMs, and possibly even fewer due to budgetary constraints.) The declarations would be made annually and would state the maximum number of long-range nuclear SLCMs each side planned to deploy for the following five years. For nuclear SLCMs with a range between 300 and 600 kilometers, the two sides agreed to have a confidential data exchange. The Soviet Union had some 600-800 short-range nuclear antiship SLCMs, whereas the United States did not have any nuclear SLCMs with a range under 600 kilometers. By keeping the SLCM agreement outside the START treaty, the United States was able to avoid the verification problem created by the prospect of Soviet inspectors boarding U.S. warships. The compromise also provided Moscow with long-sought assurances that the United States would not vastly expand its SLCM program.

There were, however, a number of issues that Baker and Shevardnaze were unable to resolve in Moscow, the most important of which were the details of a noncircumvention provision, constraints on Soviet Backfire bombers and mobile missiles, limits on the flight testing of the Soviet "heavy" SS-18 missile, and verification provisions of the START accord.[39]

Noncircumvention pertained to the process of preventing either side from getting around the provisions of a strategic arms agreement by giving weapons to another country that was not a party to the treaty. The main problem with respect to this issue concerned Britain's ongoing "special relationship" with the United States, whereby the British nuclear program received U.S. assistance, including Trident D-5 missiles. The Soviets wanted to know how far this special relationship would extend into the future and particularly how it would affect reductions and developments in strategic arms control.

One way that the United States could conceivably circumvent the provisions of a START treaty, the Soviets feared, was by cooperating with Britain in the development of a new long-range, nuclear-armed, air-launched cruise missile that was prohibited by the treaty. The British, who were in the midst of discussing a joint nuclear air-to-surface missile program with the French government, might in turn share U.S. weapons technology with France. Although the Soviets were prepared to allow the U.S.-British Trident II missile program to continue, they wanted a noncircumvention provision that would foreclose weapon transfers to other parties, such as France.[40]

With respect to the Backfire bomber, the Soviets were prepared to make a unilateral statement for the START treaty stating that the bomber would not be used for strategic missions. But the United States wanted the statement expanded to include a ceiling on the number of Backfires that could be deployed during the period of the treaty, something the Soviets were not prepared to do.

The dispute over mobile missiles was, in part, a question of numbers. The Soviet Union, which had deployed such weapons, wanted a higher limit than was desired by the United States. In Moscow, Baker proposed a limit of 800 mobile land-based missiles for each side. The Soviets initially suggested 1,600 but later reduced that figure to 1,200.

Nor could the two sides decide on how to verify the movement of mobile land-based missiles, such as the Soviet ss-24 and ss-25, or mobile versions of the American MX missile and the proposed Midgetman. Washington wanted to be notified when these Soviet missiles were taken from, and returned to, their bases in order to enable U.S. satellites to verify Soviet missile activity. However, Moscow refused to accept this U.S. condition, pointing out that the whole purpose of making missiles mobile is to make them difficult for an adversary to find.

In addition, the Soviet Union had deployed several dozen multiwarhead, rail-mobile ss-24s and about 200 single-warhead, road-mobile ss-25s. Neither of the corresponding U.S. weapons, the rail-based MX or Midgetman, were in production at that time, and both faced strong political opposition to doing so. Accordingly, the United States wanted an expanded version of the verification system that was established by the INF Treaty. It provided that each country's inspectors would be able to continually monitor factories in the other country that build key parts and assemble the missile types at issue. But Moscow was not prepared to go this far in verifying the START Treaty.

Another issue that perplexed negotiators was the problem of ICBM modernization. The United States wanted to prevent continued modernization of the ss-18, the most threatening missile in the Soviet arsenal. But the Soviets rejected this proposal, saying that the United States should be satisfied with the Soviet Union's prior commitment to reduce the then-current number (308) of ss-18 missiles by 50 percent, eliminating some 1,500 warheads in the process. Moreover, the preliminary agreement prohibited any new types of heavy missiles or any increase in the number of warheads on the ss-18 beyond the amount then present.[41]

The Washington Summit, May 31–June 3, 1990
Bush and Gorbachev were unable to clear up these unresolved issues at their Washington summit. They nevertheless reaffirmed their determination to have a START agreement "completed and ready for signature by the end of the year." They also signed a five-page joint statement delineating the major agreed START provisions. These included the compromises accepted by Baker and Shevardnaze in Moscow as well as two new agreements reached during the negotiations at the Washington summit: a sublimit of 1,100 on the number of warheads permitted on deployed mobile ICBMs and a schedule for implementing the treaty's reductions in three phases over seven years.[42]

The two presidents also signed a joint statement promising that negotiations on a START II Treaty would begin "at the earliest practical date." In the discussions leading to the joint statement, the United States had argued that START II talks should focus on the elimination of ICBMs with multiple independently targetable reentry vehicles (MIRVs), an area in which the Soviet Union had an advantage. The Soviets responded by saying that limits on MIRVed ICBMs would have to be accompanied by limits on MIRVed submarine-launched ballistic missiles. The joint statement alluded generally to reducing "the concentration of warheads on strategic delivery vehicles as a whole," but reflected U.S. priority by specifying that this would include "measures related to the question of heavy missiles and MIRVed ICBMs."[43]

In spite of the euphoria prevailing at the Washington summit, by failing to complete START at this meeting, Bush and Gorbachev gave right-wing critics of the treaty additional time to attack it. Earlier, in a May 23 letter to Bush, nine conservative Republican senators led by Jesse Helms (R-N.C.) objected to certain aspects of the cruise missile arrangement, in particular, Baker's assurance to Gorbachev that the United States would not equip the Tacit Rainbow missiles with nuclear weapons. The senators also asserted that the treaty would give the Soviet Union a numerical advantage in total delivery systems over the United States. They pointed to the provision that would permit the Soviets to deploy 210 ALCM-equipped bombers while allowing the United States only 150. Helms suggested that this provision violated the so-called Jackson Amendment of 1972, which required that any strategic arms treaty be based on "equal forces" for each party. However, the administration argued that the treaty would give each side roughly equal numbers of ALCMs because U.S. planes could carry more missiles.[44]

Conservatives also feared that the Soviets might have an advantage in regard to two other issues. One concerned the degree to which the Soviet Union would be permitted to improve its ss-18 ICBM. Conservatives argued that the START-limited force of 154 improved versions of the ss-18 would be as powerful as the pre-START force of 308 missiles. The Bush administration responded by asserting that it would be much better to have 150 ss-18s subject to modernization restrictions than 308 that were not. But the administration also stated that it was pressing the Soviets for a ban on further ss-18 production after 1992, as well as urging them to accept a prohibition on more than two ss-18 test launches per year. Eventually, administration spokesmen reasoned, Soviet military planners would lose confidence in the reliability of the aging missiles anyway.[45]

Conservatives also brought up the Backfire bomber, insisting that it could reach U.S. targets from Soviet bases and therefore should be covered by the START treaty. The Bush administration tried to satisfy this objection by demanding that the plane either be counted as a strategic bomber under START or be counted as a regional weapon that would be limited by the Conventional Forces in Europe (CFE) agreement. They also doubted the ability of the United States to verify the treaty. Reflecting this concern, a former Pentagon official in the Reagan administration, Frank J. Gaffney Jr., contended that the treaty's limits on mobile missiles were hopelessly unverifiable. His argument was reinforced by the timely disclosure of verification lapses in the INF regime. Soviet-built SS-23 missiles, banned by the INF pact, had turned up in East Germany, Czechoslovakia, and Bulgaria. Shevardnadze insisted that he and other top Soviet political leaders were unaware that the missiles had been sent to these countries. But the lapse was significant enough to bring a sharp protest from Senator Richard G. Lugar (R-Ind.), a political centrist who was a strong supporter of the INF Treaty. "The whole purpose of this [INF] treaty," he said, "was to eliminate intermediate weapons in Europe." Lugar and other senators insisted that it was imperative to ensure that this agreement could be verified before the debate on START began.[46]

Other critics of the arms control process, among them Kenneth L. Adelman, who had been director of the Arms Control and Disarmament Agency under Reagan, criticized the treaty's emphasis on "deep cuts" in existing arsenals, even though that was Reagan's cardinal goal. With Adelman undoubtedly in mind, Baker labeled most of the critics as people "who, in the past . . . have simply rejected the concept of arms control, generally." He asserted that the emerging treaty largely reflected U.S. positions and that the Soviets had made most of the concessions to complete it. Moreover, he added, the pact had the support of top U.S. military officials.[47]

Fortunately for the administration, much of the force of the hard-line attack on the START treaty was deflected by the waning of the Cold War. With the Soviet Union showing a less belligerent attitude under Gorbachev, the technical arguments of the hard-liners' attack on START carried far less weight than they had against the SALT II Treaty in 1979, when the Soviet threat seemed more menacing. Richard Perle, a chief architect of SALT II's defeat, admitted as much: "There is no treaty negotiated by a Republican so defective as to be turned down by a Democratic-dominated Senate, so it'll pass." Indeed, as the Cold War wound down, and the possibility of a Soviet-U.S. nuclear war virtually disappeared, strategic arms control gradually lost its position as the primary point of Soviet-American dialogue. By the time of

the Washington summit, the reunification of Germany, not START, dominated the Soviet-American agenda.[48]

The Reunification of Germany

Following the fall of the Berlin Wall in November 1989, the two Germanys
had moved inexorably toward unification. Gorbachev was alarmed by this
prospect, not only because of the threat he believed a reunified Germany
would pose to Soviet security, but also because he feared that hard-liners in
his own country would use it as an instrument to drive him from power.

To make German reunification digestible to the Soviets, Bush gave Gorbachev nine assurances at the Washington summit, including a promise that
Germany would reaffirm its commitments neither to produce nor to possess
nuclear, biological, and chemical weapons, and a promise to conduct negotiations on short-range nuclear forces once a CFE Treaty was signed. He also
declared that the United States would withdraw all of its nuclear artillery
shells from Europe and announced that the United States would not develop
a missile to replace the Lance. With the Soviets withdrawing their forces
from Eastern Europe, the only targets that remained for NATO SNF were
located in the newly democratic states. In effect, the SNF issue had ceased to
be a problem.[49]

On July 6, 1990, the NATO summit in London added to these assurances
by approving a declaration proclaiming the end of the Cold War and inviting
the Warsaw Pact states to establish diplomatic liaisons with NATO. NATO
countries also pledged to make nuclear forces weapons of "last resort." They
acknowledged that NATO now needed "far fewer nuclear weapons," particularly "systems of the shortest range" (SNF).[50]

With these assurances, on July 14, 1990, Gorbachev accepted the reunification of Germany as well as its membership in NATO. In exchange, West
German Chancellor Helmut Kohl promised to provide economic aid to the
Soviet Union and agreed to limit the military forces of the reunited Germany
to 370,000 personnel (in 1990 the combined forces of the two Germanys
stood at 667,000). He also assured Gorbachev that there would be no
nuclear, biological, or chemical weapons in the German arsenal. For his part,
Gorbachev promised to withdraw Soviet troops from East Germany within
four years and agreed to terminate Soviet occupation rights after reunification occured.[51]

On September 12, 1990, the four allied powers in World War II and the
two Germanys signed the Treaty on the Final Settlement with Respect to

Germany. On October 1 the World War II victors formally surrendered their four-power rights and responsibilities over Germany and Berlin. Germany was reunified two days later. "The epoch of the Cold War," Baker proclaimed, "is over. Any lingering doubts have been dispelled by the events of the past month."[52]

Demise of the START 1990 Deadline

Despite the promise made by Bush and Gorbachev at the Washington summit to finish a START treaty by the end of 1990, that deadline proved impossible to meet. Nevertheless, by the end of that year they were able to make progress toward resolving the three major problems that existed during the Washington summit: the Backfire bomber, the ss-18 ICBM, and the noncircumvention issue.

The problem of the Backfire bomber was settled in principle during October talks between Baker and Shevardnadze. The Soviets agreed to make a politically binding commitment—similar in form to the agreement on long-range nuclear sea-launched cruise missiles—to deploy no more than 500 Backfire bombers (300 nonnaval and 200 naval). The Soviets also renewed their SALT II commitment not to give the Backfire intercontinental-range capability through aerial refueling.

The noncircumvention dispute was settled at a Baker-Shevardnadze meeting in Moscow during November. Essentially, the two men agreed to "kick the can down the road." The United States agreed to make a unilateral statement that "existing patterns of cooperation" (such as the sale of U.S. submarine-launched ballistic missiles to the United Kingdom) would not be affected by START. The Soviet Union agreed to make a unilateral statement that if the strategic balance were altered by U.S. strategic arms transfers, the Soviet Union could consider such a shift as grounds for withdrawal from START. Finally, to allay Soviet concerns, the British government told Moscow that it had no intention of maintaining more than a minimum deterrent or of deploying more than the four Trident submarines they were deploying.

On the ss-18 issue, the United States abandoned its call for flight-test restraints. The Soviet Union, in turn, agreed not to increase the ss-18's throw weight and launch weight beyond those of the ss-18 model 5. Another ss-18 issue, however, cropped up. The Soviet Union indicated that it would like to reserve the right to build new ss-18 silos. Two of the Soviet Union's six ss-18 fields were in Kazakhstan (the other four were in the Russian republic) and, reportedly, these were among those being modernized with the ss-18 model 5. The Soviets wanted to keep those silos as part of their permitted 154 ss-18s, but they reserved the option of building new silos for those missiles elsewhere in the Soviet Union in the event that Kazakhstan seceded from the union or prohibited the deployment of nuclear weapons on its territory—a step the Kazakh parliament was considering at that time.[53]

As a consequence of the progress made in START, on December 12, 1990, President Bush was able to express his hope that "we'll be ready to sign a treaty at a summit in Moscow on February 11 through 13." But following another Baker-Shevardnadze meeting in Houston during December, three "endgame" issues surfaced: monitoring mobile ICBM production sites, determining how telemetric data must be transmitted during strategic ballistic missile flight tests, and verifying limits on heavy bombers.[54]

With respect to the first problem, the United States asserted that it would like to have continuous monitoring at the Soviet plants that produce solid-fuel rocket motors for the first stages of the ss-24 and ss-25 missiles. The discussions were complicated by the fact that the United States did not have any final assembly sites. Instead, it transported its strategic ballistic missiles in individual stages for assembly at their deployment sites. A second asymmetry lay in the fact that the United States still had no deployed mobile ICBMs, whereas the Soviet Union had deployed two types of mobile ICBMs. Nevertheless, the Soviets wanted to be able to examine containers large enough to carry the first stage of the Midgetman missile, a potentially mobile ICBM. But the United States argued that the Midgetman was not yet ready to be tested as a mobile missile, and thus the Soviets could only examine containers large enough to carry the first stage of the MX, another potentially mobile ICBM that had already been flight tested.

However, administration sources told reporters that it was likely that the United States would eventually accept the right of each party to inspect final assembly plants as being sufficient for verifying limits on Soviet mobile missiles, as it did under the INF Treaty. If so, the Soviet Union would also get access to two sites in the United States.

Telemetry, the engineering data broadcast from strategic ballistic missile during flight tests, also continued to be a problem. The two sides were still trying to negotiate an agreement incorporating complex trade-offs between broadcasting telemetry in an efficient and effective way for the testing party, and at the same time making telemetry easy for the other side to obtain.

The problem of doing this was aggravated by the dissimilarity in the ways the two sides monitored missile telemetry. The United States frequently transmitted telemetric data at high frequency and low power, which made telemetry more difficult for the Soviets to monitor. If adopted by the Soviet Union, these broadcasting techniques could create problems for the United States, since virtually all Soviet ICBM flight tests took place over the Siberian landmass, beyond the range and capability of U.S. sensors to intercept their low-power, high-frequency telemetry. On the other hand, U.S. ICBM test missiles flew across the Pacific Ocean from California to Kwajalein Atoll, where the Soviets could utilize surface ships with electronic eavesdropping equipment.

To deal with this asymmetry, the United States proposed a three-year moratorium on changing existing practices, effectively allowing the United States to continue using its methods but preventing the Soviet Union from following suit for three years. Subsequently, under the U.S. proposal, a change in telemetry transmission practices would be subject to discussion.

Bombers posed still another verification problem. The Soviets expressed concern that they would have difficulty determining which U.S. bombers were declared "penetrators"—bombers that carry only gravity bombs and short-range attack missiles—from those declared to be cruise missile carriers. (Penetrating bombers would count as one warhead toward START limits, but U.S. cruise missile carriers would count as ten.) The United States and the Soviet Union had already agreed to on-site inspections for two types of bombers. They agreed to allow the verifying side to look at bombers declared to be cruise missile carriers, such as B-52Hs, to determine that they did not carry more than the permitted maximum number of air-launched cruise missiles, but the agreement did not permit inspectors to examine bombers that were declared to be penetrators. The Soviets wanted the right to examine these bombers to ensure that they were not equipped with ALCMs.[55]

Gorbachev's Growing Domestic Problems

Another major reason for the inability of Bush and Gorbachev to conclude START before the end of 1990 was the Soviet leader's increasing preoccupation with growing domestic problems. *Perestroika* had not only failed to produce any visible improvement in the Soviet economy but had actually contributed to its decline. The consequences were shortages, falling productivity, strikes, and runaway inflation.

Moreover, unlike earlier Soviet leaders, Gorbachev had to contend with rising public opposition. In June and July 1988, he had been able to push a new constitution through the Supreme Soviet. One of its major features was a new Congress of People's Deputies, most of whose members would be directly selected by the Soviet people in an election during March 1989. However, the election results were a disaster for the Communist Party, as one communist establishment figure after another was defeated and replaced by antiparty candidates, the most outstanding of whom was maverick communist Boris Yeltsin. On May 29, 1990, the eve of Gorbachev's departure for the Washington summit, Yeltsin was elected the chairman of the Presidium of the Supreme Soviet of the Russian Federation—in effect, president of Russia. In that post, he would increasingly challenge Gorbachev.

Rising nationalism also contributed to Gorbachev's problems. The decline of the Communist Party deprived the Soviet empire of the glue that had held it together. In February 1988 ethnic violence broke out in Soviet Armenia and Azjerbaijan, requiring Gorbachev to dispatch troops to those republics in what turned out to be a partially successful attempt to restore order. On March 11, 1990, Lithuania, which (along with Estonia and Latvia) had been forcibly annexed by Josef Stalin in 1940, declared its independence. In an attempt to prevent the breakup of the Soviet Union, Gorbachev imposed an economic blockade on Lithuania, threatened to rule the republic by presidential degree, and sent Soviet troops to Vilnius, the Lithuanian capital, all in an ultimately unsuccessful attempt to reverse its declaration of independence.

During the fall of 1990, Gorbachev vacillated between the reformers and communist hard-liners in an increasingly desperate attempt to hold the political center. In August 1990 he accepted a Yeltsin-drafted plan to bring about a free-market economy in 500 days. However, he withdrew his support from the plan after belatedly realizing that its implementation would have eliminated the need for a centralized economic structure as well as the rationale for maintaining the Soviet Union. By scuttling the 500-Day Plan, Gorbachev was forced to rely even more heavily on the hard-liners in the Politburo. Alarmed by Gorbachev's turn to the right, Soviet Foreign Minister Shevardnadze resigned on December 20, after warning that a dictatorship was coming. He was replaced, on January 15, 1991, by the Soviet ambassador to Washington, Alexander Bessmertnykh.

During the winter of 1991, Shevardnadze's prediction appeared to be coming true. In January, Gorbachev approved a hard-line plan for what turned out to be a bloody but unsuccessful attempt to overthrow the pro-independence government of Lithuania. In March, hard-liners tried to remove Yeltsin from the Russian presidency by impeaching him, but they were thwarted by mass demonstrations on his behalf. Needless to say, the Soviet leader, facing these kind of problems, paid little attention to the START deadline.

The Persian Gulf Crisis Delays START

START was also eclipsed by a crisis in the Persian Gulf region. It began on August 2, 1990 when the armed forces of Iraq invaded neighboring Kuwait and quickly conquered the oil-rich emirate. President Bush almost immediately announced his determination to reverse Iraq's aggression. Gorbachev decided to support him, even though this meant abandoning an important Soviet client. More important to Gorbachev than Iraq was his need for Western assistance to save the Soviet economy and, indeed, the Soviet Union itself. U.N.-authorized military action against Iraq began on January 17, 1991, when the United States and its allies launched an air attack on Iraqi targets. On February 23 the allies began the ground war against Iraq, called Operation Desert Storm. In less than seventy-two hours, the allied forces routed the Iraqi forces in Kuwait and southern Iraq while suffering only very light casualties in the process. By contrast, the Iraqis lost thousands of soldiers and tanks and were forced to retreat rapidly across the Iraq-Kuwait border.

For a variety of reasons, Bush terminated the war before Iraqi president Saddam Hussein was overthrown. One was Gorbachev's pressure on him to avoid the humiliating defeat of a Soviet client state. Realizing that the Soviet president's assistance would be required on other issues such as START, Bush complied with Gorbachev's wishes. On February 24, only four days after Operation Desert Storm began, he ordered its end.

The Persian Gulf War contributed to the delay in concluding the START Treaty. On January 28, only two weeks before the scheduled Moscow summit at which the United States and the Soviet Union were expected to sign the treaty, Baker announced that the meeting would have to be postponed to "a later date." He justified the indefinite postponement of the START summit by saying that "the Gulf War makes it inappropriate for President Bush to be away from Washington." He added that the START treaty also would require "some additional time."[56]

The postponement of the Moscow summit was clearly a major setback for the START treaty. The summit had provided a deadline that would have forced both sides to resolve relatively minor remaining differences in order to complete the treaty for signing at the summit. Instead, with the additional time provided by the postponement of the summit, the "minor" issues that required "some additional time" became major differences that delayed further the completion of START.[57]

Among the new problems was one called "downloading," that is, the process of reducing the number of warheads carried by particular types of strategic ballistic missiles. The United States had initially proposed downloading as a way of avoiding spending time and money on building new systems. Downloading would also give the two sides flexibility in reconfiguring existing forces within the START ceiling of 4,900 ballistic missile warheads and 1,600 delivery vehicles. Each would be able to deploy a larger number of ballistic missiles, each with fewer warheads, thereby enhancing the survivability of their retaliatory forces by, in effect, "spreading their eggs into more baskets."

But defining the precise rules for downloading proved to be a major sticking point in the talks because the process posed major risks, as well as advantages, to deterrence. The potential danger involved was the possibility that, during a crisis, downloaded missiles might be quickly "uploaded" with additional warheads and thereby place the other side in a numerically disadvantageous position. To reduce this risk, the two sides agreed to place a ceiling on the total number of warheads that could be removed from missiles. However, they would argue for months on such issues as whether the Soviet SS-N-18 submarine-launched ballistic missile should be subject to this ceiling.

With respect to defining "new types" of strategic ballistic missiles, the United States sought a definition that would require substantial changes in certain engineering characteristics for a missile to qualify as a new type. The U.S. side was concerned that if variants of existing Soviet single-warhead missiles could qualify as new types with only small changes, such new types could be tested with multiple warheads. Consequently, in a "breakout" scenario, the Soviet Union would be able to retrofit (add) additional warheads on a force of previously deployed missiles. The Soviets, for their part, proposed a new types rule that would have made it easier for a variation of an existing missile to count as a new type.

Nor were the two sides able to reach agreement on all the terms and procedures related to the ban on encrypting telemetry. Both sides agreed in principle to transmit telemetry openly so that the other side could obtain missile test data. However, they also agreed that there would be some exemptions to the ban, but they could not decide what specifically would be exempted. The United States, for example, proposed a quota on exempted tests flights that would be permitted. But the Soviet Union maintained that certain types of its reentry vehicles and missiles did not broadcast telemetry and therefore would have to be exempted from the obligation to broadcast telemetry.[58]

The Patriot Missile

Although the Persian Gulf War contributed to the delay in concluding START, it also breathed new life into the Strategic Defense Initiative. Before the Gulf War, fear of the Soviet threat had diminished as the Cold War wound down, thereby permitting Congress to concentrate on the rising federal deficit and on cutting the defense budget as a primary way of reducing it. SDI became one of the targets of the defense reductions. In August 1990 the Senate voted to cut $1 billion from Bush's $4.7 billion proposed SDI budget.[59]

However, the reputed success of the Patriot missile in destroying Iraqi Scud missiles during the Persian Gulf War gave SDI an important lift. During that conflict, U.S. and coalition forces were subjected to attack by short-range (600 kilometer) Iraqi Scud tactical ballistic missiles. Although the Iraqi Scuds, armed only with chemical explosives and with poor accuracy, hardly affected the military outcome of the war, they had a significant psychological and political effect. They aroused great fear, particularly in Israel and Saudi Arabia, which the United States attempted to relieve by dispatching Patriot antiballistic missiles to those countries. That effort, Bush declared, had been a great success. "Patriot works," he announced. "All told, Patriot is 41 for 42—42 Scuds engaged, 41 intercepted." Transferring Patriot's alleged success to SDI, the *Wall Street Journal* stated: "The Patriot isn't full-blown 'Star Wars.' But the principle of intercepting missiles before they hit civilians is what most SDI supporters, including us, have been promoting all along."[60]

Some discounted the performance of the Patriot. A General Accounting Office report issued in September 1992 concluded that only 9 percent of the Patriot-Scud engagements "resulted in a warhead kill." According to Representative to John Conyors Jr. (D-Mich.), the chairman of the House subcommittee, "the Patriot's supposedly near-flawless performance may be one of the greatest myths in weapons history." Patriot fell short, John Pike of the Federation of Atomic Scientists explained, "precisely because of the problems that missile defense skeptics long suspected would be encountered by any antimissile system: difficulty discriminating between real and decoy targets, and the unreliability of computer software."[61]

GPALS

Others insisted that Patriot was a success and even criticized the Bush administration for pushing research on space-based strategic ABMs rather than antitactical ballistic missile defenses (ATBMD) like Patriot. Only diehards, they pointed out, still believed that a spaced-based ABM system had any chance of protecting the United States against an increasingly unlikely Soviet attack. To these critics, the Gulf War raised the specter of a more realistic threat—so-called rogue states (e.g., Iraq, Iran, North Korea, Syria, and Libya) armed with ballistic missiles carrying chemical, biological, or even nuclear weapons. Dealing with this threat and not the declining danger of a Soviet attack, they argued, should be the primary goal of SDI. Responding to this criticism, President Bush announced in his State of the Union address on January 29, 1991 that the mission of SDI would be changed from emphasizing only a defense against large-scale Soviet attack to "providing protection against limited ballistic missile strikes—whatever their source."[62]

The new component of SDI was called Global Protection Against Limited Strikes, or GPALS. Although a much less ambitious program than Brilliant Pebbles, GPALS largely preserved SDI orthodoxy. It perpetuated the old program's multilayered defenses and its use of existing SDI projects. The space-based layer, designed to intercept attacking missiles in their boost and midcourse phases, would consist of 1,000 Brilliant Pebbles, the small homing rockets that became SDI's preferred space weapon in 1989. These would circle the earth at an altitude of around 400-500 kilometers, accompanied by about fifty sensors ("Brilliant Eyes") orbiting about twice as high. However, the space-based Brilliant Pebbles interceptors would now be backed up by 750-1,000 ground-based interceptors on U.S. territory. Their task would be to destroy incoming missiles late in their flight through space or high in the atmosphere as they begin to reenter. The leading candidates for this job were derivatives of two long-standing SDI projects, the Exoatmospheric Reentry Intercept System (ERIS) and the High Endoatmospheric Defense Interceptor (HEDI). A third defense layer would consist of upgraded Patriots and other theater-missile defenses that could be transported for use by threatened allies or U.S. military forces. The major projects envisioned for this layer were the Theater High Altitude Area Defense (THAAD), the Extended Range Interceptor (ERINT), and the Arrow, which was being developed jointly with Israel. Deployment of theater defenses would begin first, by the mid-1990s, with the other layers following later in the decade.[63]

SDI officials estimated that GPALS would cost $48 billion, in addition to the more than $20 billion already spent on SDI since 1984. This represented a reduction of about a third from previous estimates for a full-fledged Phase 1 SDI system. Days after the president's State of the Union address, the administration submitted a fiscal year 1992 budget requesting almost $5.2 billion, a 66 percent increase in the SDI budget. According to administration plans, theater-missile defenses (Patriot-type programs) would increase from $218 million to $578 million in the following year and swell to $1.5 billion by the mid-1990s.[64]

GPALS, however, was no more popular with the critics of SDI than Brilliant Pebbles had been. They argued that pursuing the GPALS concept would require abrogating the ABM Treaty, since the program would violate the treaty's fundamental ban on nationwide missile defenses, its ban on the development, testing, and deployment of space-based ABM components, and its limits on ground-based ABM launchers and ABM sites. They also questioned the urgency of SDI's new mission, arguing that building ICBMs posed such difficult problems that many years would pass before a developing nation could threaten the United States with such weapons. As former secretary of defense Harold Brown put it, "If Third World and terrorist weapons of mass destruction emerge as a threat to the United States, they are far more likely to be delivered by aircraft, ships sailed into our harbors, or packing crates smuggled across our borders, than by ballistic missiles."[65]

Critics also rejected another argument of SDI proponents—that the breakdown of central authority in the Soviet Union provided a primary reason for concern about an unauthorized launch of a ballistic missile. They referred to a statement by General Colin Powell, chairman of the Joint Chiefs of Staff, who said that on the basis of his "knowledge of how the Soviets manage their nuclear systems," he was "fairly comfortable that those weapons will not get into improper hands," and would be "unusable" if they did.[66]

Nevertheless, in March 1991 congressional Republicans called for the elimination of all, or at least most, of the provisions of the ABM Treaty in order to make the deployment of GPALS possible. In a March 5 floor speech, Senator John Warner (R-Va.), ranking minority member of the Senate Armed Services Committee, pointed to the "success" of the Patriot system in the Gulf War as justification for Congress to "unleash American ingenuity" by removing all ABM Treaty development and testing restraints. Warner proposed an amendment to a supplemental defense authorization bill that would have directed the secretary of defense to "immediately undertake"

ABM development and testing "not withstanding any other provision of law (including the provisions of the ABM Treaty)." However, after several senators pointed out that the amendment's language effectively directed a member of the cabinet, sworn to uphold the law, to immediately begin violating a law, the ABM Treaty, Warner brought a significantly different measure to the Senate floor on March 13.[67]

The new bill, in the form of a nonbinding "sense of Congress" resolution, concluded that article 5 of the ABM Treaty, which prohibits development and testing of space-based and other mobile ABM systems and components, was no longer "in the national interest." It urged the president to negotiate a new agreement within two years that "would clearly remove any limitations on the United States having effective defenses against ballistic missiles." Should the Soviet Union not agree to such changes within two years, the bill stated, the president would be called on to decide "immediately" whether the ABM Treaty remained in the U.S. interest. With this nonbinding language, Warner succeeded in gaining White House approval for his effort. In a letter to the senator, Brent Scowcroft, the president's national security adviser, wrote that the administration "strongly supports your sense of the Congress resolution," citing the need for defenses against Third World missile attacks or unauthorized missile launches.[68]

However, Warner's amendment was opposed by Senator Sam Nunn, chairman of the Armed Services Committee. Nunn, who was one of the strongest champions of the ABM Treaty, argued that ground-based systems, which were permitted by the treaty, could provide protection against limited threats—such as Third World missile strikes—more quickly and effectively than space-based systems, which were barred by the treaty. As early as 1989, Nunn had urged Congress to fund an Accidental Launch Protection System (ALPS) to shield the United States in the event of unauthorized launches of ballistic missiles or even deliberate attacks by emerging nuclear powers.

In response to Warner's bill, Nunn put forward an alternative amendment that called for providing an additional $224 million in fiscal year 1991 for Patriot procurement and for shifting funds within the Strategic Defense Initiative to develop ground-based interceptors. However, he also stated that he hoped to be able to "make some bridges" with Warner and said that he was "totally prepared to support, and indeed would encourage, modest amendments" to the ABM Treaty to permit more effective limited defenses, if the Soviet Union would agree to them. But after it became apparent that Nunn's amendment would unleash a flood of other amendments that would delay passage of the supplementary defense authorization bill, he and Warner agreed to drop both of their amendments without a vote. However, supporters of the new ABM measures indicated that they would bring up similar legislation later in the year, when the defense budget came up for debate.[69]

Return to START, Spring 1991

As the winter of 1991 turned to spring, the prospect that START would be completed by that summer began to look increasingly doubtful. Part of the reason was Gorbachev's increasing reliance on the hard-liners in the Politburo, who were vehemently opposed to Lithuanian independence. The Bush administration did not want to attend a summit with Gorbachev if Lithuania remained a stumbling block. In addition, the Americans and the Soviets disagreed on the interpretation of the CFE Treaty. The president bluntly stated that it would not sign a START agreement until a dispute over the interpretation of the CFE Treaty was concluded first.[70]

By June, however, it was evident that Gorbachev's turn to the hard-liners had been a temporary flirtation. Yeltsin's overwhelming victory in the Russian presidential election on June 12, combined with the determination of Politburo hard-liners to turn back the clock, alarmed Gorbachev and again pushed him back to the left. In an attempt to regain the favor of reformers and appease restive Soviet nationalities as well, Gorbachev embraced democracy, radical economic reform, and a proposal for greater autonomy for the republics within a new union of the Soviet republics. Prompted by these developments in the Soviet Union, as well as by the resolution of the CFE Treaty interpretation dispute on June 1, Bush expressed hope that the START Treaty could be completed in time for signing at a Moscow summit during the summer. With that goal in mind, the administration held top-level meetings from June 5–6 to hammer out an interagency consensus on the remaining issues in START.

The following day, in Geneva, Baker presented Soviet foreign minister Alexander Bessmertnykh, Shevardnadze's successor, with a letter from Bush to Gorbachev outlining the new U.S. proposals. After the meeting, Bessmertnykh said that the two sides had "singled out two or three points" that they believed were "critical for the outcome of the treaty" and added that Bush's letter contained "several new ideas." Ten days after the Baker-Bessmertnykh meeting, Bush announced that he had received a positive response to his letter to Gorbachev that allowed him to say that the treaty was "96 percent, or close to it, concluded."[71]

The Washington Ministerial Meeting, July 1991

Baker and Bessmertnykh set the stage for the Moscow summit at a marathon session in Washington from July 11–14, at which the two sides resolved the downloading and telemetry issues and most of the questions related to new types of missiles—the three issues that had been in dispute since the preceding December.

The downloading issue was resolved with a compromise on the ss-n-18 problem. In December 1987 the Soviet Union had declared that the ss-n-18 would be counted as having seven warheads. The ss-n-18 had been deployed in two versions: the Model 1 had a three-warhead front end, or "bus," and the Model 3 a seven-warhead bus. But that fall (1987), when the two sides exchanged data on strategic forces, the Soviet Union claimed it had withdrawn the Model 3s and would deploy only the Model 1 in the future. The Soviets wanted the ss-n-18 counted as having only three warheads. The United States maintained that if the ss-n-18 were counted as having only three warheads, it should be counted toward the total Soviet downloading quota on removed warheads. Otherwise, the United States argued, the Soviets could quickly add up to 896 extra warheads by replacing the ss-n-18's three-warhead bus with the seven-warhead bus.

At the outset of the Washington meeting in July, the United States suggested that the ss-n-18's empty slots should be counted as part of the Soviets' overall "empty space" quota of 1,000. The Soviet Union had proposed that downloading could create a maximum of 750 empty warhead spaces, not counting the ss-n-18. In the end, the two parties agreed that each side could remove 1,250 warheads but must leave only 500 unmodified empty spaces. In the case of downloaded ss-n-18s and U.S. Minuteman iiis, the bus would have to be altered to conform to the actual number of warheads. The two sides would be permitted to download two additional missile types, presumably, the Soviet ss-24 icbm and the ss-n-20 slbm; the U.S. Trident ii d-5 would be downloaded by simply removing warheads from the bus. Each side would also be permitted to download individual missiles by as many as four warheads, but the bus would have to be altered if any missile were downloaded by more than two warheads. The significance of the downloading issue had always been overstated. Militarily significant cheating on downloading could easily be detected by reconnaissance satellites. But, as Richard Burt put it, "The last remaining issues in a negotiation take on a political importance that is disproportionate to their military importance because neither side wants to be seen in the last stage ... as caving in."[72]

The second problem resolved at the Washington meeting concerned telemetry. In December 1987 each side had agreed in principle to broadcast telemetry in the clear, without encoding the data or making other efforts to conceal information. But the technical details involved in implementing that principle had been hard to nail down. Exchanging data raised a host of problems. For example, some older missiles—the U.S. Minuteman II and the Soviet ss-11 and ss-13—did not broadcast telemetry during flight tests. Instead, these missiles recorded flight-test data on tapes that were stored in capsules and recovered after the tests. In addition, the Soviet Union, unlike the United States, flight-tested some of its ICBMs from operational deployment sites. These missiles were not configured to broadcast telemetry. The Soviet Union also had some missiles that broadcast during their boost and postboost phases, but not during their reentry phase. The United States, for its part, wanted to avoid broadcasting telemetry when using some retired Minuteman ICBMs and Poseidon SLBMs in SDI experiments.

To deal with these complications, the two sides agreed to exempt the broadcast requirement for older missiles and missiles tested from operational launchers. In addition, they both acknowledged that there would be no obligation to provide formulas to interpret reentry flight-test data. Finally, it was agreed that the United States would not be required to broadcast data from a limited number of treaty-covered missiles used in SDI tests. The U.S. and Soviet delegations in Geneva also had struggled for a provision that would be tight enough to ensure treaty compliance but loose enough to protect secrets not covered by the treaty. After these efforts failed to produce results, the two sides settled on a simpler approach at the Washington meeting, agreeing to exchange tapes from all strategic ballistic missile flights. This provision, combined with the commitment to broadcast telemetry in the clear, gave both sides confidence that they would be able to obtain enough flight-test data to monitor treaty compliance.

The problem of defining a new type of missile, as opposed to a "modification" of an existing type, was the final sticking point. The United States had argued that allowing a missile to be declared a new type with only minor design changes from an existing type could create the potential for breakout. One side might modify an existing single-warhead missile, such as the Soviet ss-25, and test this new type with multiple warheads. But by designating the missile as a new type, it would not have to count the already deployed missiles as MIRved. At the same time, that side would gain the capability to "backfit"—reequip—its existing single-warhead force rapidly with multiple warheads. An opposite outcome was also a possibility: if a new type were counted as having fewer warheads than an existing type with the same basic design, such as a six-warhead missile similar to the existing ten-warhead ss-24, the new type might have the capacity to be rapidly modified to carry the larger number of warheads carried by the existing system.

The United States wanted a definition that precluded classifying a missile with only minor design changes as a new missile. The Americans believed that the Soviet ss-25 single-warhead missile had surplus throw weight. If true, the Soviet Union could have modified the ss-25 slightly, declared it a new type, and legally tested it with multiple reentry vehicles. Consequently, the Soviet Union might be able to quickly convert already deployed ss-25s from single- to multiple-warhead systems. The United States was also concerned about the ten-warhead ss-24. If a new type of this missile were tested and counted as having fewer warheads, it might still have the capacity to carry a larger number of warheads. The United States wanted a definition of a new missile that would require substantial changes from an existing type in order to guard against rapid "treaty breakout."

During the Washington ministerial meeting, the two delegations agreed that, to be considered a new type, a missile must meet any of the following criteria: a different number of stages, a different type of propellant, a 10 percent change in either length or launch weight, a 5 percent change in diameter, or—the most contentious provision—a 5 percent change in the length of the first stage combined with a 21 percent change in throw weight. But the United States was still concerned about the ss-25, that is, that its surplus power might be used to increase its throw weight by 21 percent, with the Soviets declaring it a new type and then testing it without any actual modifications. The United States proposed longer-range testing as the solution to this problem. In Washington, the two sides wrangled over the testing range for new missiles. This issue was not resolved until July 17, just in time for a Bush-Gorbachev meeting in London, when the Soviet Union reportedly accepted a U.S. proposal requiring the ss-25 to be flight-tested over a range of at least 11,000 kilometers. At that distance, the Soviet Union would have to expend surplus throw weight on distance rather than payload.[73]

The START I Treaty

The agreements reached at the Washington ministerial meeting made it possible for Bush and Gorbachev to sign a finished START treaty on July 31 during a Moscow summit. The two presidents signed the two hundred fifty pages of documents (including nineteen treaty articles and additional annexes, agreed statements and definitions, protocols, related agreements, letters, joint statements, unilateral statements, and declarations, along with a memorandum of understanding establishing basic data on each side's strategic forces) with pens made out of metal that had been melted down from Pershing II and ss-20 missiles destroyed under the 1987 INF Treaty.

START I, which took nine years of negotiation to complete, was the first accord in the nuclear age to require reductions in the number of warheads deployed on strategic offensive weapons. The two sides would reduce their strategic arsenals to 6,000 "accountable" warheads on no more than 1,600 nuclear delivery vehicles, that is, deployed ICBMs, SLBMs, their associated launchers, and heavy bombers. (At the end of 1990, the United States had slightly fewer than 12,778 strategic warheads on 1,876 launchers and the Soviet Union had 10,880 warheads on 2,354 launchers.) The two sides also agreed to a sublimit of 4,900 on the aggregate number of ICBM and SLBM warheads, a sublimit of 1,100 on the number of mobile ICBM warheads, a sublimit of 1,540 warheads on 154 heavy ICBMs, and a 46 percent cut in the aggregate throw weight of Soviet ICBMs and SLBMs. (In 1990 total Soviet throw weight for these missiles was about 12 million pounds, whereas that of the United States was 4.4 million pounds.) The United States and the Soviet Union agreed to carry out these reductions over a period of seven years.

The Soviet Union's agreement to cut in half (to 154) the number of its heavy ICBMs was a major concession to the United States. It reduced by half the most threatening weapon in the Soviet arsenal, the ss-18, and required the total force to carry no more than 1,540 warheads. The Soviets also agreed not to give future modifications of the ss-18 ICBM any greater throw weight or launch weight than the existing ss-18 model. By placing a cap on the throw weight and the number of ballistic warheads each side could field, START complicated the task of planning a first-strike attack and severely limited Soviet capability to barrage large areas that contained bombers, submarines, or mobile missiles. As a result of START, U.S. retaliatory capability would become appreciably more survivable than it was.

Paradoxically, although the formal treaty limited each side to 6,000 warheads, the counting rules established by START actually allowed each side to deploy more warheads. This was due to the fact that a bomber would count as only one warhead no matter how many nuclear bombs or short-range attack missiles (SRAMs) it actually had on board. By counting ballistic missile warheads one for one while heavily discounting the number of bomber-carried weapons, the treaty gave the Soviet Union a strong incentive to shift the relative emphasis of its strategic forces from ballistic missiles toward slower-flying bombers, which posed less threat of a surprise attack because they required many hours of flight to deliver their nuclear weapons. If the Soviets decided not to take full advantage of the permissive bomber rules, the result would be fewer deployed strategic warheads for the Soviet Union than the United States.

All totaled, the treaty required the United States to cut its ballistic missile warheads by about 38 percent, and the Soviet Union by about 48 percent. Overall strategic force cuts would be smaller because of the discounts on bomber-delivered weapons and would be determined largely by bomber modernization decisions. By most estimates, the United States would cut its strategic warheads by about 25 percent, whereas the Soviet cut would be about 35 percent.

With respect to air-launched cruise missiles, the treaty provided that existing and future U.S. heavy bombers could be equipped to carry no more than twenty long-range nuclear ALCMs; existing and future Soviet heavy bombers could be equipped for no more than sixteen long-range nuclear ALCMs. Each of the first 150 U.S. ALCM-carrying bombers would count as carrying ten warheads. Beyond 150, they would count as having the number of ALCMs for which they were actually equipped. Each of the first 180 Soviet ALCM-carrying bombers would count as carrying eight warheads. Beyond 180, they would count as having the number of ALCMs for which they were actually equipped. Existing ALCMs with a range of more than 600 kilometers would be subject to START limits. (The U.S. conventionally-armed Tacit Rainbow missile, which had a range of over 600 kilometers, was exempted from this provision.) Future conventionally armed ALCMs with a range greater than 600 kilometers would not be accountable under START if they were externally distinguishable from long-range nuclear-armed ALCMs.

Nuclear-armed, sea-launched cruise missiles (SLCMs) with a range of over 600 kilometers would be limited under START I to a maximum of 880 deployed missiles in a separate "politically binding" agreement. Each year the two sides would declare the maximum number of long-range nuclear-armed SLCMs they planned to deploy over the succeeding five years. The two sides would also exchange data annually on the types of SLCM platforms and the number of deployed nuclear-armed SLCMs with a range between 300 and 600 kilometers.

Warhead loadings for existing ballistic missile types also were established by the treaty. For example, each MX ICBM and SS-18 ICBM would be counted as having ten warheads and would not be permitted to be flight-tested or deployed with more than ten warheads.

The START Treaty also regulated mobile ICBMs. It defined the Soviet SS-24s and SS-25s as mobile missiles. For the purposes of reciprocity, the MX ICBM also would be treated as mobile, although it had not been tested in that mode. Neither side was permitted to keep more than 250 nondeployed ballistic missiles of types that had been flight-tested from mobile launchers. Of those retained, no more than 125 could be nondeployed missiles for rail-mobile launchers. There was also a numerical limit of 110 nondeployed launchers for mobile missiles, of which no more than eighteen could be nondeployed launchers for rail-mobile ICBMs. In addition, road-mobile ICBMs could only be based in "restricted areas" of five square kilometers. No more than ten road-mobile ICBMs would be permitted in each restricted area, and each area's garages could not be capable of containing more mobile missiles than declared for that area. When road-mobile ICBMs left their restricted areas for "routine movements" and "exercise dispersals," they would have to be confined to "deployment areas" covering 125,000 square kilometers. Further, no more than seven rail garrisons would be permitted. Each garrison could have no more "parking sites" than the number of trains specified for that garrison, which could not be more than five. Garrisons could have no more than two rail exits. Provisions regulating movements would parallel those for road-mobile ICBMs. No more than 50 percent of rail-mobile launchers could be engaged in a routine movement at any one time.

The treaty also stated that "exercise dispersals" from restricted areas or garrisons into the deployment areas or railways could take place no more than twice every two years, and they could not last for more than thirty days at a time. After an exercise dispersal was completed, each party would have the right to conduct inspections to confirm that the number of mobile ICBMs at the inspected base, and those that had not returned to it, did not exceed the number specified for that base. During "operational dispersals," which could take place only in a severe crisis that raised fears over missile survivability, the parties had the right to suspend the limits on mobile ICBM dispersals temporarily.

The treaty also established limits on the number of nondeployed mobile ICBMs and launchers. (Under START, restrictions on the total number of nondeployed missiles applied only to mobile ICBMs.) Each side was allowed no more than 250 nondeployed mobile ICBMs, of which no more than 125 could be for rail-mobile launchers. Nondeployed mobile ICBM launchers were limited to 110, of which no more than eighteen could be rail-mobile launchers. There were also numerous limits on where nondeployed ballistic missiles could be stored, so as to limit each side's ability to quickly reload operational launchers. The treaty also required nondeployed mobile ICBMs to be stored some distance from mobile ICBM deployment sites and from any facility in which mobile missile launchers are stored. Factory serial numbers would be used to identify legally produced missiles.

The number of ICBM and SLBM launchers at test, training, and space-launch sites were also limited. However, the United States was permitted to exempt two specially modified Poseidon submarines, without their missiles, for use by special forces.

A separate politically binding agreement limited the number of Soviet Backfire bombers to 500. In addition, the Soviet Union agreed to operational constraints that would make it more difficult for the Backfire to strike the United States. Rules for counting the number of warheads on future ballistic missile types also were agreed to in principle.

Under the downloading provision, the parties were permitted to reduce by up to 1,250 the number of warheads carried by three existing types of missiles. For the United States, these were the Minuteman III ICBM and two other missiles. For the Soviet Union, they were the SS-N-18 SLBM and two other missiles. Under the treaty, each Soviet SS-N-18 SLBM would be counted as having three warheads, although the SS-N-18 was developed with both a three- and a seven-warhead platform. However, 896 SS-N-18 warheads would count toward the Soviet overall downloading limit. U.S. Minuteman IIIs could be downloaded by one or two warheads. Within the 1,250 limit, up to 500 other reentry vehicles could be downloaded on two other existing ballistic missile types, but no missile could be downloaded by more than four reentry vehicles.

In the case of the Minuteman III and the SS-N-18, the warhead dispensing mechanism (or bus) had to be destroyed and replaced with one that conformed to the actual, reduced number of permitted warheads. Similarly, although the other two types of missiles could be downloaded by as many as four warheads, the bus for any missile downloaded by more than two warheads had to be replaced and destroyed. The parties could download the two other types of missiles by up to 500 warheads, so long as the total number of downloaded warheads on all three types of missiles did not exceed 1,250 at any time.

New types of multiple-warhead missiles could not be developed and later downloaded. Nor would either side be permitted to develop new missiles designed to carry more warheads than on any downloaded type, with the exception of the Minuteman III and the SS-N-18. Any ICBM downloaded by more than two reentry vehicles had to be equipped with a new front section platform, and all old platforms were required to be destroyed.

The basic structure of the START I Treaty was designed to facilitate verification by national technical means (NTM), primarily space-based surveillance satellites. Noninterference provisions explicitly prohibited interference with NTM or the use of concealment measures that might impede verification by NTM. Other detailed, interlocking, and mutually reinforcing provisions would be used to supplement NTM verification. These included data exchanges and notifications on strategic systems and facilities covered by the treaty; a ban on the denial of data from telemetry; twelve types of on-site inspection and exhibitions; continuous monitoring at mobile ICBM final assembly facilities; and other cooperative measures. Compliance concerns could be raised by either side in the Joint Compliance and Inspection Commission or any other appropriate forum.

With respect to circumvention, START provided that strategic offensive arms may not be transferred to Third World countries, with the exception that existing patterns of cooperation may be maintained. START also prohibited the permanent basing of strategic offensive arms outside national territory and inspections outside national territory. Temporary stationing of heavy bombers overseas would be permitted, but certain notifications would apply.

The treaty would have a duration of fifteen years unless superseded earlier by a subsequent agreement. If the sides agreed, the treaty would be extended for successive five-year periods. The two sides did agree that the treaty could be signed and ratified without completing the Defense and Space Treaty regulating antiballistic missile activities. If "extraordinary events" related to the accord "jeopardize" a party's "supreme interests," it was permitted to withdraw from the treaty after giving six months prior notification. The treaty could be amended by mutual consent.[74]

The START I Debate

Administration spokesmen championed the START treaty as an important step toward a safer twenty-first century. It would reduce the nuclear attack potential of both sides and exact deep cuts in the most destabilizing and dangerous U.S. and Soviet strategic weapons, such as the Soviet ss-18. It contained incentives for both nations to preferentially reduce the number of warheads carried on multiple-warhead ballistic missiles, and it limited MIRVs to ten warheads. In addition, START heavily discounted the numbers of gravity bombs and air-launched cruise missiles loaded on long-range strategic bombers. This would produce a more balanced mix of forces less capable of threatening a first strike, especially on the Soviet side. The treaty also permitted both nations to improve the survivability of their deterrent forces, thereby enhancing the stability of the U.S.-Soviet strategic balance. START I would also institutionalize unprecedented cooperative verification measures, which some supporters regarded as its greatest achievement. Its detailed provisions not only would meet the requirements for verifying compliance with the treaty's numerical limits and operational restrictions, but also would guard against using verification procedures as intelligence "fishing expeditions."

With the Soviet Union in disarray, many argued that the treaty would create a formal, structured, and predictable strategic environment. It would also impose on the Soviet Union a legally binding set of obligations that would be in effect for many years, regardless of changes in its leadership or form of government. In addition, START's extensive series of intrusive, cooperative, and technical verification measures would greatly enhance U.S. knowledge about Soviet strategic nuclear forces and activities. The force reductions, predictability, and transparency that START would lock into international law would be especially valuable if the Soviet Union broke up into independent states or if communist hard-liners gained control of the government. In addition, START would provide a framework for deeper reductions that could lessen further the risk of nuclear war, stimulate an increasingly cooperative relationship between the United States and the Soviet Union or its successors, and save tens of billions of dollars as well.

Finally, by demonstrating a U.S. and Soviet commitment to reversing the arms race, START would reinforce efforts to stem the proliferation of nuclear weapons among the Soviet republics and nuclear "threshold" states, and it would ensure success at the Nuclear Nonproliferation Treaty extension conference, which was scheduled to occur in 1995.

Although arms controllers considered START I an important step in reducing the risks of a nuclear war, they pointed out that the treaty did not do a number of things it should have done, in most cases because the United States refused to go further. Among START's shortcomings was the fact that even after the substantial reductions required by the treaty were implemented, both sides still had massive arsenals of strategic weapons. As a result of U.S. insistence on permissive counting rules for heavy-bomber weapons and on separate quotas for sea-launched cruise missiles, each side would retain between 8,000 and 10,000 warheads, about the same number they possessed when the START process began in 1982.

Second, START by itself did not eliminate the vulnerability of the U.S. silo-based ICBM force. As long as large numbers of highly accurate warheads could attack a considerably smaller number of fixed targets (that is, in a ratio of 2 to 1 or more), ICBM silos on both sides would be vulnerable to destruction, at least in theory. However, START I did limit the number of attacking warheads and at the same time permitted the deployment of both fixed and mobile single-warhead ICBMs. The combination of these two measures undercut the advantages of a 2 to 1 attack on silos and permitted both sides to enhance the survivability of their ICBM forces.

Third, and again mainly at U.S. insistence, START allowed both sides an ample number of both treaty-compliant delivery systems that could accommodate additional warheads and treaty-exempt weapons that could enter the force on short notice. As a result, START did not eliminate the capability for a relatively rapid expansion of strategic forces—breakout—in the event the treaty regime collapsed. START was most permissive in this respect with regards to second-strike systems such as cruise missiles and short-range bomber armament, categories in which the United States had traditionally concentrated more of its forces.

Fourth, START did not create an absolutely foolproof verification regime. No reasonable arms control agreement that would have been mutually acceptable to both sides could have done so. Ultimately, a certain degree of mutual trust was required to make START a reality.

Finally, and again mainly at U.S. insistence, START did not prohibit the modernization of delivery systems or warheads. With the exception of some specific constraints on heavy missiles and bans on nonexistent systems like air-to-surface ballistic missiles (ASBMs) and MIRVed cruise missiles, and on exotic basing modes, U.S. and Soviet modernization programs—as well as programs to make the forces more survivable—were permitted to go forward unhindered.[75]

The Missile Defense Act of 1991

Although Bush and Gorbachev agreed that the START Treaty could be signed and ratified without completing the Defense and Space Treaty, in June 1991

Soviet negotiators insisted that START could only be viable if the ABM Treaty were not violated. They also stated that U.S. abrogation, or material breach, of the ABM Treaty would be grounds for Soviet withdrawal from the START Treaty. Despite this warning, the U.S. Senate, only hours after Bush and Gorbachev signed the treaty, approved the Missile Defense Act, which made the deployment of a limited nationwide defense system a national goal. It also required the Bush administration to negotiate changes in the ABM Treaty that would permit its deployment.

The Missile Defense Act, which was fashioned by Senators Sam Nunn and John Warner, was a "compromise" position between the administration's proposed GPALS, which called for an extensive deployment of space-based "Brilliant Pebbles" interceptors as well as ground-based components, and a House authorization bill that provided zero funding for the Brilliant Pebbles program. In the short term, the act called for upgrading the Patriot system, despite its debatable performance in the Persian Gulf War. In the long term, the act provided for the deployment of a Theater High Altitude Area Defense system by the turn of the century. It also called for the construction of a single treaty-compliant, ground-based ABM site (at Grand Forks, N.D.) that would be equipped with 100 ABM interceptors by 1996. This would be the "initial step" toward a nationwide missile defense incorporating "one or an adequate additional number" of ABM sites. To make way for the larger system, designed to defend against limited ICBM strikes, the measure also called for treaty amendments to permit more ABM sites and ABM interceptors, space-based battle-management sensors, and an unspecified relaxation of the limits on ABM testing. If the Soviet Union did not agree to make the required changes in the ABM Treaty by the mid-1990s, the president and Congress were to "consider the options available," including withdrawal from the treaty.[76]

Critics pounced on the Missile Defense Act when it was still a bill. They argued that it would not only unravel the ABM Treaty but would put the ratification of the START Treaty at risk. Senator Albert Gore (D-Tenn.) tried unsuccessfully to amend the act by removing all language supporting ABM deployments and any references to amending the ABM Treaty. Although Nunn had described the treaty amendments proposed in the committee bill as "modest," Gore charged that, to meet the bill's stated goals, "the ABM Treaty would have to be ripped up, rewritten from start to finish, from goals and definitions all the way to the end." Furthermore, "if the language of this bill as it is currently written becomes law," he warned, "we will never see a second START treaty." Nunn and other supporters of the bill, however, argued that the threat of unauthorized use was real and, therefore, an ABM "insurance policy" was necessary. After six hours of debate, Gore's amendment was defeated by a vote of 60 to 39.[77]

The following morning, Senators Levin and Biden proposed yet another amendment, which provided that nothing in the bill could be construed to imply authorization for any activities that would violate the ABM Treaty. Since the bill did not authorize funds for such purposes, Nunn and Warner accepted the amendment, and it passed unanimously. Efforts to cut back SDI funding then failed, leaving the bill's original approach largely intact.[78]

4

Bush and START II

The Unsuccessful Coup against Gorbachev

Passage of the Missile Defense Act was undoubtedly helped by the unsuccessful coup against Gorbachev in August 1991. The coup was attempted by Politburo hard-liners who were particularly upset by Gorbachev's effort to preserve the Soviet Union by increasing the powers of the republics at the expense of the central government. The new union treaty would have reduced the power (if not eliminated the jobs) of the hard-liners. Shortly before the treaty was scheduled to be signed on August 20, the hard-liners took advantage of Gorbachev's absence from Moscow and attempted to overthrow him.

But the hard-liners underestimated the extent of popular support for democracy and popular antipathy toward communism. They also failed to get the military support they needed to overthrow Russian president Boris Yeltsin, who rallied the democratic forces against them. As a result, the coup quickly collapsed and on August 21 Yeltsin reported that its leaders were under arrest. The next day, a fatigued and disheveled Gorbachev returned to Moscow and declared that he was in full control of the government. Yeltsin, however, did not wait for him to regain his balance. On August 21 he labeled the Communist Party the organizing and inspiring force behind the coup, suspended its activities in Russia, and seized its property. In other republics,

the local leadership—in almost all cases made up of former communist leaders—followed suit and banned or suspended the Communist Party.

After belatedly realizing how the public mood had changed, on August 24
Gorbachev resigned as the party's general secretary, disbanded its Central
Committee, and ordered the members of the Council of Ministers to resign.
He then instructed the Congress of People's Deputies to take control of the
party's property, and he banned the party's activities within the central government and the security organs. On August 29 the Congress voted (283 to
29 with 52 abstentions) to suspend all Communist Party activities in the
Soviet Union until the party's role in the coup was investigated. Although
the party itself was not abolished immediately, the events of August spelled
the end not only of communism in the Soviet Union but, ultimately, of the
Soviet Union itself.

Loose Nukes

In the aftermath of the unsuccessful coup attempt, both the Bush administration and Soviet officials tried to assuage any concern that an accidental or
unauthorized use of Soviet nuclear weapons could have occurred during the
confusion that ensued during the coup attempt. On August 29 Secretary of
Defense Richard Cheney stated that the United States had "no reason to
doubt" that Soviet nuclear systems remained "under central authority."[1]

Nevertheless, the reliability of Soviet command and control did erode
during the coup attempt. Before the crisis, three sets of codes—one held by
Gorbachev, one by defense minister Dimitry Yazov, and one by the chief of
the General Staff, Marshal Moiseev—had to be used to launch the missiles
of the Soviet Union. But during the coup attempt, from August 18 until
August 22, Gorbachev was deprived of his codes. During this period—one of
the most critical in Russian history—the only guarantee against the concentration of all sets of codes in one pair of hands was their division between
Yazov and Moiseev. But Yazov lost his codes on the morning of August 21,
when he was completely demoralized by the failure of the coup and fled
Moscow. Evidently, all the keys were then transferred to Marshal Moiseev.
After the coup failed, Moiseev was replaced by General Shaposhnikov, who
received a set of the codes. Another set was given to the commander of the
Strategic Rocket Force, General Maksimov, who had stayed loyal to Gor-
bachev during the coup attempt.[2]

Yet the danger of an unauthorized launch of Soviet nuclear forces by a
rogue general was not the only risk that may have existed during the failed

coup against Gorbachev. As one Soviet republic after another moved toward independence, the disintegration of the Soviet Union created the danger that Soviet nuclear weapons would come under the control of a multiplicity of political leaders, specifically, the presidents of Russia, Ukraine, Belarus, and Kazakhstan. On September 5, however, Gorbachev was successful in persuading the presidents of these "nuclear" republics to support a resolution passed by the Congress of People's Deputies that called for the maintenance of central command over all weapons of mass destruction. The resolution also required any republic seeking complete independence to give up its nuclear weapons and sign the Nuclear Nonproliferation Treaty.

There was disagreement about the ultimate fate of the nuclear weapons deployed in the non-Russian republics. Belarus prime minister Vyacheslav Kebich said that his republic favored becoming a nuclear weapon-free zone, but his government had not decided whether nuclear weapons located on its soil should be transferred to Russia. The presidents of Kazakhstan and Ukraine stated flatly that they were not prepared to transfer the nuclear weapons within their republics to Russia. The Ukrainians wanted Soviet nuclear weapons in their republic to be registered with an international commission and then destroyed in Ukraine rather than be transferred to Russian territory. Some analysts believed that Kazakhstan and Ukraine were prepared to use the nuclear weapons on their soil as bargaining chips to gain economic and political concessions from Russia and the United States.

As a result of this squabbling among the Soviet republics, the "loose nukes" problem did not disappear, and the United States felt compelled to try to do something about it. On September 12, 1991, Representative Les Aspin released a report that proposed taking $1 billion from the U.S. defense budget and giving it to the Soviet Union for the purpose of strengthening the central government's control over its nuclear weapons. Among other things, the report recommended employing permission action links (PALs) on all U.S. and Soviet nuclear weapons to prevent unauthorized launchings, placing postlaunch destruct switches on ballistic missiles, giving high priority to nuclear security in future arms talks, and increasing openness of nuclear command and control, including discussing "rules of the road" for nuclear alerts.[3]

Further Cuts
As the Soviet Union crumbled, President Bush became increasingly concerned about the security of Soviet nuclear weapons. Of paramount impor-

tance to the president was preventing the creation of three new nuclear weapon states—Ukraine, Kazakhstan, and Belarus—in addition to Russia. An independent Ukraine alone would possess the world's third-largest nuclear arsenal—approximately 1,700 strategic weapons and some 2,200 tactical weapons. And some of these weapons were aimed at the United States. Bush was also determined to prevent any "leakage" of nuclear warheads, technology, or expertise from any of the Soviet republics to "rogue" countries like Iran, Iraq, and Libya.[4]

Bush's concern about the security of Soviet nuclear weapons motivated him to propose the most far-reaching and one-sided reductions and restraints ever made in the nuclear age. On September 27, 1991, he announced that the United States would dismantle or destroy all tactical nuclear weapons that were deployed in Europe, in Asia, and on U.S. warships. These included some 2,150 sea-based and land-based naval nuclear weapons, including sea-launched cruise missiles, bombs, and depth charges, but not strategic sea-launched ballistic missiles. The involved weapons, together with similar systems stored in the United States, had been the weapons of choice for "first use" in a crisis situation and had long been viewed as among the most dangerous of all nuclear systems. The disintegration of the Warsaw Pact, the withdrawal of Soviet forces from Central Europe, and the overall East-West disengagement made their military rationale not only obsolete but dangerous to maintain. Nevertheless, Bush did indicate that the United States intended to retain air-launched nuclear weapons in Europe (the United States deployed about 1,400 nuclear bombs with NATO forces) and maintain thirty to forty air-delivered nuclear weapons for use in Korea.

Bush's request that the Soviet Union reciprocate these reductions also reflected his concern that Soviet tactical nuclear weapons would be misused by political schismatics or ethnic terrorists. Tactical nuclear arms were more numerous, more widely dispersed, and generally less tightly controlled than Soviet strategic nuclear weapons. According to Soviet authorities, several thousand of the estimated 10,000 ground-based tactical nuclear warheads in their arsenal remained in the non-Russian republics.

The president also announced three unilateral decisions affecting strategic nuclear forces. First, he said that he was taking U.S. strategic bombers off alert in order to "reduce tensions." According to the Defense Department, the U.S. strategic bomber force of 280 aircraft normally had about 40 aircraft on "strip alert," loaded with nuclear weapons and ready to take off within five minutes. Bush also announced that several hundred weapons from these aircraft would be placed in storage with nonalert bomber weapons. Since Soviet bombers were not kept on strip alert, Bush asked the Soviet Union to reciprocate by "confining" its mobile ICBMs to garrisons in which they would be "safer and more secure." However, since bombers off alert and mobile ICBMs confined to garrisons would not make them "safer and more secure" but rather more vulnerable to surprise attack, Bush was implicitly predicating his decision on the realization that a "bolt from the blue" attack was no longer a credible scenario. Moreover, he was explicitly urging the Soviets to garrison their mobile missiles in order to ensure that they remained under the strictest command and control. Both the bombers and the mobile missiles could, of course, return to alert status on short notice. Cheney indicated that he could have the U.S. bomber force back on alert "within 24 hours."[5]

Bush's second unilateral decision was to take off alert "immediately" the 450 Minuteman II single-warhead ICBMs scheduled for elimination under the START Treaty. The next day, the Pentagon announced that the United States would also "stand down from alert" ten Poseidon submarines with 1,600 SLBM warheads that also were scheduled for elimination under START. The president also declared that the United States intended to implement its strategic force cutbacks more quickly than the seven-year schedule agreed to in START, and he invited the Soviet Union to follow suit.

The not-so-hidden motive behind the immediate stand-down was analogous to U.S. concerns regarding Soviet tactical nuclear weapons. It was to provide the Soviet Union with a sound reason for immediately removing from operational status the several hundred strategic missiles, particularly ss-18s and ss-19s, that were deployed in Kazakhstan and Ukraine. Removing these weapons would not only meet the terms of START earlier than required, it would prevent the missiles from being used as bargaining chips by the political leaders of the Soviet republics in which they were deployed.

Bush's third unilateral decision was to terminate the MX and mobile (but not the silo-based) Midgetman ICBM programs, as well as the SRAM-II missile (a follow-on short-range attack missile designed for use on strategic bombers) and the SRAM-T tactical air-to-surface missile that was a part of the NATO missile modernization program. All of these programs had encountered either serious technical problems (e.g., the SRAM-II missile) or serious opposition on Capitol Hill (e.g., the mobile MX). Simultaneously, the European allies did not want the SRAM-II deployed on their territory, and the U.S.

Air Force did not want to deploy a mobile version of the Midgetman. The president pointed out that the silo-based, single-warhead Midgetman option was currently the only U.S. ICBM modernization program. He urged the Soviets to limit their ICBM modernization to "one type of single-warhead missile."

In the area of command and control, Bush announced the formation of a new, consolidated U.S. Strategic Command with operational control of all strategic weapons (ICBMS, SLBMS, and heavy bombers). The Defense Department later indicated that the new unified command would be located at Offut Air Force Base in Omaha, Nebraska, where the Strategic Air Command had long been based. Bush also proposed bilateral discussions to explore cooperation on nuclear command and control, warhead security and safety, and safe and environmentally responsible storage, transportation, dismantling, and destruction of nuclear warheads. These discussions would be a logical result of what the president described as a shift of "focus away from the prospect of global confrontation."

President Bush also stated that the United States would propose additional initiatives in the area of ballistic missile early warning. But he did not make clear whether those initiatives would be technological ones (such as space-based sensors or a joint warning system), declaratory ones (such as prelaunch announcements), or both.

Bush also plugged for a revision of the ABM Treaty that would permit the deployment of his GPALS system. Arguing that up to twenty nations could have ballistic missiles by the end of the century, the president asked the Soviet leadership to join the United States "in taking immediate, concrete steps to permit the deployment of nonnuclear defenses to protect against limited ballistic missile strikes—whatever their source—without undermining the credibility of existing deterrent forces." The next day, Cheney indicated that Bush was simply reaffirming a U.S. proposal in the Defense and Space Talks which, if adopted, would mean "basically an end to the ABM Treaty."[6]

Gorbachev's Response, October 5, 1991

On October 5, 1991, Gorbachev matched U.S. unilateral cuts in tactical nuclear arms, strategic alerts, and missile modernization. The Soviet president announced that all nuclear warheads for artillery and land-based tactical missiles would be destroyed while all naval tactical-nuclear weapons would be withdrawn and either stored or destroyed. All Soviet nuclear land mines also would be destroyed; some nuclear warheads for air-defense missiles would be stored, and some destroyed. The Defense Department estimated that the Soviet Union had as many as 10,000 land-based nuclear weapons and 2,000 naval tactical-nuclear weapons.

Gorbachev challenged Bush to go further and agree that both sides should destroy, rather than store, all their naval tactical weapons and withdraw all air-delivered tactical nuclear weapons "from combat units [of] frontal aviation." He also urged other nuclear nations to join in the tactical nuclear reductions. Britain and France had already announced some cutbacks in their tactical nuclear arms while insisting that they would continue to maintain their independent nuclear deterrents.

The Soviet president emphasized his support for quick ratification of START and said that over the seven-year START reduction period the Soviet Union would unilaterally reduce its forces to 5,000 warheads, 1,000 less than the 6,000 accountable-warhead limit established by the treaty. The Soviet Union, he said, would "welcome a similar approach from the U.S. side."[7]

Gorbachev also indicated that all Soviet strategic bombers would "not be on alert status," but in fact Soviet bombers had never been on alert status. Nevertheless, all their weapons would be placed in storage at their bases. In addition, 503 ICBMs (134 of them carrying multiple warheads) and six missile submarines, carrying a total of ninety-two missile launchers, would stand down from alert, roughly half of the missiles the Soviet Union would have to eliminate under START.

Matching Bush's cancellation of new ICBM mobility-enhancing programs, Gorbachev announced that modernization programs for both "small mobile" and "rail-mobile" ICBMs would be canceled. He was referring to the follow-on systems to the road-mobile ss-25 and the larger ten-warhead, rail-mobile ss-24 that had been in development. Gorbachev also halted modernization of short-range attack missiles for Soviet bombers, again paralleling a Bush step. The Soviet leader also announced a cutoff of additional deployments of the rail-based ss-24 while confining the existing missiles to their permanent garrisons. Bush had called for both the ss-25 and the ss-24 ICBMs to be kept in garrisons rather than out in the field.

Although Bush had asked the Soviet Union to limit ICBM modernization to one new type of single-warhead ICBM, Gorbachev did not indicate whether existing follow-on programs for the silo-based ss-24 variant, or the Soviet Union planned future modifications for its "heavy" ss-18 ICBMs, would be the missile of choice.

Gorbachev also proposed that "intensive" START II negotiations on deeper strategic cuts begin "immediately after the ratification of the START treaty." It should aim, he suggested, at reducing the strategic forces remaining after START "by approximately one-half." Soviet negotiators had long been pushing to accelerate such talks. However, before the August coup attempt, the United States had reportedly favored a prolonged pause, similar to the U.S.-imposed delay in the nuclear test ban talks. Suggesting a U.S.-Soviet summit, Gorbachev put forward an array of proposals for follow-on negotiations, including a proposal for cutting each side's strategic arsenals to roughly one-half the levels agreed to under the START Treaty.[8]

Gorbachev also called for "a substantive dialogue" on both "safe and ecologically sound technologies" for handling nuclear weapons and measures designed to enhance "nuclear security." In addition, he said that the Soviet Union would bring all strategic nuclear weapons under one operational command to enhance "the reliability of control over nuclear weapons." He also suggested a joint U.S.-Soviet early warning system, again echoing a Bush proposal.[9]

The Soviet leader also repeated a number of earlier proposals the United States had resisted. He again proposed a comprehensive ban on nuclear testing and announced a year-long unilateral testing halt, which continued an unannounced Soviet moratorium under way since October 1990. In addition, he proposed an agreement to end production of highly enriched uranium and plutonium, which could be used to make nuclear weapons, an idea the Bush administration had resisted even though the United States had no plan to produce such materials for weapons in the foreseeable future. Gorbachev also called on all nuclear powers to join in the Soviet Union's nuclear no-first-use pledge, a step the United States, Britain, and France had long refused to take, despite NATO's announcement the previous year that nuclear weapons would henceforth be only "weapons of last resort."[10]

Surprisingly, Gorbachev also expressed a willingness to consider modifying the ABM Treaty to permit limited deployment of SDI, but he said he would do so only if the United States agreed to share SDI technology with the Soviet Union. At meetings in Moscow in early October and in Washington in late November, the two sides discussed arms reduction and the ABM issue, with the United States saying for the first time that it was willing to accept some limits on ABM deployments. At the November meeting, the United States tabled an outline of a treaty regime permitting widespread defense development and deployment, but limiting the number of interceptors.

However, no Soviet response was received before the Soviet Union expired at the end of December 1991.[11]

Despite their inability to achieve agreements on ABM deployments, Bush and Gorbachev had initiated the largest changes ever made in nonstrategic nuclear forces, and they did this unilaterally, without prolonged negotiation. The reductions provided the basis for the even deeper strategic arms cuts—roughly two-thirds of the pre-START I levels—which the United States and Russia would accept in the START II agreement, signed by Bush and Yeltsin in January 1993. This achievement was not only a product of the improvement in U.S.-Soviet relations that followed the end of the Cold War but also of the shared realization that these weapons were not only unnecessary but dangerous. It was also prompted by the turmoil that confronted the Soviet Union in the wake of the failed coup against Gorbachev, turmoil that eventually contributed to the breakup of the Soviet Union itself.

Verification and the Nunn–Lugar Act

Although the main motive behind the unilateral reduction and restructuring of U.S. nuclear forces that Bush announced on September 27 was a desire to ensure the elimination of hazardous nuclear weapons, surprisingly he did not raise the topic of how the destruction of warheads was to be verified. Instead, he proposed discussions with the Soviet Union to explore physical security arrangements, command, and control, and "joint technical cooperation on the safe and environmentally responsible storage, transportation, dismantling, and destruction of nuclear warheads." But an administration paper stated that "with regard to the SNF [short-range nuclear forces] and naval systems, we do not envision any formal verification regime, although we are willing to discuss possible confidence building measures with the Soviets."[12]

This new flexibility was an abrupt (and to some, welcome) departure from previous statements by both Bush and Reagan that insisted on "effective verification" of arms control agreements. On September 28 Cheney stated that verification was "no longer a fundamental U.S. arms control policy." He explained "that we can undertake these [nuclear arms reduction] efforts and know that the Soviets are, in fact, responding." The reasons he gave included increased freedom of information and debate within the Soviet Union, the collapsing Soviet economy, and the "twelve different types of on-site inspection" provided for in START. He also spoke about a process of "consulting" on the "safe and environmentally sound destruction of nuclear weapons" and on "safeguarding systems." But he described these discussions as "more a sharing of information than it would be a treaty" and suggested that one result might be negotiation of "some kind of memorandum of understanding."[13]

More than a few arms control experts were alarmed that the administration was suggesting, as the Soviet Union fell apart, that a mere "exchange of information" would suffice to establish the whereabouts and eventual elimination of about 15,000 nonstrategic Soviet nuclear weapons (including artillery shells, land mines, short-range missile warheads, air defense warheads, and naval weapons) that were deployed throughout Russia, Ukraine, Belarus, and Kazakhstan. START, they pointed out, made no provision for verifying the dismantlement of warheads or for safeguarding excess nuclear weapons materials so that they could be disposed of or converted to peaceful use. They also were concerned that the Soviet nuclear arsenal might be parceled out to the republics, an action that would not be conducive to nuclear stability or to the safe custody of nuclear weapons. It would also create a danger that nuclear weapons or their components would be seized, stolen, or sold, particularly if the nuclear weapon operating and custodial system disintegrated.

Among the nuclear material in the Soviet Union was an estimated 700-1,000 tons of plutonium and highly-enriched uranium. Although these materials were under the nominal central authority of the Soviet Ministry of Atomic Power and Industry (MAPI), that agency's effectiveness was eroding as the government's financial support for it declined. The result was the creation of both the conditions and incentives for unsafeguarded exports to be sold abroad in order to earn hard currency for the financially strapped Soviet government. A related concern was that highly trained Soviet nuclear engineers and technicians would emigrate and sell their skills to the highest bidders. Evgeni Mikerin, deputy minister in charge of nuclear materials production, reported that "two or three" of his top nuclear fuel cycle scientists had already been approached to work for foreign countries. Some 3,000-5,000 MAPI technical employees held sensitive clearances providing significant access to plutonium fuel cycle and enrichment technology.

Considering the risk that the weakening of Soviet nuclear controls might result in the transfer of nuclear materials to areas outside Soviet territory, some found it amazing that the Bush administration would not insist on rigid verification procedures for the dismantlement of Soviet nuclear weapons. One explanation is that Russian officials were not prepared to accept international verification of the movement and disposal of their nuclear warheads and materials unless the United States reciprocated, something the Bush administration would not accept. A senior Soviet arms expert tried to explain the U.S. position: "The Bush administration is trying to avoid institutionalization of the warhead elimination process" so that nuclear materials and warhead production facilities could be converted to other uses without Soviet interference.[14]

Administration critics argued that it was high time to set aside lingering Cold War fears about Russia. More important, they insisted, was the creation of an international control system that would work against the dangers of diversion or theft of nuclear weapons or materials from the far-flung Soviet arsenal as well as lay the groundwork for even deeper nuclear weapon cutbacks later. Verified controls on nuclear warheads and materials, they pointed out, would give the international community an inventory of Soviet stockpiles, along with firm knowledge of which weapons had been destroyed and which remained.

In the end, it was the Congress that finally compelled the administration to accept the need to verify the nuclear arms reductions called for in the president's September 27 initiative. In November 1991 it passed the Soviet Nuclear Threat Reduction Act, commonly known as the Nunn-Lugar Act in honor of its two chief sponsors. The legislation authorized the Defense Department to transfer $400 million from other programs to assist the safe dismantlement and storage of nuclear weapons and materials in the republics of the former Soviet Union (FSU). However, the funds were tied to presidential certification that the FSU were committed to not reusing the fissile materials from dismantled warheads in new weapons and to facilitating U.S. verification of warhead dismantlement. As a result, the Bush administration was forced to accept the need for inspection of the Soviet Union's nuclear weapon stockpile, as well as that of the United States as well.[15]

The Cooperative Threat Reduction Program (CTRP), as the Nunn-Lugar assistance was formally called, was renewed and expanded in subsequent years. The program covered seven major areas: nuclear warhead safety and transportation, nuclear material storage facilities, nonproliferation, strategic delivery vehicle launcher elimination, chemical weapons destruction, and defense conversion. As of January 1996, $612 million (50 percent) was allocated for Russia, $349 million (28 percent) for Ukraine, $131 million (11 percent) for Kazakhstan, and $105 million (9 percent) for Belarus.[16]

The Commonwealth of Independent States and the Control of Nuclear Weapons
By the time Nunn-Lugar was enacted, the Soviet Union was in its final death

throes. Despite the efforts of Gorbachev and Yeltsin to preserve some form of union among the republics, the centrifugal force of nationalism that was released by the unsuccessful August coup and the overthrow of the Communist Party proved much too strong to overcome. One republic after another followed the lead of the Baltic States and declared their independence. The straw that broke the Soviet Union's frail back was Ukraine's nationwide referendum, on December 1, 1991, in which more than 90 percent of the Ukrainian people voted for independence. Without Ukraine, Yeltsin decided, there was no point in trying to preserve the union. On December 8 the Russian president met with Leonid Kravchuk and Stanislav Shushkevich, respectively the leaders of Ukraine and Belarus. They concluded that "the USSR, as a subject of international law and geopolitical reality, is ceasing its existence." In its place they announced the formation of the Commonwealth of Independent States (CIS). On December 25 Gorbachev resigned the presidency of the Soviet Union and transferred his nuclear "button" to Yeltsin.[17]

The demise of the Soviet Union complicated the task of verifying nuclear weapon dismantlements and of ensuring continued control over the nuclear weapons of the former Soviet Union. On December 21, 1991, in a meeting in Alma Ata, the capital of Kazakhstan, the Commonwealth states agreed that any decision to use CIS nuclear weapons would only be made with the agreement of the leader of the states with nuclear weapons, that is, Russia, Ukraine, Kazakhstan, and Belarus. On December 30, 1991, one day before the Soviet Union's official demise, the CIS further modified their nuclear weapon policies at a meeting in Minsk, Belarus. They agreed to maintain single, unified control over all nuclear weapons, with Yeltsin in charge of the nuclear "button" but with the presidents of Ukraine, Belarus, and Kazakhstan having the right to veto any use of nuclear weapons as long as such weapons remained on their soil. In theory, before making a decision about launching nuclear forces, the Russian president was to call the other three nuclear presidents and ask their approval before launching the strategic forces of the CIS. In reality, however, it was highly doubtful that a Russian president, faced with the threat of incoming missiles, would spend an extra five to seven minutes to call the other three republic leaders.[18]

Yet the unanimity of the CIS nuclear weapon states was soon disrupted by a dispute between Russia and Ukraine on the disposition of the Soviet Black Sea Fleet. This dispute erupted on January 4, 1992, when Ukrainian president Leonid Kravchuk asserted that since the ships and submarines of that fleet did not carry long-range nuclear weapons, they were not "strategic" forces and therefore should be controlled by Ukraine and not the CIS. Russia, on the other hand, insisted that the ships were strategic weapons and should be under CIS control. In early April, the dispute escalated when both Russia and Ukraine claimed control over the fleet, but it seemed to simmer down after Yeltsin and Kravchuk agreed to establish a commission to negotiate how the fleet's 300 ships and submarines would be divided between the two countries.[19]

The Surrender of Tactical Nuclear Weapons
Another source of friction between Russia and Ukraine concerned the dismantlement of tactical nuclear weapons. In December, the CIS had agreed that all tactical nuclear weapons would be transferred to Russia by July 1, 1992. This process appeared to be moving along smoothly until March 12 of that year, when Kravchuk announced that he was suspending the withdrawal of tactical nuclear warheads from Ukraine. He was prompted to do so by the Ukrainian parliament, which disliked the prospect of handing over nuclear weapons to the Russians and receiving nothing in return for the highly enriched uranium that the weapons contained. The Ukrainians wanted to sell the uranium to the Russians for hard currency, which they intended to use in building new Ukrainian embassies around the world.[20]

Moreover, the Ukrainians were concerned that there was no procedure to ensure that the weapons they sent to Russia would be dismantled and feared that they would be incorporated into the Russian nuclear arsenal. They realized increasingly that international, especially American, interest in Ukraine was almost wholly confined to nuclear matters and that once the Ukraine was denuclearized, it might find itself isolated and dependent on Russia's mercy for its independence. Finally, the Ukrainians realized that holding up the removal of their tactical nuclear weapons would guarantee them a share of Nunn-Lugar aid. This hope was reinforced by Senator Nunn who, after returning from a trip to Ukraine, criticized the Bush administration for focusing too much of its attention on Russia. Nunn suggested that some of the $400 million of the CPR should go to Ukraine, Belarus, and Kazakhstan.[21]

On April 8, 1992, the Bush administration accepted Nunn's suggestion. It certified to Congress that Belarus, Russia, and Ukraine had met the requirements for up to $400 million in Nunn-Lugar assistance for dismantling their nuclear and chemical warheads and for funding nonmilitary projects for their weapons scientists and engineers. Kazakhstan was not certified until July, apparently because of U.S. uncertainty over its commitment to join the NPT as a nonnuclear-weapon state and to eliminate the nuclear weapons on its soil. The administration had applied the carrot and the stick in attempting to denuclearize Ukraine. It offered the Ukrainians $175 million in Nunn-Lugar aid, primarily for the purpose of dismantling Ukrainian-based ss-19 and ss-24 ICBMs and their silos. But the aid was contingent on Ukrainian ratification of the START Treaty and accession to the NPT. Applying the stick, Secretary of State Baker told Kravchuk that U.S. aid to Ukraine could be reduced and a planned Bush-Kravchuk meeting canceled if Kiev did not fulfill its commitment to return its tactical nuclear weapons to Russia.[22]

A week later, Kravchuk caved in to U.S. pressure. He and Yeltsin signed an agreement permitting Ukraine to monitor the removal and dismantlement of tactical nuclear weapons from its territory. Kravchuk announced the resumption of the tactical nuclear weapon withdrawals and said they would be completed in July, as scheduled. Ukraine and Russia also signed agreements providing for the servicing of the strategic nuclear missiles still in Ukraine and for the redeployment of their warheads to Russia. However, there was no mention in the agreements of compensation to Ukraine for the fissile material the warheads contained.

Kravchuk's decision to resume the withdrawal of tactical nuclear weapons enabled him to meet with President Bush, as scheduled, on May 6. However, when the Ukrainian leader arrived in Washington, he was surprised and embarrassed to learn that the last train carrying tactical nuclear weapons from Ukraine had crossed into Russia the same day, long before the July deadline for their removal. It was soon apparent that the Russians had ignored Kravchuk's March 12 withdrawal suspension order and clandestinely continued to remove the weapons from Ukraine. Although the Russians no doubt gloated over Kravchuk's embarrassment, the clandestine removal of the tactical nuclear weapons from Ukraine was ultimately counterproductive for Russia. It made the Ukrainian leadership much more wary of dealing with the Russians and also made Washington more sensitive to Kiev's anxieties about Russia. The Russian subterfuge would also make the removal of strategic nuclear warheads from Ukraine a much more contentious issue.[23]

The Ratification of the START Treaty

The dissolution of the Soviet Union in December 1991 severely complicated the task of ratifying the START Treaty, which was signed on July 31, 1991, and submitted to the U.S. Senate for its advice and consent on November 25. Instead of requiring only two legislatures to ratify the agreement, the treaty now required ratification by four newly independent states in addition to the United States. Over 70 percent of the strategic arsenal of the former Soviet Union was deployed in Russia, including 1,067 ICBMs equipped with some 4,308 warheads, the entire Soviet missile submarine force, including 892 missiles carrying some 2,828 warheads, and 22 heavy bombers, probably carrying some 350 warheads. Ukraine deployed 130 SS-19 ICBMs and 46 SS-24s, along with 33 heavy bombers, for an estimated total of over 1,700 warheads. Kazakhstan was home to 1,400 warheads mounted on 104 SS-18 ICBMs, considered the most threatening weapons in the Soviet arsenal, and forty bombers. The only strategic weapons in Belarus were 72 single-warhead, road-mobile SS-25 ICBMs. To make matters even more difficult, Russia insisted that it would not ratify the START treaty until Ukraine, Belarus, and Kazakhstan surrendered their nuclear weapons and ratified the Nuclear Nonproliferation Treaty.[24]

Initially, the administration had favored making START a bilateral treaty between the United States and the Russian Republic, thereby making Moscow the sole "agent" for START implementation and giving Russia the responsibility for working out implementation arrangements with Belarus, Kazakhstan, and Ukraine. But when two high-level CIS meetings—a March 20 summit in Kiev and an April 11 foreign ministers meeting in Moscow—failed to reach agreement, it became clear that Ukraine and Kazakhstan wanted equal status under the treaty. The challenge became one of accommodating this desire without seeming to grant the new nations the status of nuclear-weapon states.[25]

To this end, the United States proposed that the three non-Russian states with nuclear weapons become parties to START while simultaneously making legally binding commitments to join the NPT as nonnuclear weapon states and to eliminate all of the nuclear weapons based on their territories within the START seven-year reduction period. In late April 1992, Washington drafted a protocol to the START Treaty (called the Lisbon Protocol, after the city in which it eventually was signed on May 23) recognizing the new situation. Fortunately for the United States, obtaining Kravchuk's agreement to its terms was eased by the protocol's formal recognition of Ukraine—as well as Russia, Belarus, and Kazakhstan—as a successor to the Soviet Union for START purposes. In addition to the status this conferred on Ukraine, it allowed Kiev to make a stronger claim for its fair share of the former Soviet Union's assets, especially its buildings and properties overseas.[26]

Kazakhstan was also a problem for the administration. Whether due to anxiety over being a nonnuclear state wedged between nuclear-armed Russia and China, a desire to be included in the START negotiations, or a policy decision about how best to win financial concessions and security guarantees from Washington and Moscow (or for all these reasons), it was obvious by the beginning of May 1992 that Kazakhstan intended to retain strategic nuclear weapons on its territory. Yet on May 19, Kazakh president Nursultan Nazarbayev stood by President Bush's side in the White House and pledged, for the first time, to ratify the START agreement, join the NPT "in the shortest possible time," and eliminate all nuclear weapons on Kazakh territory within seven years.[27]

A number of events were responsible for Nazarbayev's change of mind. In April, Bush had agreed to recognize Kazakhstan, Ukraine, and Belarus, in addition to Russia, as legal successors to the Soviet Union under START, a move these countries had long sought. In addition, the week before the Washington summit, Nazarbayev had signed a collective security treaty with Russia and other CIS countries. The treaty reduced Nazarbayev's fear of China, which had made claims on Kazakh territory, thereby making it possible for Kazakhstan to surrender its nuclear weapons. In addition, Secretary of State Baker consistently emphasized that Kazakhstan's relationship with the United States would improve only if its nuclear weapons went to Russia. Following Nazarbayev's pledges at the White House, the Kazakh leader and Bush signed a host of economic and trade agreements.[28]

In early July 1992, Kazakhstan ratified the START agreement. The U.S. Senate, for its part, approved the START Treaty on October 1, 1992, by a vote of 93 to 6. The Russian parliament ratified it on November 4. But the Duma stipulated that the actual exchange of instruments of ratification—the final step necessary to bring the treaty into force—would not occur until the other CIS republics with nuclear weapons acceded (as nonnuclear weapon states) to the Nuclear Nonproliferation Treaty and agreed to the START implementation measures.[29]

Ukraine and START

With the adherence of Kazakhstan and Belarus, only Ukraine prevented the implementation of the START Treaty. The Ukrainians were angered by the way the Russians had removed tactical nuclear weapons from their soil and by their inability to resolve the Black Sea Fleet dispute. They were also increasingly concerned about the larger pattern of Russia's behavior in its "near abroad," that is, the former republics of the Soviet Union. The Russian military was intervening in Moldova, Georgia, and Tajikistan, where it claimed a "special responsibility" to maintain peace. In the minds of Ukrainians, Russia's regional military interventions raised the specter of Russian aggression against their own country, perhaps a replay of Russia's absorbing Ukraine into the Soviet empire in 1922. The fact that Ukraine had a substantial Russian minority and that Russian ultranationals were demanding the return of the Crimea to Russia (which Nikita Khrushchev had magnanimously awarded to Ukraine in 1955) only heightened Ukrainian concerns about their Russian neighbor.[30]

That Ukraine did not belong to any security alliance magnified its sense of isolation. Kiev had decided not to join the CIS security arrangement, which was formed in May 1992. Although the Ukrainians were not specific about the security assurances they sought, they indicated that they wanted the same protection accorded NATO members: an attack on one member is considered an attack on all members of the alliance. The United States, however, was only willing to provide limited security assurances to Ukraine. Baker reminded the Ukrainians that in 1968 the United States made a commitment to go to the U.N. Security Council to act as "a friend in court" on behalf of nonnuclear signatories to the NPT that were subjected to nuclear threats. The Soviet Union, for its part, made a unilateral commitment in 1982 not to be the first country to use nuclear weapons.[31]

Ukraine also made it clear to Washington that it expected to receive a share of the money provided by the Nunn-Lugar Act. Senators Nunn and Lugar had proposed during their trip to the former Soviet Union that Kiev might receive $100 million to $150 million for dismantling SS-19 and SS-24 missiles and silos based on Ukrainian territory. However, Senator Lugar cautioned Kiev that the United States would not spend "one penny until START I and the nonproliferation treaty are, in fact, affirmed by Ukraine and the other states." And the United States would not do so for the balance of Bush's one term in the presidency, leaving the problem of gaining Ukraine's adherence to START and the NPT to his successor, William Clinton. Not until the end of 1993 would Ukraine meet the conditions required to make the START Treaty effective.[32]

On to START II

On February 1, 1992, President Bush met with President Boris Yeltsin in a brief summit at Camp David. The two leaders proclaimed the creation of a new U.S.-Russian relationship "characterized by friendship and partnership and founded on mutual trust." They agreed to take steps to reduce strategic arsenals and to "work actively" to "curb the proliferation of weapons of mass destruction and associated technology" as well as "the spread of advanced conventional arms." It was also announced that Yeltsin would travel to Washington for a full-scale summit in the first half of the year, and that Bush would go to Moscow before the end of 1992.[33]

Shortly after the Camp David summit, both presidents announced new unilateral cutbacks in strategic modernization and proposed a new round of bilateral nuclear reductions. President Bush's proposals, outlined in his State of the Union address on January 28, 1992, focused on strategic nuclear weapons, since tactical weapons had been dealt with in the previous fall's reciprocal nuclear cutbacks. Bush repeated his call for an agreement to eliminate all land-based missiles with multiple warheads; as an incentive to the Russians, he added an offer to cut U.S. submarine-based warheads by "about a third" to balance the one-sided cuts in Russian missiles that land-based de-MIRVing would require.

Bush also announced a number of unilateral cuts in ongoing U.S. strategic programs. He offered to stop the production of the costly and controversial b-2 "Stealth" bomber at twenty planes, five less than Congress had approved. He also announced that production of new w-88 nuclear warheads for the Trident II submarine-launched ballistic missile would be canceled, leaving no U.S. nuclear warheads in production for the first time in the nuclear age. In addition, Trident II missiles would be equipped with the 400 w-88s already produced and the lower-yield w-76 warhead in use on Trident I missiles.

Bush also said the Midgetman missile, whose mobile basing mode he canceled in the fall, would not be produced at all. Production of MX test missiles, already cut off in the fall, would not be resumed. Further, the advanced cruise missile program would be halted at the 640 missiles paid for to date, rather than the 1,000 previously planned. Finally, a "substantial portion" of the U.S. bomber force would be shifted to "primarily conventional use."[34]

The following day, General Colin Powell, chairman of the Joint Chiefs of Staff, estimated that Bush's proposals, if accepted by the Russians, would leave the United States with some 4,700 strategic warheads, compared to 9,500 previously planned under START and 13,000 in the U.S. strategic arsenal as of September 1990. The reduced level would correspond roughly to the level of strategic forces the United States possessed in 1971, before the first strategic arms treaty (SALT I) was signed. Bush's proposals would leave Russia with roughly 4,400 strategic warheads, taking into account the various production cutbacks announced by Yeltsin and Gorbachev. Yet unless Russia undertook a massive program to build single-warhead ICBMs, Bush's suggestion would have required a drastic reorientation of Russian forces, leaving the Russians with nearly four-fifths of their missile warheads at sea, compared to fewer than one-third at that time. While announcing these substantial cutbacks in offensive strategic nuclear weapons, however, Bush called on Congress to approve an increase of nearly $1.3 billion for the Strategic Defense Initiative.[35]

Just hours after Bush's address, Yeltsin offered a sweeping response that spanned the entire spectrum of arms control. Like Bush, Yeltsin combined unilateral steps with a call for bilateral reductions. He announced that some 600 Russian ICBMs and SLBMs carrying "nearly 1,250 nuclear charges" had been taken off alert; that 130 missile silos and six missile submarines had been "liquidated" or were being prepared for liquidation; that all production of heavy bombers, including both the Bear-H and Blackjack, would be stopped; and that all production of both air- and sea-launched nuclear cruise missiles would end.

In the way of bilateral proposals, Yeltsin called for cuts in strategic nuclear warheads to a level of 2,000-2,500 on each side. He also repeated earlier proposals for a comprehensive test ban, a cutoff in production of plutonium and highly enriched uranium, and a ban on antisatellite weapons. In addition, he suggested that all missile submarines be kept in port instead of patrolling at sea. He also proposed that "after the reductions" remaining weapons in Russia and the United States "should not be aimed at American and Russian targets." A Yeltsin spokesman later indicated that the targeting codes had already been removed from all Russian long-range missiles.[36]

The Russian president, however, did not address Bush's proposal to eliminate land-based MIRVs. The *New York Times* reported that Yeltsin had sent Bush a letter calling the idea "lopsided." Yeltsin did announce that he had submitted the START Treaty to the Russian parliament for ratification and that he would unilaterally take the weapons to be retired off "combat duty" in three years, rather than the seven years specified for eliminating these launchers in the treaty. "If there is mutual understanding with the United States," he said, "we could achieve this even faster."[37]

Yeltsin also addressed U.S. concerns over the potential for proliferation of nuclear weapons and other dangerous technology once belonging to the

Soviet Union. He said that Russia was preparing to require full-scope International Atomic Energy Agency safeguards as a condition of all nuclear exports. He also announced that a new "state system" to monitor exports was being created and that domestic legislation to regulate all exports of dual-use "materials, equipment, and technologies" that could be used for nuclear, chemical, or biological weapons and missiles would soon be passed. In addition, Yeltsin said that Russia intended to join the Missile Technology Control Regime as a full participant, an arrangement the major Western powers had created in 1987 to prevent the spread of ballistic missiles to "rogue" states. Yeltsin also stated that Russia supported and would abide by the arms trade principles agreed to among the Big Five arms exporters in October of the previous year. Yeltsin then proposed "an international agency for ensuring nuclear arms reduction," which would ultimately control "the whole nuclear cycle, from the production of uranium, deuterium, and tritium to the dumping of nuclear waste." Later, he also announced that he had ordered the salaries of nuclear experts increased from 1,000 to 5,000 rubles a month to encourage them not to leave the country.[38]

At the same time, however, the Russian president seemed to go in conflicting directions on the matter of missile defenses. He reaffirmed Russia's "allegiance" to the ABM Treaty, which bans space-based missile defenses, but called for "a global system for protection from space" that would be jointly developed, built, and operated by Russia and the United States.[39]

President Bush described Yeltsin's response as "very positive," but the administration quickly played down, or rejected, virtually all of his specific proposals. Cheney called his proposed level of 2,000-2,500 strategic warheads "too low." He said such levels "could ultimately destabilize" the strategic balance and that Bush's proposal was preferable. Cheney also rejected the suggestion that the United States refrain from targeting missiles on Russia. He said missiles could be retargeted in a crisis anyway and that detargeting "would delay response time [and] probably weaken the value of the deterrent." Cheney also dismissed Yeltsin's proposals for a comprehensive test ban as "a mistake, as long as we rely on nuclear weapons," brushed off a ban on submarine patrols as "not a good idea," and criticized the idea of an antisatellite weapon ban.[40]

Baker and Kozyrev Discuss Deep Cuts, February–March 1992
Kozyrev also held meetings with Baker in February and March 1992 to discuss the U.S. and Russian January proposals for additional cuts in strategic

weapons well beyond those required by START. Initially expressing optimism that a new accord could be completed in time for a Bush-Yeltsin summit in Washington from June 16-17, the administration soon backpedaled, indicating that no new arms pact should be expected at that time.

After another Baker and Kozyrev meeting in Brussels on March 11, there were two main sticking points impeding progress toward an agreement on deep cuts in strategic forces. First, Russia had proposed a ban on *both* MIRVed ICBMs *and* MIRVed SLBMs. The United States, on the other hand, had proposed a ban on MIRVed ICBMs *only*, with a commitment to reduce the number of U.S. SLBM warheads by about a third below the number planned under START. Under the Russian proposal, the two sides would each deploy 2,000-2,500 strategic warheads, much lower than the level the Pentagon would accept. Accordingly, the U.S. proposal called for a limit of 4,700 strategic warheads. Second, Russia had proposed that cuts in MIRVed missiles be implemented within the seven-year START reduction period, whereas the United States wanted any new cuts to begin after the initial START reductions had been completed.

Little progress was made in meshing U.S. plans for the Strategic Defense Initiative and Yeltsin's undefined concept of a jointly designed, produced, and operated missile defense. The two sides did, however, agree to consider setting up a facility that would, in Baker's words, "integrate and display ballistic-missile-early-warning information" from each side's sensors. Russia's interest in cooperative early warning efforts may have stemmed from the dismantlement of the Krasnoyarsk radar and the fact that many of the former Soviet Union's early warning radars were located outside Russian territory.[41]

The Washington Summit, June 1992
On June 4, 1992, Baker met with Scowcroft, Cheney, and General Powell to discuss where to go next with START II. "De-MIRVing will be a major substantive and political triumph for the President, something he needs," Baker argued. He added: "This is *his* issue." Baker bluntly stated the president's bottom line: "They [the Russians] have offered us what we want and what no one else has ever come close to: zero MIRVed ICBMs, and without eliminating MIRVed SLBMs. We can't let this slip through our fingers because we think we need a higher total number. That is not sustainable with the public or the Congress." As a result of his blunt presentation of the political realities, Baker won his colleagues' approval to invite Kozyrev to Washington to determine whether he had any "give" in the Russian position.[42]

In their Washington meeting, Baker and Kozyrev agreed on a 4,700-warhead limit, but the two men could not agree on the sublimits for ICBMS, SLBMS, and bombers under the overall 4,700-warhead ceiling. In addition, their time frames for destroying weapons were different. Baker told Kozyrev he was willing to go to Moscow to eliminate any differences. "That just won't work," Kozyrev replied. "We're accepting twenty-four billion dollars in aid, and the U.S. Secretary of State comes to Moscow to get what he wants." Kozyrev also warned Baker that the Russian reformers' room for maneuver was limited. He noted, "I've been outvoted seven to two on many issues" in Yeltsin's Security Council. "We have some hard-line thinkers who say moderate things to Westerners, but in private, there is no change."[43]

On June 11 in London, Kozyrev told Baker that Yeltsin had ordered him to appear at a Kremlin meeting of all top Russian national security advisers, including the military leaders. "Explain to us," Yeltsin instructed Kozyrev, "why the U.S. will not take our proposal and why it will not cost money to do what the U.S. proposal suggests." Kozyrev was able to convince the generals that the U.S. proposal would not cost the hard-pressed Russian treasury more money to produce additional nuclear weapons. As a result, Yeltsin was able to give Kozyrev more room in which to maneuver in the negotiations, and, as a result, he and Baker were able to narrow their differences in London.[44]

Nevertheless, the two sides remained divided over the U.S. demand to eliminate all land-based MIRVs while making only modest cuts in overall force levels. Only a week before the impending Washington summit, Yeltsin bitterly criticized the U.S. position. Speaking before a group of Russian military officers, he said that "if such a decision is made, the United States would find itself in a more advantageous position." "Russia supports the idea of strategic parity," he told the officers, "while the U.S. side is moving along a different way." For Baker, the Pentagon, not the Russians, was the chief obstacle to a START II treaty. He recalled: "I was beginning to lose patience with our side. The Russians had moved as far as they were going to, and the arms control theologians at the Pentagon seemed to prefer no agreement than one that got us 'only' ninety percent of what we wanted."[45]

During the Washington summit, June 16-17, 1992, Yeltsin offered a way out of the stalemate. Instead of agreeing to a specified numerical ceiling, he asked, why not agree to a "range?" As Yeltsin put it, "each country will elect a figure that it will consider appropriate to ensure its defense and security." He proposed that in phase 1, each side lower its number of warheads to between

3,800 and 4,250 total warheads; in phase 2, the range would drop to between 3,000 and 3,500 warheads. The benefits of this approach were immediately apparent to the U.S. side. It would allow the Russians to go to lower limits (which they wanted to do for economic reasons), and it would allow the United States to have slightly higher numbers (which was consistent with the U.S. force structure). Above all, Yeltsin's approach recognized that, in the realm of nuclear weapons, when both sides had over 3,000 warheads, a few-hundred-warhead advantage was not all that important. Equally, if not more important, Yeltsin agreed to eliminate all land-based MIRVed ICBMs, the backbone of the Russian strategic force. Furthermore, he agreed to permit both sides to retain MIRVed submarine-launched ballistic missiles, a traditional area of U.S. advantage. However, the United States agreed to cut SLBM warheads to 1,750, half the level it had previously planned to retain under the START Treaty. In effect, both sides would cut their forces well below the 4,700-warhead level President Bush had proposed in January.[46]

Baker urged Bush to accept Yeltsin's proposal. He told the president, "I think this will be a significant achievement for your presidency, but you're going to have to tell the arms-control theologians you want it to happen. I've done all I can trying to roll this rock uphill."

"I hear you," Bush responded. He would accept Yeltsin's proposal. "With this agreement," the president announced later, "the nuclear nightmare recedes more and more for ourselves, for our children, and our grandchildren."[47]

In START II, the two sides would lower their total nuclear warheads to between 3,800 and 4,250 warheads by the year 2000, and to between 3,000 and 3,500 warheads by the year 2003. The accord would reduce the number of strategic weapons held by both sides to the lowest levels since 1969 and, more importantly, fundamentally reverse the arms race by eliminating land-based MIRVs. These weapons, which required each side to adopt a hair trigger posture of "use 'em or lose 'em," would disappear, much as the Cold War, the Soviet empire, and the Soviet Union itself had disappeared.

The two sides also agreed to create a high-level group to pursue further discussions of the concept of cooperation on early warning and ballistic missile defense, but they did not agree on any specific measures. Although administration officials had publicly expressed hope that Yeltsin would agree to radically alter the ABM Treaty to permit deployment of the GPALS system, including roughly 1,000 space-based interceptors and 750 ground-based interceptors, the administration confirmed that no agreement to change the

1972 accord had been reached. Yeltsin had reiterated Russia's "allegiance" to the ABM Treaty in his January disarmament address and several times subsequently. In the weeks before the summit, senior Russian officials restated both the previous Soviet link between the ABM Treaty's limits on defenses and reductions in offensive forces and long-standing Soviet opposition to any deployment of weapons in space.[48]

Like the START I Treaty, the new agreement did not require dismantling warheads on missiles that were to be retired. Launchers, including ICBM silos and missile tubes on submarines, had to be eliminated, but warheads could be "downloaded" from missiles that remained deployed. However, in a separate letter, Baker and Kozyrev agreed to lift the restrictions on downloading practices imposed in START I. Those restrictions had allowed each side to remove as many warheads as it chose without being required to dismantle the missile buses designed to carry the previous number of warheads. Only the SS-18 ICBM could not be downloaded at all.

Although the United States planned to retire its force of fifty MX ICBMs, it also intended to download all of its Minuteman III ICBMs from three warheads to one. Similarly, the Pentagon planned to deploy eighteen Trident submarines, meeting the SLBM-warhead START limit either by deploying each missile with four warheads rather than eight or by changing START rules to allow some missile tubes to be "plugged." Russia would be able to keep the same SLBM force it was likely to have retained under START I.

While START I allowed each side to exempt up to seventy-five bombers, by converting them to conventional missions (but requiring that the bombers be modified to make them unable to easily carry nuclear weapons), the new pact allowed each side an additional 100 bombers that never had been equipped with cruise missiles to be exempted without such modifications, as long as the nuclear weapons were removed and the aircrafts were kept at conventional force bases. The air force said that the entire U.S. B-1B force would be converted to conventional roles under this provision, leaving only fifteen to twenty B-2 bombers and a small force of B-52Hs armed with cruise missiles in the U.S. arsenal. Thus few (if any) U.S. bombers or bomber weapons would actually have to be eliminated under the new accord. Similarly, Russia would be able to keep its small strategic bomber force in tact.[49]

Yeltsin told a joint session of Congress that "without waiting for the treaty to be signed, we have begun taking off alert the heavy SS-18 missiles targeted on the United States of America." In reciprocation, the Pentagon indicated later that more U.S. missile stand-downs were a possibility.[50]

START II was fashioned in the form of a "joint understanding" that was signed by both presidents in Washington. However, administration officials reported that the two sides hoped to work out a formal bilateral treaty of no more than a few pages within the following one to three months, since all of the "grunt work," as one official put it, had been done in START I. Some analysts, however, expressed concern that the bilateral approach would offend the sensibilities of the non-Russian nuclear-weapon states, which had just been made party to the START agreement by the Lisbon Protocol. Before the summit, Ukrainian president Leonid Kravchuk and Kazakh president Nursultan Nazarbayev had both publicly asserted their right to participate in future arms talks. After the summit, however, Kravchuk publicly praised the new accord, which would cut Russian forces on Ukrainian soil as their nuclear weapons were eliminated, and he reaffirmed his country's commitment to denuclearization. But he also warned that Russia's "imperial ambitions constitute a menace to peace."[51]

In other arms control-related issues, the two sides agreed on a "charter for American-Russian partnership and friendship," with pledges of cooperation on a broad range of issues, including tightening existing nonproliferation regimes. A joint declaration called defense conversion "a key challenge of the post-Cold War era and essential for building a democratic peace." It also established a U.S.-Russian Defense Conversion Committee to facilitate U.S. private investment in conversion projects. There was also an agreement on nuclear weapons security and dismantlements, under which the United States agreed to provide 450 armored blankets to protect weapons containers, accident response clothing and equipment, and containers for the fissile components of nuclear weapons to be produced by the end of 1995. Discussions also began regarding U.S. assistance to Russia for building a storage site for plutonium and highly enriched uranium, improving the security features of Russian warhead-transport rail cars, using or disposing of fissile material from warheads, and setting up a system for accounting for fissile materials.[52]

Russian Resistance to START II

Progress on putting the Bush-Yeltsin Washington agreement into its final form was sluggish. Despite Baker's June prediction that the treaty would be done by September 1, the United States did not submit its version of a draft START II treaty to Russia until late July. The negotiating process then languished for about a month, with no response to the U.S. draft from Moscow.

In the Russian capital, the Bush-Yeltsin agreement was sharply criticized in the Russian military press and by a conservative faction in the Duma that attacked Yeltsin for making too many concessions to the United States. Since the most powerful component of Russia's triad was MIRVed ICBMs, particularly heavy missiles, Russian resistance to the core treaty obligation to eliminate all MIRVed missiles was understandable. When START II was fully implemented, it could force Russia, which was already beset by economic and other difficulties, to reduce ICBM warheads from over 60 percent of the pre-START I Soviet force structure to 15 to 20 percent of the Russian force structure. The military's view was that, in its effort to comply with the ban on MIRVed ICBMs, Russia should have the right to download as many of its 170 SS-19 missiles to single-warhead status as it wished and convert all of its remaining 154 SS-18 silos (after START I limits had been reached) for use by lighter, single-warhead missiles of the SS-25 type. The military also feared that the treaty provision allowing either side to reorient strategic bombers to conventional roles (an option that as a practical matter would be available only to the United States) could be used to circumvent the treaty.

To accommodate the Russian military's concerns about strategic equality and implementation costs, the United States agreed to several modifications in the framework agreement. For one, it permitted Russia to keep in place up to 105 of its 170 SS-19 ICBMs by downloading five of the six warheads from each missile. For another, Russia was permitted to retain up to ninety SS-18 (heavy ICBM) silos (of the 154 remaining after START I reductions), provided the silos were physically converted for use only by single-warhead ICBMs of the SS-25 type, and provided all the SS-18 heavy missiles were physically eliminated. In addition, the United States accepted a restriction that strategic aircraft designated as conventional bombers could be reoriented to nuclear roles only once. Finally, the U.S. B-2 bomber, exempt from inspection under START I, would be subject to inspection under START II.[53]

Signing START II in Moscow on January 3, 1993, Bush was able to announce near the end of his tenure in office that he and Yeltsin had concluded an agreement unprecedented in the history of international relations. The United States and Russia were taking another huge step toward mutually divesting the bulk of their massive strategic nuclear arsenals. By January 1, 2003, each would retain only a quarter of the nuclear warheads it possessed at the beginning of the 1990s. They would be left with 3,000 to 3,500 warheads each. As significant as the numerical limits were, the new treaty's ban on the deployment of multiple warhead ICBMs—the principal first-strike weapons in each side's arsenal—was a major result. This ban made real the standard claims that strategic forces existed only for the purpose of deterring a strategic attack from the other side.[54]

Although the START I Treaty was approved overwhelmingly by the Senate in November 1992, the deeper cuts called for by START II made the agreement much more controversial in the Russian Duma.

The Iraqi Challenge

In addition to the administration's policy toward the Soviet Union, Bush also changed his mind about how to deal with nuclear proliferation in the Third World. When he entered the White House in 1989, he assumed, as Reagan had, that nothing could be done to control the horizontal proliferation of nuclear weapons. But this view began to change, particularly after Iraq's invasion of Kuwait. Not only had Iraq become an enemy (after being treated as a useful counterbalance to Iran by both Reagan and Bush), it was also considered a nuclear threat.

How close Iraq came to building a nuclear weapon has been a matter of considerable debate. In August 1995, Hussein Kamel, Saddam Hussein's son-in-law, defected to Jordan and revealed significant details about the Iraqi nuclear weapon program. The Iraqis admitted that shortly after their invasion of Kuwait they had engaged in a crash program to turn a stock of safe-guarded, highly enriched uranium into a nuclear weapon, which they intended to use as a nuclear warhead on an intermediate-range ballistic missile. The general consensus seems to be that Iraq would probably have needed a year or two to master its weapon design if the Gulf War had not occurred.[55]

Needless to say, the destruction of Iraq's nuclear weapons facilities was a high U.S. priority during the Gulf War. Bush initially expressed confidence that Iraq's nuclear capability had been destroyed during Desert Storm, but on June 15, 1991, he stated that "probably some of it did survive." After the Gulf War, inspectors associated with the U.N. Special Commission (UNSCOM), which was set up by the Security Council to prevent Iraq from reacquiring the potential to develop weapons of mass destruction, discovered over twenty undamaged Iraqi nuclear weapon facilities. Over 1,000 hours of allied air strikes had left much of the Iraqi nuclear infrastructure untouched.[56]

As a consequence of the Gulf War, the Bush administration upgraded its nonproliferation staff at the National Security Council, brought back several nonproliferation experts who had been effectively banned by the Reagan administration, and placed nonproliferation on the president's own diplomatic agenda with various world leaders. In addition to seeking tightened controls on the export of materials related to weapons of mass destruction, U.S. officials sought to enhance international monitoring of proliferation activities and to stiffen the penalties for those found in violation of established nonproliferation controls.

In the meantime, quite independently of the administration's own counterproliferation efforts, considerable progress was made on the international front. South Africa, which had conducted a secret nuclear weapon program in the 1970s and 1980s and, by its own admission, had produced six nuclear bombs by 1991, agreed to terminate its nuclear weapon program and become a party to the Nuclear Nonproliferation Treaty. South Africa's action went a long way toward assuring that the African continent would remain free of nuclear weapons. In addition, in November 1990, Argentina and Brazil, the only Latin American countries with the potential to develop nuclear weapons, agreed to establish a mutual system of comprehensive safeguards and to take steps to implement the Treaty of Tlatelolco, Latin America's nuclear-weapon-free zone agreement. Later, both countries would join the NPT.

India and Pakistan

Neither the international community nor the Bush administration was able to persuade either India or Pakistan to abandon its nuclear development programs. India had first tested a nuclear weapon in 1974 and was suspected of having a small nuclear arsenal. Moreover, the Indians had refused to ratify the NPT, ostensibly because it discriminated against nonweapon states by forbidding them to acquire nuclear weapons while permitting Russia, China, Britain, France, and the United States to have them. In response to the Indian nuclear weapon test, Pakistan began to develop its own nuclear weapon capability.

For years, the United States had refused to admit the existence of the clandestine Pakistani nuclear weapon program because Pakistan was an important Cold War ally of the United States, particularly during the Afghanistan rebellion against the Soviet Union. However, after Gorbachev withdrew Soviet forces from Afghanistan in February 1989, Pakistan's nuclear weapons became a major concern of the Bush administration. During that year, the administration was able to extract two promises from the

Pakistani government: first, that Pakistan would stop enriching uranium to weapon-grade quality and second, that it would not convert its existing stock of weapon-grade uranium from gas to metal, which could then be machined into nuclear bomb cores. However, in early 1990 the freeze on the Pakistan nuclear program was removed and the program began to move forward again. As a consequence, the administration believed it had no choice but to apply the Pressler Amendment, requiring a cutoff of U.S. military and economic aid to Pakistan unless the president could certify annually that Pakistan does not "possess a nuclear explosive device."[57]

The administration also urged both Pakistan and India to take steps to end their nuclear weapon programs, to eliminate their nuclear weapon capabilities, and to sign the Nuclear Nonproliferation Treaty. In addition, in late 1991 the administration began promoting a five-nation conference—designed to include India, Pakistan, China, Russia, and the United States—aimed at creating a regional nuclear-weapon-free zone on the South Asian subcontinent. But in March 1992 the Indians rejected the U.S. initiative for a regional disarmament conference. They also said they would not sign the NPT or accept safeguards on their most important nuclear facilities in exchange for the resumption of U.S. economic aid. Instead, the Indians called for global constraints on nuclear-weapon activities, particularly a comprehensive nuclear test ban and a ban on the production of plutonium and highly enriched uranium for weapons, both of which the Bush administration opposed.[58]

In the past Pakistan had offered to sign the NPT if India agreed to do so. Now it signaled that if it attended a U.S.-sponsored nuclear disarmament conference, it would want its nuclear status recognized by the international community. The Pakistanis believed that recognition would make possible the renewal of U.S. aid. After much U.S.-Pakistani discussion, Pakistan tentatively and unilaterally agreed to "cap" its nuclear program, but the two countries were unable to work out an agreement on how to verify the cap. The Pakistanis wanted the United States to use national technical means, primarily spy satellites, but the Americans wanted to use intrusive, on-the-ground inspections.[59]

North Korea
Perhaps the most frustrating test of the Bush counterproliferation strategy was North Korea. The North Koreans were believed to possess sufficient bomb-grade plutonium to produce one or two nuclear weapons. In addition,

they had developed and tested a long-range derivative of the Scud missile and were thought to be developing missiles with even longer ranges. Even though North Korea, under Soviet pressure, had signed the NPT in 1985, it refused to open its nuclear facilities to international inspection.

Partly as a way of getting the North Koreans to abandon their nuclear weapons program, Bush's initiative of September 27, 1991, announcing the withdrawal of all U.S. ground- and sea-based tactical nuclear weapons from outside the United States, included the land-based portion of U.S. nuclear weapons deployed in South Korea. Although the North Koreans welcomed this move, they quickly attached new conditions for permitting the inspection of their nuclear facilities. They included South Korea's withdrawal from the U.S. nuclear umbrella, termination of South Korean port calls by U.S. warships, and an end to all flights by U.S. military aircraft over South Korea. As a result, the Bush administration was unable to eliminate, before it left office in January 1993, the possibility that North Korea would eventually become a nuclear power.[60]

Bush and the MTCR

As another way of curbing the horizontal proliferation of nuclear weapons, the Bush administration championed the Missile Technology Control Regime. The MTCR was created in 1987 by Western countries, including the United States, Canada, the United Kingdom, France, West Germany, Italy, and Japan, as a way of blocking the export of ballistic missiles capable of carrying at least 500 kilograms to a range of at least 300 kilometers, along with certain missile-related technologies. In spite of this international action, the threat of ballistic missile proliferation grew by the time Bush was president. Iraq used modified Scud missiles during the 1991 Gulf War. In addition, China transferred M-11 missile technology to Pakistan, Israel collaborated with South Africa to develop a medium-range rocket, North Korea was developing the 1,000 kilometer-range Nodong 1 missile and was also exporting Scud B and C missiles to Iran and Syria, and India had tested the 2,500 kilometer range Agni missile.

In response to this growing threat, shortly after taking office, the Bush administration began emphasizing the need to include all remaining European Community (EC) states in the MTCR. It wanted to prevent exports of technology to the community's non-MTCR members, from whose territory controlled items might be shipped to would-be proliferators. By January 1993, the remaining EC countries—Belgium, Denmark, Greece, Ireland,

Luxembourg, the Netherlands, Portugal, and Spain—as well as Austria, Australia, Finland, New Zealand, Norway, Sweden, and Switzerland had joined the MTCR.

The administration also tried to persuade states that continued to remain outside the MTCR to at least adhere to the regime's guidelines. In June 1990 the Soviet Union, largely as a result of Gorbachev's "new thinking," agreed to do so. China, in 1992, also agreed to abide by the guidelines, but only after the administration promised to lift certain restrictions on high-tech U.S. exports to the Chinese. However, China adopted such an ambiguous stance on missile nonproliferation that the administration was never really sure where the Chinese stood on the issue.

The United States also gained Israel's adherence to the MTCR. It did so by threatening to impose sanctions on those Israeli entities involved in transferring missile technology to South Africa and by warning that it would curtail America's defense-related business with other Israeli firms. Fearing the loss of Israel's military edge over its Arab neighbors if U.S. military aid were terminated, the Israelis agreed to adhere to the regime's guidelines.

North Korea remained the only country that was still prepared to export complete systems in violation of the MTCR's guidelines. Although North Korea's isolated status in this respect highlighted the relative success of the administration's effort to gain international adherence to the MTCR, it also illustrated a major weakness of the regime, that is, its inability to prevent determined proliferators from providing missile technology and assistance to other countries. North Korea continued to export Scud B and C missiles and the related production technology and components to Iran and Syria, despite the U.S. administration's imposition of sanctions against North Korean, Iranian, and Syrian entities. Because North Korea was isolated internationally and subject to a comprehensive embargo, MTCR members had little chance of persuading Pyongyang to forgo its missile sales, especially since they constituted a major source of income for the economically beleaguered North Korean regime.[61]

Strengthening the MTCR

In an effort to strengthen the MTCR, the Bush administration called for a number of changes in the regime's guidelines that would respond to ongoing technological developments and definition problems. The MTCR's scope, for example, was expanded to include missiles capable of delivering all weapons of mass destruction, thereby addressing growing international concern about chemical and biological weapon proliferation. The focus of the MTCR thus became the "intention" of potential recipients, regardless of the range and payload of the missile systems in question.

The administration was also successful in tightening restrictions on the export of space launch vehicle (SLV) technology. The administration successfully pressured South Africa to terminate its SLV program, which the United States considered a proliferation risk. The U.S. government imposed two-year-long sanctions on the Armaments Corporation of South Africa for receiving rocket technology from Israel. The administration also tried to convince South Africans that it is was not economically worthwhile to develop a commercial SLV capacity by arguing that the launch market was already dominated by proven rocket producers.

The administration persuaded France to halt the planned transfer of rocket engines to both the Indian and Brazilian space launch programs because the engines also could be used in ballistic missiles. The administration also successfully used this logic to persuade Taiwan and South Korea to suspend their space launch projects. It was instrumental in persuading Argentina to terminate its Condor II missile project in 1990, although an MTCR-imposed embargo on SLV technology transfers to Argentina was certainly a more important reason behind Argentina's decision to do so. The regime's embargo on SLV technology transfers to Brazil was important in restricting that country's space launch and missile programs as well.

Russia's missile technology transfers posed a continuing problem for the Bush administration. Even though the Russians had pledged to adhere to the MTCR guidelines, in late 1990 the Russian Space Agency signed an agreement to supply cryogenic rocket engines and associated production technology to the Indian Space Research Organization. Although Moscow said the deal conformed with MTCR guidelines, the Bush administration argued that it did not. As a result, the United States imposed sanctions on both Russian and Indian space entities. Subsequently, it linked Russia's willingness to terminate its deal with the Indian Space Agency to America's willingness to allow Russian participation in the construction of an international space station. But this pressure on Russia did not produce any concrete results during the final months of the Bush presidency, primarily because Russia's military-industrial complex did not want to jeopardize its freedom to export SLV technology and tactical missiles by conforming to U.S. wishes.

In addition to these measures to remove the loopholes in MTCR guidelines, the Bush administration acted to strengthen U.S. missile technology export controls. In December 1990 it inaugurated the Enhanced Proliferation Control Initiative (EPCI), which required American exporters to obtain licenses for "any export destined for a publicly-listed company, ministry, project, or other entity" that was engaged in missile or chemical-biological weapon "activities of proliferation concern." Licenses were required if an exporter "knew" (or was informed by the government) that a "proposed export may be destined to a project of concern," copying a similar provision already in place in the nuclear field.[62]

After the Gulf War, the administration began encouraging other MTCR members to adopt comparable EPCI-type controls. For example, it pressured and assisted Italy and West Germany to improve their export control systems in response to revelations about both countries' lax enforcement of MTCR guidelines. This problem had contributed to several high profile cases of missile proliferation to South America and the Middle East, including exports of technology and assistance to Argentina and Iraq. Italian and West German laxity in enforcing MTCR guidelines was fed by trade policies and mechanisms that favored export promotion over export control.

The Bush administration did not act alone in strengthening the MTCR. In November 1990 Congress enacted a new law, the Missile Control Act, which required the U.S. government to impose sanctions automatically on American or foreign persons, companies, or any other entities that participated in MTCR-prohibited activities. Congress was especially concerned about the role that companies from several MTCR member states had played in supplying technology and assistance to Argentina's Condor II project. The Bush administration at first opposed the congressional action. It argued that the new law deprived the executive branch of the ability to treat missile nonproliferation issues in isolation from commercial and other foreign policy interests. Nevertheless, the administration subsequently used the new law to gain nonproliferation pledges from nonregime suppliers, including Israel, China, and Russia.

By January 1993 the effectiveness of the MTCR had been enhanced considerably. Its members were meeting regularly to discuss common issues of concern, the guidelines had been revised and updated, and the export control systems and compliance of several member states, including the United States, had been strengthened. In addition, the guidelines had been expanded to cover missiles capable of delivering all WMD, a reflection of increased international concern with the proliferation of chemical and biological weapons. The regime's expansion to twenty-two countries by 1993 also helped strengthen international efforts to curb the proliferation of ballistic missiles.[63]

Still, the regime retained a number of significant shortcomings. Some countries adopted less stringent national controls than the United States. And Chinese firms continued to provide restricted parts and materials to Iran, Pakistan, and Syria, prompting the new Clinton administration to impose limited trade sanctions on several Chinese missile and space companies. The MTCR was also limited by the fact that a number of Third World missile producers, including China and North Korea, were not members. The MTCR was not perfect, but it helped prevent countries like Iraq from gaining access to longer-range missile technology.[64]

Toward a Comprehensive Test Ban

One suggestion that the Bush administration refused to implement was making the United States a party to a comprehensive test ban treaty. By 1992 international pressure to do so had become almost irresistible. Boris Yeltsin reaffirmed Gorbachev's nuclear test moratorium and extended it through the remainder of the year. France followed suit. And so too did China, after conducting a nuclear weapon test that May, which was reportedly the largest in Chinese underground testing history. Moreover, China, the last declared nuclear weapon state that still refused to join the NPT—and once one of that treaty's harshest critics—announced that it would become a party to the treaty as a nuclear weapon state.

Congress also pressured the administration to participate in a CTBT. On June 4 the House approved an amendment to the fiscal year 1993 defense authorization bill that would prohibit U.S. nuclear testing for one year if the former Soviet republics did not test. The amendment, which passed by a vote of 237 to 167, marked the first time either chamber of Congress had passed a complete and binding ban on nuclear testing. In the Senate, virtually identical legislation, sponsored by majority leader George Mitchell (D-Maine) and Mark Hatfield (R-Oreg.), gained fifty-one cosponsors, including eight Republicans, virtually assuring its passage.[65]

To head off a congressionally mandated moratorium, on July 10, 1992, the administration sent a letter to Congress announcing that "the President had decided to modify U.S. nuclear testing policy immediately." The letter stated: "We do not anticipate, under currently foreseen circumstances, more than six tests per year over the next five years, or more than three tests per year in excess of 35 kilotons." The letter also said that "all U.S. nuclear tests of our weapons will henceforth be for the safety and reliability of our deterrent forces." But since the United States had already stopped producing new types of warheads, there were no plans to conduct nuclear tests for modernization purposes. Finally, the letter said that, if current efforts to maintain the reliability of the U.S. nuclear stockpile under additional limits on testing were "successful" and "the international security environment" continued to improve, "further reductions in these numbers [may be] possible."[66]

Critics, however, contended that the limits imposed by the president on the purpose, number, and yield of the nuclear tests would require few, if any, changes in current U.S. nuclear testing practices. They pointed out that the Reagan administration had put forward initiatives on nuclear testing just before Congress was scheduled to vote on more stringent limitations. Moreover, the critics argued that despite the administration's insistence that future tests would be conducted only for safety and reliability purposes, government documents distributed to Capitol Hill staffers by administration officials indicated that only four of the next ten scheduled tests had safety or reliability as their principal objective. According to *Time* magazine, at least three of the ten scheduled tests were intended to support research for the Strategic Defense Initiative.[67]

The administration's gambit failed. On August 3, by an overwhelming margin of 68 to 26, the Senate approved legislation (an amendment to an Energy Department bill) that would suspend U.S. nuclear testing for nine months, limit the number and purpose of tests for the next three years, and halt all testing in 1996, provided Russia did not test after that date. It was the first time the Senate had voted to end U.S. nuclear testing. In fact, the last time the Senate had considered any kind of nuclear test ban, in 1988, it handily rejected, by a 57 to 39 vote, a resolution to ban nuclear tests with yields over five kilotons. Although the Senate moratorium was shorter than the one-year moratorium called for in the House version of the test ban resolution that was passed in June, the Senate bill also required the Energy Department to end all testing by September 30, 1996, unless Russia conducted a nuclear test after that date. Until then, the administration could conduct up to fifteen tests, all for safety reasons, except for one "reliability test" each year.[68]

Although antinuclear activists preferred a one-year moratorium, the *Washington Post* called the Senate vote for an end to nuclear explosions "a sweeping reversal of its Cold War-era opposition to any constraints on underground nuclear explosions." Equally important, the Senate amendment called for the resumption of U.S.-Russian negotiations for a comprehensive test ban treaty by 1996. In effect, the Senate rejected the Bush administration argument that continued nuclear testing was necessary as long as the United States relied on a nuclear deterrent. Test ban advocates had apparently succeeded in making their case that testing is not required to ensure either the reliability or the safety of the U.S. arsenal.[69]

The Senate was also motivated by international pressure to conclude a comprehensive test ban before the Nuclear Nonproliferation Treaty Review Conference took place in 1995. Many nations had threatened to oppose renewal of the treaty, which otherwise would have expired that year, if the United States continued to reject treaty provisions calling for the major nuclear powers to terminate nuclear testing as a prerequisite to ending the nuclear arms race. The previous NPT Review Conference in September 1990 failed to reach consensus on a final document due to a deadlock between pro-CTBT signatories, led by Mexico, and the two major opponents of a ban, the United States and Britain. The Senate realized that it would be difficult, if not impossible, to preserve the NPT if the United States continued to oppose a CTBT.[70]

After a conference committee bill ironing out differences in Senate and House versions of the test moratorium amendment passed in both chambers, President Bush signed it into law on October 2. Although he said that the provision limiting testing "unwisely restricts the number and purpose of U.S. nuclear tests and will make future U.S. nuclear testing dependent on actions by another country, rather than on our own national security requirements," he nevertheless decided not to veto the bill, reportedly because it included $517 million for the superconducting super collider, an $8 billion project located in Texas, a key state in Bush's reelection bid. However, he did promise that he would "work for new legislation to permit the conduct of a modest number of necessary underground nuclear tests." In spite of Bush's promise, one former nuclear weapons designer remarked, "I don't think we will ever test again."[71]

The Decline of SDI
Equally surprising, four days after the Senate passed a resolution ending nuclear testing, it stunned the White House by casting a preliminary vote to chop almost a billion dollars from the Strategic Defense Initiative. The administration had requested $3.8 billion for SDI, but Congress provided only $2.9 billion. Before it left office, the Bush administration had revealed plans for a significant expansion of the program. It had planned to request $39 bil-

lion over the next five fiscal years. The Bush plan envisioned a slightly larger tactical missile defense program and a far more ambitious national missile defense system, including the deployment of a ground-based interceptor system around the turn of the century, and continued research and development of the space-based Brilliant Pebbles boost-phase interceptor. With a Congress and a Democratic president hostile to SDI due to take office, the prospects for implementing the ambitious Bush program were virtually nil.[72]

5
Clinton, START II,
and the ABM Treaty

Candidate Clinton

Unlike Ronald Reagan, William Jefferson Clinton entered the White House determined to reduce the number of nuclear weapons. He also promised to go much farther than the Bush administration in ending the nuclear arms race. He indicated that his administration would continue to reduce the risks of vertical nuclear proliferation by giving the START I and START II treaties high priority.

As for ballistic missile defenses, Clinton's campaign statements strongly suggested that his administration would continue to adhere to the 1972 ABM Treaty. Although he believed the United States should conduct missile defense research and development, he insisted it should be done "in strict compliance" with the ABM Treaty. However, he also said that he "would consider modest changes in it that clearly enhanced U.S. security interests and were negotiated in good faith with Russia." "At present," he added, "such changes are not needed." Clinton also promised that his administration would spend far less money on the Strategic Defense Initiative than the previous administration had wanted (as much as $8 billion per year on SDI). Clinton stated that the deployment of a massive space-based defense, such as the Bush Brilliant Pebbles program, was not necessary. In addition to scaling back SDI, Clinton said that he would support negotiated limits on antisatellite weapons.[1]

Throughout his presidential campaign, Clinton also made it clear that stemming the proliferation of nuclear, biological, and chemical weapons, as well as the ballistic missiles that could deliver them, would be a top priority of his administration. Yet many of the antiproliferation steps he initially described built on and reinforced Bush administration policies. These included commitments to bolster the capacity of the International Atomic Energy Agency to inspect suspicious facilities and to encourage more nations to abide by the Missile Technology Control Regime. He also said that his administration would not permit American firms to sell key technology to "outlaw" states such as Iraq. Regarding China's missile sales, Clinton said that his administration would "link China's trading privileges to its human rights record, and its conduct of trade and weapons sales." Clinton also explicitly endorsed a comprehensive test ban treaty, a step that his predecessor had vehemently opposed.[2]

Clinton and START

By the time Clinton entered the White House in January 1993, the legislatures of the United States, Russia, and Kazakhstan had all approved the START I Treaty. On February 4, 1993, the Belarusan parliament ratified the treaty and voted to accede to the Nuclear Nonproliferation Treaty. But Ukraine, which had 176 ICBMs on its soil, continued to delay ratification until it received money and security guarantees from the United States. More troubling, hardline nationalists in the Rada (parliament) were talking about permanently retaining the nuclear weapons still on Ukrainian territory, a sentiment that, if implemented, would have killed both the START I and START II treaties.[3]

As an incentive to persuade Ukraine to ratify START I, on October 25, 1993, the United States signed an umbrella agreement with the Ukrainians under which the administration promised $135 million in Nunn-Lugar assistance for dismantling their strategic nuclear weapons. In response, on November 18, 1993, the Rada ratified START I, but the ratification instrument lacked a precise commitment to eliminate all its strategic nuclear weapons within the seven-year period required by the treaty. The Rada also rejected article 5 of the Bush-negotiated Lisbon Protocol, which required Ukraine's accession to the NPT as a nonnuclear weapon state. President Clinton reacted by saying that the Rada's instrument of ratification made it impossible to put the START I treaty into force. In addition, Senator Sam Nunn stated that Nunn-Lugar assistance would not be provided to Ukraine unless the Rada "corrected" the instrument of ratification.

American pressure helped to bring the Ukrainians around. President Leonid Kravchuk pledged to resubmit START I and the NPT to the Rada after new elections were held in December. As a result of that election, the Ukrainian president was able to join Clinton and Yeltsin in Moscow on January 14, 1994 to sign a trilateral statement designed to facilitate the removal of nuclear weapons from Ukraine. In the statement, the United States and Russia agreed, contingent upon START I entering into force and Ukrainian accession to the NPT, to provide Kiev with a number of security assurances, including commitments to respect Ukraine's existing borders and to refrain from economic coercion.

In addition, the three states outlined the terms for compensating Ukraine for transferring to Russia the highly enriched uranium (HEU) contained in its strategic nuclear warheads. Ukraine also agreed to transport to Russia 200 ICBM warheads and to deactivate all forty-six ss-24s on its territory within ten months. In exchange, Russia agreed to send Ukraine 100 tons of low enriched uranium (LEU) for use in commercial nuclear reactors. To help cover the expense of transportation and dismantlement, the United States agreed to pay the Ukrainians $60 million as an advance on payments due to Russia under the HEU contract. The United States also reaffirmed its commitment to provide Ukraine with technical and financial assistance for the dismantlement of its nuclear weapons. Finally, through confidential correspondence, Ukraine agreed that all strategic nuclear warheads would be withdrawn from its territory and sent to Russia within three years. Russia agreed to write off some of Ukraine's debt for past oil and natural gas deliveries as compensation for the tactical warheads the Ukrainians had already transferred to Russia.

On February 3, 1994, three weeks after the Moscow summit, the Rada passed a two-part resolution instructing Kravchuk to exchange the instruments of ratification for START I and to acknowledge that Ukraine was obligated, under the Lisbon Protocol, to accede to the NPT as a nonnuclear weapon state. On March 4, 1994, during a meeting with Kravchuk in Washington, Clinton pledged to increase significantly the amount of economic and Nunn-Lugar assistance to Ukraine. Two days later, U.S. and Russian officials confirmed that the first trainload of sixty nuclear warheads removed from ss-19 and ss-24 missiles in Ukraine had arrived in Russia in accordance with the trilateral statement. By September 1994, Ukraine had transferred over three hundred warheads to Russia, more than meeting its obligation to transfer two hundred warheads in the first ten months of the accord.[4]

On June 1, 1996, Kravchuk's successor as president, Leonid Kuchma, announced that Ukraine had transferred the last of the former Soviet strategic nuclear warheads on its territory to Russia, thereby making it the second republic of the former Soviet Union to become completely nuclear free. Finally, on November 16, 1994, the Rada voted by an overwhelming margin of 301 to 8 to accede to the NPT as a nonnuclear weapon state. However, the Rada made its approval contingent on two key conditions: written security assurances from the nuclear-weapon states and recognition of Ukraine's "ownership" of the fissile material in the nuclear weapons still on its territory. U.S. officials expressed confidence that these conditions would be met.[5]

The Clinton administration responded to Kuchma's commitment to denuclearize Ukraine by obtaining international financial assistance for the Ukrainians and by agreeing to provide the Ukrainians with $100 million to help implement their domestic reform program. The security assurances were worked out in a flurry of eleventh-hour diplomacy just prior to the Rada vote. They included the standard assurances nuclear weapon states provide to all nonnuclear weapon state that are parties to the NPT, as well as commitments from the parties to the 1975 Final Act of the Conference on Security and Cooperation in Europe (CSCE) to respect existing borders and to refrain from economic coercion. After the security assurances were signed on December 5, 1994, in ceremonies at a CSCE summit in Budapest, Ukraine provided the instruments of accession to the NPT, thereby making it possible for the START I Treaty to enter into force—almost three and a half years after it was signed.[6]

START II in the U.S. Senate

Ukraine's adherence to the NPT and its ratification of the START I Treaty dramatically improved the prospects for U.S. nuclear cooperation with Russia. It also cleared the way for the U.S. Senate and the Russian parliament to begin deliberating the ratification of a START II agreement.

Initially, the prospects for Senate ratification of START II looked good. Shortly after hearings began on the treaty in January 1995, Senator Jesse Helms (R-N.C.), chair of the Foreign Relations Committee, made it clear that he would support START II. He even appointed a pro-arms control Republican, Senator Richard Lugar of Indiana, to guide it through the Senate. In March, Lugar said that he expected the full Senate to consider the treaty no later than May. However, by late March, the treaty had become a political football between Helms and the Clinton administration. Helms had introduced a bill that would incorporate three independent agencies—

the Arms Control and Disarmament Agency, the Agency for International Development, and the U.S. Information Agency—into the State Department. Helms decided to make a hostage of START II until Senate Democrats ended a filibuster against his bill. He refused to permit his committee to act on the START II Treaty as well as the Chemical Weapons Convention until the Democrats yielded. On August 1, Helms told reporters: "They [the Clinton administration and its supporters] want to play hardball; we can play hardball, too. They get no more ambassadors, they don't get any treaties, they don't get anything." As a result, the START II Treaty would stay in Helms's deep freeze for months.[7]

Finally, on December 7, 1995, Helms and Senator John Kerry (D-Mass.) worked out a deal: the Democrats would permit a vote on Helms's State Department reorganization bill. In return, the Foreign Relations Committee would vote promptly on START II, and the full Senate would take up the treaty before the end of the year, or it would be the first item on the 1996 agenda. Five days later, on December 12, the Foreign Relations Committee approved START II by an 18 to 0 vote. Ten days later, the full Senate considered the treaty and prepared for a final vote. At that point, however, Armed Services Committee chair Strom Thurmond (R-S.C.) blocked the vote on the treaty in an unsuccessful attempt to pressure President Clinton to sign the 1996 defense authorization bill.

START II continued to be a political football as the new year began. Republican senators James Inhofe of Oklahoma and Robert Smith of New Hampshire threatened to hold up the final vote on the treaty until the president committed the United States to deploy a national missile defense system. The Republican caveat was triggered by a threat from Democrats, who said they would delay approval of a second version of the defense authorization bill until the START II Treaty was approved. Finally, on January 26, 1996, the treaty was brought to a vote, three years after Bush and Yeltsin signed it. The Senate overwhelmingly approved the ratification resolution by an 87 to 4 margin.

However, eight conditions and twelve declarations were attached to the ratification resolution. Fortunately for START II, none of the conditions required Russian action, which would have necessitated reopening the negotiations. One condition stated that ratification should not be construed as a guarantee that the United States would finance the destruction and dismantlement of Russian missiles required by START II. One of the declarations prohibited asymmetrical reductions; in other words, neither side could get ahead of the other in missile numbers as the reductions were being implemented. Another declaration accused both the former Soviet Union and the Russian Federation of continued noncompliance with arms control agreements and called for annual reports by the president on compliance issues. The Senate also declared that missile defenses were essential and enjoined the United States and Russia to move ahead cooperatively in this field. Interestingly enough, while calling for the construction of ABMs, the Senate also requested the president to work with the Russians to achieve further strategic offensive arms reductions.[8]

The Russian Duma and START II

On the Russian side, the discussion of the START II Treaty began in the Supreme (Russian) Soviet, where its members raised questions concerning the cost to Russia of implementing the agreement as well as the treaty's effect on the strategic balance. One semiofficial estimate projected the cost of implementing the START I reductions at 30 billion rubles (using first-quarter 1992 prices), with START II requiring an additional 20-30 percent of that amount. This was an enormous sum of money, considering that the annual expenditure on Russian strategic forces was only some 20 billion rubles, an amount that was scheduled to decline to 15 billion rubles after the START reductions were implemented. However, another estimate suggested an implementation cost for START II of 80-90 billion rubles over and above the cost of implementing START I. However, as in the Ukrainian Rada, supporters of the treaty in the Russian Duma tended to overestimate the implementation cost in order to demand larger financial assistance from the United States and other Western states. At the same time, treaty opponents advanced inflated cost estimates in order to defeat the treaty by making its implementation conditional on unrealistic levels of Western funding.[9]

In terms of the effects of the START II reductions on the strategic force balance, opponents of the treaty argued that it would force Russia to give up its great advantage in heavy MIRved ICBMs while allowing the United States to retain its advantage in bombers and SLBMs. To eliminate its land-based MIRved ICBM missiles and still have only the maximum 3,500 deployed warheads permitted by START II, the Russians would have to build hundreds of new single-warhead missiles, which they obviously could not afford. Perhaps more disconcerting to the Russians was the fact that their entire strategic nuclear force was aging, leading many to believe that it would degrade to a level of 2,000–2,500 warheads within ten years with or without START, purely through attrition. Sergei Kortunov, a top Kremlin defense aide, wrote that "with a lot of effort" Russia might reach 1,000 warheads by 2015. By contrast, the Soviet Union in 1990 had 10,779 strategic nuclear warheads. U.S. strategic forces, by comparison, are relatively modern. The land-based Minuteman missiles, Trident submarines, and B-52 bombers are expected to remain in service for the foreseeable future. When combined with the conventional threat posed by NATO, the Russian opponents of START II argued, the treaty would be dangerous to Russia's security. The Russian military leadership, which had been supportive of the treaty initially (in part because they expected it to free funds for conventional forces) increasingly became concerned that the passage of the much lower defense budgets that were in the offing would leave funding for both Russian conventional and strategic forces inadequate.[10]

START II was also stalled by political squabbles between Yeltsin and the communist-dominated parliament. In the Supreme (Russian) Soviet, Chairman Ruslan Khasbulatov stated that the treaty would be endorsed only if it were presented by a foreign minister who enjoyed the respect of the public, a direct attack on Kozyrev's alleged attempts to "appease" the Western powers at Russia's expense. Indeed, the ratification proceedings ground to a halt when, in March 1993, Yeltsin attempted to bypass the parliament and rule by decree. As a result, START II languished in the Russian parliament. The forceful dissolution of the parliament by Yeltsin in October 1993, the implementation of a new Yeltsin-drafted Russian constitution, and the election of a new parliament in December 1993 did not improve START II's ratification chances. If anything, the new parliament made ratification of the treaty even more difficult.

According to the new constitution, the ratification of treaties requires a simple majority in both houses of the new Russian Federal Assembly, composed of a lower house, the State Duma, and an upper house, the Federation Council. Unfortunately for START II, one consequence of the December parliamentary election was that opponents of the treaty controlled about 188 votes of the 450 total in the Duma. As a result, obtaining a majority (226 votes) for START II in the Duma required the complete support of the centrist parties. But their members were split on the treaty. Realizing that the treaty would, in all likelihood, fail to win a majority vote in the Duma, Yeltsin decided not to push for ratification after the treaty was sent to the Duma on June 20, 1995. There it continues to languish until this writing.[11]

The Expansion of NATO

START II's ratification chances were also hurt by the Clinton administration's decision to expand NATO's membership to include three former Soviet satellite states—Poland, the Czech Republic, and Hungary. Without question, this move increased hostility toward the West and specifically toward START II in the Duma.

Clinton initiated the expansion of NATO in 1994, ostensibly to encourage the development of democracy, human rights, and free market economies in Central and Eastern Europe by offering the countries of those regions the protection of NATO's shield. But the proposal to include Poland, Hungary, and the Czech Republic in the alliance also had domestic political ramifications. Clinton announced it at a campaign rally of Polish Americans in 1996, obviously to attract the support of American ethnic voters in the approaching presidential election. The effort to expand NATO also served to divert public attention from Clinton's inability to enact major provisions of his domestic reform program, particularly national health care. Clinton also hoped that NATO expansion would be remembered as one of the hallmarks of his presidency. Ronald Reagan was recalled as the president who ended the Cold War and George Bush as the one who helped reunify Germany. Clinton wanted to be remembered as the president who united Europe.[12]

George Kennan, who authored the containment strategy, called the decision to expand NATO into Eastern Europe "the most fateful error of American policy in the entire post-cold-war era." NATO expansion, he predicted, would "inflame nationalistic, anti-Western and militaristic tendencies in Russian opinion, adversely affect the development of Russian democracy, restore the atmosphere of the Cold War to East-West relations, and impel Russian foreign policy in directions decidedly not to our liking." Last but not least, he added, "it might make it much more difficult, if not impossible, to secure the Russian Duma's ratification of the START II agreement and to achieve further reductions of nuclear weaponry."[13]

If ordinary Russians, who were more concerned about economic problems, were not particularly upset by NATO's action, the Russian political elite was. They considered it, among other things, a violation of the tacit understanding they believed had been reached by Mikhail Gorbachev and George Bush. Gorbachev agreed to give up the Soviet buffer zone in East Europe and accepted the overthrow of communist regimes in the Soviet Union's satellites, as well as the liquidation of the Warsaw Pact. He even permitted the reunification of the Soviet Union's archenemy, Germany, and the expansion of NATO into what was once East Germany. In return, Gorbachev expected the West to refrain from expanding NATO into the vacuum created by the Soviet military withdrawal.

In an attempt to take the sting out of NATO's decision to expand, Washington offered Russia a more intensive relationship with, but not the prospect of, membership in the Western alliance. Hoping to obtain badly needed Western economic assistance and make the best of Russia's isolation, on May 27, 1997, Yeltsin met with Clinton at a Helsinki summit and signed an agreement known as the Founding Act on Mutual Relations, Cooperation, and Security between NATO and the Russian Federation. As its preamble notes, the act "defines the goals and mechanism of consultation, cooperation, joint decision-making and joint action that will constitute the core of the mutual relations between NATO and Russia." The act established a NATO-Russian Permanent Joint Council, which would be a mechanism for consultations, coordination, and, where appropriate, joint decisions and joint action with respect to security issues of common concern.[14]

As predicted by Kennan, one consequence of NATO's expansion was the continued refusal by the Duma to ratify the START II Treaty. Although Yeltsin promised at the March 1997 Helsinki summit with Clinton that he would move quickly on gaining ratification of the treaty, when he came back to Moscow, according to Alexei Arbatov, "he immediately 'forgot' about it." He did so because there was no chance of getting the Duma to ratify it. Moreover, even moderate Russian strategists argued that, with NATO expanding and Russia's army being downsized, Russia would have to rely more heavily on nuclear deterrence along with a military doctrine permitting the first use of nuclear weapons, a strategy the Soviet Union had forsworn. In short, instead of gaining Russian cooperation in reducing the major threat to European peace—the menace of nuclear weapons—NATO enlargement was helping, as Senator Sam Nunn put it, "to create the very threat we are trying to guard against," that is, a potentially hostile, nuclear-armed power.[15]

Theater Ballistic Missile Defenses
During his 1992 campaign for the presidency, Clinton strongly suggested that his administration would continue to adhere to the ABM Treaty. He also said that his administration would move away from Reagan's and Bush's apparent obsession with space-based Star Wars weapons, whose planned testing and deployment would have violated the treaty. Although Clinton declared that the debate over Star Wars was over, his administration planned

to continue a broad-based ABM research and development program. The Reagan-Bush Strategic Defense Initiative Organization (SDIO) was changed to the Ballistic Missile Defense Organization (BMDO) and it was given a budget of $3.8 billion (which was reduced to $2.9 billion by the Democratically controlled Congress). The five-year BMDO appropriation was $18 billion (a reduction of $11 billion from the last Bush request).[16]

The Clinton administration also changed the focus of U.S. ABM activities. In contrast to the Reagan-Bush plans for a national ballistic missile defense, which were designed to counter the threat to U.S. territory posed by ICBMs, the primary focus of the Clinton ABM program has been on theater missile defenses (TMD), which are intended to protect U.S. forces deployed overseas from the threat posed by theater-range ballistic missiles. Again, the intense U.S. interest in TMD stemmed from the Persian Gulf War, in which U.S. and coalition forces were, for the first time, subjected to attack by short-range (600 kilometer) tactical ballistic missiles. Although Iraqi Scuds, armed only with chemical explosives and having poor accuracy, hardly affected the military outcome of the war, they exerted a significant psychological and political effect. They aroused great fear, particularly in Israel and Saudi Arabia, that prompted the United States to dispatch Patriot missiles to those countries and to make the destruction of the Iraqi Scuds one of the major priorities of the air and ground forces of the allied coalition. The Gulf War also raised the specter of more accurate, longer-range ballistic missiles armed with chemical, biological, or even nuclear weapons in the hands of so-called rogue states like Iraq, Iran, North Korea, Syria, and Libya. The Pentagon stated that more than fifteen countries possessed theater ballistic missiles, and the list was growing. In addition, more than twenty-five countries possessed or might be developing weapons of mass destruction (chemical, biological, or nuclear) that could be delivered by ballistic missiles.[17]

To counter this threat, the administration's plan envisioned the deployment of three "core" TMD systems, at a cost of about $10 billion. These programs consisted of two point-defense systems and one area-defense system. Point defenses are relatively short-range systems intended to protect targets like airfields and port facilities. Because of the relatively short range of these systems, to be effective, they must be deployed near the targets they are intended to protect. The two point-defense systems were the Patriot Advanced Capability, Level 3 (PAC-3) system and the Navy Lower Tier Sea-Based TMD system. Both programs involved the modification of surface-to-air missile systems originally designed to shoot down attacking aircraft.

The third core system, designed for area rather than point defense, is the Army's Theater High Altitude Area Defense (THAAD) system, which is scheduled to be deployed by 2006. Unlike the PAC-3 and the navy's Lower Tier Sea-Based TMD systems, THAAD is an entirely new system rather than an upgrade of an existing system. Its supporters argued that it would have the capability to intercept tactical ballistic missiles with a range of up to 3,500 kilometers traveling up to 5 kilometers per second. Unlike the other two core systems, THAAD was designed to protect targets over a far larger area, that is, as much as 140 kilometers by 130 kilometers. Initial plans called for procurement of 1,422 missiles, 99 launchers, and 18 radar units to equip eight batteries at a cost of $10 billion. However, in 1994 the Congressional Budget Office estimated that overall TMD development and procurement would cost around $50 billion through the year 2010.[18]

But compared to PAC-3 & PAC-2 GEM plus ?

TMD and the ABM Treaty

Critics again called theater ballistic missile defenses a waste of money and a threat to the ABM Treaty, which has been the bedrock of the U.S. effort to control the nuclear arms race since 1972. Although the treaty applies only to strategic antiballistic missiles, arms controllers feared that TMDs are only the first step toward a NMD designed to shoot down Russian or Chinese strategic ballistic missiles.

NMD critics believe that if THAAD were coupled with a satellite tracking system, such as the U.S. Brilliant Eyes system, its interceptors could defend much of the continental United States, thereby making it a nationwide system—and a violation of the ABM Treaty. The Clinton administration planned to store the THAAD missiles in the United States for rapid deployment abroad, but the missiles could be quickly deployed in the United States to defend urban areas against strategic attacks. In addition, the navy's plan to supplement its seaborne, low-altitude missile defense system with an advanced high-altitude interceptor called the Light Exoatmospheric Projectile (LEAP), could have, with appropriate tracking data, significant capability against strategic missiles, a potential some navy spokesmen have advertised.[19]

The air force planned an even more ambitious system. It would attack ballistic missiles in their boost phase with interceptor missiles launched from fighter aircraft that would travel twice the speed of THAAD interceptors. The air force predicted that this advanced system would be effective in countering enemy measures to foil the interception of their ballistic missiles, including the use of multiple warheads and decoys. However, by extending the interceptor missile's range, or by deploying it on "stealth" aircraft, the advanced air force system could become a major threat to Russian or Chinese strategic missiles. With the United States building a potential NMD, the Russians would be unlikely to reduce further their arsenal of offensive nuclear weapons, as called for in the START treaties. Indeed, the Russians would need more, not less, offensive missiles to overcome the U.S. NMD. The result would be the deployment of more, rather than less, Russian nuclear-armed missiles pointed at the United States.[20]

The TMD Demarcation Talks

In an attempt to continue developing tactical ballistic missile defense systems without vitiating the ABM Treaty, in November 1993 the Clinton administration initiated talks with the Russians to establish a "demarcation line" between permitted TMD and restricted ABM systems. Article 6 (a) of the ABM Treaty states that the parties may not test a non-ABM system in an "ABM mode" and may not give a non-ABM system "ABM capability." But the treaty does not define "ABM capability"; before the United States could proceed with TMD development, it wanted the Russians to accept that TMD did not have an "ABM capability" that would violate the ABM Treaty.[21]

One of the issues raised in the TMD demarcation talks concerned the peak velocity of the THAAD interceptor missile. When the ABM Treaty was being negotiated in the early 1970s, a senior Defense Department official, John Foster, proposed that interceptor missiles with a velocity of no more than five kilometers per second and with a capability to destroy missiles with a maximum range of 3,500 kilometers should be considered theater antiballistic missiles (ATBMs). Those above that velocity and range should be considered strategic ABMs. The Clinton administration accepted Foster's demarcation line but added an important modification: Instead of interceptors being limited to a velocity of five kilometers per second, it proposed that ATBMs be defined as systems that had not demonstrated a capability to intercept targets moving faster than five kilometers per second.[22]

The Russians were pleased with the Clinton administration's adherence to the "traditional interpretation" of the ABM Treaty. They also accepted the Clinton idea that it was necessary to draw a demarcation line between ABM and ATBM systems. But they argued that the velocity and range criteria suggested by the United States were not sufficient to differentiate between ATBMS and ABMS. They feared that the U.S. position would permit the deployment of missile defenses with much greater capability than THAAD, thereby undermining the ABM Treaty and ruling out additional cuts in strategic offensive missiles, something the Russians badly wanted, not only to enhance nuclear stability but also to relieve the hard-pressed Russian economy.

As a consequence, the Russians suggested additional technical criteria. Specifically, the Russians proposed that ATBM interceptor missile speeds should be limited to three kilometers per second and that ATBMs should be defined, as the United States had suggested, as systems that had not demonstrated a capability to intercept targets moving faster than five kilometers per second. However, the U.S. delegation rejected the Russian counterproposal. Although it would not have precluded the testing and deployment of THAAD, it would have prevented development of some interceptors under consideration, for example, the navy's Upper Tier system.[23]

Unwilling to permit the demarcation stalemate to delay THAAD development, the Clinton administration changed its initial position on THAAD flight tests. The Americans originally had stated that the tests would not take place until the Russians had agreed that they would not violate the ABM Treaty. Now the Russians were informed that the United States did not consider the testing of THAAD components, which was scheduled for early 1995, a violation of the ABM Treaty, since the initial tests would not include all the elements of the final system, such as targeting information from space-based sensors. Predictably, the Russians reacted by asserting that the flight tests of THAAD components would violate article 5 of the ABM Treaty, which prohibits the development and testing of mobile, land-based ABM systems or components. The Russians also said the U.S. test plan "worsens the atmosphere" of the ongoing demarcation talks and may have a "negative effect on the entire complex of security negotiations in general."[24]

The administration's decision to proceed with THAAD flight tests, the first of which occurred on April 21, 1995, was motivated in part by the election of a Republican-controlled Congress in November 1994. Conservative Republicans, in particular, denounced the administration's effort to place any restrictions on ABM development and deployment and, in their so-called Contract with America, called for the construction of a national ballistic missile defense system, even if it required scrapping the ABM Treaty. In a letter to President Clinton on March 25, 1994, all forty-four Republican members of the Senate had urged him to resist any restrictions on ATBM systems beyond the original U.S. proposal. The senators' letter also warned the president that "there is an emerging consensus in the Senate that any agreement to substantively modify the ABM Treaty should be submitted by the administration for Senate advice and consent." Senior Democratic senators expressed a similar view, and several questioned the wisdom of trying to make any changes to the treaty without the Senate's approval. However, the administration preferred not to classify the new demarcation line between ABMS and ATBMS as an "amendment" because the new definitions would have to be approved by the legislatures of all the parties to the ABM Treaty, possibly including Belarus, Kazakhstan, and Ukraine.[25]

Faced with the vigorous advocacy of missile defenses by the new Republican majority in Congress, as well as by the possibility that they might use a demarcation amendment to cripple or kill the ABM Treaty, the Clinton administration decided in early 1995 to concentrate on bilateral discussions with the Russian government before proceeding further with talks in the Standing Consultative Commission, the usual forum for ABM matters. The product of those discussions was a joint statement issued by Clinton and Yeltsin at a May 1995 summit. It included a set of principles designed to establish the basis for a demarcation agreement. It also reaffirmed the commitment of both governments to preserve the ABM Treaty as the cornerstone of strategic nuclear stability. And, for the first time publicly, it established the principle that an effective theater missile defense could be deployed within the framework of the ABM Treaty.

The joint statement also asserted that although theater missile defense systems might have a theoretical capability against strategic missiles, they could not be regarded as having a practical ABM capability. In other words, TMDs could not be militarily significant, in terms of numbers, location, system characteristics, or any realistic engagement scenario, against strategic ballistic missiles. Further, both sides accepted the proposition that missiles carrying decoys and other countermeasures could easily overwhelm ATBMS. Both sides also were aware that the defense does not control engagement factors, such as the ability of the offensive force to choose the scale, timing, and location of an attack. Finally, both sides realized that defensive missiles deployed in the vicinity of ICBM fields— which could influence the strategic balance—would raise military, political, and legal issues that the other side would not ignore. Accordingly, each side accepted the proposition that ATBMS did not pose a threat to the strategic nuclear force of the other side. And they agreed that TMDs would not be tested to give them that capability. Although the principles enunciated in the joint statement were not legally binding on either party, they did provide the foundation for continued TMD discussions between the two governments.[26]

Nevertheless, talks to formalize the TMD demarcation line languished in the Standing Consultative Committee during most of 1995. Since the Russians had accepted the U.S. position that flight-testing of THAAD components would not violate the ABM Treaty, the Clinton administration apparently was no longer in any rush to complete the talks. It was not until spring 1996 that progress was possible. On April 21, 1996, during a summit meeting in Moscow, Clinton and Yeltsin promised to try to complete a demarcation agreement on lower-velocity TMD systems by June, and a follow-on agreement covering higher velocity systems by October.[27]

The first objective was essentially achieved during the May 20 to June 24 session of the Standing Consultative Commission. The five parties affected by the ABM Treaty—Ukraine, Belarus, Kazakhstan, as well as the United States and Russia—reached preliminary agreement that the deployment of TMD systems with interceptor speeds of three kilometers per second or less would be permitted, provided that the systems were not tested against ballistic missile targets with velocities above five kilometers per second or ranges that exceed 3,500 kilometers. In addition to these parameters, the parties reaffirmed a 1978 U.S.-Soviet agreed statement clarifying the meaning of the treaty term "tested in an ABM mode." This initial demarcation agreement would clear the way for the deployment of the THAAD system, as well as lower-velocity systems like the army's PAC-3 system and the navy's Lower-Tier system.[28]

The five governments also reached preliminary agreement on a memorandum of understanding that would formally multilateralize the ABM Treaty, thereby officially making Ukraine, Belarus, and Kazakhstan parties to the ABM Treaty. In addition, the United States and Russia reached agreement on a series of confidence-building measures to accompany the agreed statement on lower-velocity TMD systems. These measures included advance notification of theater ballistic missile target launches and tests, invitations to observe TMD test launches, and assurances that TMD systems would not be deployed against the forces of the other side. The United States and Russia also agreed to regulations governing the multilateral operation of the Standing Consultative Commission.[29]

However, in 1996 the parties were not able to complete an agreement on high-velocity TMD systems, that is, interceptors above the five-kilometer velocity. Until such an agreement was concluded, the United States insisted that each side had the right to decide whether or not a missile system it was developing was in compliance with the ABM Treaty. The Clinton administration had already declared unilaterally that the navy's Upper-Tier system, which would have an interceptor velocity of up to 4.5 kilometers per second, was treaty compliant. The Russians, on the other hand, insisted that no unilateral decisions to flight-test higher-velocity systems should be made until an agreement regarding their compliance with the ABM Treaty had been concluded.

In this regard, Russian foreign minister Yevgeny Primakov sent a letter to Secretary of State Warren Christopher referring to previous assurances that he alleged the United States had made to the effect that it would not "conduct flight tests of high-velocity systems against any kind of targets for the next three years." Primakov also proposed an agreement affecting higher-velocity TMD systems that included these restrictions or exemptions: (1) limits on the velocity (5 kilometers per second) and the range (3,500 kilometers) of ballistic missile targets during tests of high-velocity TMD systems; (2) a ban on the use of targets with multiple reentry vehicles and strategic ballistic missile reentry vehicles during tests of high-velocity TMD systems; (3) a ban on space-based TMD interceptors; (4) a ban on space-based tracking and guidance sensors; (5) a ban on space-based TMD systems that make use of other physical principles; (6) no ban on TMD interceptors equipped with nuclear warheads; (7) discussion of limits on the basing of air-launched, high-velocity TMD systems; (8) limits on the parameters (maximum allowed velocity) for high-velocity TMD interceptors; (9) limits on testing conditions for high-velocity TMD systems; and (10) limits on the number and geographic deployment of high-velocity TMD systems.[30]

The Primakov letter elicited sharp criticism from congressional Republicans. Representative Robert Livingston (R-La.) said, "It's obvious the Russians want to close down our missile defenses." Likewise, Representative Curt Weldon (R-Pa.) claimed that Russia's proposed restrictions on high-velocity TMD systems were "outrageous." "If we give into what Primakov wants," he said, "this will be the single biggest cave-in in the history of American diplomacy."[31]

In spite of their differences over high-velocity TMDs, on September 23 Christopher and Primakov reaffirmed their commitment to the low-velocity TMD agreements and announced that the documents would be ready for signature by the end of October. They also agreed that the Standing Consultative Commission would reconvene on October 7 to prepare the low-velocity TMD documents for signature and begin negotiations on higher-velocity

TMD systems. However, on October 25 the Russians announced that they would not permit implementation of the low-velocity TMD agreement until a second-phase agreement dealing with higher-velocity systems had been concluded. The United States, strongly objecting to such linkage, said it was "inconsistent" with the understanding reached by Christopher and Primakov in September and called off the signing ceremony, leaving the talks once again in limbo.[32]

The Helsinki Summit, March 1997

Clinton and Yeltsin again attempted to break the demarcation stalemate at the Helsinki summit meeting in March 1997. In a joint statement issued at the end of the summit, the two presidents expressed their commitment to strengthening strategic stability and international security, emphasized the importance of further reductions in strategic offensive arms, and recognized the fundamental significance of the ABM Treaty for the fulfillment of these objectives. They also reaffirmed the principles of their May 10, 1995, Joint Statement and stated that they had instructed their respective delegations to complete the preparation of a TMD agreement on higher-velocity TMD systems as soon as possible.

The Helsinki Joint Summit statement also included a number of agreed statements: (1) that neither side had plans before April 1999 to flight-test, against a ballistic target missile, TMD interceptor missiles subject to the agreement on demarcation with respect to higher-velocity TMD systems; (2) that neither side had plans for TMD systems with interceptor missiles faster than 5.5 kilometers/second for land-based and air-based systems or 4.5 kilometers/second for sea-based systems; and (3) that neither side had plans to test TMD systems against target missiles with MIRVs or against reentry vehicles deployed or planned to be deployed on strategic ballistic missiles.

Clinton and Yeltsin also accepted the following elements for the agreement on higher-velocity TMD systems: (1) the velocity of the ballistic target missiles would not exceed five kilometers per second; (2) the flight range of the ballistic target missiles would not exceed 3,500 kilometers; (3) the two sides would not develop, test, or deploy space-based TMD interceptor missiles or components based on other physical principles that are capable of substituting for such interceptor missiles; and (4) the two sides would exchange detailed information annually on TMD plans and programs. The two presidents also noted that TMD technology was in its early stages and would continue to evolve.

Clinton and Yeltsin also agreed that developing effective TMDs, while maintaining a viable ABM Treaty, would require continued consultations. To this end, they reaffirmed that their representatives to the Standing Consultative Commission would discuss, as foreseen under the ABM Treaty, any questions or concerns either side may have regarding TMD activities, including matters related to the agreement to be completed on higher-velocity systems. Such an agreement would be based on this joint statement. The two presidents also recognized that there was considerable scope for cooperation in theater missile defense. They stated that they were prepared to explore integrated cooperative defense efforts, inter alia, in the provision of early warning support for TMD activities, technology cooperation in areas related to TMD, and expansion of the ongoing program of cooperation in TMD exercises. They also resolved to act in a spirit of cooperation, mutual openness, and commitment to the ABM Treaty.[33]

Despite the fact that the Russians essentially adopted the U.S. position on high-velocity TMD systems at Helsinki, Republican members of Congress reacted negatively. In a March 23 statement, House Speaker Newt Gingrich (R-Ga.), Representative Robert Livingston (R-La.), and Representative Chris Cox (R-Ca.) argued that the agreement "will halt the development of the most effective possible ballistic missile defense," a reference to space-based systems. "If allowed to stand, this agreement will place the lives of our brave fighting men and women—and ultimately millions of Americans—in jeopardy."[34]

The administration attempted to counter Republican criticism that the Helsinki summit crippled the U.S. TMD program. Rejecting the notion that there is a distinction between space-based interceptors deployed on TMD or ABM systems, Secretary of Defense William Cohen argued that the agreement's prohibition on the former is not a new restriction on U.S. missile defense capabilities because the ABM Treaty already explicitly bans space-based ABM interceptors.

Arms controllers, on the other hand, argued that the administration's position on high-velocity TMD systems would almost certainly have a deleterious impact on the ABM Treaty in the long term. Although the Helsinki agreement placed limitations on the parameters of ballistic missile targets and prohibited space-based TMD interceptors, arms controllers argued that it would allow the United States and Russia to deploy highly capable TMD systems that could become the basis for an NMD that would undercut the ABM Treaty and complicate the effort to achieve further nuclear force reductions.[35]

The Demarcation Agreement

In spite of Republican objections, on August 21, 1997, the five participating states in the Geneva-based Standing Consultative Commission—the United States, Russia, Belarus, Kazakhstan, and Ukraine—completed an agreed statement on so-called higher-velocity theater missile defense systems, marking the conclusion of nearly four years of complex negotiations to establish a "demarcation line" between permitted TMD and restricted ABM systems.

The agreed statement on higher-velocity TMD systems reiterated the ban on testing such systems against ballistic missile targets with velocities above five kilometers per second or ranges that exceed 3,500 kilometers. The statement also banned the development, testing, or deployment of space-based TMD interceptor missiles, and required an annual data exchange of TMD plans and programs. Each side agreed to continue to make deployment decisions on higher-velocity TMD systems based on their own national compliance determinations. The United States had already declared that the navy's Theater-Wide Defense system, scheduled for deployment in 2008, would be compliant with the ABM Treaty. A supplementary agreement on TMD confidence-building measures (which applies to both lower- and higher-velocity systems) attempted to reassure the United States and Russia that TMD systems are not being developed for national missile defense purposes.

In an effort to increase the transparency of TMD activities, these confidence-building measures required prior notification of TMD test launches as well as data exchanges pertaining to TMD plans, programs, and production. The memorandum of understanding on ABM succession designated the United States, Russia, Belarus, Kazakhstan, and Ukraine as the only parties to the ABM Treaty, thereby resolving the issue of which states would assume the rights and obligations of the former Soviet Union under the treaty. The latter four states collectively would be limited to ABM deployment at a single site. Finally, the agreement on SCC regulations details the new procedures under which the body will operate. This agreement became necessary in light of the multilateralization of the ABM Treaty.

However, before the SCC agreements could enter into force, they had to be ratified by the five involved parties. At this writing, it still remains unclear whether the TMD agreements are restrictive enough to placate the Russian Duma, which generally is skeptical of U.S. missile defense efforts, or are too restrictive to appease the U.S. Senate, which generally is opposed to any limitations on TMD programs. Some senators also oppose the agreement that multilateralizes the ABM Treaty, fearing that adding new states to the treaty will make amending the accord virtually impossible in the future.[36]

However, the successful development of the TMD systems approved in the Standing Consultative Commission agreements proved even more difficult to achieve than the negotiated agreement. As of early 1999, the army's THAAD system had consistently failed to intercept a ballistic missile in repeated tests. As a result, the schedule for deploying THAAD was set back from 2001 to 2006, although a limited version could be available earlier. The air force's airborne laser (ABL) was also experiencing serious problems. At issue is whether the laser is underpowered due to the amount of turbulence it encounters in the atmosphere, which diffuses the laser beam, resulting in insufficient destructive energy on the target. If the ABL's power is degraded, the system will have to be moved closer to the battlefield, making it much more vulnerable to enemy air attack. The study also noted that "the enemy can hit key targets in most scenarios by moving launch sites outside ABL range."[37]

Even the PAC-3, long considered the most technically mature TMD system, has experienced problems. A PAC-3 intercept test, initially scheduled for late February 1998, was postponed until later in the spring due to preflight software problems. In addition, the system was expected to amass $43 million in cost overruns above its fiscal year 1999 allocation of $343 million for procurement and $137 million for research and development. These difficulties, critics argued, demonstrated the immaturity of the TMD program.[38]

The Republican NMD Plan

Although Republicans supported (and even pushed the Clinton administration to build) tactical ballistic defenses, they were even more aggressive in advocating strategic ballistic missile defenses. Early in 1995, Republicans brought to the House floor Resolution 7, the national security portion of the so-called Contract with America. It contained a pledge to deploy both a national missile defense as well as theater missile defense systems "as soon as practical." But in a major surprise to its supporters, this renewed drive for Reagan's SDI stalled even while other elements of the contract went flying through the House. On February 15 the House voted 218 to 212 for an amendment offered by John Spratt (D-S.C.) that eliminated the commitment to deploy NMD. In a shrewd maneuver, Spratt forced the House to choose between military "readiness" and NMD—and readiness won out.

Sobered by this defeat, and aware of bipartisan skepticism about NMD, in

May 1995 the House National Security Committee (previously named the Armed Services Committee) tried to expand funds for an NMD in the annual defense authorization bill. The Republican-dominated committee pumped up funding for NMD by $628 million, almost double the Clinton administration's original request of $371 million. The committee also added $135 million to Brilliant Eyes, the space-based sensor that could replace ground-based radars.

Republicans argued that they were not out to destroy the ABM Treaty. Nevertheless, the Senate Armed Services Committee passed a resolution declaring that it was the policy of the United States to deploy multiple-site national missile defenses by 2003, an action that would have violated the treaty. The committee also added $500 million to the administration's original $2.9 billion request, bringing the total appropriation to $3.4 billion. Included in the increase was $300 million for NMD and $170 million for the navy's Upper-Tier long-range antimissile system. The bill also called for the creation of a new $145 million anticruise missile defense program and added $135 million to the administration's request for Brilliant Eyes.[39]

Critics immediately warned that the committee's effort to discard the ABM Treaty would kill both START I and START II. Unilateral U.S. action on the ABM Treaty, they asserted, would inflame hard-liners in the Duma, who already opposed START II ratification and thereby jeopardized an opportunity to eliminate between 5,000 and 6,000 Russian nuclear weapons aimed at the United States. Nevertheless, in an August 1 letter to other Republicans, Senate majority leader Robert Dole (R-Kans.) urged his party to "remain united behind the fundamental principle that America, Americans, and American interests must be defended."[40]

Dole largely got his wish. On August 3 an amendment by Senator Carl Levin (D-Mich.) to delete the anti-ABM Treaty portions of the bill lost 51 to 48. Only four Republicans voted with Levin; one Democrat voted with the majority. Almost every other amendment offered by Democrats on this bill was defeated. After the defeat of the Levin amendment, most Democrats joined together to threaten a filibuster of the defense authorization bill unless it was substantially changed. To this was added the threat of a presidential veto, which was made on August 4. As a result, the Republican majority felt compelled to seek a compromise with the Democrats.

The compromise bill excised the Republican commitment to deploy a nationwide defense and replaced it with new language that would commit the United States to "develop for deployment a multiple site" defense rather than commit the United States to "deploy." The compromise also deleted the 2003 deadline for an initial operational capability. Instead, it simply required the secretary of defense to develop a system "capable of attaining" that capability by 2003. Moreover, the new bill stated that before a final decision to deploy NMD, Congress would have to review the system for "affordability and operational effectiveness," as well as for the threat the system would address and its impact on the ABM Treaty. Finally, the compromise removed the prohibition on the president's negotiating with the Russians on the demarcation line between theater and national defenses. The newer version stated that if the president negotiated a new understanding on the matter, he would have to seek prior congressional approval before implementing it.[41]

Many Democrats criticized the compromise bill. They argued that it would have been better to spurn compromise with the Republicans precisely to avoid blurring the differences in the Republican and Democratic positions on the ABM Treaty. Accordingly, they urged the president to veto the bill, and Clinton obliged them by doing so later in the year. After Republican leaders were unable to muster enough votes to override his veto, they were forced to strip out the controversial ABM provisions from the defense authorization bill in order to get it enacted. Nevertheless, the Republican leadership announced that they intended to make NMD a key issue in their bid to defeat Clinton in his November reelection bid.[42]

The 1996 Defend America Act

On March 21, 1996, Senate majority leader Robert Dole and House Speaker Newt Gingrich introduced the Defend America Act, mandating deployment by 2003 of a nationwide system of satellites, radars, and missile interceptors. The bill stated that it was U.S. policy to deploy an NMD system by 2003 that "is capable of providing a highly-effective defense of the territory of the United States against limited, unauthorized, or accidental ballistic missile attacks" and that "will be augmented over time to provide a layered defense against larger and more sophisticated ballistic missile threats as they emerge." The legislation also called for an amendment to the ABM Treaty to permit the deployment of such an NMD system and, if the Russians refused to go along, for the United States to consider withdrawing from the treaty. Dole called the bill "one of the key defining pieces of legislation the Congress will consider this year," adding that "national missile defense must be America's top defense priority." Gingrich promised that it would be "the most important national defense debate since Churchill argued for building radar."[43]

The Congressional Budget Office (CBO) was asked to estimate the costs of implementing the act. Their answer, and the resulting sticker shock, halted efforts to pass the Defend America Act in the 104th Congress. According to CBO, "through 2010, total acquisition costs would range from $31 billion to $60 billion." CBO also estimated that it would cost an additional $2-$4 billion annually to operate and support the system. Congressional leaders asked CBO to recalculate the costs of several extremely limited single-site NMD systems. Deploying these systems would range between $4 billion and $13 billion. Operating and supporting the systems once deployed would add to the price tag. Most in Congress who favored the deployment of an NMD system, however, saw these options merely as a down payment on a much broader plan for a layered approach to defending the entire country from the potential threat of ballistic missiles. Moreover, none of the CBO estimates included planned spending on TMD.[44]

The Defend America Act obviously was designed to trigger another Clinton veto and provoke a confrontation with him during the presidential campaign. As a result, by May 1996 missile defense had become a major theme for conservative columnists, talk-show hosts, and editors. The *Wall Street Journal* lauded the bill in a series of editorials, as did the *New York Times* columnist William Safire. The Republican Party platform and its presidential and vice presidential candidate Robert Dole and Jack Kemp also embraced the issue. The entire conservative defense establishment was sure that the bill would be the wedge issue that would expose President Clinton's weakness in "failing to defend America."[45]

But NMD failed to work for the Republicans as an election issue. Independent polls and focus groups showed little public interest in the issue, and it was soon abandoned by Republican congressional candidates. Dole and Kemp barely mentioned the topic after the convention, even in their debates with Clinton and Vice President Al Gore. Although Congress pumped extra ABM funding into the budget, legislation mandating deployment of an NMD system never made it out of the House. Moreover, the missile defense issue never made a difference in the November election, with Clinton and Gore winning reelection."[46]

The Eclipse of NMD

What happened? Defense analyst Joseph Cirincione identified a number of reasons for the Republican failure to sell NMD. First, he contended, there was no credible threat that was easily perceivable to the public, nor was there likely to be one in the foreseeable future. Government intelligence assessments concluded that there were only two potential enemies that could strike the continental United States with land-based ballistic missile warheads: Russia, which would have 3,500 warheads under START II, and China, which had seven. Many felt that the certainty of swift U.S. retaliation was sufficient to deter a deliberate nuclear attack from either country. Although the danger of an accidental or unauthorized launch was real, it was not considered a major threat.

Like critics of TMD, critics of NMD argued that the Republican-advertised system would not work. In thirteen attempts against a variety of targets in tests conducted by the Department of Defense between 1982 and 1996, only two hits were achieved. Moreover, in both successful tests, the target was artificially enhanced to make interception easier. "If antimissile interceptors have such a poor record in controlled experiments, where their designers have months to create the ideal circumstances for success," Cirincione asked, "how can such complicated systems be expected to function in the white heat of combat?" The prodigious amount of money that has been spent, together with the modest results that expenditure has produced, he added, "is in itself testimony to the magnitude of the challenge at hand."[47]

Moreover, deploying the type of "thin" NMD that was now possible, whether at one site or several, whether ground based or sea based, could trigger unintended consequences. The Chinese, for example, might be prompted to protect the deterrent value of their nuclear weapons by equipping them with countermeasures designed to overcome U.S. defenses. Or they might speed up their ICBM modernization program to increase the quantity and quality of their missiles. It was precisely this kind of outcome that persuaded President Richard Nixon to negotiate the ABM treaty in the first place.

The absence of a credible threat, and the lack of effective NMD technology, might have been overcome had the military strongly supported the program. But the Joint Chiefs of Staff were more concerned about maintaining the existing force structure, modernizing existing weaponry, and defending against the current short-range missile threat to deployed troops. In January 1996, the JCS wrote that since "Russia and China are the only countries able to field a threat against the U.S. homeland, the funding level for [NMD] should be no more than $500 million per year and [TMD] should be no more than $2.3 billion per year." Such funding levels, they stated, would allow a "balanced and proportional" program that could meet war-fighting needs and still "save dollars that can be given back to the Services to be used for critical recapitalization programs." In other words, the JCS did not want to divert critical funds into a program that promised little real defense against a threat that might not develop for decades.[48]

In addition, the Joint Chiefs did not want premature deployment of a national defense system to scuttle nuclear arms reduction efforts. In May 1996 JCS chairman John Shalikashvili wrote Senator Sam Nunn that the Defend America Act might cause changes to the ABM Treaty that would trigger Russian withdrawal from the START process. "I am concerned," Shalikashvili wrote, "that failure of either START initiative will result in Russian retention of hundreds or even thousands more nuclear weapons, thereby increasing both the costs and risks we may face."[49]

Ignoring JCS opposition, in 1996 the Congress added $855 million to the President's $2.8 billion request for ballistic missile defense. This boosted the amount earmarked for NMD from $508 million to $833 million. Despite his opposition, President Clinton acceded to the funding increase in September, since it was part of the overall spending bill for the Department of Defense and included a pay raise for the troops.

The most important reason for the failure of the Defend America Act was the cost of the program. Between 1983 and 1993 the Strategic Defense Initiative Organization had spent $44 billion without producing any deployable systems or technological breakthroughs. Overall, according to a Brookings Institute study, the country had spent more than $100 billion in current dollars on missile defense efforts since the mid-1950s plus $17 billion on the Patriot system. In mid-May 1996, the Congressional Budget Office estimated that the new program would involve acquisition costs amounting to an additional $31 billion to $60 billion through 2010—much more than Republican leaders had estimated. A Heritage Foundation study had stated that an NMD would require only $7.3 billion over requested missile defense budgets through the year 2001—about what the Senate and House had planned to add to the missile defense accounts. However, the CBO estimated that its requirement for a "highly effective defense of all 50 states . . . augmented over time to provide a layered defense against larger and more sophisticated ballistic missile threats" would cost up to $60 billion for the deployment of ground-based interceptors, tracking stations, satellite sensors, and hundreds of yet-to-be-invented space-based interceptors and space lasers. Another CBO report, in July 1996, estimated the total cost of the proposed system at $116 billion over twenty years, including operation and support costs. The CBO estimates caused freshmen Republican deficit hawks in the House to revolt. They refused to support a major new government program, even one for national defense, causing the Republican leadership to pull the legislation from floor consideration. Despite efforts to reintroduce the bill, they could never muster sufficient support to do so.[50]

Clinton's Three-Plus-Three Program
In an attempt to take some of the steam out of the Republican effort to build a national missile defense system, the Clinton administration introduced its own NMD program in February 1996. Called the Three-Plus-Three plan, it proposed to develop an NMD within three years and, if necessary, to deploy the system within the following three years. If, as the administration expected, the threat had not materialized during that period, research would continue but deployment would not begin. Most of the $3 billion per year that would be spent on the program would be devoted to the development of THAAD and other medium-range interceptors.

However, the Clinton plan also included an NMD program but one that would conform to the ABM Treaty. It would consist of 100 interceptors deployed at a single launch site. The focus of the Clinton program was on the development of an exoatmospheric kill vehicle capable of intercepting incoming ballistic missile warheads before they could enter the atmosphere. The interceptors would be designed to counter an ICBM attack of several missiles launched at the United States from one of the so-called rogue states, such as North Korea, or a small, accidental launch from the more nuclear-capable states, such as China. If, by 1999, it was determined that the ballistic missile threat to the United States warranted the deployment of an NMD system, that system could be deployed three years later, that is, by the year 2003. However, if by 1999 the threat were judged insufficient to warrant deployment, the Three-Plus-Three program would preserve the option to deploy an NMD system within three years of a decision to do so by allowing continued development and testing of the system's elements.

In defending the Three-Plus-Three program, Secretary of Defense William Perry enunciated a new deterrent strategy that he claimed would replace mutual assured destruction (MAD). Called mutual assured safety (MAS), the new strategy implied that both the United States and Russia would develop NMDs with the capability to protect their homelands from limited nuclear attacks. But the administration did not intend to rely solely on ABMs to protect the United States against missile attacks. "Our first line of defense," Perry said, "is to prevent the spread of weapons and missile technology through a range of arms control and nonproliferation treaties, export controls and sanctions." These included the Nuclear Nonproliferation Treaty, the Intermediate-range Nuclear Forces Treaty, the Strategic Arms Reduction Treaties, a Comprehensive Test Ban Treaty, and the Missile Technology Control Regime, as well as other nuclear export controls. In addition, the Nunn-Lugar Cooperative Threat Reduction program would continue to "intercept" missiles on the ground by removing missiles with nuclear warheads from operational status in the former nuclear republics of the Soviet Union.[51]

The second line of defense outlined by Perry was designed "to deter the use of these weapons by maintaining strong conventional and nuclear forces and the willingness to retaliate" against an attacker. The conventional armed forces of the United States, he promised, could destroy any foe that used or threatened to use weapons of mass destruction. Conventional forces could also be employed to seek out and destroy missiles before they were launched. He said the only remaining logical role for nuclear weapons was as a deterrent against the use of nuclear weapons by others. Finally, Perry said, if these two lines fail, "we must also have a third line of defense—a program to deploy systems to defeat the threat by shooting down missiles of mass destruction." This option would be provided by the administration's Three-Plus-Three program.[52]

The 1996 National Intelligence Estimate
The gradual pace of developing ballistic missile defenses called for by the Clinton's administration's Three-Plus-Three program was supported by the U.S. intelligence agencies. They all agreed that any country other than Russia or China was unlikely to acquire a capability to strike the continental United States "during the next 15 years." Most missile-equipped countries, including Iran, Libya, and North Korea, they asserted, had only Scud-like missiles with a range of a few hundred kilometers, incapable of reaching the United States or Europe. Moreover, making the change from a short- or medium-range missile that could pose a threat to U.S. troops located abroad, to a long-range ICBM capable of threatening the continental United States, would require a major technological leap that the intelligence agencies did not think these states were capable of making quickly. In 1993 the CIA concluded that, at a minimum, North Korea would require nearly ten years to develop an ICBM capable of delivering a chemical or biological warhead and ten to fifteen years to develop an ICBM that could carry a nuclear warhead. In

1996 a national intelligence estimate concluded that the North Korean missile program would move more slowly than projected earlier.[53]

In response to these findings, conservative advocates of NMD accused the Clinton administration of "politicizing" the "intelligence assessment to hide the truth about the missile threat." Congress then mandated a special panel to critique the intelligence assessment, but the move backfired. In December 1996, the panel, which was headed by Bush CIA director Robert Gates, concluded that there was "no evidence of politicization." Moreover, the panel blasted as irresponsible "unsubstantiated allegations challenging the integrity of intelligence community analysts by those who simply disagree with their conclusions, including members of Congress." Finally, the panel agreed that the United States is unlikely to face an ICBM threat from the Third World before 2010, "even taking into account the acquisition of foreign hardware and technical assistance, and that case is even stronger than was presented in the estimate."[54]

The National Missile Defense Act of 1997

Nevertheless, Republicans continued to insist that the Clinton Three-Plus-Three plan was inadequate to meet what they considered to be the far more imminent threat of a ballistic missile attack upon the United States, its armed forces, or its allies by Russia, China, or rogue states. In an attempt to redress this "deficiency," on April 24, 1997, the Senate Armed Services Committee approved the "National Missile Defense Act of 1997." The vote was close, 10 to 8, and was divided along party lines.

Sponsored by the new Senate majority leader, Trent Lott (R-Miss.), the bill would require the United States to deploy an NMD by the end of 2003. The NMD would be capable of defending the territory of the United States against limited ballistic missile attack, "whether accidental, unauthorized, or deliberate," and "could be augmented over time to provide a layered defense against larger and more sophisticated ballistic missile threats if they emerge." Rather than the 100 interceptors at a single site called for in the Clinton plan, however, the Republican bill mandated the deployment of hundreds of interceptors at as many as half a dozen separate launch sites. Its layered defense would also include Reagan-era, space-based weapons such as lasers or kinetic energy interceptors. Moreover, the Republican plan required an immediate decision to proceed with deployment rather than the less demanding time line contained in the Clinton plan. While Lott's legislation "urged" the president to pursue negotiations with the Russians to amend the ABM Treaty, in order to permit deployment of the NMD system, it also required the United States to consider withdrawing from the treaty if the negotiations did not succeed within one year of the bill's enactment. However, the Lott bill did require another congressional vote on NMD deployment in 2000.[55]

In voting against the National Missile Defense Act, the committee's eight Democratic senators repeated the same arguments that they had used against the Defend America Act in the previous year. Again they insisted that NMD was unnecessary, unworkable, wasteful, and a threat to the nuclear arms control regime. Not surprisingly, Republican committee members took the opposite line on each Democratic criticism. They insisted NMD could work, was affordable, and was needed. Nor would it undermine nuclear arms control agreements or nuclear stability. Moreover, Republicans insisted, it was necessary to specify a firm deployment date in order to "provide focus and establish a sense of priority and urgency," something they charged the Clinton administration had failed to do.[56]

The Welch and Rumsfeld Panels and the American Missile Protection Act of 1998
In response to stepped-up pressure from Republicans to accelerate the testing and deployment of U.S. missile defense systems, the Pentagon released a report, dated February 27, 1998, which warned that accelerating missile defense testing schedules "is far more likely to cause program slips, increased costs, and even program failure" than to prove successful. Written by an independent panel composed primarily of former military officers and defense contractors, and headed by retired general Larry Welch, the study found serious problems with abbreviated testing schedules and reduced number of flight tests. The result, the report predicted, would be "a rush to failure."[57]

Not satisfied with the findings of the Welch Report, congressional Republicans decided to get a second opinion. They appointed a panel headed by Donald Rumsfeld, a former defense secretary. Released on July 15, 1998, the Rumsfeld Report challenged the official intelligence estimates. It stated that Iran and North Korea could develop weapons capable of striking U.S. territory sooner—within about five years of a decision to acquire—than government analysts had predicted and with little or no warning. The direct threat to the U.S. population, it concluded, "is broader, more mature and evolving more rapidly than has been reported in estimates and reports by the intelligence community." Not only are Iran and other terrorist states capable of producing a nuclear-tipped missile within five years, they are capable of bypassing extensive testing, which means, the Rumsfeld Report concluded, the warning time the U.S. will have to develop and deploy a missile defense is near zero. Adding force to the Rumsfeld Report were a number of ballistic missile launchings by Iran and Korea. On July 22, Iran tested its 1,300-kilometer-range Shahab 3, which was capable of reaching Israel, Turkey, and Saudi Arabia. Then, on August 31, North Korea tested its Taepodong 1 missile, with a range of 1,500-2,000 kilometers, sufficient to strike targets throughout Japan.[58]

Democrats countered by citing an August 24 letter to Senator James Inhofe (R-Okla.) by General Henry Shelton, chairman of the Joint Chiefs of Staff, which challenged the Rumsfeld Commission's assessment of the missile threat. Shelton wrote that the JCS "remain confident that the Intelligence Community can provide the necessary warning of the indigenous development and deployment by a rogue state of an ICBM threat to the United States." He concluded by reiterating his support for the administration's Three-Plus-Three program.[59]

Nevertheless, Republicans continued to push for rapid deployment of an NMD. In March 1998 Senator Thad Cochran (R-Miss.) introduced the American Missile Protection Act of 1998, which stated that it is U.S. policy "to deploy as soon as is technologically possible an effective National Missile Defense system capable of defending the territory of the United States against limited ballistic missile attack (whether accidental, unauthorized, or deliberate)." However, twice, in May and September, fifty-five Republican senators, and four Democrats, failed to end a Democratic filibuster against the bill by only one vote less than the sixty required for cloture. As a result, the Republicans would have to push for their NMD plan in the new Congress, which took office in January 1999.[60]

Antisatellite Weapons

Both the Clinton administration and the Republican-controlled Congress did agree on one point: that control of space had become critical to national security. But they disagreed over the right course to accomplish that mission. Clinton believed that the safety of America's satellites stood on U.S. and Russian willingness to refrain from taking aggressive steps against each other's satellites. As a result, the president used his newly acquired line-item veto power in October 1997 to kill a Republican-sponsored $37-million program to develop a kinetic energy antisatellite weapon. He also approved the Pentagon's decision to eliminate funding for concept work on an air force space plane—similar to the space shuttle—that could destroy enemy satellites.

The Republicans responded by charging that the president's actions were part of secret negotiations with Russia aimed at concluding an ASAT ban. However, General Howell M. Estes, commander in chief of the North American Air Defense (NORAD) and Space Command, said that no such negotiations were going on or were even contemplated. Yet discussions had been under way with Russia on a possible reporting agreement among countries that operate ground and space lasers. The reporting program for ground lasers would be much like the one in use for intercontinental ballistic missile tests, wherein warnings are given by the launching country so that planes and ships stay away from areas at which dummy warheads are aimed.

Under the U.S.-proposed agreement, laser operators in Russia and elsewhere could ask the U.S. Space Command, which maintains coverage of all items in space, whether the use of laser illumination in a particular area of space at a specific time might inadvertently hit an orbiting object such as a satellite, space shuttle, or space station. Space Command already performs this service for U.S. laser operators. "If such an agreement were reached with Russia," stated Robert G. Bell, counselor to the assistant to the president for national security affairs, "no details about the vulnerabilities of our satellites need or would be divulged."[61]

The impetus for discussions on a reporting agreement came from an October 17, 1997 test of the U.S. ground-based Mid-Infrared Advanced Chemical Laser (MIRACL) against an orbiting U.S. satellite. Army scientists hoped to use test data to assess how much destructive power could be trained on a satellite from a ground-based laser. Such weapons could prove useful in a war, given the ability of satellites to pinpoint arms and troops. The laser beam used in the MIRACL test generated some heat when it struck the satellite, but the craft was not seriously damaged. Nevertheless, the test prompted the Russian foreign ministry to warn that laser programs "may become a step toward creating an antisatellite potential." Although ASATs are not banned by treaty (U.S.-Soviet attempts to negotiate an ASAT treaty in the late 1970s failed), both sides had exercised restraint in the development and deployment of systems that could threaten satellite functions considered vital to intelligence collection as well as commercial communications. Under a 1971 agreement, neither the United States nor Russia can interfere with each other's space-based missile early-warning systems. But such obligations are not binding in the event of war or self-defense.

The Russians also warned that the MIRACL test could undermine the ABM Treaty, which prohibits space-based ballistic missile interceptors, including lasers. The deployment of ASATs, the Russians added, would threaten the mutual retaliatory capabilities of both sides. In response, a Pentagon spokesman said the MIRACL test "had nothing to do with attempting to shoot down satellites and absolutely nothing to do with ballistic missile defenses." He said U.S. officials had sought to make it clear to Russian officials that the test's object was "to evaluate the vulnerability of U.S. satellites to lasers." Pentagon critics, however, argued that the test clearly threatened the goal of maintaining space as a sanctuary for earth-orbiting satellites.[62]

In 1989 a Democratic Congress, concerned about the costly and provocative nature of such ASAT activities, passed an amendment to the fiscal year 1990 defense authorization bill that specifically prohibited test-firing MIRACL at a satellite in space. However, in 1995 the Republican-dominated Congress, interested in sustaining the laser project and exploring its ASAT and ABM potential, refused to renew the five-year prohibition. Shortly before Secretary of Defense Cohen's October 2 decision to permit the MIRACL test, some congressional Democrats, including minority leader Richard Gephardt, Ronald Dellums, and John Spratt, called for its postponement. In a September 26 letter to President Clinton, they said, "We are deeply troubled that a test of a ground-based laser system with such obvious ASAT warfare capabilities would proceed ahead of any debate or deliberate policy development." Senator Tom Harkin (D-Iowa) also warned that "the United States should not start an unnecessary and expensive ASAT arms race." However, Cohen obviously accepted the explanation offered by General Estes that the test was necessary to give the United States the capability to "enforce the peace" in space by deploying defense systems against enemy ASATs.[63]

Accidental Nuclear War

Yet the potential threat to satellites posed by lasers may not be the greatest danger that the command, control, and intelligence-gathering systems of the United States and Russia will face in future years, as an incident on January 25, 1995 demonstrated. On that day, Russian early warning radar detected the launch of a rocket from the Norwegian coast. The rocket was a four-stage Norwegian-U.S. joint research missile, called Black Brant XII. Ninety-three seconds after launch, the fourth stage of the rocket burned out, hurling it and its payload nearly straight up into the atmosphere before they fell back into the sea. Although the Russian government had been notified of the launch several weeks before, inexplicably the news never reached Russia's Strategic Rocket Forces Command. As a result, Russian radar operators mistakenly believed the scientific rocket was a missile heading for Russian territory. They also misinterpreted the separation of the rocket's multiple stages for an attack by several missiles. These errors immediately raised the specter of an American first strike.

According to Nikolai Devyanin, chief designer of the Russian nuclear "suitcase" (the nickname for the codes required to launch Russian nuclear forces), the radar operators experienced crushing pressure while deciding how to treat the missile launch. They realized that they could have been reprimanded for a panicky, false reaction. But they also remembered how Mathias Rust, a young German civilian, flew a small plane through Soviet air defenses in 1987 and landed it in Red Square, an incident that led to the dismissal of the top military officers responsible for Soviet air defense. Consequently, the radar operators decided to issue an alert of an unidentified missile with an unknown destination. The alert was sent up the chain of command all the way to President Yeltsin, who felt compelled to call for his nuclear suitcase for the first time in his presidency. Fortunately, most probably because tensions between Russia and the United States had been quite low for some time, Yeltsin prudently waited for more information. Had U.S.-Russian relations been strained, the dangerous situation caused by having nuclear forces on a hair-trigger status could have ended in a nuclear holocaust.

Bruce Blair, a senior fellow at the Brookings Institution in Washington, who has written extensively on Soviet and Russian command and control systems, said the significance of the episode was the confusion that marked the period during which Yeltsin would have had to make a real "launch-on-warning" decision. He pointed out that the Soviet Union and Russia have experienced attempted coups, rebellions, and even collapse over the last decade, and it is possible in the future that a Russian leader could be called upon to make crucial decisions concerning nuclear weapons during another upheaval. Even though the Cold War has ended, the high-alert, nuclear-launch mechanism that existed throughout the Cold War still remains in place.[64]

"The prospect of a mistake," Vladimir Belous, a retired general and leading Russian strategist, wrote recently, "has become particularly dangerous." "A fateful accident," he warned, "could plunge the world into the chaos of a thermonuclear catastrophe, contrary to political leaders' wishes." This possibility is even more likely now than before because Russia's command and control system is suffering from many of the problems that confront its entire military establishment. Russia's early warning radar and command infrastructure is old and crumbling, raising the possibility that it will be even less able to discern between future civilian rocket activities and a real nuclear attack. Electronic circuits and computers that control Russia's nuclear forces, for example, frequently, and for no apparent reason, switch to a combat mode. In addition, the economic depression that has plagued the Russian people also has produced hardship for those who work in nuclear command installations. Moreover, the breakup of the Soviet Union has left many Russian radar installations in other republics. The resulting gap in radar coverage has grown more serious as these installations have been closed. Colonel General Vladimir Yakovlev, commander of Russia's strategic rocket forces, has predicted that the shutdown of the Russian radar station at Skrunde, Latvia, by the Latvians, will seriously strain Russia's warning network.[65]

In September 1998 Clinton and Yeltsin signed an accord designed to help fill the developing gaps in the Russian early warning system. It provided for the instantaneous sharing of data about the launch of ballistic missiles and space payloads. If Norway launched another scientific rocket, for example, the United States would quickly provide data on the origin and time of the launch, its trajectory, and moment of expected impact. There would no longer be tense moments for Russian commanders struggling to figure out if a foreign missile launch was malevolent or benign. Bruce Blair said the accord also would help Moscow and Washington better understand the spread of missile technology in the Third World and could be the basis for cooperation on ABM defenses.[66]

However, a 1998 report by the Carnegie Commission on Preventing Deadly Conflict concluded that "the current operational conditions of much of the Russian [nuclear] inventory cannot be safely sustained." Due to this worsening situation, the Carnegie report endorsed a proposal by several prominent analysts that the United States and Russia "eliminate the practice of alert procedures and set an immediate goal to remove all weapons from active deployment."[67]

The Carnegie proposal would go much further than a 1994 Clinton-Yeltsin joint statement, announcing that U.S. and Russian missiles would no longer be targeted on one another. Sergei Rogov, director of the USA-Canada Institute and a leading strategic analyst, called the joint statement "a step back from a trigger-happy situation" but also "a gimmick, because it's reversible in one or two minutes." In fact, according to a Russian specialist, Russian missiles can be retargeted in ten to fifteen seconds. Nor does the 1994 agreement alleviate concern about an accidental Russian launch, since an unprogrammed missile would automatically switch back to its primary wartime target, which might be a Minuteman silo in Montana or a command center in Washington, London, Paris, or Beijing. And Russian missiles, like their U.S. counterparts, cannot be ordered to self-destruct once they are launched.[68]

Like Russia, the United States also maintains a launch-on-warning policy that was put into place during the Cold War. However, the Clinton administration slowly realized that keeping over 5,000 U.S. and Russian strategic nuclear weapons in a hair-trigger posture was dangerous. As a result, the Pentagon began studying ways by which the United States could verifiably and safely take its nuclear weapons off alert. Options included pinning open the switches that allow a missile's engine to fire, immobilizing silo lids, requiring that submarines receive two command messages authorizing the firing of submarine-launched ballistic missiles, and sharing real-time early warning information with the Russians. The ultimate goal of these ideas is to ensure that national command authorities have stricter control of nuclear weapons so that in a crisis "automatic" responses are slow enough to allow the opportunity to defuse the unfolding situation and reduce the potential for a nuclear holocaust "by mistake."[69]

Others have suggested that the United States, because it possesses the most robust forces and cohesive command structure, should take the lead in a new round of voluntary actions by announcing that it will withdraw the warheads that most threaten Russia's nuclear deterrent forces, particularly those capable of hitting Russian missile silos and underground command posts. The most menacing warheads are those deployed on the fifty MX silo-based missiles, which are armed with ten warheads each, and the 400 high-yield w-88 warheads fitted atop some of the missiles on Trident submarines. They would also immobilize all of the land-based Minuteman IIIs (about 500 missiles), which are armed with three warheads each, reduce by half the number of submarines deployed in peacetime, and cut the number of warheads on each submarine-borne missile from eight to four. They also recommended altering the operation of ballistic missile submarines so that crews would require approximately one day to ready missiles for launching. These measures would still leave almost 600 U.S. warheads remaining invulnerable at sea, each capable of destroying a great city, more than enough to deter any nuclear aggressor. Such a dramatic shift would demonstrate that the United States does not pose a first-strike threat to Russia and do much to persuade the Russians to follow suit and take most of their missiles off hair-trigger alert.[70]

The Decline of Russia's Strategic Nuclear Arsenal
What makes Russia's command and control problems even more worrisome is the fact that, with its conventional military capability having deteriorated significantly in the wake of the Cold War's end, the Russians have come to rely even more than before on their nuclear forces and on a launch-on-warning policy as the mainstay of their strategic defense policy. On December 17, 1997, Yeltsin signed Russia's first post-Soviet national security "concept," which stated that Russia "reserves to itself the right to use all the means and powers it has in its possession, including nuclear weapons, if as a result of unleashing an armed aggression, there will appear a threat to the very existence" of the state. This policy repealed a pledge made by Mikhail Gorbachev that the Soviet Union would not to be the first to use nuclear weapons, a pledge the United States has never made. Defending the new policy, Lev Volkov, a prominent Russian military strategist, said that, with Russia's conventional forces drastically reduced, "all we have is the nuclear stick . . . we have nothing else. We're naked. Can you imagine that?"[71]

Paradoxically, however, in the years ahead, Russia will have less nuclear weapons on which to rely for its defense. According to Russian and Western specialists, Russia will have an arsenal of 1,000-1,500 warheads a decade from now, fewer than the limit envisioned in START III. Lev Volkov estimates that even with robust economic growth, Russia will have only 700 warheads a decade from now. Sergei Kortunov, a top Kremlin defense aide, has written that "with a lot of effort" Russia might reach 1,000 warheads by 2015. However, it could fall to half that number if the economy does not recover. That would put Russia in league with China, which is estimated to have 400 warheads today—a number roughly equivalent to the total held by Britain, with 260, and France, with 440. By contrast, in 1990 the Soviet Union had 10,779 strategic nuclear warheads—a figure that does not include Russia's estimated 6,000-13,000 nonstrategic, smaller nuclear weapons, which have never been covered by arms control treaties.[72]

The main reason for this precipitous decline in the size of the Russian strategic nuclear arsenal lies in the fact that Russia is not replacing the nuclear-armed submarines, long-range bombers, and intercontinental ballistic missiles that the Soviets built during the Cold War. As a result, they are declining dramatically in both number and quality. The Russian landscape is littered with stark evidence of this decline.

At Russia's northern and far eastern ports, nuclear-powered submarines are piling up in watery junkyards. Of sixty-two strategic submarines deployed by the Soviet Union in 1990, the Russian navy currently has only twenty-eight, of which, twenty-three are operational, according to some reports. Most of the rest have been junked or are waiting to be scrapped. At the peak of the Cold War, twenty to twenty-two Soviet submarines were at sea. Today, there are usually only two on patrol, and they do not go far from their bases. One of the most fearsome symbols of Soviet power was the Typhoon, the largest submarine ever built, carrying twenty missiles armed with ten warheads each. In the event of a nuclear attack, the six Typhoons completed between 1980 and 1989 could have launched 1,200 nuclear warheads. But in 1998 only half the Typhoons were operational. Three of the huge boats have been taken out of service. A new missile planned for them has yet to materialize, and it is unclear whether they will ever sail again. Russia started construction in November 1996 on a new generation of strategic submarine, the Borey Class, but only 1 percent of the first submarine was completed in the first fifteen months of work. The new missile planned for the submarine has failed four times.

Once the pride of the Soviet Air Force, the Blackjack bomber has also fallen on hard times. The largest group of Blackjack bombers is rusting away in Ukraine. Russia has only six Blackjacks, built in 1991, currently deployed at Engels Air Base in the Volga region. A Russian military source said that only four of them are combat ready. A few more Blackjacks are partially finished or are being used as trainers. Even the core of the Russian strategic deterrent, the missile force, is expected to shrink dramatically in the years ahead. Most of the missiles built in the 1970s and 1980s are due to be retired or decommissioned if the START II treaty is ratified. This includes the ten-warhead "heavy" missile, the ss-18, which embodied the destabilizing threat of multiple-warhead missiles. Russia's force of ss-19 six-warhead missiles also would be reduced and fixed with only one warhead each. The abolition of multiple warheads was the chief accomplishment of the START II Treaty.

Even if START II is not ratified, obsolescence will overtake Russian missile forces in the next decade. Lev Volkov explains, "Everything ends. In 22 or 23 years, a moment comes when everything starts to collapse or fall apart. Each piece of equipment has a moment when the construction simply gets old . . .

the silo, the container, the body of the missile . . . are corroded, fungus eats through the metal, things start to grow on it—God knows what." General Vladimir Yakovlev, chief of strategic rocket forces, said that 62 percent of Russia's missiles are already beyond their guaranteed service life. Moreover, as the factories that made the missiles grind to a halt and the workers and designers leave for other jobs, the problem of maintaining the existing force becomes acute. Scavenging for spare parts has become the usual practice.[73]

Another Russian specialist on strategic missiles, Yuri Balashov, warned that Russia's older SLBMs are also wearing out. He publicly criticized the military leadership for prolonging their use, which he said risks a catastrophe. Balashov said that liquid-fueled intercontinental ballistic missiles have become corroded and degraded by age, making them potentially unreliable. He said corrosion and "natural weakening" of the missiles' metal parts heightens the risk of an unintended explosion. Russia, he charged, is risking "hundreds of Chernobyls" by keeping the rockets in service.[74]

Balashov's comments were made in the wake of an unexplained incident aboard a Russian nuclear missile submarine in the Barents Sea on May 5, 1998. According to a Western source, the stricken nuclear-powered submarine sent an emergency call for help and had to be escorted to its base on the Kola Peninsula in northern Russia. As a result, panic swept the nearby cities of Murmansk and Severomorsk, where schools were closed and residents bought iodine to counter the effects of a possible radiation leak. Two days later, however, Russian officials said there had been no accident and there was no reason for panic. Yet the Western source said that there had been a leak or an explosion in the fuel tank of one of the missiles aboard the submarine. This source said there was no radiation leak but that the missile was damaged, apparently by its highly toxic fuel.[75]

U.S. strategic forces, by contrast, are relatively modern. And even older systems, like the land-based Minuteman missiles and B-52 bombers, have been upgraded and are expected to remain in service for many years to come. General Eugene Habiger, commander of U.S. strategic forces, does not "see the United States even thinking about having to modernize any of our forces until the year 2020."[76]

The decline of Russia's strategic forces explains, in part, the eagerness of some prominent Russian military and political analysts to find a way out of their country's cocked-trigger nuclear embrace with the United States—if only because Russia's dwindling forces demand it. "The model of nuclear deterrence that existed during the Cold War must be radically changed," said

Vladimir Dvorkin, director of a Russian think tank, "since it is senseless right now to deter the United States from an attack, nuclear or conventional, on Russia." But the traditional arms control process is at an impasse as a result of the Duma's failure to ratify the START II agreement. As a consequence, some Russians are now suggesting that Russia abandon bilateral negotiations with the United States and unilaterally create a small and "sufficient" nuclear force similar to France's *force de frappe*.[77]

As an apparent step in this direction, in December 1997 Yeltsin surprised many when he declared that "we, in a unilateral manner, are reducing by another third the number of nuclear warheads." Yeltsin's press secretary, Sergei Yastrzhembsky, said he was referring to a future START III arms control treaty with the United States. But later, back in Moscow, a senior Russian defense strategist shook his head at Yastrzhembsky's explanation. Yeltsin's comment, he said, captured perfectly what is happening to Russian strategic forces. "They are running out of steam, out of money, and out of time."[78]

The Future of START

It seems obvious that the decline of the Russian nuclear threat offers an unprecedented opportunity to end the nuclear arms race once and for all. Yet some still argue that the United States, as the only global superpower, does not need to match the steep Russian decline. Indeed, proponents of ballistic missile defenses see Russia's declining strategic forces as an opportunity to make the United States invulnerable to nuclear attack by building an NMD that could deal effectively with a much smaller Russian nuclear attack. But, opponents of NMD fear that if the prospect of its deployment threatens to render Russia incapable of retaliating in the response to a U.S. first strike, the Duma will never ratify START II, let alone a START III that calls for even fewer Russian nuclear warheads.

On the other hand, if the ABM Treaty remains intact, there will continue to be compelling reasons for the Duma to ratify the START II Treaty. Failure to ratify the treaty would leave Russia at a strategic disadvantage relative to the United States. If the Duma ratifies START II, the parity ratio of strategic nuclear forces between Russia and the United States will be 1:1. If they fail to do so, Russia will be in a position of nuclear inferiority at the strategic level by a ratio of 1:3. Yet even if the Duma does approve START II—and this is the irony of ironies—the potential for blocking its implementation will shift back to the U.S. Senate, which must approve a protocol to give the Russians more time to make the reductions required by the START II TREATY.[79]

As an even more difficult obstacle that will have to be overcome before START II goes into effect, the theater missile defense agreements will have to be attached to the ABM Treaty. Senator Jesse Helms and other conservative Republican senators have made it quite clear that they want to take a "careful look" (meaning they would like to defeat) some aspects of the TMD package, including the second agreed statement on higher-velocity TMD systems. The Republicans also want to look at the multilateralization of the ABM Treaty that is called for in the memorandum of understanding signed by the United States, Russia, Ukraine, Belarus, and Kazakhstan. They believe that multilateralization will make more difficult any future amendment of the ABM Treaty, including amendments that could make "legal" a national ballistic missile defense system. For another, some Republicans believe that if they defeat multilateralization, they will in effect kill the ABM Treaty. Oklahoma senator James Inhofe, for example, called the treaty "a mistake in 1972 and even worse policy today." He called consideration of the ABM Treaty amendments "an opportunity [to] kill the ABM Treaty, which certainly is outdated."[80]

The Clinton administration, on the other hand, had hoped to win Senate approval of the amendments by tying them to the prospect of major Russian strategic force reductions called for in START II and proposed for START III. "If you want further nuclear reductions," the administration was telling Republican senators, "you have to go along with the ABM Treaty amendments." However, with the Russian nuclear arsenal shrinking of its own accord through aging and attrition, Republican opponents of the ABM Treaty may feel they do not have to accept Clinton's alternative. The future of START, needless to say, is tied to the outcome of the battle over the ABM Treaty amendments.[81]

6

Clinton and Counterproliferation

NPT Extension

Throughout his presidential campaign, President Clinton made the elimination of nuclear, biological, and chemical weapons—as well as the ballistic missiles that could deliver them—a top priority of his administration. Perhaps the most important counterproliferation program of the Clinton administration was the effort to gain international support for the indefinite extension of the Nuclear Nonproliferation Treaty. With 181 parties in 1995, the NPT had entered into force in 1970 but was scheduled to expire in 1995 if not renewed. The administration argued that indefinite extension of the NPT was essential for global and regional stability, for preventing the spread of nuclear weapons, and for facilitating and regulating cooperation among states in the peaceful uses of nuclear energy.[1]

Although the nonweapon states as a whole supported the idea of renewing the NPT, several of them demanded concessions by the weapon states before they would approve its indefinite extension. The Arab states, led by Egypt, refused to endorse any proposal for the extension of the NPT unless pressure was brought on Israel to accede to the NPT and to accept full-scope safeguards. At the same time, the Iranians accused the developed states of violating their obligation (under article 4 of the NPT) to permit Iran access to peaceful nuclear technology. The failure of the weapon states to negotiate a comprehensive test ban treaty, as called for in article 6 and the preamble of the NPT, was another source of friction. Indeed, two of the four review conferences (in 1980 and 1990) broke up without achieving a consensus on a final declaration because of disagreement over language relating to the failure to negotiate a CTBT.[2]

But the core issue in any debate extending the NPT indefinitely hinged on the willingness of the weapon states to implement their promise to bring about nuclear disarmament. To be sure, Russia and the United States were able to point to their significant nuclear arms control achievements as proof that they were heading in that direction. They had eliminated their intermediate-range nuclear forces and would substantially reduce their long-range nuclear weapons in START. Shorter-range weapons also were reduced and withdrawn from operation without a formal treaty. Yet even if strategic warheads on each side fell to about 3,500, as called for in the START II Treaty, there would still be more nuclear warheads deployed on land- and submarine-launched strategic missiles than there had been in 1970, when the NPT went into effect. Although welcoming the START agreements, the nonweapon states expressed the hope that "the ultimate goal of the complete elimination of nuclear arsenals will be attained within a specific time frame," and called upon Britain, China, and France "to actively participate in this endeavor."[3]

As a way of putting pressure on the weapon states to move toward nuclear disarmament, a core group of fourteen nonaligned states led by Indonesia suggested extending the NPT for a series of rolling fixed periods of twenty-five years each. The decision to renew the treaty after each of these intervals would depend on the achievement of certain goals, including the implementation of a CTBT and legally binding assurances by the weapon states that they would not use or threaten to use nuclear weapons against nonweapon states. The nonweapon states also wanted an international agreement calling for the cutoff of weapons-usable fissile material production as well as the elimination of nuclear weapons and other weapons of mass destruction.[4]

Among the other measures favored by the nonweapon states was the achievement of NPT universality, that is, bringing under the treaty's coverage Israel, India, and Pakistan—at the time, all undeclared nuclear powers. Mexico, for its part, said it would accept an indefinite extension of the NPT only if a CTBT were completed by 1996 and the nuclear powers halted the production of nuclear weapons and began serious work toward reducing their arsenals to zero. In addition, the Mexicans demanded that all states (and the weapon states in particular) promise to respect all nuclear weapon-free zones. Among the nuclear-free zones in effect or in the process of being implemented in 1998 were those in Latin America (Treaty of Tloltelolco) and Southeast Asia (Treaty of Bangkok). Progress also was made toward securing the entry into force of the African Nuclear Weapon-Free Zone Treaty (Treaty of Pelind-aba). It was signed by forty-seven African states and ratified by six as of April 1998.[5]

As a way of encouraging indefinite extension of the NPT, the Clinton administration gave strong support to a CTBT "as soon as possible." On January 30, 1995, the president extended the moratorium on U.S. nuclear testing (which he had continued in 1993) through at least September 1996, when the nuclear powers were expected to sign a CTBT. The United States also urged all other nuclear-weapon states to observe a moratorium on testing. All except China and France agreed to do so.[6]

Clinton also directed a review of U.S. policy on security assurances. In 1978 the United States and Britain had provided certain limited negative security assurances expressly to NPT nonnuclear weapon states. France and the Soviet Union also issued limited negative security assurances in 1978, but they did not link them specifically to the NPT. China, for its part, declared as early as 1964, when it exploded its first nuclear device, that it would not use nuclear weapons against any nonweapon state. However, many nonweapon states considered these assurances inadequate; they wanted the adoption of a common and legally binding agreement by all the nuclear weapon states. They specifically called for a more explicit role for the U.N. Security Council in the event of nuclear aggression against NPT nonweapon states. In an attempt to satisfy these concerns, each of the nuclear weapon states made additional comprehensive security assurances. In addition, on April 11, 1995, the Security Council unanimously adopted Resolution 984, recognizing these national declarations. The action did much to ease the security concerns of the nonweapon states.[7]

Going one step further, a November 1997 presidential decision directive "reaffirmed" the negative security assurance that was given by the United States in 1995, just before the indefinite extension of the NPT. That pledge stated that "the United States reaffirms that it will not use nuclear weapons against non-nuclear-weapon States Parties to the [NPT] except in the case of an invasion or any other attack on the United States, its territories, its armed forces or other troops, its allies, or on a State toward which it has a security commitment, carried out or sustained by such a nonnuclear-weapon State in association or alliance with a nuclear-weapon State."[8]

At the NPT Extension Conference, which was held in New York from April 17 to May 12, 1995, the nonweapon states presented three documents to the assembled delegates. The first provided for a review conference every five years, as had been the case for the previous twenty-five years. But in the future, before each review conference, there would be more systematic preparation for discussion on substantive issues.

The second document contained a set of twenty principles and objectives for nuclear nonproliferation and disarmament. Among them was a call for the completion of a CTBT no later than 1996, "systematic and progressive efforts to reduce nuclear weapons globally, with the ultimate goal of eliminating those weapons," and general and complete disarmament under strict and effective international controls. The document also recommended that parties to the NPT which had been slow to sign and bring into force comprehensive safeguards agreements should do so "without delay." It also asserted that research into (and the production and use of) nuclear energy for peaceful purposes is an "inalienable right of all parties to the treaty."

The third document in the compromise package, "Extension of the Treaty," simply noted that the treaty would be extended indefinitely because a majority favored it.

On May 11, 1995, conference president Jayantha Dhanapala of Sri Lanka employed a procedure sometimes used at the United Nations when there is no consensus for a proposal. He obtained the consent of the delegations to proceed with the adoption of the three draft documents without a vote. He then declared each of the decisions adopted. Partly because of these efforts, and fear of the consequences if the NPT were allowed to expire, the NPT Review and Extension Conference voted overwhelmingly to indefinitely extend the treaty.[9]

Disarmament versus Deterrence

Many delegates from the nonweapon states, however, were angry that the nuclear weapon states had obtained an indefinite extension of the NPT without themselves being required to accept a deadline for the complete elimination of their nuclear weapons, as called for in article 6 of the treaty. The nonweapon states argued that the fulfillment of this obligation was the key to successful nuclear nonproliferation policy. Simply put, their argument was that if the "haves" gave up their nuclear weapons, the "have-nots" would no longer seek them. By disarming, the nuclear weapon states would provide an example for would-be proliferators to follow. The latter, then, would have no reason to seek nuclear weapons as a deterrent against the weapon states. The possession of nuclear weapons would be discredited and would no longer be an acceptable means of acquiring international prestige.

Moved by this reasoning, in late 1995, for the first time ever, a majority in the U.N. General Assembly called for the elimination of nuclear weapons within a fixed time period. The resolution, introduced by Myanmar (formerly Burma), called on the nuclear weapon states "to stop immediately the qualitative improvement, development, stockpiling, and production of nuclear warheads and their delivery systems." The resolution also called on the U.N. Conference on Disarmament to establish a committee that would "commence negotiations early in 1996 on a phased program of nuclear disarmament, and for the eventual elimination of nuclear weapons within a time-bound framework." After a divisive debate in the General Assembly, the Myanmar resolution was adopted on December 12, 1995, by a vote of 106 to 39, with seventeen abstentions. However, Britain, France, and the United States strongly opposed the resolution and voted against it. China voted for the resolution and Russia abstained, as did U.S. allies Australia, New Zealand, and Japan.

The debate at the United Nations made clear that the nuclear weapon states had no intention of eliminating their nuclear arsenals, at least not in the foreseeable future. Rather than disarmament, the weapon states obviously believed that nuclear deterrence would be necessary for the indefinite future. The resumption of French and Chinese nuclear testing shortly after the close of the NPT conference only rubbed salt into the wounds of the non-weapon states. The tests, they argued, were inconsistent with the political commitment made by the nuclear powers at the NPT extension conference to "exercise the utmost restraint" regarding testing pending the completion of a CTBT.

Japan then proposed a compromise resolution that proved easier for the nuclear weapon states to swallow. It reaffirmed the notion that nuclear weapons should be ultimately eliminated but without calling for the imposition of a deadline. It received a larger affirmative vote than the Myanmar resolution—154, with 10 abstentions. The United States, Russia, Britain, and France voted for the resolution, and China abstained. In response to the watering down of the Myanmar resolution, however, the nonweapon states reminded the weapon states that proliferation could not be stopped unless they were willing to eliminate their own nuclear arsenals.[10]

Cutting Off the Production of Fissile Materials

Partly to reduce the pressure for nuclear disarmament, in September 1993 the Clinton administration proposed a ban on the production of fissile material for use in nuclear explosives. At the Geneva-based Conference on Disarmament, the U.S. delegation proposed three bilateral measures to implement a fissile material cutoff treaty (FMCT). The first called for negotiations to establish a regime that would monitor the inventories of fissile material obtained from the nuclear warhead dismantlement process. The second proposed the exchange of the names and locations of all facilities used to dismantle nuclear warheads, as well as the places their fissile material would be stored. The third proposal recommended that each party be permitted to conduct reciprocal "familiarization" visits and inspections at all facilities containing highly enriched uranium obtained from dismantled nuclear warheads.

Clinton was not the first to propose a fissile material cutoff. President Dwight Eisenhower did so in 1956. But Eisenhower's proposal was rejected by the Soviet Union, which feared being frozen into a status of quantitative nuclear inferiority relative to the United States. However, in January 1989 Mikhail Gorbachev embraced the cutoff idea, as did Boris Yeltsin. This time, however, the United States rejected the idea; the Bush administration believed it would undermine the U.S. ability to maintain a credible nuclear deterrent. By adopting the FMCT, Clinton changed the U.S. position dramatically: instead of an isolated opponent of a fissile cutoff, the United States became its leading proponent.

The Clinton administration argued that an FMCT would constitute a decisive check to the nuclear arms race by ending the production of the material used in nuclear weapons. Moreover, a fissile cutoff would also reduce the discriminatory nature of the nonproliferation regime by stripping the nuclear weapon states of their exclusive title to produce unsafeguarded fissile materials. Thus an FMCT would make universal the basic commitments already undertaken by the nonweapon states that had signed the NPT. In addition, it would limit the development of incipient weapon programs in the de facto nuclear weapon states (India, Israel, and Pakistan), whose stocks of fissile materials were believed to be relatively small. Finally, a cutoff, along with a comprehensive nuclear test ban, would represent a major step toward the ultimate goal of nuclear disarmament.[11]

In December 1993 the U.N. General Assembly responded to the Clinton initiative by passing a resolution, without opposition, calling for talks on an FMCT. To build support for it, Washington tried to orchestrate a joint announcement by the five weapon states to the effect that they were halting the production of fissile materials for weapons. The United States, for its part, was already observing a fissile material cutoff, since it had stopped producing highly enriched uranium for weapons in 1964 and ceased producing plutonium for nuclear weapons in 1988.

The Russians also were willing to sign an FMCT. In the late 1980s, the Soviet Union had terminated production of highly enriched uranium and had drastically reduced the production of plutonium. Deep cuts in Russia's nuclear arsenal eliminated the strategic need for additional plutonium. Moreover, the Russians realized that a positive position on the issue would help persuade the other former Soviet republics to become responsible members of the international nonproliferation community. Finally, the Russians could hardly ignore Congress's action tying the release of Nunn-Lugar funds for the construction of a plutonium storage facility in Russia to presidential certification that the Russians were committed to terminating the production of weapons-grade plutonium.[12]

In a June 1994 meeting of U.S. Vice President Al Gore and Russian Prime Minister Viktor Chernomyrdin, the two sides formally agreed to halt the production of plutonium for nuclear weapons. Under the agreement, Russia would shut down its three remaining plutonium-production reactors by 2000 and allow the United States to verify that any plutonium produced by these reactors in the interim was not being used for weapons. In exchange, the United States agreed to "facilitate" Russian acquisition of alternative energy sources to replace the closed-down reactors.

Britain also agreed to participate in a fissile material cutoff. It announced at the NPT extension conference that it had "ceased the production of fissile material for explosive purposes." But China and France declined to make such an announcement, even though the Chinese privately had informed the United States that they had stopped fissile material production, and the French had announced in May 1993 that they had halted the production of plutonium for weapons. China was reluctant to sign any agreement that would permanently establish its quantitative inferiority to the United States and Russia, especially when it appeared that the United States was developing antiballistic missile systems that could negate the Chinese nuclear retaliatory capability.[13]

But a more important obstacle to progress on a fissile material cutoff was the opposition of Pakistan, India, and Israel. The Pakistanis did not want to lock their fissile material stockpile into a position of permanent inferiority relative to India. Pakistan's stockpile of weapon-grade uranium at the time was probably 100-200 kilograms. India, by comparison, had an estimated stockpile of 300-400 kilograms of weapon-grade plutonium. Moreover, India's government was under increasing pressure from nationalist forces to delay a fissile cutoff that would cap its stockpile of weapon material at a level far lower than China's. Israel, for its part, was not interested in even discussing the subject, and the United States was reluctant to press the Israelis on the issue, wanting to keep their attention focused on their peacemaking effort with Syria and the Palestinians.

The Clinton administration did attempt to change the minds of the Pakistanis and Indians, however. It offered to resume U.S. military assistance to Pakistan, which had been terminated by the Bush administration in 1990 because of concern about Pakistan's nuclear program. Specifically, Bush suspended the delivery to Pakistan of thirty-eight F-16 fighter planes that the Pakistanis had bought from the United States in the late 1980s. In March 1994 the Clinton administration suggested that it would finally deliver the planes if Pakistan would agree to produce only low-enriched uranium, agree to do so under IAEA safeguards, and forswear the production of fissile materials for either military or civilian purposes. But Pakistani prime minister Benazir Bhutto rejected the plan because it did not place similar restrictions on India until a later date. Pakistan also threatened to complete and operate a half-finished plutonium production reactor unless India agreed to halt its production of plutonium and reduce its stocks to the same level as Pakistan's. However, in late 1994, the Pakistanis agreed to support a fissile cutoff in exchange for a statement that existing stockpiles would be discussed during the negotiations.[14]

The Pakistanis were not the only ones who insisted that mandatory fissile material reductions be a part of an FMCT. Algeria, Egypt, and Iran, along with Pakistan, led an effort to broaden the Conference on Disarmament's mandate to include negotiations of reductions so that "unsafeguarded stocks are equalized at the lowest possible level." They were prompted to do so by a realization that the proposed FMCT would result neither in the elimination nor the safer management of a single kilogram of the estimated 248 metric tons of weapon-grade plutonium and 2,285 metric tons of highly enriched uranium on the planet (of which 104 and 994 metric tons, respectively, were produced by the United States). Even after the planned elimination of hundreds of tons of weapon-grade plutonium and uranium by START, the United States alone would still retain as much as fifty tons of plutonium and a few hundred tons of weapon-grade uranium—enough to make more than 10,000 thermonuclear warheads.

Nor would the cutoff under consideration in Geneva address the tons of nuclear material used in, or recovered from, civilian power and research reactors. As of 1990, the planet was home to 122 metric tons of reactor-grade civilian plutonium, which had been separated (recovered from) spent or irradiated nuclear fuel, and another 532 metric tons of reactor-grade plutonium in civilian, spent-nuclear fuel that had not been separated. Moreover, the amount of plutonium on the planet continued to grow by 60-70 tons per year, as plutonium was separated from spent nuclear fuel to be used as reactor fuel.

However, the expansion of the negotiations to include existing stockpiles of fissile materials was unacceptable to the nuclear-weapon states. They insisted that the negotiations concentrate only on future production of fissile materials for military purposes. Britain, France, and China, in particular, stated that they would not support a fissile-material cutoff if their existing stocks were involved. In fact, their support for the fissile material ban was tenuous at best because they regarded their own stockpiles as relatively small compared to those of the United States and Russia. In the end, the negotiating mandate adopted for the Conference on Disarmament in March 1995 gained consensus because it blurred whether a cutoff regime would apply solely to future production, as advocated by most nuclear weapon states, or include stockpiles, which some conference members (particularly Egypt and Pakistan) desired.[15]

In an overture aimed at getting the talks moving, on March 1, 1995, President Clinton ordered a major reduction in the U.S. stockpile of materials used to make nuclear warheads. Under the order, the U.S. government's stores of highly enriched uranium and plutonium would be reduced by 200 tons, roughly half the total U.S. stockpile, and enough for thousands of nuclear weapons. Clinton pledged that the 200 tons of material would "never again be used to build a nuclear weapon." Administration officials said the highly enriched uranium removed from weapons stockpiles would be converted to civilian use.[16]

It seemed unlikely, however, that even such dramatic reductions were going to be sufficient to persuade China to reduce its stockpile to India's level or to persuade India to reduce to Pakistan's amount. The only way to eliminate completely the discriminatory nature of the NPT, many argued, was to eliminate all nuclear warheads and unsafeguarded fissile material. And since the nuclear weapon states are opposed to what is for them such a drastic measure, the prospect of implementing an FMCT in the foreseeable future remains bleak. Given the lack of progress made on the FMCT, it is understandable why the Clinton administration was eager to turn its attention to the effort to conclude a comprehensive test ban treaty.[17]

The Demise of Nuclear Testing

Although President Clinton entered office with a positive attitude toward a comprehensive test ban, he permitted both sides to express their arguments before announcing his administration's position. The law passed by Congress in 1992 allowed fifteen safety and reliability tests before September 30, 1996. Pressing for those tests to be conducted before the cutoff deadline took effect were the Energy Department, the Joint Chiefs of Staff, the Defense and State Departments, and the National Security Council. These organizations also recommended that the administration push for a one-kiloton-threshold version of a CTBT, a "CTBT Lite," that would enable the United States to continue nuclear testing.[18]

Advocates of a CTBT were appalled by these recommendations. They asserted that testing after September 30, 1996, would be a clear violation of Congress's intention, that is, the end of all U.S. tests by 1996. They pointed out that legislation passed in 1992 permitted the United States to resume testing only if "a foreign state conducts a nuclear test after this date." Concerning the legislation, Sen. Mark Hatfield (R-Ore.) said, "It's not a limited ban. It's a ban. B-A-N." Furthermore, if the Clinton administration had pushed for a one-kiloton test threshold, the Russians and the French (both of whom had testing moratoria in place) would have resumed testing. This might have doomed efforts to achieve a true CTBT and could have torpedoed the prospects for an indefinite extension of the NPT.[19]

President Clinton decided that additional nuclear tests were unnecessary. On July 3, 1993, he announced that "after a thorough review," his administration had "determined that the nuclear weapons in the U.S. arsenal are safe and reliable." Moreover, he announced that he had decided to extend the moratorium on U.S. nuclear testing until at least September 30, 1994, "as long as no other nation tested." In response, France and Russia immediately extended their previously declared moratoria. However, the British, who had lobbied for a continuation of testing in order to put improved safety devices on their D-5 submarine-launched ballistic missile warhead, were compelled to become a partner in the international moratorium because they used U.S. test facilities.[20]

The Chinese responded to these moratoria by conducting a nuclear test on October 5, 1993, a step that provoked an international outcry. However, the Chinese called the criticism leveled at their country unjustified, pointing out that of the five declared nuclear weapon states, China had conducted the smallest number of nuclear tests. (By the time the United States stopped testing on September 23, 1992, it had conducted 1,030 tests, 51 percent of all tests. The Soviet Union, which conducted its last test on October 24, 1990, had accumulated a total of 715 tests. Russia had not tested since becoming the nuclear successor state to the former Soviet Union. When France finally stopped testing on January 27, 1996, it had tested 210 nuclear devices, 10 percent of all tests. When Britain halted its tests on November 26, 1991, its total was 45 tests, 2 percent of the total. After conducting a nuclear test on June 8, 1996, China announced that it would test one more device before beginning a unilateral moratorium and joining a CTB. That final test was conducted on July 29, 1996, bringing China's total to 45 tests, 2 percent of all tests.) President Clinton, in a reversal of his initial position, did not use the Chinese test to justify resuming U.S. testing. Instead, he renewed his commitment to complete a CTBT by 1996, and he urged China to refrain from further tests. Britain, France, and Russia took a similar line.[21]

A Zero-Yield Ban

The CTBT negotiations began on January 25, 1994, in the Conference on Disarmament in Geneva, with all five nuclear weapon states participating. By September 1994 the rough outline of a treaty was ready, but it contained tiers of brackets denoting major remaining disagreements, including (1) whether tests related to warhead safety, as demanded by France and Britain in "exceptional circumstances," or "peaceful" nuclear explosions, as desired by China, would be permitted; (2) whether the United States would get a ten-year "easy-out" clause to facilitate withdrawal from the treaty at the mandated ten-year review conference, if the resumption of testing were deemed necessary by the president; (3) whether China, supported by the nonweapon countries, would get language related to no first use, the "complete prohibition and thorough destruction of nuclear weapons," and universal security assurances to nonweapon states.[22]

Prospects for a CTBT were boosted by the extension of the NPT in the spring of 1995. To get it, the United States abandoned its CTBT easy-out proposal, and France and Britain dropped their demands for safety tests. However, within days of the vote for an indefinite extension of the NPT, China exploded another nuclear weapon. A few weeks later, the new French president, Jacques Chirac, announced that France would break its moratorium and conduct up to eight tests in the South Pacific between September 1995 and May 1996. Both nations asserted that they would be ready to sign a CTBT after their respective test series ended.

The Pentagon, in turn, began pushing the administration to propose that the treaty permit tests with yields equivalent to as much as 500 tons of TNT. Had that proposal been accepted by the administration, it would almost certainly have derailed the CTBT talks by converting a "comprehensive" test ban into a "low-threshold" test ban. The other nuclear powers also wanted a low-threshold test capability. Russia advocated a ten-ton threshold, France one of 200-300 tons, and Britain one of 40-50 kilograms. The administration remained officially committed to a "zero yield" ban, but it defined zero yield as being no more than four pounds of TNT equivalent. This definition would have preserved the U.S. right to conduct so-called hydronuclear experiments, that is, tests that produce data from minuscule fission yields. China did not engage directly in the threshold debate because it wanted the treaty to permit peaceful nuclear explosions. But the Chinese let it be known that they would not accept the very low thresholds advocated by the United States and Britain because they believed that such tests would benefit only the powers with the most sophisticated nuclear weapons-testing technology.

To the nonweapon state delegations in Geneva, many of whom had opposed indefinite extension of the NPT because they discounted the weapon states' commitment to nuclear disarmament, the desire of the weapon states to preserve a test capability was another example of their arrogance and bad faith. In response, Indonesia and India each introduced proposals that would have widened the scope of the CTBT to include all tests related to nuclear weapons, whether explosive or not. By mid-1995, the prospect for concluding a CTBT looked bleak indeed.

Yet on August 11, the deadlock on low-yield testing began to break down after the United States released a report by the so-called Jason Committee, which consisted of fourteen nuclear and security experts commissioned by the Energy Department, revealed that subkiloton tests would be of only marginal utility in ensuring stockpile safety. The report prompted the Clinton administration to support a true zero-yield ban. Under the new Clinton plan, no hydronuclear tests would be permitted. France, which had announced its own zero-yield decision, reacted favorably. But the Russians and British were furious that they had not been adequately consulted before the U.S. announcement. However, lacking an independent test site, Britain had no alternative but to adopt the zero-yield concept, a step they took in September 1995. The Russians, however, did not do so until the Moscow nuclear summit, the following May.

Thanks to the new zero-yield positions assumed by the weapon states, the possibility that a CTBT would be concluded in 1996 improved. However, India, which had supported a CTBT for more than four decades, began to have second thoughts about it. The Indians now faced the prospect that their nuclear program would be frozen. In the fall of 1995, the Indian government initiated preparatory work for nuclear testing at its Pokharan site, where the 1974 nuclear explosion had taken place. News of these preparations led to accusations in the Western media that India was planning a test, although no final decision to do so had actually been made. This in turn touched off a public debate in India, fanned by a hotly contested election campaign in which opposition to a CTBT, the retention of a full nuclear option, and the right to test were equated with India's independence and international status by the nationalist Hindu Bharatiya Janata Party.

When test-ban negotiations resumed in Geneva in January 1996, India presented a set of proposals to prohibit the "qualitative improvement and development" of nuclear weapons and to make the treaty's conclusion and implementation dependent on a commitment by the signatories to a timetable for nuclear disarmament. Many viewed New Delhi's gambit as an attempt to scuttle the treaty so as to permit India to resume nuclear testing. Nevertheless, a number of nonaligned delegations also pushed for stronger language on nuclear disarmament. But the nuclear powers dismissed this effort by saying it was solely motivated by India's desire to resume testing. This caused more resentment on the part of the nonweapon states toward the nuclear powers.[23]

Subcritical Tests

Nonweapon states' fear that the nuclear powers might use technological advances to circumvent the purpose of a CTBT, which had been somewhat allayed following the zero-yield decisions in 1995, were revived with a vengeance after an announcement by the U.S. Energy Department that a program of "subcritical" tests using chemical rather than nuclear explosions would begin in June 1996. The Energy Department argued that, in addition to their scientific value, the proposed tests would have the additional advantage of employing "many of the facilities and skills necessary for [a] resumption of nuclear testing . . . at a cost comparable to exercises that would be necessary in the absence of subcritical experimentation."[24]

The decision to perform the tests underground was partly a response to political and economic pressure from the state of Nevada. Its congressional delegation had lobbied for continued use of the Nevada test site, which had suffered layoffs as a result of the nuclear testing moratorium. In 1995 the Energy Department awarded the Bechtel Nevada Corporation a five-year, $1.5 billion contract to manage and operate the site, which employed about 3,500 people. When the subcritical experiments (at $20 million apiece) were announced, the *Reno Gazette-Journal* reported that Nevada Senators Richard Bryan and Harry Reid believed that "the tests should stabilize employment at the test site."[25]

Although subcritical experiments were not banned by the proposed CTBT (because they employed chemical rather than nuclear explosives), they raised concern that they would complicate the effort to verify compliance with a CTBT, since some fissile material would be involved. Observed from earth-orbiting satellites, a subcritical test would be virtually indistinguishable from any other underground experiment, including a hydronuclear test. Moreover, seismic data would not be able to determine what fraction of the energy from an explosion was chemical in nature and what amount was nuclear.

However, following appeals to President Clinton from key Western allies, who were afraid that subcritical tests could derail the CTBT negotiations, the tests were quietly postponed. But much damage had been done. The credibility gained by the weapon states when they adopted the zero-yield provision was undermined by the U.S. proposal to permit subcritical tests. The nonnuclear weapon states, as a whole, wanted a total ban on testing. A number of them called for closing all nuclear test sites. In response to this pressure, the French test site was closed. But the Clinton administration made it clear that the United States intended to preserve "the basic capability to resume nuclear test activities prohibited by the CTBT" should it ever be in the country's "supreme national interests" to do so. However, China finally agreed to the prohibition against peaceful nuclear explosions, requiring only that the issue be reviewed in ten years.[26]

Remaining CTBT Issues

There were two other issues that confronted the CTBT conference at this point. One was the proposed treaty's entry-into-force provision; the other was its on-site inspection provisions. With respect to the first issue, Russia, Britain, China, Pakistan, and Egypt wanted to make sure that the CTBT could not take effect until all eight nuclear weapon states, declared and undeclared, agreed to participate. However, the majority of states at the Geneva Conference disliked the coercive entry-into-force proposal. The United States and France, in particular, feared that such a provision would give India the power to kill the treaty. The United States preferred a more flexible provision based on the ratification by a certain number of states, including the five declared nuclear powers. This would avoid backing India into a diplomatic corner. India itself suggested sixty-five ratifying states, the number named in the entry-into-force provision of the 1992 Chemical Weapons Convention. However, Britain, Russia, China, and Pakistan were adamant that India must sign and ratify the treaty, making the prospect that a CTBT would be implemented in the foreseeable future poor indeed.

Meanwhile, the United States had its own "treaty breaking" issue: on-site inspection. The Clinton administration wanted quick and unrestricted U.S. access to foreign nuclear facilities, and it wanted the right to use information gained by national technical means—earth-orbiting satellites—to support an inspection request. China, however, opposed the use of national technical means and insisted that an inspection be authorized only if agreed to by two-thirds of the executive council of the Comprehensive Test Ban Treaty Organization. During negotiations among the declared nuclear powers in June and July, Britain, France, and Russia had been willing to accept an on-site inspection decision-making procedure based on an affirmative "three-fifths" majority vote of the executive council's membership. After hard bargaining, however, during which China's support for the treaty seemed to hang in the balance, the United States accepted China's proposal that at least thirty members of the fifty-one-member executive council would have to approve an on-site inspection before it could occur. India's delegate, Arundhati Ghose, was furious that the treaty text had been amended at the behest of the United States and China, whereas India's disarmament or entry-into-force proposals were ignored. Editorials in Indian newspapers reacted by warning that India would not be ignored in the future if it conducted a nuclear test, built nuclear weapons, and declared itself a nuclear weapon state.[27]

In mid-August, India carried out its threat to prevent adoption of the CTBT by the Geneva Conference. The treaty was finally rescued on August 22, 1996 when Australia sponsored a resolution in the General Assembly calling upon all countries to sign and become parties to the treaty "at the earliest possible date." On September 9 Australia's resolution, to which the treaty draft was attached, was cosponsored by 127 nations. The next day, the General Assembly endorsed the treaty by a vote of 158 to 3. Only India, Bhutan, and Libya voted against it. The General Assembly's action set the stage for individual countries to sign the treaty. On September 24 President Clinton became the first world leader to do so. Within one week, ninety-four nations had followed suit, including the other four declared nuclear powers (Russia, China, France, and Britain) and Israel, one of the three so-called threshold states. The other two, India and Pakistan, refused to sign, despite appeals from the international community. Arundhati Ghose, India's chief test-ban negotiator, declared that India would "never sign this unequal treaty, not now, nor later."[28]

Having signed the CTBT, the Clinton administration focused its attention on getting the Senate to ratify it. But given the opposition to the treaty in the Republican-controlled Senate, that task did not appear easy. Unlike the Chemical Weapons Convention, which was largely negotiated during Republican administrations and signed by President Bush, the negotiation of a comprehensive test ban was opposed by both Reagan and Bush, as well as by the 1996 Republican Party platform on which Robert Dole ran for president. Moreover, the CTBT was signed by the Republicans' archrival, President Clinton.

Even though France and Britain became the first nuclear weapon states to ratify the treaty, in April 1998, the CTBT remained locked in the Senate. By then, the treaty had been signed by 149 countries and ratified by 13. However, the CTBT cannot enter into force until it has been signed and ratified by the five declared nuclear weapon states, in addition to India and Pakistan, which tested nuclear weapons in May 1998, Israel, which is still an undeclared nuclear weapon state, and thirty-six other countries that are participating members of the U.N. Conference on Disarmament and are recognized by the IAEA as possessing nuclear power and/or research reactors. Whereas all forty-four key states—with the exception of India, North Korea and Pakistan—had signed the treaty by 1998, only six states had ratified it. They are

Austria, Japan, Peru, Slovakia, Britain, and France. India argued that the treaty did not go far enough in spelling out a timetable for global nuclear disarmament, whereas Pakistan said it would not sign unless India did. If the required forty-four countries do not ratify the treaty before September 1999, a conference will be convened to explore ways to accelerate the treaty's entry into force. Until the CTBT enters into force, however, all signatories are bound by article 18 of the Vienna Convention on Treaties, which requires them not to undertake any action that violates the treaty's purpose or intent.[29]

As if this were not enough, some believed that the Pentagon and the intelligence community would go to any length to scuttle the treaty. In August 1997 they reported that the Russians had conducted a nuclear test at their Novaya Zemlya site near the Arctic Circle that was equivalent to an underground explosion of less than 100 tons of TNT. Later data analysis, however, determined that the event was an earthquake centered about eighty miles southeast of Novaya Zemlya, in the Kara Sea. But ten weeks passed before the CIA acknowledged this. Some believed that the CIA was unnecessarily slow in clarifying the true nature of the event, intentionally casting unfounded doubt on the U.S. ability to monitor international compliance with the CTBT.[30]

To counter this impression, which was accepted by Republicans in Congress, the Clinton administration said it had insisted on—and had obtained—the inclusion of very high standards of verification in the CTBT. The treaty provided for four major types of global monitoring systems: seismological, underwater sound, atmospheric infrasound, and the sampling of radionuclides produced by nuclear explosions. In addition to these monitoring systems, the treaty permitted the United States to use its national technical means of verification, that is, intelligence gathering systems that included satellite imagery and other types of sensors. With regard to seismology, the treaty provided for a global network of 170 stations and also an international data center. In addition, auxiliary seismic stations would be built around the world and particularly in areas (e.g., the Middle East) in which there is great concern about proliferation. In an effort to counter opposition to the CTBT in the Congress, the Clinton administration agreed to spend $45 million over ten years to enable U.S. weapon laboratories to develop ways to check the reliability of bombs without detonating them, including computer simulation.[31]

During his January 1998 State of the Union address, President Clinton urged the Senate to give its advice and consent to allow ratification during that year. He also announced that four former chairmen of the Joint Chiefs of Staff—Generals John Shalikashvili, Colin Powell and David Jones, and Admiral William Crowe—had endorsed the treaty. However, the former JCS chairmen conditioned their support for the treaty on the "six safeguards" established by Clinton in August 1995 and reiterated in his September 1997 transmittal letter to the Senate. Under these safeguards, the United States would conduct a stockpile stewardship and management program to ensure the safety and reliability of its nuclear arsenal. The United States would also maintain modern nuclear laboratory facilities and programs in theoretical and exploratory nuclear technology, and it would preserve the basic capability to resume nuclear testing, if necessary. The United States would also continue a comprehensive research and development program to improve its treaty monitoring capabilities and operations. It would continue developing intelligence gathering and analytical capabilities and operations on worldwide nuclear arsenals and programs. Finally, the United States would retain the option of withdrawing from the CTBT under the "supreme national interests" clause in the event that a type of nuclear weapon critical to the U.S. nuclear deterrent could no longer be certified as safe and reliable.[32]

Yet the endorsement of the CTBT by the former chiefs of the JCS was not nearly enough to persuade Sen. Jesse Helms, chairman of the Foreign Relations Committee, to even begin the ratification process. In a January 21, 1998, letter to Clinton, Helms announced that his committee would only consider the treaty after it had voted on the ABM demarcation and multilateralization agreements. This condition obviously would delay Senate action on the CTBT because the administration had stated that it did not intend to submit the ABM agreements (along with the START II extension protocol) to the Senate for its advice and consent to ratification until after Russia had approved the START II Treaty—a move that might not occur for some time. In his letter to Clinton, Helms stated that the CTBT was "very low" on the Senate Foreign Relations Committee's list of priorities. He added that it had "no chance of entering into force for a decade or more," considering that at least two of the states required to ratify it before it could go into force, Pakistan and India, were unlikely to do so.[33]

In his reply to the Helm letter, Clinton restated his strong support for the test ban. "Rather than waiting to see if others ratify the CTBT," he wrote, "I believe America must lead in bringing the CTBT into force." With regard to India and Pakistan, Clinton added that when he traveled to the subcontinent, later in that year, it would be important that he do so "with U.S. ratification in hand." But by then, the CTBT had become a part of the Duma-Senate nuclear arms control logjam. The Duma appeared to be waiting on the Senate's ratification of the CTBT before acting itself, and the Senate appeared to be in no rush to approve the CTBT until the Duma ratified the START II Treaty.[34]

Dealing with Rogue States: North Korea
While pushing multilateral efforts to prevent the proliferation of nuclear weapons, the Clinton administration also took unilateral and punitive action against states that threatened to "go nuclear." This involved more overt forms of pressure on noncooperating states and a greater readiness to impose sanctions and threaten military action when such states failed to heed Washington's warnings.

North Korea experienced the first application of the more aggressive Clinton counterproliferation policy. When Clinton entered the White House in 1993, the North Koreans were operating a twenty-five-megawatt reactor at Yongbyon, some sixty miles north of the North Korean capital of Pyongyang, which was ideally configured to produce plutonium for nuclear weapons. They also were building two larger reactors and were expanding a large reprocessing facility, which eventually could have produced enough plutonium for dozens of nuclear weapons every year. Suspecting that the North Koreans had hidden some of the plutonium believed to have been extracted from fuel rods that were removed from the Yongbyon reactor in 1989, the IAEA demanded access to the facility. But North Korea refused, saying IAEA inspection would be an infringement on its sovereignty. More ominously, on March 12, 1993, North Korea announced its intention to withdraw from the NPT. The result was an international crisis that continued well into 1994.[35]

In a series of speeches during July 1993, Clinton warned that the United States was prepared to use force—even extreme force—to punish unacceptable proliferation behavior by "outlaw regimes." In a visit to the demilitarized zone separating North and South Korea, he took an even more aggressive stance. It would be "pointless," he said, for the North Koreans to build nuclear weapons in the face of certain U.S. retaliation in the event of their use. "It will be the end of their country," he threatened. Clinton also reinforced U.S. military capabilities in South Korea and threatened to impose tough economic sanctions on North Korea if it failed to discontinue its efforts to manufacture nuclear weapons.[36]

At the same time, however, Clinton also indicated that his preferred approach to the North Korean threat was diplomacy, and he offered the North Koreans economic incentives to persuade them to discontinue their nuclear weapon program. He made some progress. The North Koreans, who were seeking international assistance for their disintegrating economy, were willing to talk to the United States. In June 1993, after a round of intense negotiations, the United States persuaded the North Koreans to suspend their withdrawal from the NPT. However, the North Koreans continued to block IAEA inspections of their nuclear facilities. As a result, in early December 1993, IAEA director general Hans Blix declared that his agency's safeguards in North Korea could no longer provide "any meaningful assurances" that nuclear materials were not being diverted to weapons uses.[37]

Yet on December 29, 1993, the United States and North Korea reached an agreement designed to end the stalemate. It was based on four points: (1) the United States would suspend a joint U.S.-South Korean military exercise called Team Spirit; (2) the North Koreans would permit the resumption of IAEA inspections; (3) "working-level contacts" between North and South Korea would "resume in Panmunjom"; and (4) the third round of high-level U.S.-North Korea talks would begin March 21. The U.S.-North Korean agreement, however, did not take into account the wishes of the South Koreans. They insisted that they would not call off Team Spirit until a North-South exchange of special envoys took place and the North agreed "to full nuclear inspections." When the United States accepted the South Korean conditions, Pyongyang reacted by accusing the Americans of reneging on the December 29 agreement. The North Koreans again refused to permit the IAEA inspections.[38]

In mid-May 1994, the North Koreans escalated the confrontation with the United States by abruptly shutting down the Yongbyon reactor and initiating the removal of its spent fuel rods. Once the rods cooled, they could be reprocessed, extracting four or five bombs' worth of plutonium. The reactor could also be refueled and restarted, generating even more spent fuel. The United States responded by obtaining the U.N. Security Council's endorsement of sanctions against the North Koreans. The United States also dispatched military reinforcements to Korea. The reactor shutdown and the threat of sanctions led to the most acute crisis in U.S.-North Korean relations since the end of the Korean War.[39]

The North Korean crisis eased, however, after former President Jimmy Carter conducted a personal peacemaking mission to Pyongyang on June 16-

17, 1994. Carter persuaded North Korea's leader, Kim Il Sung, to freeze North Korea's nuclear program in return for a promise of fresh talks with the United States. These negotiations, which did not take place until early August because of Kim's sudden death on July 9, proved successful in hammering out an agreed statement on August 12, 1994. Under its terms, North Korea agreed to dismantle the parts of its nuclear program that could be linked to the production of nuclear arms. In return, the United States agreed to supply North Korea with two less proliferation-prone light-water reactors and provide interim energy supplies until the reactors were operational. North Korea also said it would remain bound by the NPT and would implement its safeguards agreement. The two sides also agreed to establish liaison offices in Washington and Pyongyang and to reduce barriers to trade and investment as moves toward the full normalization of political and economic relations. In addition, the United States promised that it would not use, or threaten to use, nuclear weapons against North Korea. The North Koreans, in turn, reaffirmed their commitment to implement the 1992 North-South Joint Declaration on the Denuclearization of the Korean Peninsula.[40]

But this latest U.S.-North Korean agreement was again stymied by the South Koreans. They decried the absence of any specific North Korean commitment to special IAEA inspections, which they believed to be essential in order to determine whether or not North Korea had a bomb. The South Koreans also opposed any moves toward diplomatic normalization between North Korea and the United States. South Korean president Kim Young Sam formally offered to supply North Korea with the two nuclear reactors promised by the United States, but he attached conditions sufficient to ensure that North Korea would not accept them, including special inspections of North Korea's nuclear facilities. Predictably, the North Koreans rejected the South Korean demand for special IAEA inspections. They also objected to getting South Korean reactors, calling them "unsafe, uneconomical, and politically unsuitable." However, the North Koreans did agree to accept reactors from an international consortium, as long as an American firm acted as its prime contractor. But the United States insisted that the only country willing to supply replacement reactors was South Korea.[41]

After a period of continued stalemate, the parties finally signed the Agreed Framework on October 21, 1994. In mid-January 1995 the United States began delivery of nearly $5 million worth of heavy fuel oil to the North and partially lifted decades-old sanctions against Pyongyang. The U.S. moves followed the IAEA's confirmation that North Korea had halted construction of its two nuclear reactors, sealed its reprocessing facility, and had not refueled its small nuclear reactor or diverted any of the spent fuel it unloaded.[42]

In April 1998, however, the Clinton administration said that lack of money could bring to a halt work in North Korea on one of the two nuclear power plants under construction, which are the centerpieces of the four-year-old deal to stop that country's nuclear weapons program. The United States, Japan, and South Korea had difficulty working out a payment plan for the $5.1 billion project. The accord calls for South Korea to pay about 70 percent, Japan about 20 percent, and assorted countries the remainder of the costs of a nuclear plant that would supply power for energy-starved North Korea. But the governments in Seoul and Tokyo, both struggling to cope with a financial crisis afflicting Asia, had trouble winning parliamentary approval for their share of the money. As a result, in May 1998 North Korea suspended compliance with the 1994 nuclear freeze agreement, contending that the United States is behind schedule in heavy fuel shipments and in its preparations to build the new reactors, which were to be completed by 2003. The North Korean government decided to unseal the nuclear reactor at Yongbyon, which under the agreement was to have been closed permanently. They also barred technicians from packing the last of the reactor's spent fuel rods for shipment out of the country. In addition, as 1998 came to an end, they continued to refuse to allow international inspection of a tunnel complex that was suspected of housing a nuclear facility.[43]

Not surprisingly, considering North Korea's past efforts to build nuclear weapons, that country is also a ballistic missile threat. On August 31, 1998, the North Koreans fired a missile over Japan during a failed attempt to put a satellite into orbit. The missile was believed to be a new class of ballistic missile, the Taepodong 1, with an intermediate range of 937 miles to as much as 1,875 miles. U.S. intelligence officials were surprised by the third-stage capability of the missile, which could give it a 2,408-3,720 mile range. In addition, in June 1998, the North Koreans announced (as U.S. intelligence already suspected) that they were selling missile technology to Syria, Iran, and Iraq. In response to the North Korean missile launch on August 31, the Japanese announced that they were suspending talks to establish diplomatic ties with North Korea, halting food aid to that country, and withdrawing from the project to finance, with the United States and South Korea, the construction of two nuclear reactors in North Korea. Republican critics called for the agreement to be scuttled. If not resolved, the financial wrangling could call into question the viability of the reactor project and, with it, the entire 1994 agreement by which North Korea agreed to place under international safeguards nuclear material it could use to produce bombs.[44]

The Iranian Nuclear Threat

In 1995 the U.S. nuclear proliferation spotlight swung away from North Korea and onto Iran. Although Western intelligence agencies did not discover clandestine Iranian nuclear weapon facilities, they did assemble a substantial body of evidence suggesting that Iran was secretly pursuing a broad, organized effort to develop nuclear weapons. But because Iran's industrial infrastructure could not support a nuclear weapon effort, it had to seek important weapon-related equipment and materials from abroad.

The United States had attempted to prevent that from happening by seeking approval for an international embargo on the transfer of nuclear goods to Iran. Western governments agreed to participate in the nuclear embargo, but both China and Russia refused. On January 8, 1995, Russia signed a $1 billion deal with Iran in which the Russians agreed to complete one, and possibly two, partially constructed nuclear power reactors, a project that had been suspended by the Germans in 1979. Although the reactors would not contribute directly to weapons development, U.S. officials worried that the training and technology supplied to the civilian side of the project would spill over into a military program. They also were concerned that plutonium embedded in the reactor's spent fuel could be reprocessed into bomb material, if Iran somehow obtained the necessary technology. China, for its part, had agreed in 1992 to supply Iran with two reactors. However, the Chinese insisted that the reactors were being sold for "peaceful purposes" and would be placed under IAEA safeguards, as required by the NPT, to which Iran adheres. But the administration, remembering how Iraq had circumvented IAEA safeguards, did not believe they would deter the Iranians from using the reactors for military purposes.[45]

Many in Congress wanted to punish both Russia and China. Several Republican congresspersons suggested that the United States substantially curtail its Nunn-Lugar aid to Russia unless it canceled the deal. But the administration argued that this step would impair the U.S. effort to dismantle Russian nuclear warheads and therefore would be tantamount "to shooting ourselves in the foot." Nevertheless, Clinton did convey U.S. displeasure over the Russian reactor sales to Boris Yeltsin at the Moscow summit in May 1995. He gave the Russian president a five-page, single-spaced U.S. intelligence document describing Iran's nuclear program. As an incentive to cancel the Iranian deal, Clinton also offered the Russians limited participation in the international effort to build two reactors in North Korea. But the administration also warned the Russians that if they went ahead with the sale, the United States would not renew a twenty-two-year-old pact on nuclear safety projects. The administration also threatened to cancel ongoing negotiations for a broad nuclear cooperation agreement involving joint ventures to finance new Russian reactors and the opening of U.S. markets to Russian nuclear equipment, which could amount to $100 million in business for Russia's hard-pressed economy. Nevertheless, the Americans were able to persuade the Russians to cancel only part of the Iranian deal: the building of a gas centrifuge plant that could produce highly enriched uranium. As a result, most of the Russian-Iranian deal remained intact, a continuing sore point between the United States and Russia.[46]

Some experts believe the United States was overreacting to the Iranian nuclear threat. To date, the IAEA has not found Iran to be in violation of its safeguards obligation, possibly because much of its activities have been at levels below anything that could be considered a violation. In addition, Iran's nuclear program is still relatively primitive. The Iranians lack the knowledge and equipment to successfully build or operate most of the required fuel cycle facilities. Furthermore, despite attempts to procure equipment and materials that would suggest an active nuclear weapon development program, the Iranians have had only limited success in doing so. The imposition of tighter export controls by the nuclear supplier states following the Gulf War played a large role in restraining Iran's nuclear ambitions. As a result, some experts found it difficult to substantiate a U.S. intelligence estimate that Iran would have the capability to build nuclear weapons within five to ten years. They believed, instead, that Iran is unlikely to have the ability to field even simple nuclear weapons for at least ten to fifteen years—unless it secures sufficient quantities of weapons-grade fissile material on the black market, a prospect that is not totally implausible.[47]

Clinton and the MTCR

Like the Bush administration, Clinton also placed great emphasis on curbing the proliferation of ballistic missiles. The administration had encouraged nonparticipating states to join, or to comply with the guidelines of, the Missile Technology Control Regime (MTCR), which was formed in 1987 by the

United States and its G-7 allies as a voluntary arrangement designed to restrain the proliferation of nuclear-capable ballistic and cruise missiles. By November 1997, the MTCR had twenty-nine members, including Russia, which had joined in 1995. Ukraine and China had pledged in 1994 to follow the regime's guidelines. Moreover, in 1993 member states had broadened the regime's coverage to encompass missiles capable of delivering all weapons of mass destruction as a means of combating increased chemical and biological weapons proliferation.

To get Russia, Ukraine, and China to abide by the MTCR guidelines, the Clinton administration offered them a guaranteed share of the satellite-launch market and invited them to participate in international space projects. A U.S.-Chinese pact signed on January 27, 1995, permitted Beijing to launch American geostationary satellites through 2001. A 1993 U.S.-Russian agreement permitted Moscow to launch nine American geostationary satellites through the year 2000. In late January 1996, the United States and Russia concluded a deal that allowed Russia to orbit from sixteen to twenty commercial payloads through the end of the century.

Making Russia a part of the effort to build an international space station was also an important aspect of the Clinton administration's missile counterproliferation program. However, the cash-strapped Russian government has had trouble funding its share of the project, causing the other international partners in the project to consider whether Russia should withdraw as a full partner and serve only as a subcontractor for specific jobs. This action has been resisted by the Clinton administration, however, because it would cause Russian space firms to lose expected revenue and acquire a poor reputation in the space market—results that could tempt them to engage in missile proliferation.

Ukraine was also offered a share of the satellite-launching business. However, under the U.S.-Ukrainian launch pact, which extends through 2001, Ukraine will have launched only three to four rockets with American payloads annually, far below expectations. Competition from U.S. and foreign space programs has been too stiff, and joint space projects are not a reliable source of income due to the potential for launch mishaps. In short, the joint U.S.-Russian and U.S.-Ukrainian space projects have not provided sufficient revenue to serve as a nonproliferation incentive. Moreover, because both countries lack comprehensive export control systems, there is a substantial risk that neither government is capable of preventing the illicit sale of missile components.[48]

China and the Ballistic Missile Market

For a number of reasons, China has refused to join the MTCR, even though it has promised to observe the regime's guidelines. For one, Beijing argues that the MTCR is a discriminatory arrangement that does not cover delivery systems of greater concern to China, such as jet fighters purchased from the United States by Taiwan. China views Taiwan as a rogue province and has not ruled out using force to return it to the mainland. The United States, on the other hand, has said publicly that it follows a "one China" policy, but U.S. law mandates that the U.S. government take all necessary action to defend Taiwan if its security is threatened. "If you want us to join the missile regime," a Chinese official said, "you have to do something on Taiwan."[49]

In addition, Beijing views the sale of its military technology—including missiles—as a means of realizing its strategic goals, increasing its diplomatic influence, and funding its defense modernization. In 1984, while Western nations were negotiating the creation of the MTCR, China was designing an export program for its short-range M-9 missile. Pakistan was a major customer. The test of its Ghauri missile in April 1998, a missile capable of delivering a nuclear weapon to virtually any target in India, was responsible in part for India's decision to test nuclear weapons the following month. U.S. analysts believe that China also was primarily responsible for kick starting Pakistan's nuclear weapons program in 1980 by providing a bomb design and some weapon-grade uranium. In addition, the Chinese gave technical assistance to the Pakistanis in the construction of a plutonium production reactor, which could produce plutonium and tritium, key materials in nuclear weapons.[50]

As a way of pressuring China to abide by the MTCR guidelines, both the Bush and Clinton administrations imposed trade sanctions against China (in 1991 and 1993 respectively) for selling Pakistan finished components of launchers for its M-11 missile. However, in 1994 the Clinton administration lifted the sanctions on China in exchange for Beijing's promise to abide by the MTCR guidelines and stop missile deals with Pakistan. Nevertheless, in 1996 China was accused of three major missile transfers: (1) the export of M-11 missiles and guidance equipment to Syria; (2) the sale of C-802 cruise missiles to Iran; and (3) the supply of blueprints and equipment to Pakistan for a missile factory. Pakistan's test firing of the Hatf III missile (with a projected range of 600 kilometres) in July 1997 provided further evidence of China's assistance to Islamabad. In June 1998 President Jiang Zemin told President Clinton that China would consider joining the MTCR, but in November of that year U.S. officials were still expressing concern about Chinese missile transfers to Pakistan.[51]

The Iranian Ballistic Missile Program

In addition to Pakistan, China also has sold missiles to Iran. In January 1990 China and Iran signed a ten-year agreement for scientific cooperation and the transfer of military technology. Subsequently, China was reported to be shipping Iran the M 1-B surface-to-surface missile, which has a hundred-kilometer range. Although these missiles have a short range, the transaction indicated a growing relationship between the two countries. A CIA report said that China had provided the ballistic missile programs of Iran, as well as Pakistan, with "a tremendous variety of assistance" in the second half of 1996. U.S. officials are concerned that transfers of missile technology to Iran would enable the radical Islamic regime to interdict shipping in the Persian Gulf and threaten U.S. Arab allies if it possessed accurate medium-range missiles.[52]

Russia also has assisted the Iranian ballistic missile program, particularly on engine technology, guidance systems, and special materials. For example, Iran's Shahab-4, with a range of 2,000 kilometers and a capability of carrying a thousand-kilogram payload, is alleged to be based on the Soviet ss-4 missile. On July 23, 1998, Iran tested its Shahab-3 missile, with a range of approximately 800 miles, that could strike Israel, Iraq, and thousands of U.S. troops stationed in Saudi Arabia. The test contradicted estimates by the U.S. intelligence community in 1997 that Iran would need up to ten years to develop a medium-range missile. On Capitol Hill, some Republicans said the test showed the need to build missile defenses against long-range attack.

Beginning in 1997 the Clinton administration intensified pressure on Russia to terminate its assistance to the Iranians. Although the Russians have continued to reject U.S. requests to halt work on the Iranian light-water reactor it is completing, in early 1998 they promised to end their assistance to the Iranian ballistic missile program. On January 22, 1998, Russian prime minister Viktor Chernomyrdin issued a new "catchall" regulation cutting off the flow of Russian technology and materials to Iran's ballistic missile development effort. The Russian crackdown, the Clinton administration hoped, would end congressional efforts to impose sanctions on Russia for past transfers of missile technology to Iran. On November 12, 1997, the House of Representatives adopted, by a voice vote, the Iran Missile Proliferation Sanctions Act of 1997. It was designed to punish any entity (namely, Russia) that provides technology or assistance to Iran's ballistic missile program. It would give the president thirty days to send Congress a list of violators. Automatic sanctions then would be imposed, ranging from denial of arms licenses to denial of U.S. foreign aid for up to two years. However, the president could grant a waiver if he cited national interest grounds. Democratic senators were able to delay Senate action on the bill by arguing that the administration needed more time to work with Moscow on concrete steps to stop the missile technology leaks. But on May 22, 1998, the Senate lost patience with that effort and passed the measure by a 90 to 4 margin. The legislation passed in both houses well above the two-thirds majority needed to override a promised presidential veto. In response, President Clinton cut off aid to seven Russian research and manufacturing enterprises accused of selling sensitive weapons technology to Iran, Libya, and North Korea.[53]

Russia, Iraq, and India

Even more ominous than Russia's assistance to Iran has been its aid to Iraq. On April 11, 1998, not long after Chernomyrdin announced the crackdown on the export of Russian missile technology to Iran, the *Washington Post* reported that the Russians also were sending missile parts to Iraq, including more than 800 sophisticated gyroscopes for intercontinental ballistic missiles. The gyroscopes had been removed from the command modules of Russian SS-N-18 submarine-launched ballistic missiles that were being destroyed under START. However, the gyroscopes were intercepted by Jordanian authorities in November 1995, before they could be delivered to Iraq. Russia at first denied that the gyroscopes were from its missiles, but after Rolf Ekeus, head of the U.N. Special Commission (UNSCOM) in charge of probing Iraq's weapons programs, came to Moscow with detailed evidence in February 1996, Russian officials acknowledged that the guidance systems indeed had come from Russia. However, they denied that the Russian government had given approval for the transfer. The Iraqi case nevertheless seemed to support the suspicion that Russia's vast military-industrial complex, facing hard times, had become fertile ground for countries shopping for ballistic missile technology. Moreover, Western politicians and intelligence experts expressed skepticism that such leaks of know-how and equipment could occur without the knowledge of high-ranking Russian government officials. The factory in which the missiles were dismantled was state owned, as is most of the military-industrial complex.[54]

The Russians have also been helping India's ballistic missile program, particularly India's effort to build a sea-launched ballistic missile, the Sagarika, which is believed to have a range of nearly 200 miles and the capability to carry a nuclear warhead, a potent weapon against Pakistan. U.S. officials disagreed about whether Russian assistance violated the MTCR guidelines, which could prompt sanctions against both Russia and India. However, Henry Sokolski, executive director of the Nonproliferation Policy Education Center, said that "anything that encourages the Indians to play around with strategic technology is bad business."[55]

The Indian and Pakistani Nuclear Tests

On May 11, 1998, India tested three nuclear devices, including a forty-three-kiloton thermonuclear explosion, a twelve-kiloton fission explosion and a 0.2-kiloton fission explosion. They were India's first nuclear tests since 1974. Two days later, the Indians conducted two more tests, with reported yields in the range of 0.2 to 0.6 kilotons. Indian prime minister Atal Bihari Vajpayee, whose Bharatiya Janata Party had come to power the previous March, said that the tests were prompted by security concerns. What he was alluding to was Pakistan's April 6 test of the medium-range Ghauri ballistic missile. But defense minister George Fernandes said that China, not Pakistan, is India's "potential enemy number one." The Indian government accused China of supplying Pakistan with the missile technology for its April test, even though the United States reported that the North Koreans, not the Chinese, were Pakistan's missile supplier. The Indians were convinced, however, that the United States was lying to protect its relationship with China.[56]

Yet experts believe that China has no designs on its southern neighbor. The Indian action, they believe, was largely motivated by the ruling party's efforts to gain support for its fragile coalition government by appealing to nationalistic pride, not by fear of China. "India is now a nuclear weapon state," Prime Minister Vajpayee said. "It is India's due, the right of one-sixth of humankind." For years, Indians of all political persuasions have complained that the world, and particularly the United States, has refused to consider India a great power. India's demand for a permanent seat on the United Nations Security Council, for example, was consistently ignored. Consequently, Indians resolutely refused to sign international nuclear arms control pacts—specifically the NPT and the CTBT—because they would deny India its "rightful" status.[57]

Moreover, Indians have argued for years that the NPT and the CTBT discriminated against India and other nonweapon states. The NPT permitted the five declared nuclear powers to keep their weapons while requiring others to promise never to develop any. The Indians were offended by the provision in the CTBT stating that the treaty could not enter into force unless India signed and ratified it, along with forty-three other "nuclear capable" nations. India was included in this list in the face of its repeated statements that it would never sign the CTBT unless it was accompanied by a "time-bound" commitment to complete nuclear disarmamentmt by the nuclear powers.[58]

The hyporcritical devotion of the nuclear weapon states to the CTBT was demonstrated, the Indians charged, by the "stewardship" programs that have enabled the weapon states to continue to modernize their nuclear arsenals. They pointed to the Clinton administration's program to spend $45 million over ten years to enable U.S. weapons laboratories to develop ways, including computer simulation, to check the reliability of bombs without detonating them. In the opinion of the Indians, the nuclear weapon states had finally succeeded in converting the CTBT from a tool for nuclear disarmament—as originally envisioned by Indian prime minister Jawaharlal Nehru in 1954—into nothing more than a nonproliferation instrument. The Indians also realized that they would be the primary target of a CTBT review conference scheduled for September 1999. Parties that had ratified the treaty by then would be in a position to pressure India by various means, including sanctions, to sign and ratify it. In other words, by the time the Bharatiya Janata Party came to power in March 1998, the Indian political scene had already shifted in favor of testing nuclear weapons.[59]

Ironically, instead of enhancing India's international status, the Indian nuclear tests may have weakened it. The tests were met with almost universal condemnation by the U.N. Security Council, the G-7 industrialized countries, and most members of the Conference on Disarmament. President Clinton said India's test "not only threatens the stability of the region, it directly challenges the firm international consensus to stop the proliferation of weapons of mass destruction." He then imposed economic sanctions on India, in accordance with the 1994 Nuclear Proliferation Prevention Act, which mandates that all direct aid to India—more than $140 million a year— be suspended, bars U.S. banks from making loans to the Indian government, and restricts exports of U.S. computers that could be used for military purposes. Clinton also recalled the U.S. ambassador to India and subsequently canceled his planned visit to India, which had been scheduled to take place later in the year.[60]

Yet, in spite of the president's strong reaction to the Indian tests, his administration may have unwittingly assisted the Indians in conducting them. Over the objections of some Pentagon officials, the administration had permitted U.S. companies to export to India sensitive equipment and nuclear technologies, such as high-powered computers, nuclear safety equipment for bomb makers, and robotics technology for use in nuclear facilities not subject to international inspections. The administration approved all these exports ostensibly to improve safety conditions for Indian civilian nuclear workers. The United States also allowed Indian scientists to work at the three U.S. national nuclear laboratories—Los Alamos, Lawrence Livermore, and Sandia.[61]

Clinton also was unable to persuade the Pakistanis to avoid reacting in kind to the Indian tests. On May 28 Pakistan conducted five nuclear tests, and one on May 30. The announced total yield of the first day's tests was forty to forty-five kilotons, including a large explosion of thirty to thirty-five kilotons, and fifteen to eighteen kilotons for the second day. As with India, however, the seismically estimated yields were significantly lower. Nevertheless, the international community reacted harshly. On June 2 forty-seven members of the Conference on Disarmament, including all five nuclear weapon states, issued a statement accusing India and Pakistan of "blatantly" undermining the international nonproliferation regime. The statement demanded that both states renounce their nuclear weapons programs, accede unconditionally to the CTBT and the NPT, and begin negotiations on a fissile material cutoff treaty.[62]

Many feared that the tests would touch off a nuclear war on the subcontinent that would kill millions. The London-based *Jane's Intelligence Review*, a leading defense journal, reported that if India used reactor-grade, as well as weapon-grade plutonium, it might have enough fissile material to build 455 atomic bombs, far more than previously believed. The journal also estimated that Pakistan could build up to 100 bombs, four times more than previously believed. President Clinton also expressed concern over the prospect of escalating tensions in South Asia. "I cannot believe," he said, "that we are about to start the 21st century by having the Indian Subcontinent repeat the worst mistakes of the 20th century." He then announced that the United States would impose economic sanctions against Pakistan, as it had against India. However, in July the administration was able to persuade Congress to lift sanctions on food for India and Pakistan, primarily because they were hurting American farmers.[63]

Some analysts, like John Mearsheimer, believe that the development of

nuclear weapons by India and Pakistan will not necessarily lead to a doomsday scenario but could be the way to prevent another conflict between the
two antagonists, whether nuclear or conventional. "Nuclear weapons,"
Mearsheimer argued, "are a superb deterrent for states that feel threatened by
rival powers." The end result, he predicted, is "that the United States will
have to learn to live with the spread of nuclear weapons in the decades ahead.
We should try to manage and contain this process," he advised, "but we cannot stop it."[64]

Others objected strongly to Mearsheimer's analysis. "If both India and
Pakistan deployed nuclear weapons," argued Joseph Cirincione, director of
the Nonproliferation Project at the Carnegie Endowment, "I think it would
almost certainly lead to a nuclear exchange in combat." Unlike other nuclear
weapon states, neither India nor Pakistan is likely to have the command-
and-control capabilities that help reduce the risks of a nuclear war. "What
worries military people the most," observed Michael Krepon, president of
the Henry L. Stimson Center, "isn't detonation by design, but by unauthorized use, screw-up and miscalculation, a stray electron or misreading the
screen." When asked why Washington and Moscow should not provide
India and Pakistan with the training and equipment necessary to maintain a
safe deterrence strategy, Deputy Secretary of State Strobe Talbott replied
that they would be "tempted—like us—into a considerable escalation of the
arms race." Accordingly, the administration put pressure on the Indians and
Pakistanis to ratify the comprehensive test ban treaty.[65]

India and Pakistan Move Toward the CTBT
Apparently, the pressure paid off. On September 23, 1998, Pakistan's prime
minister, Nawaz Sharif, said his country would unilaterally adhere to the
CTBT within one year, as long as India did not resume testing and the United
States lifted economic sanctions. Pakistan obviously wanted to be part of the
September 1999 CTBT review conference in order to prevent a change in the
rules that would allow the treaty to go into effect without ratification by
India. The next day, Indian prime minister Vajpayee joined Pakistan in
declaring that his country was "prepared to bring discussions" on the CTBT
"to a successful conclusion" so that the treaty can go into effect by September
1999. Although this did not amount to a promise to sign the treaty, a senior
U.S. official called it "movement in the right direction."[66]

However, in a letter to President Clinton, three Republican senators—
Jesse Helms, Trent Lott, and Jon Kyl of Arizona—said they opposed lifting

sanctions as a price for adhering to nuclear agreements. "As the recent Indian nuclear tests demonstrated," they asserted, "the CTBT is not adequately verifiable." Others rejected this charge. They argued that although India's tests took the U.S. intelligence community by surprise, the seismic waves that they created were recorded by sixty-two stations. With the advent of digital data, global communication networks, global positioning systems, geosynchronous time, and other technologies, intelligence gathering and the monitoring of arms control agreements was bound to get only better.[67]

Not all Republicans took the party line on the CTBT. Senator Arlen Specter of Pennsylvania, who had previously declined to endorse the treaty, argued on May 13 that "consideration and ratification of the Comprehensive Test Ban Treaty ought to be a very high priority on the Senate's agenda." Specter joined Joseph Biden (D-Del.) in cosponsoring a nonbinding sense of the Senate resolution calling on the Foreign Relations Committee to hold a hearing, or hearings, on the CTBT and the full Senate to debate and vote on its ratification "as expeditiously as possible." Senator Helms, however, continued to block a vote on the CTBT. He insisted that the administration must first submit for ratification the ABM demarcation agreement, which would specify what forms of theater missile defenses would be permitted without violating the ABM Treaty. Helms, and other conservatives, want to use the missile demarcation issue to get rid of the ABM Treaty, thereby eliminating all restrictions on the capabilities of a missile defense system.[68]

The Continuing Problem of Iraq

Iraq continued to perplex the United States during the Clinton administration. In October 1997 Iraq attempted to end U.N.-imposed sanctions by accusing American UNSCOM inspectors of spying and then announcing that it would bar Americans from future inspections. On November 13 the Iraqis said that American inspectors must leave immediately. In response, UNSCOM chief inspector Richard Butler ordered all inspectors out of Iraq. President Clinton reacted the next day by ordering additional military forces to the region. The crisis ebbed on November 20 after Russia persuaded Iraq to allow U.S. UNSCOM inspectors to return to the country. In return, Russia assured the Iraqis that it would work to have the U.N. economic sanctions lifted. President Clinton warned, however, that if Iraq reneged on its promise to comply, "everyone would understand that then the United States, and hopefully all of our allies, would have the unilateral right to respond at a time, place, and manner of our own choosing."[69]

Two months later, Clinton appeared ready to do just that. Iraq again provoked a confrontation by threatening to block the work of a new inspection team led by William S. ("Scott") Ritter Jr. of the United States. Seeking to defuse the crisis, U.N. secretary-general Kofi Annan and Saddam Hussein signed an agreement establishing new rules for the inspections. Secretary of State Madeleine Albright said the United States would reserve judgment and allow the agreement to be "tested." Ritter said that although he and other inspection officials were deeply worried about the agreement's impact, they too had decided to test Iraq's willingness to comply with the agreement. Ritter later recounted that he was encouraged by the Security Council's warning of "severest consequences" if Iraq again blocked the inspectors.[70]

Yet on August 3, 1998, Iraq again announced that it was ceasing cooperation with UNSCOM inspectors. This time, however, there were no U.S. threats of military action to force compliance, primarily because the Clinton administration could obtain virtually no international support for it. In response, Ritter resigned from the inspection team on August 26, accusing the United States and Britain of failing to back up their stated claims of wanting to disarm Baghdad. Between November 1997 and August 1998, he charged, the Clinton administration had been secretly trying to find a diplomatic solution for its confrontation with Iraq. He also accused the administration of making at least seven efforts to delay or stop an investigation or block a line of inquiry. The Clinton administration heatedly denied Ritter's charges, saying that it had faithfully backed the inspections and was "keeping up the pressure on Iraq."[71]

In November 1998 Iraq again brought UNSCOM inspections to an end, and again President Clinton reacted by sending military reinforcements to the Persian Gulf region. The president ordered a military attack on Iraqi targets but canceled it virtually at the last minute, on November 15, after Iraq agreed to resume UNSCOM inspections unconditionally. However, on December 15, U.S. cruise missile attacked Iraq after Butler, the day before, abruptly withdrew UNSCOM inspectors because he concluded that the Iraqis were again not cooperating with the inspections. The U.S. cruise missile attacks, which were supplemented by both U.S. and British aircraft strikes beginning the next day, lasted until December 19. The president, who was impeached by the House of Representatives the same day, stated that the attacks were terminated because the WMD threat posed by Iraq was substantially degraded. Yet almost no one, apparently, believed that they had eliminated Iraq as a nuclear menace.[72]

Nuclear Terrorism

As scary as the prospect of an Iraqi nuclear arsenal might be, the ultimate nuclear nightmare may be a terrorist group armed with a nuclear weapon and threatening a city. The bomb that terrorists exploded in front of New York's World Trade Center in February 1993, for example, turned three levels of parking garage into a tangle of steel beams and killed six people. It contained 1,200 pounds of fuel oil and fertilizer. By contrast, a nuclear weapon would ignite a holocaust that would incinerate every bit of steel, concrete, and human flesh for miles. The rubble would be highly radioactive for weeks if not months.

For would-be terrorists, making a crude bomb would be difficult but not impossible. The basic information necessary to design a simple fission weapon has been available in public literature for many years. Moreover, there are thousands of people around the world with sufficient nuclear experience, and tens of thousands with the appropriate skills in physical chemistry and explosives, to build a nuclear weapon. One can only guess how many nuclear physicists, engineers, and technicians have already made this know-how available to would-be terrorists. The Japanese cult responsible for releasing sarin gas in Tokyo's subway in 1995 was also studying uranium enrichment and laser technology, potential steps to producing nuclear weapons. The cult had at least one follower on the staff of Kurchatov Institute, a nuclear physics laboratory in Russia. Even if they were unable to design and build a bomb, terrorists might construct a dispersal device or package radioactive material with conventional explosives to contaminate their targets. Highly radioactive plutonium dropped in a city's water supply would fulfill a terrorist's dream.[73]

By far, the hardest part of building a nuclear weapon is obtaining fissile material. It is estimated that a bomb could be made with as little as three kilograms of enriched uranium or between one and eight kilograms of plutonium. A kilogram of plutonium occupies about one-seventh the volume of a standard aluminum soft drink can. However, producing fissile material is extremely difficult, costly, and time-consuming—as Iraq discovered before its nuclear program was crippled by coalition bombing during the Persian Gulf War. It would seem to be far easier to buy or steal fissile material than to produce it.[74]

The Russian Nuclear Market

For at least three reasons, Russia is now considered the major potential source of fissile material through illicit purchase or theft. First, there is abundant fissile material in Russia. Second, security over fissile materials has lessened since the Soviet Union disintegrated. Third, Russia has long, porous borders that are close to states eager to obtain Russian fissile material.

In the republics of the former Soviet Union (FSU), there were until recently nearly 30,000 nuclear warheads, mostly in Russia. Estimates of the Russian stockpile of weapons-grade materials exceed 1,200 tons of uranium and 150 tons of plutonium. Ukraine recently possessed about 100 kilograms of highly enriched uranium but no plutonium, and Kazakhstan approximately 300 kilograms of HEU and perhaps 100 kilograms of plutonium. Weapons-usable plutonium-239 is also a by-product of most commercial nuclear power reactors, of which forty-six are operating in the FSU today. Because primitive nuclear weapons require relatively small amounts of plutonium or highly enriched uranium, the diversion of only a small fraction of this fissile material from Russian could have dangerous consequences.[75]

Another reason for would-be nuclear terrorists to consider Russia a prime source for fissile material is the poor condition of the Russian security system. Prior to its breakup in 1991, the Soviet Union had a highly effective mechanism for protecting nuclear weapons and materials—a totalitarian government. Strong central control and intrusive oversight, combined with accepted political authority and a well-disciplined military establishment, appeared to make sophisticated material control and accounting systems unnecessary. Moreover, because the Soviet Union had been a nuclear weapon state, it had never been required by the NPT to develop the kind of system of safeguards and security required of nonweapon states who were parties to that treaty. Indeed, the accountability of Russian nuclear materials is highly uncertain. According to Viktor Mikhailov, former director of MINATOM, the Russian ministry of atomic energy, "Nobody knows the exact capacities for the production of these materials [or] the exact quantity of the produced materials themselves due to technological losses in production."[76]

There have also been questions about the system used by the Russian ministry of defense for protecting nuclear warheads that are deployed or stored at more than 100 locations, due to the deteriorating conditions under which military forces are serving. Declining morale and discipline problems resulting from budget cuts, displacement, and inadequate pay and housing have taken their toll on the Russian military, increasing the risk that a disaffected group in the military could subvert the security system from within.[77]

Reinforcing this fear, General Alexander Lebed (who was the head of Russia's Security Council briefly and now is the governor of Krasnoyarsk province and a leading contender for the Russian presidency in 2000) once said that more than a hundred suitcase-sized nuclear bombs were missing from Russian military inventories. He also said that the Soviet Union had produced 132 portable nuclear weapons and that 84 were missing. Lebed's allegations were vehemently denied by Russian military authorities. General Igor Volynkin, who heads the Defense Ministry department responsible for nuclear security, denied that nuclear "suitcase bombs" of the sort described by General Lebed even existed. U.S. officials also have expressed confidence in Russia's ability to control its nuclear arsenal. After touring weapon sites across Russia in 1998, General Eugene Habiger, head of the U.S. Strategic Command, concluded that Russia keeps its deadly nuclear arsenal in safe hands, monitoring it with as much vigilance as the United States safeguards its own missiles. "I want to put to bed this concern that there are loose nukes in Russia," Habiger said.[78]

Still, there are factors that may encourage nuclear theft and trafficking within the FSU. The economic collapse these countries have experienced has left some nuclear enterprises without work or payrolls, putting intense pressures on managers to find some way to sustain their facilities, production lines, and workforce. Glen E. Schweitzer, a former head of the Moscow-based International Science and Technology Center that employed Russian weapons scientists, testified before Congress that many of the some 60,000 scientists and engineers in Russia with direct experience building weapons systems are out of jobs and out of money. But Schweitzer added that, to the best of his knowledge, "there has been no major emigration of core weapons scientists." He admitted, however, that "short-term visits abroad and meetings [between Russian weapons scientists] and foreign visitors in Moscow or other capitals" are a subject of concern.[79]

If anything, considering the continuing downward spiral of the Russian economy, the prospects for recovery and expansion of state funding for nuclear programs, with concomitant improvements in worker morale and pay, are not good. The former director of MINATOM, Viktor Mikhailov, claimed his ministry received only 48 percent of its budget in 1997. In fact, budget shortfalls have forced many facilities to cut spending for nuclear material security systems in order to retain key scientific staff. In addition, many nuclear workers are still not receiving wages for long periods of time, and the quality of available food, housing, and medical care remains poor. These conditions increase the chance that "insider" personnel could be tempted to divert nuclear material for financial gain. As a way of preventing smuggling and a brain drain from Russia to countries like Iran, Iraq, or North Korea, in September 1998 the United States promised to provide Russia with $20 million toward retraining 30,000-50,000 Russian nuclear scientists for civilian work in ten so-called closed cities. The money would also be used to convert nuclear weapons and missile manufacturing plants to commercial operations.[80]

Official corruption and organized criminal activity are also a concern. In May 1994 the Russian Interior Ministry reported the existence of 5,691 organized crime groups in Russia, with an estimated total membership of 100,000 people. However, in April 1995 the FBI noted that "no definitive proof of international organized crime involvement in trafficking in actual weapons-grade nuclear materials has been noted to date." Yet the potential for trafficking in nuclear materials is there. According to Rensselaer Lee, president of Global Advisory Services, Russian investigators reported that "some 35 to 40 suspected dealers in nuclear substances were operating around Moscow." If large organized crime groups, particularly those centered in the FSU and having international ties, would engage in nuclear smuggling, the task of preventing the illicit transfer of Russian nuclear materials would be virtually impossible.[81]

Nuclear Smuggling

In fact, there have been numerous reports of stolen fissile material from Russia. The German government alone reported more than 700 cases of attempted illicit nuclear sales between 1991 and 1994. In 1994 almost a pound of plutonium was seized by German police at the Munich airport. The plutonium had been carried in a suitcase on a flight from Moscow. Two passengers on the plane were arrested, as was a third man who was identified as the buyer of the nuclear material. During the same year, six pounds of highly enriched uranium was seized in Prague. It was found in two plastic-wrapped metal containers in the backseat of a car parked on a side street. A Czech nuclear scientist, a Russian, and a Belarussian were arrested in connection with this seizure. Russian documents were found with the nuclear material.[82]

Although Moscow has denied that any weapons-grade material has been smuggled out of Russia, in 1995 Russian law enforcement authorities acknowledged that they had cracked twenty-one cases of theft of fissile materials, some of it enriched, since mid-1992 and had prosecuted nineteen Russian citizens. Interior Ministry officials report twenty cases of theft in 1993 and twenty-seven in 1994, all by insiders with access to nuclear materials. In one case, in November 1993, a Russian naval officer entered the Sevmorput shipyard (in Murmansk), located a building used for naval reactor fuel storage, removed about ten pounds of highly enriched uranium, put the fuel in a briefcase, and walked out of the shipyard the way he came in.[83]

U.S. officials, nevertheless, have backed up the Russian assessment that large amounts of weapon-grade material has not left the country. Apparently, the quantities of weapon-usable materials that have been seized would not be enough to make a nuclear weapon. Even the largest seizures of weapon-grade material, such as the 2.7 kilograms of highly enriched uranium seized in Prague in December 1994, involved quantities smaller than the minimum needed for a nuclear explosive. Yet accumulated thefts of small amounts of fissile materials could give a rogue state (or a terrorist group) bent on acquiring fissile material a sufficient amount to build a nuclear weapon.

Moreover, it is quite possible that all the material smuggled out of Russia has not been detected. Smugglers could be getting nuclear materials to potential buyers by taking routes through the Central Asian republics and across the Black Sea, where border controls are weak and potential customers are close to the sources of supply. A congressional report noted widespread concern within the international intelligence and nonproliferation communities that the Central Asian republics "are being used as transit routes for nuclear materials coming out of Russia." It also reported that many border points lack controls and that corrupt customs officials can be bribed with as little as a bottle of vodka in others. The congressional report concluded that Iran, Iraq, and North Korea tried to recruit nuclear specialists in these countries to help them develop the materials, technology, and expertise needed for their "nuclear programs."[84]

Seizures of nuclear material made in Germany and Turkey support the conclusion of the congressional report that outlaw states such as Iran may be looking for high-quality nuclear material. In May 1995 Secretary of State Warren Christopher told the press that Iran has had an organized structure dedicated to acquiring and developing nuclear weapons since the mid-1980s. Iranian agents have scoured the FSU searching for nuclear materials, technologies, and scientists. In 1992 Iran unsuccessfully approached a plant in Kazakhstan for a substantial quantity of enriched uranium. Rensselaer Lee, president of Global Advisory Services, cited a 1991 letter faxed to Russia's Arzamas 16, a nuclear research center, purportedly from the Islamic Jihad, offering to buy a nuclear weapon. He quoted the center's director as saying that in 1993 Iraqi representatives offered $2 billion for a warhead.[85]

How Vulnerable is America to Nuclear Terror?

If rogue states or terrorist groups were able to make bombs from leaked fissile material, could they be used against targets in the United States? Unfortunately, the answers appears to be yes. For a number of reasons, the problem of bringing nuclear materials into the United States, where they could be assembled, is not great. First, U.S. borders, like those in the FSU, are porous. The volume of people and commodities that flow through the legal points of entry into the United States is enormous and largely uninspected. In 1995, there were 301 U.S. ports of entry and fewer than 10,000 customs inspectors, that is, roughly thirty inspectors per port of entry, none of whom were trained or equipped to detect nuclear materials. Each day, roughly 1.25 million people enter the United States, 1.36 billion kilograms of cargo arrive by sea, and 4.66 million kilograms enter by air. Fewer than 5 percent of everything entering the United States is physically inspected, and then only after arriving on U.S. territory. Given the volume of the daily inflow of people and material into the United States, it is difficult to believe that the U.S. Customs Service can be counted on to prevent the entry of fissile material and other weapon components into the United States.

Second, detection of nuclear weapons or fissile material is not easy. Technologies designed to detect nuclear materials operate over very short ranges and are used only at secure storage facilities by a few special search teams. Although existing technology can detect some of the material used in nuclear weapons at a range of 30-300 feet, this is possible only if the material is not shielded. Moreover, radioactive sensors of this type are not usually found at U.S. ports of entry. And some nuclear weapons, especially those employing highly enriched uranium, can be designed to be all but undetectable. Thus, to reliably detect a nuclear weapon or component hidden in a freight container, the container must be physically searched by personnel who know what to look for. It is also quite possible that detection of smuggled nuclear weapons would occur only at the moment of detonation.

Third, the means of delivering weapons to the United States are essentially infinite. Because terrorists and most rogue states do not possess the intercontinental delivery systems preferred by the nuclear superpowers, they would almost certainly rely on unconventional means of delivery if they decided to threaten the United States with a nuclear weapon. For example, a nuclear weapon could be shipped in a container by sea and exploded in a harbor, or driven by truck to any location in the continental United States. Nuclear weapons or components also could be flown into the United States in private aircraft or smuggled across the border on foot. A criminal or terrorist group could even ship a weapon into the United States in pieces small and light enough to go by Federal Express, United Parcel Service, or even the U.S. Postal Service. If it possessed enough fissile material for several weapons, such a group could even afford to fail once or twice before getting the material for one weapon into the United States.

Certainly, every effort should be made to police America's borders, but this is unlikely to be foolproof regardless of the level of resources employed. The extent of the nuclear smuggling threat to the United States depends largely on the probability of success that a group or state would face if it attempted to bring fifteen pounds of plutonium or thirty pounds of HEU into the United States. However, the effort to detect and interdict nuclear smugglers is extremely unlikely to reduce the potential of successful smuggling to anywhere close to zero. As a result, most experts believe that the best way to reduce the threat of nuclear terrorism against the United States is to reduce the risks of nuclear leakage from the source. And the primary potential source of such material is Russia.[86]

The MPC&A Program

To ensure that all nuclear weapons and weapons-usable materials in the FSU are secure and accounted for, the U.S. Department of Energy was entrusted with the task of conducting the International Materials Protection Control and Accounting (MPC&A) program. The program is designed to protect fissile materials at civil and military sites in the nuclear FUS, expand U.S. cooperation with Russian organizations responsible for monitoring the safety and security of nuclear materials, protect nuclear materials in Russian naval reactors, and help protect intersite shipments of nuclear materials. This involves facility-level security and accounting systems for both weapons-usable materials and nuclear weapons themselves, new, secure storage facilities, consolidation of weapons and materials at a smaller number of locations, high security for transport of weapons and materials (often the most vulnerable point in their life cycle), effective national-level systems of accounting, control, and regulation, and, ultimately, more stringent international standards.

Much has been done already. In cooperation with the Russian nuclear regulatory agency, Gosatomnadzor (GAN), and the Russian Ministry of Atomic Energy (MINATOM), the U.S. government has initiated a broad array of programs to upgrade the security of nuclear materials and warheads. U.S. assistance has included training in using enhanced security techniques and equipment, such as computerized accounting, radiation measurement, seals, physical inventory procedures, sensors, video surveillance, fences, gates, barriers, alarm systems, portal monitoring, and access control. In 1994 the United States and Russia agreed to exchange unclassified information to enhance the safety and security of warheads and materials during dismantlement. The United States also sent 1,300 emergency response items to Russia to help assess and mitigate the effects of accidents involving warheads or fissile materials being transported for storage and dismantlement. The United States has also developed and shipped hundreds of conversion kits to upgrade the safety and security of Russian railroad cars transporting nuclear warheads to storage and dismantlement facilities. In addition, the United States has provided Russia with thousands of fissile material storage containers. In one of the biggest projects to date, the United States has earmarked $75 million to help Russia build at Chelyabinsk a new safe and secure storage facility for plutonium and highly enriched uranium from dismantled weapons. The new facility would offer greatly improved security and accounting compared to the locations at which these materials are currently being stored.[87]

Although Russia and the United States have dismantled thousands of nuclear warheads since the end of the Cold War, all the plutonium from those warheads is stored in bomb-ready form. Thus there is still a risk that some of this plutonium could end up in the hands of rogue states or terrorists. One way to eliminate or reduce this threat would be to make the plutonium less useful for military purposes by irradiating it and mixing it with other elements. The facilities to do this are expensive, costing hundreds of millions of dollars each, but the cost might be worth the cure, particularly if terrorists are prevented from obtaining deadly plutonium.[88]

It is certainly helpful for security purposes that the Russians have greatly reduced the number of sites at which nuclear weapons are stored—according to the CIA, from over 600 sites in 1989 to roughly 100 in 1995. Nevertheless, a similar consolidation is needed in the number of sites with weapons-usable nuclear materials. In fact, MPC&A experts now believe that the scope of the security problem is much larger than was originally anticipated. In 1994 the U.S. government estimated that approximately eighty to a hundred facilities at several dozen sites in FSU contained weapons-usable nuclear materials. However, by early 1998, the Department of Energy had identified over 150 facilities at 53 sites containing such materials. By then, joint MPC&A upgrades were completed or under way at more than 100 of these facilities and planning had begun for work at the remaining ones.

Since 1993 the United States has been purchasing highly enriched uranium from Russia as one way of disposing of weapon-grade material that could be smuggled out of the country. By 2001 Russia is expected to have converted to low enriched uranium (for use in civilian reactors) the highly enriched uranium equivalent to about 7,500 nuclear warheads. As part of this agreement, Russia was awarded an advance payment of $100 million against future deliveries of HEU. Still, there are dozens of research reactors in the FSU that use weapons-usable fuel. To deal with the problem, the Department of Energy is conducting a program to develop low enriched uranium fuels for these reactors, called the Reduced Enrichment for Research and Test Reactors (RERTR). Because the conversion of HEU to LEU fuel is costly, however, it will take time to end these reactors' reliance on HEU.[89]

In addition, the Clinton administration has attempted to eliminate Russian plutonium stockpiles. In September 1998, Russia and the United States signed an agreement that would require each country to remove fifty tons of plutonium from its military stockpile and dispose of it by using it as fuel in nuclear reactors or mixing it with waste. The fifty tons of Russian plutonium to be disposed of represents only a quarter of Russia's estimated supply, but U.S. officials called the accord an important precedent: plutonium is not a resource to be husbanded, as the Russian nuclear establishment often claimed, but a very dangerous material.[90]

In addition to helping Russia defray the cost of eliminating strategic nuclear weapons, as called for in the START treaties, the Nunn-Lugar program has offered assistance to reduce the threat of illicit transfers of nuclear materials. This assistance has included armored blankets to enhance the safety and security of weapons and fissile material during transport; safety and security enhancements for railcars used in transporting nuclear weapons and fissile material; emergency response equipment to upgrade capabilities to respond in case of a nuclear accident; transportation and storage containers for fissile material removed from dismantled nuclear weapons; assistance in the design of a storage facility for fissile material; assistance in chemical weapon destruction; and establishment of a science center to employ former weapon scientists. In addition, the United States has assisted Russia in constructing and purchasing operating equipment for a fissile material storage facility and has helped establish national and facility-level systems for material control and accountability and for physical protection of civil nuclear material.[91]

However, because the government-to-government program was slow to start (due to Russian intransigence, sluggish leadership within the U.S. government, and funding restrictions that were unacceptable to Russia), in April 1994 the Department of Energy initiated a new "laboratory-to-laboratory" MPC&A program. The essence of this approach was to build on the highly successful scientific collaborations between U.S. and Russian nuclear laboratories and extend that success to interlaboratory cooperation on MPC&A. Three major pilot projects were completed in 1995: at Arzamas 16, a nuclear weapon design laboratory, at the Obninsk nuclear research facility, and at the Kurchatov Institute. Since then, the program has been expanded to include more than fifty nuclear sites in the FSU. Only a small number of additional sites are expected to emerge as cooperation continues.

Although the Department of Energy and other U.S. government agencies have programs under way that deal with nuclear smuggling (funded separately from the MPC&A program), some experts believe there is still a need for the United States to help create a stronger second line of defense to prevent the unauthorized removal of nuclear material from the FSU. Accordingly, the Department of Energy has initiated planning for the purpose of working with the national laboratories to provide FSU customs officials and border guards with significantly improved capabilities for deterring, detecting, and interdicting the smuggling of weapons of mass destruction at ports and border crossings in the former republics of the Soviet Union. However, due to the length of these borders, and the fact that large quantities of goods move across them at uncontrolled points, a second line of defense program can only be expected to make incremental improvements in the overall security of nuclear materials.[92]

Continuing Problems and Prospects
Effective counterproliferation will require more U.S. and international economic assistance to the FSU. The lack of financial resources prevents Russian nuclear facilities from investing in MPC&A improvements. In 1995 the U.S. Department of Energy estimated that rapid improvements to MPC&A systems for all weapons-usable nuclear material in the FSU could be completed by the end of 2002, at a total cost of approximately $800 million. Moreover, the original Department of Energy estimate projected that Russia and the other nuclear republics would be able to devote an increasing share of resources to sustaining and expanding MPC&A improvements during the second half of the "rapid upgrade" phase (roughly 1999-2002). However, the

near collapse of the Russian economy in 1998 means that the financial situation of most sites requiring MPC&A upgrades is not likely to improve significantly before the end of 2002.

By the end of 1998, the installation of new MPC&A systems at the largest sites—those with the greatest quantities of nuclear materials and the most restrictions on cooperation—was a long way from completion. In addition, at many of the sites that will have new MPC&A systems in place, cooperative work will have to continue well past 1998 in order to complete training and to support the early phases of system operation. Thus the accomplishment of original program goals is likely to require continued increases in the level of effort for the MPC&A program in 1999-2002. If FUS officials are faced with the prospect of sharply reduced U.S. funding for the MPC&A program, on the other hand, they may decide that modern systems are unaffordable and attempt to rely on outmoded safeguards approaches. Making sure that an indigenous foundation for modern MPC&A systems is established is crucial to sustaining the effectiveness of the systems that have been jointly installed during the past four years. It is inevitable that the U.S. financial commitment to this program will eventually decrease, but it certainly is not in the U.S. interest to cut back until the national security threat posed by loose nuclear materials has been sufficiently addressed.[93]

Moreover, the supporters of the Nunn-Lugar Program insist that if the counterproliferation programs being implemented in the FSU are to succeed, they must be based on genuine cooperation, mutual trust, and maximum flexibility. This, they insist, means that Congress must resist the temptation to impose burdensome restrictions on the assistance. In 1997, for example, an amendment sponsored by Representatives Gerald Solomon (R-N.Y.) and Dana Rohrbacher (R-Calif.) nearly succeeded in cutting off all CTR funding unless Russia canceled plans to sell the 1970s-era short-range nuclear capable Sunburn antiship missile to China. The Rohrbacher-Solomon amendment initially passed by a vote of 213 to 205, but in a rare revote was subsequently defeated 215 to 206. The reversal showed that, even for those who share the amendment sponsors' concern about Russia's exporting practices, the national interest of the United States in continued funding for the CTR transcends this concern. In addition, the continuation of the MPC&A program will facilitate another round of U.S-Russian nuclear arms reductions, in START III. Without effective controls over nuclear materials, on the other hand, the dismantlement of nuclear weapons required under START III could actually increase rather than decrease proliferation threats because there would be greater potential for loose nukes.[94]

Above all, the fulfillment of the U.S. counterproliferation programs in the FSU will require patience. The scope of the problem means that it will take years to eliminate the nuclear threat in the FSU. And smugglers are not going to sit by idly in the meantime. As a result, for the immediate future, there will be a premium on good intelligence and law enforcement. Unfortunately, international agencies with nuclear expertise are not yet cooperating effectively with those who are responsible for stopping illicit trade. The IAEA and the U.N. Crime Prevention and Criminal Justice Branch are both located in Vienna's International Center, but the IAEA mandate does not allow it to engage in investigative activity. As a result, contacts between the two have been little more than desultory. Obviously, this arrangement will have to change if the task of collecting intelligence on would-be terrorists is to be performed effectively.[95]

Conclusion
The Enduring Nuclear Threat

The Reagan Years

For some time to come, historians and political scientists are likely to ponder the reasons for the transformation that occurred in Reagan's Soviet policy
beginning late in his first administration. One interpretation, the so-called Reagan victory school, contends that his administration's military buildup
during his first term was motivated by a preconceived
plan to bankrupt the Soviet Union. Even Reagan supported this interpretation. On December 16, 1988,
almost a month before leaving office, he said that the
changes that were taking place in the Soviet Union
were in part the result of U.S. firmness, a strong
defense, healthy alliances, and a willingness to use
force when necessary.[1]

The Strategic Defense Initiative, this school of thought argues, was the
real key to the transformation in U.S.-Soviet relations. Reagan's Arms
Control and Disarmament Agency director, Kenneth Adelman, asserted
that "SDI played into our comparative advantage—technological
prowess—and discounted theirs—big ballistic missiles." When "the Soviets realized that we intended to capitalize on our high-tech, embodied by
SDI," he added, then and only then did they become willing to deal. Even

some former Soviet leaders support this assessment. In February 1993 former Soviet foreign minister Alexander Bessmertnykh said that SDI "made us realize we were in a very dangerous spot." Gorbachev was convinced that any attempt to match SDI would have done "irreparable harm to the Soviet economy."[2]

Beth Fischer, on the other hand, makes a compelling case that Reagan was the stimulus for the new approach to the Soviet Union that began late in his first term. Much to the surprise of Reagan's hard-line advisers, he was serious about eliminating nuclear weapons, and this became the primary goal of the new policy he adopted toward the Soviet Union. Fischer points to a number of incidents late in the summer and the fall of 1983 for Reagan's turnabout. The first was the KAL 007 disaster in September. The second was Reagan's viewing of the TV movie *The Day After* during the following month. Still another, in October 1993, was his participation in a Pentagon briefing on U.S. nuclear war plans. And, finally, Reagan was exposed to an even more frightening nuclear scare, the Able Archer 83 military exercise, which he learned later had led the Kremlin to believe that the United States might be preparing a nuclear strike on the Soviet Union.

Within one week after the conclusion of Able Archer 83, Fischer points out, Reagan took the reins of power away from the hard-liners and began to play a direct and primary role in formulating his administration's Soviet policy. The result was a more conciliatory approach toward the Soviet Union, which led to the INF Treaty. Reagan failed to conclude a START treaty before he left office only because the Soviets refused to accept a defensive strategy, the basis of SDI, which he believed would allow the elimination of all nuclear weapons.

Fischer, however, deemphasizes the role of Secretary of State George Shultz, Robert McFarlane, and Nancy Reagan in bringing about the transformation in Reagan's Soviet policy. Nancy Reagan wanted her husband to be remembered as a peacemaker more than cold warrior; McFarlane believed the United States could enhance its national security as well as gain political advantages by negotiating with the Soviet Union. George Shultz, usually but not always with McFarlane's support, gave the president a strategy for escaping the "clutches" of the cold warriors who had formulated the administration's initial, hard-line approach to the Soviet Union. Indeed, it was Shultz who first proposed the new approach. In a memorandum to the president on January 19, 1983, he recommended, and Reagan reacted positively to, "an intensified dialogue with Moscow."[3]

However, as Shultz expected, his initiative ran into the stonewall opposition of administration hard-liners. The new policy was also hindered by the KAL 007 tragedy in September 1983 and by the death of Yuri Andropov the following February. Nevertheless, on January 16, 1984, Reagan delivered an address on superpower relations that proved to be the turning point in his administration's approach to the Kremlin. By March 1984, Reagan had virtually excluded the foreign policy bureaucracy from the conduct of U.S.-Soviet relations.

But progress toward an INF agreement would not have been possible without a receptive Soviet leader in the Kremlin. That did not happen until Mikhail Gorbachev was elected general secretary of the Soviet Communist Party in March 1985. Like Reagan and Shultz, Gorbachev also wanted to end the nuclear arms race. Its termination, he believed, would not only reduce Soviet defense expenditure but also would diminish tensions with the West and facilitate badly needed Western economic assistance to the Soviet Union. In fact, Gorbachev seized the arms reduction initiative from Reagan by accepting, and often surpassing, the president's proposals. The INF negotiations were concluded successfully primarily because of concessions the Soviet leader made—in the face of considerable opposition from hard-liners within his own government and military.

Yet Gorbachev and Reagan were not able to conclude a START treaty. This failure resulted primarily because the Soviet leader refused to water down the ABM Treaty by permitting SDI, and Reagan refused to curtail SDI in order to achieve substantial cuts in the Soviet strategic nuclear arsenal. Still, both men contributed to a winding down of the superpower nuclear arms race and, soon thereafter, the Cold War itself.

The role that domestic politics played in the transformation of Reagan's Soviet policy cannot be discounted. Neither Reagan nor the Democratic Party, which had initially backed the president's military buildup, could ignore the impact of the nuclear freeze movement. The Democrats embraced the freeze; the president initially fought it and then subverted it by means of advancing SDI and a more conciliatory approach to the Soviet Union which emphasized his desire to eliminate nuclear weapons as a better alternative to freezing the status quo. Reagan's astute ability to defuse the antinuclear weapons movement by pressing the Soviets to return to the negotiating table was a major contributing factor behind his landslide reelection victory in November 1984.

Although Reagan was successful in concluding the INF Treaty, he failed to achieve his goal of reducing—let alone eliminating—nuclear weapons. He failed in achieving the less ambitious goal, strategic arms reductions, primarily because he refused to abandon SDI, which still remains, albeit in much altered form, an impediment to further strategic arms reduction. Gorbachev, for a variety of reasons, feared SDI. Not only would it have undermined the ABM Treaty, it would have made START reductions politically impossible. In addition, of course, Gorbachev realized there was no way the Soviet Union—and now Russia even less—could match its more technologically advanced adversary. Nevertheless, Reagan's attachment to SDI prevented implementation, during his administration, of the kind of massive reductions that were called for in START I and START II, agreements that his successor, George Bush, would conclude.

The Bush Administration

The START I and START II treaties were the hallmarks of Bush's administration in the area of nuclear arms control. The first agreement provided for reductions in warhead numbers to approximalty 6,000; START II would cut that number roughly in half. In addition, Bush took the initiative in virtually eliminating the tactical nuclear weapons that were not covered by the INF Treaty. His initiative was emulated by Gorbachev.

As a result of the nuclear arms reductions that Bush initiated or completed by 1993, when he left the White House, the total active U.S. nuclear stockpile was reduced by 59 percent from its 1988 level and the number of U.S. tactical nuclear weapons by 90 percent. Moreover, no nuclear weapons remained in the custody of U.S. ground forces, nor did the U.S. Navy deploy any tactical nuclear weapons at sea. In addition, by 1993, no U.S. nuclear systems were targeted on Russia, or any other country, and U.S. heavy bombers were no longer deployed on alert status. Furthermore, a smaller number of U.S. ballistic missile submarines were on alert than ever before, and U.S. airborne command posts were operating on a significantly reduced operations tempo. Finally, no new U.S. nuclear warhead designs were under consideration.[4]

These measures were matched by the Soviet Union and its primary nuclear-weapon successor state, Russia. The withdrawal of Soviet tactical warheads from the territory of former Warsaw Pact allies and non-Russian republics was completed in December 1991. The last shipment of tactical warheads from Ukraine took place in May 1992. By the end of 1993, the transfer of tactical weapons from frontline Russian military units to central depots on the territory of Russia was largely completed. The Bush administration, as a result of prompting by Congress, which passed the Nunn-Lugar Cooperative Threat Reduction Act in 1991, also facilitated action to dismantle the nuclear warheads of the former Soviet Union.

During the Bush presidency, the United States also initiated a major effort to prevent the proliferation of nuclear weapons to nonweapon states. It facilitated the denuclearization of the former Soviet republics with nuclear weapon, Ukraine, Belarus, and Kazakhstan, as well as their adherence to NPT. The Bush administration also expanded and strengthened the Missile Technology Control Regime and tightened U.S. controls on nuclear exports. The administration also used force to degrade (but apparently not eliminate) the nuclear threat posed by Iraq. It also was instrumental in persuading Argentina, Brazil, and South Africa to forgo the development of nuclear weapons.

But the Bush administration was unsuccessful in getting India or Pakistan to sign the NPT, primarily because, like Reagan, Bush needed Pakistani assistance in getting aid to the Afghan rebels. He did not put economic pressure on Pakistan until after the Cold War, and by then it was perhaps too late to prevent Pakistan from "going nuclear." Indeed, it was the Congress that finally pressured him into cutting off economic aid to Pakistan in 1990.

Moreover, the Bush administration refused to take a step that arms controllers believed would be most effective in ending the nuclear arms race, signing a comprehensive test-ban treaty. It argued that continued testing was necessary to maintain the reliability of the U.S. nuclear deterrent. It was the Congress, again, that compelled the president to sign a bill ultimately ending (in 1996) U.S. nuclear weapon tests. However, Bush and Gorbachev did sign verification protocols that made possible the ratification of the Threshold Test Ban and Peaceful Nuclear Explosions Treaties in 1990, two agreements that had been negotiated in the mid-1970s.

Like Reagan, Bush continued research on (and development of) a ballistic missile defense system and tried, unsuccessfully, to expand the program shortly before he left office. Justifiably, more than a few critics considered continued work on the SDI not only a threat to the ABM Treaty but also the main obstacle to ending the strategic nuclear arms race. The Russians did not appear likely to end the offensive nuclear arms race while the United States prepared to develop and ultimately deploy ABM defenses designed to eliminate or at least degrade their value as a deterrent.

The Clinton Administration

Unlike Reagan, Clinton entered the White House determined to reduce the number of nuclear weapons, not build them. He has only partially fulfilled that promise. His administration was successful in gaining the ratification of the START I Treaty by getting Ukraine to surrender its nuclear weapons to Russia and join the NPT as a nonweapon state. However, he has been unable, as of this writing, to gain the ratification of the START II Treaty.

A variety of reasons are responsible. For one, the treaty is a hostage of the lower house of the Russian parliament. Many members of the Duma believe that the agreement's reductions favor the U.S. side. For example, it would force Russia to give up its great advantage in heavy MIRVed ICBMs while allowing the United States to retain its advantage in bombers and SLBMs. The ratification effort has also been hurt by the Clinton administration's decision to expand NATO's membership to include three former Soviet satellite states—Poland, the Czech Republic, and Hungary. Without question, this move increased hostility in the Duma toward the West and specifically toward arms control agreements with the United States. More recently, the Duma again shelved consideration of the treaty to express its displeasure with U.S. bombing of Iraq in December 1998.

Ratification of the START II Treaty has also been complicated by the Clinton administration's decision to develop and deploy theater ballistic missile defenses. Fearing that it was only a step from TMD deployment to the deployment of a nationwide ballistic missile defense, some Russians have argued that it would be unwise to reduce Russia's offensive nuclear weapon systems while the United States was building a defensive system that could neutralize the Russian retaliatory capability.

To relieve these concerns, the Clinton administration persuaded the Yeltsin government to accept a "demarcation line" between permitted TMD and restricted ABM systems. However, the agreement, which was concluded in 1998, displeased many Republican members of Congress, who felt it placed too many restrictions on the development and deployment of an NMD. They insist that an NMD is necessary to protect the United States from the growing threat of a ballistic missile attack from a rogue country such as Iran, North Korea, or Iraq. Republican senators have said that they want to take a "careful look" at the demarcation agreement before approving it.

The Republicans also want to look at the agreement designed to multilateralize the ABM Treaty by making Russia, Ukraine, Belarus, and Kazakhstan parties to it in place of the defunct Soviet Union. Republicans fear multilateralization will complicate any future amendment of the ABM Treaty, including amendments that could make "legal" a national ballistic missile defense system. Some Republicans believe that if they defeat multilateralization, they will be able to kill the entire ABM Treaty, a result they would not lament.

The Clinton administration, on the other hand, has hoped to win Senate approval of the amendments by tying them to the prospect of the major Russian strategic force reductions that are called for in the START II Treaty and in the proposed START III agreement. However, with the Russian nuclear arsenal shrinking of its own accord through aging and attrition, Republican opponents of the ABM Treaty may feel that they do not have to accept Clinton's alternative. The future of START, needless to say, is tied to the outcome of the battle over the ABM Treaty amendments.

President Clinton also has made stemming the proliferation of nuclear, biological, and chemical weapons, as well as the ballistic missiles that deliver them, a major goal of his administration. To this end, he has succeeded in persuading many nations to join (or to abide by) the Missile Technology Control Regime. However, he has not been totally successful in getting the Russians, the Chinese, nor the North Koreans, in particular, to abide by MTCR guidelines. And ballistic missile proliferation continues to be a problem. North Korea, Iraq, and also Iran appear determined to develop at least intermediate-range ballistic missiles.

Clinton, however, was successful in gaining international agreement to extend the Nonproliferation Treaty indefinitely, and he successfully negotiated a Comprehensive Test Ban Treaty. Nevertheless, both agreements could be in jeopardy if the Senate does not ratify the CTBT, which the Republican majority in the Senate is reluctant to do. The refusal of the Senate to ratify the CTBT is still another reason why the START II Treaty has been stuck in the Russian Duma.

The failure of the nuclear weapon states to ratify the CTBT, in turn, could undermine international support for the NPT, and soon. In the past year, India and Pakistan have become declared nuclear weapon states, and others are likely to follow suit if the NPT unravels. Iran and North Korea seem prepared to produce nuclear weapons. Will Japan continue to rely on the U.S. nuclear deterrent if the North Koreans develop a nuclear arsenal and the ballistic missiles to deliver them? In addition, the Arab nations are angry that virtually nothing has been done to persuade Israel to dismantle its undeclared nuclear arsenal. Why, they argue, should Arab countries refrain from developing a nuclear deterrent as long as Israel maintains one? This argument has been used repeatedly by Iraq, which is the one Arab country that so far has attempted to build nuclear weapons. The NPT is not likely to endure if other states follow the Iraqi example.

Many wonder if Clinton's Iraqi strategy—maintaining U.N. economic sanctions against Iraq, combined with military strikes against suspected Iraqi WMD facilities—is the best way to prevent Iraq from threatening its neighbors with nuclear, chemical, or biological weapons. Yet there does not seem to be a better alternative in sight. Clearly, the UNSCOM inspection system did much to reveal the extent of Iraq's WMD program and also destroyed significant parts of it. UNSCOM, however, could not ensure that Iraq was no longer a WMD threat primarily because the Iraqis refused to cooperate unconditionally with the inspectors.

To be sure, the Clinton administration has made great strides in reducing the risks of illicit nuclear transfers from Russia to rogue states or would-be terrorist groups. The Nunn-Lugar Cooperative Threat Reduction Program has been responsible for facilitating the safe dismantling of thousands of nuclear weapons in the FSU. Still, there is a substantial risk that the by-products of those warheads, thousands of tons of plutonium and highly enriched uranium, could fall into the "wrong" hands. Russia, in short, remains a major potential source of nuclear weapon materials and know-how.

Moreover, the overwhelming majority of the world's states believe that the threat posed by nuclear weapons will not be removed until the nuclear powers eliminate their own arsenals. Yet this seems highly unlikely as long as the nation-state, with its emphasis on military power as the foundation of national security, endures. The alternative to the nation-state, world government, is not much in favor these days, considering the inability of the United Nations to deal effectively with Saddam Hussein, due in no small part to conflicting national interests among the members of the Security Council. In the absence of effective international cooperation to deal with the nuclear proliferation threat, the United States seems destined to play the role of the world's policeman. But this alternative also has its drawbacks. Americans will have to bear the cost of a larger military establishments and risk their sons and daughters in combat with rogue states or terrorist groups, and playing the role of world's policeman will undoubtedly expose Americans both at home and abroad to the possibility of terrorist attack. Yet in the absence of a revival of cooperation with Russia, China, and France in the U.N. Security Council, there does not seem to be a better alternative.

ACRONYMS
AND TECHNICAL TERMS

ABM   Antiballistic missile; a system designed to destroy or incapacitate strategic (offensive) ballistic missiles

ACDA   Arms Control and Disarmament Agency

ALCM   Air-launched cruise missile (see cruise missile)

ASAT   Anti-satellite weapon: a weapon system designed to destroy or incapacitate enemy satellites

ASBMS   Air-to-surface ballistic missiles

ATBMD   Antitactical ballistic missile defenses

Ballistic missile   A missile that does not rely on aerodynamic surfaces to produce lift and follows a ballistic trajectory when thrust is terminated.

BMDO   Ballistic missile defense organization

BMD   Ballistic missile defense; a system for defending against an attack by ballistic missiles

c3i   Command, control, communication, and intelligence systems

CFE   Treaty Conventional Forces in Europe Treaty

CORRTEX   Continuous reflectometry for radius versus time experiments, a method for detecting underground nuclear explosions

CIS   Commonwealth of Independent States; an association of former republics of the Soviet Union

Counterforce   Use of strategic nuclear forces to destroy or disable enemy military capabilities

Cruise missile   A guided missile that uses aerodynamic lift

CTBT   Comprehensive Test Ban; an agreement that prohibits all nuclear testing

CTPR   Cooperative Threat Reduction Program, also known as the Nunn-Lugar program, designed to reduce the threat posed by nuclear weapons and materiel in the former republics of the Soviet Union

Damage limitation   A strategy designed to reduce damage to population centers and other nonmilitary sites during a nuclear exchange

Downloading   The process of reducing the number of warheads carried by particular types of strategic ballistic missiles

DST   Defense and Space Talks

Dual-capable weapons   Systems capable of delivering either conventional or nuclear weapons

Encryption   The encoding of communications or other data (e.g., telemetric data) for the purpose of concealing information

Enrichment   The process of increasing the quantity of highly fissionable uranium-235 isotopes in uranium fuel or explosives

ERIS   Exoatmospheric reentry vehicle interceptor system; an Antiballistic missile system

FSU   Republics of the former Soviet Union

GPALS   Global Protection Against Limited Strikes; an ABM system proposed by the Bush administration

GLCM   Ground-launched cruise missile *See* cruise missile

HEDI   High endoatmospheric defense interceptor; an ABM system

HEU   Highly enriched uranium

Horizontal proliferation   The acquisition of nuclear weapons by nonweapon states

ICBM   Intercontinental ballistic missile; a fixed or mobile land-based missile capable of delivering a warhead to intercontinental ranges defined in the SALT I and II agreements as those in excess of 5,500 kilometers

IAEA   International Atomic Energy Agency

INF   Intermediate-range nuclear forces; land-based missiles and aircraft with a range/combat radius between the battlefield range of tactical nuclear weapons and 5,500 kilometers

IRBM   Intermediate-range ballistic missile; a ballistic missile with a range of between 1,500 and 3,000 nautical miles

JVE   Joint Verification Experiment, provided for exchange visits to American and Russian nuclear weapon test sites

Kiloton   Nuclear yield equal to that of 1,000 tons of TNT

LPAR   Large phased-array radar; designed to detect and track incoming ballistic missiles

LEU   Low enriched uranium

Light-water reactor   The most common type of nuclear reactor, fueled with enriched uranium

LTBT   Limited Test Ban Treaty; prohibited all but underground nuclear weapon tests

MAD   Mutual assured destruction; a concept of strategic stability under which rivals are deterred from launching a nuclear attack because each possesses the capability to devastate the other's homeland in a retaliatory attack

Megaton   Nuclear yield equal to that of one million tons of TNT

MIRV   Multiple independently targetable reentry vehicle; multiple reentry vehicles carried by a ballistic missile, each of which can be directed to a separate target

MRBM   Medium-range ballistic missile; a ballistic missile with a range between 500 and 1,500 nautical miles

MTCR   Missile Technology Control Regime

MX ICBM   An intercontinental ballistic missile capable of carrying ten nuclear warheads; also called "Peacekeeper"

NATO   North Atlantic Treaty Organization

NMD   National ballistic missile defense system

National technical means   Assets under national control, including photo-reconnaissance satellites and radars, used to monitor compliance with arms agreements

NPT   Nuclear Nonproliferation Treaty; an international agreement designed to check the horizontal and vertical proliferation of nuclear weapons

NSC   National Security Council

NST   Nuclear and Space Talks

PALS   Permission action links; mechanisms designed to prevent the unauthorized use of nuclear weapons

PAC-3   Patriot advanced capability, level 3, an advanced version of the Patriot ABM

PNE   Peaceful nuclear explosion

Reentry vehicle   The part(s) of a ballistic missile containing primarily the warhead(s) and guidance system

Reprocessing   The process of separating uranium and plutonium from spent nuclear fuel

SAC   Strategic Air Command

SALT   Strategic Arms Limitation Talks

SDI   Strategic Defense Initiative; a ballistic missile defense program begun by President Reagan; also known as Star Wars

SDIO   Strategic Defense Initiative Organization

SIOP   Single Integrated Operational Plan; the U.S. strategic nuclear war plan

SLBM   Submarine-launched ballistic missile

SLCM   Sea-launched cruise missile; see cruise missile

SLV   Space-launched vehicle

SNDV   Strategic nuclear delivery vehicle

SNF   Short-range nuclear forces

SRINF   Short-range, intermediate nuclear forces; land-based missiles with a 500-1,000 kilometer range

Standing Consultative Commission   A permanent U.S.-Soviet commission established to implement and maintain SALT agreements

START   Strategic Arms Reduction Talks

Tactical nuclear weapon   A short-range, low-yield nuclear weapon designed for battlefield use

Telemetry Data   transmitted from missiles by electronic means

THAAD   Theater High Altitude Area Defense; the army's tactical ballistic missile defense system

Throw weight   The weight of a missile that can be placed on a target trajectory

TMD   Theater missile defenses

TTBT   Threshold Test Ban Treaty; an agreement that limits U.S. and FSU nuclear tests to 150 kilotons

UNSCOM   U.N. Special Commission on Iraq; charged with monitoring the dismantling of Iraq's weapons of mass destruction

Verification   The process of determining whether parties to an agreement are in compliance with their obligations

Vertical proliferation   The increase in numbers of nuclear weapons possessed by nuclear weapon states

Warhead   The explosive part of a missile, projectile, torpedo, or rocket

WMD   Weapons of massive destruction, including nuclear, biological, and chemical weapons

Yield   The energy released in an explosion, usually expressed in terms of TNT equivalent

Notes

Introduction

1. *Public Papers of the Presidents of the United States: Dwight D. Eisenhower: 1960-61* (1961):1038.

Chapter 1

1. *Public Papers of the Presidents of the United States: Ronald W. Reagan, 1983* (1984), 362. (Hereafter cited as *RPP.*)
2. *RPP: 1981* (1982), 57. *RPP: 1982* (1983), 487.
3. Ronald W. Reagan, *An American Life* (1990), 267; Daniel Wirls, *Buildup: The Politics of Defense in the Reagan Era* (1992), 35.
4. Jeffrey Richelson, "PD-59, NSDD-13, and the Reagan Strategic Modernization Program," *Journal of Strategic Studies* 6 (June 1983):128-146.
5. *New York Times*, May 30, 1982; NSDD-12: "Strategic Forces Modernization," and NSDD 32: "U.S. National Security Strategy," in Christopher Simpson, ed., *National Security Directives of the Reagan and Bush Administrations: The Declassified History of U.S. Political and Military Policy, 1981-1991* (1995), 14-15, 46-49.
6. Caspar W. Weinberger, *Report of Secretary of Defense to the Congress on the FY 1983 Budget, FY Authorization Request and FY 1983-1987 Defense Programs* (1982), III-57-63, 77-89; U.S. Senate, Committee on Foreign Relations, Hearings: *Strategic Weapons Proposals:* Part 1, 97th Cong., 1st sess. (1981), 8-14.
7. NSDD-68: "Nuclear Weapons Stockpile," in Simpson, *National Security Directives*, 81-82.
8. Simpson, 82.
9. Laurence I. Barrett, *Gambling with History: Reagan in the White House* (1983), 308; Kennan is quoted in L. Bruce Van Voorst, "The Critical Masses," *Foreign Policy* 48 (Fall 1982):86.

10. Reagan *Life,* 550, 585; Beth A. Fischer, *Reversal: Foreign Policy and the End of the Cold War* (1997), 103-109.

11. *Gallup Reports* 188 (May 1981); 208 (January 1983).

12. Wirls, *Buildup,* 109.

13. U.S. Arms Control and Disarmament Agency, *Documents on Disarmament, 1982* (1985), 109-110. (Hereafter cited as *DD.*)

14. National Conference of Catholic Bishops, *The Challenge of Peace: God's Promise and Our Response* (1983).

15. *New York Times,* October 5, 1982; March 26, 1983.

16. Ibid., May 10, 1982.

17. *Time,* April 18, 1983, 29.

18. Alexander M. Haig Jr., *Caveat: Realism, Reagan, and Foreign Policy* (1984), 223.

19. *New York Times,* May 19, 1982.

20. Ibid.

21. U.S. Arms Control and Disarmament Agency, *1983 Annual Report,* Joint Committee Print, 98th Cong., 2d sess. (1984), 12. (Hereafter cited as ACDA, *1983 Report.*)

22. *New York Times,* March 5, 1981; October 22, 1981; *Washington Post,* October 21, 1981.

23. Strobe Talbott, *Deadly Gambits: The Reagan Administration and the Stalemate in Nuclear Arms Control* (1983), 56-61; NSDD-15: "Theater Nuclear Force Negotiations with the USSR," in Simpson, *National Security Directives,* 16-17, 52.

24. *New York Times,* November 30, 1981.

25. ACDA, *1983 Report,* 27-28; *New York Times,* December 22, 1982; January 16, 20, 24, 1983; February 14, 1983; Talbott, *Deadly Gambits,* 161-162.

26. NSDD 56: "Intermediate-Range Nuclear Force Negotiations," in Simpson, *National Security Directives,* 75, 199; Talbott, *Deadly Gambits,* 124-141; Strobe Talbott, *The Master of the Game: Paul Nitze and the Nuclear Peace* (1988), 18.

27. *DD: 1982* (1986), 223-225, 260; *New York Times,* March 31, 1983; April 3, 1983.

28. *American Foreign Policy: Current Documents, 1983* (1985), 545-547. (Hereafter cited as *AFP:CD New York Times,* June 16, 1993.

29. NSDD-102: "Soviet Destruction of the KAL-007 Airliner," in Simpson, *National Security Directives,* 240-241; NSDD-104: "Intermediate-Range Nuclear Forces Negotiations," in Simpson, 111, 142, 327-331; NSDD-106: "START Negotiations," in Simpson, *National Security Directives,* 335.

30. *DD:1983,* 910-914.

31. *New York Times,* November 23, 1983; January 12, 1984.

32. Ibid., June 1, 1982.

33. Ibid., July 21, 1982.

34. NSDD-51: "U.S. Nuclear Testing Limitations Policy-Abandonment of Comprehensive Test Ban Treaty Negotiations," in Simpson, *National Security Directives,* 73-74; NSDD-173: "Proportionate U.S. Responses to Soviet Treaty Violations," in Simpson, *National Security Directives,* 450-451, 549-555.

35. *DD:1978* (1980), 118-164.

36. NSDD-76: "Nuclear Cooperation With China," in Simpson, *National Security Directives*, 228-229, 264; *New York Times*, July 7, 1981.

37. *RRP: 1983* (1984), 437-443.

38. Fischer, *Reversal*, 104.

39. George Shultz, *Turmoil and Triumph* (1993), 466, 509; *Weekly Compilation of Presidential Documents* (1983), 448. (Hereafter cited as WCPD.)

40. Daniel O. Graham, *The Non-Nuclear Defense of Cities* (1983); Teller is quoted in the *New York Times*, November 5, 1983.

41. Wirls, *Buildup*, 143. De Lauer is quoted in Michael R. Gordon, "Reagan's `Star Wars' Proposals Prompt Debate over Future Nuclear Strategy," *National Journal* 7 (January 1984):16.

42. Talbott, *Master of the Game*, 193.

43. Wirls, "Buildup," 146. The Fletcher study, entitled "The Strategic Defense Initiative Defensive Technologies Study," is reprinted in U.S. Senate, Committee on Foreign Relations, *Strategic Defense and Anti-Satellite Weapons*, 98th Cong., 2d sess. (1984), 141-175. The Hoffman study, entitled "Ballistic Missile Defenses and U.S. National Security, Summary Report," is reprinted in the same volume, 125-140.

44. Martin Anderson, *Revolution* (1988), 98.

45. Wirls, *Buildup*, 62. *RPP:1983*, (1984) 437-443.

46. Kerry L. Hunter, *The Reign of Fantasy: The Political Roots of Reagan's Star Wars Policy* (1997), 122.

47. *Washington Post*, March 28, 1983.

48. U.S. Congress, Senate, Committee on Foreign Relations, Hearings: *Strategic Defense and Anti-Satellite Weapons*, 98th Cong., 2d sess. (1984), 30.

49. Arms Control Association, *Star Wars Quotes* (1986), 34.

50. Keith L. Shimko, *Images and Arms Control: Perceptions of the Soviet Union in the Reagan Administration* (1991), 218.

51. *DD:1972* (1973), 197-201.

52. Shultz, *Turmoil*, 250, 253. Shimko, *Images*, 202.

53. Shimko, *Images*, 201.

54. Fischer, *Reversal*, 105.

55. *Time*, October 7, 1985, 48; Hunter, *Reign of Fantasy*, 141; William Hartung, "Star Wars Pork Barrel," *Bulletin of the Atomic Scientists* (January 1986):20-24.

56. *DD:1979* (1982), 565-567; *New York Times*, March 3, 1980; Bernard T. Feld and Kosta Tsipis, "Land-based Intercontinental Ballistic Missiles," *Scientific American* 241 (November 1979):51-61.

57. Gerard C. Smith, *Doubletalk: The Story of the First Strategic Arms Limitations Talks* (1980), 341-343.

58. Hunter, *Reign of Fantasy*, 41.

59. NSDD-35: "Strategic Forces Modernization—MX Missile," in Simpson, *National Security Directives*, 65, 123-124.

60. Brent Scowcroft, chair, President's Commission on Strategic Forces, *Report of the President's Commission on Strategic Forces*, April 6, 1983.

61. *New York Times,* May 25, 1983; U.S. Senate, Committee on Armed Services, Hearing: *MX Missile Basing System and Related Issues,* 98th Cong., 1st sess. (1983).

62. NSDD-73: "Strategic Forces Modernization—MX Missile," in Simpson, *National Security Directives,* 227.   NSDD-91: "Strategic Force Modernization Changes," in Simpson, *National Security Directives,* 235.   NSDD-98: "START Negotiations—VI," in Simpson, *National Security Directives,* 238.

Chapter 2

1. Ronald W. Reagan, *An American Life* (1990), 584.

2. Beth A. Fischer, *The Reagan Reversal: Foreign Policy and the End of the Cold War* (1997), 119.

3. Fischer, *Reversal,* 122; Reagan, *Life,* 580.

4. Fischer, *Reversal,* 124-134; "Christopher Andrew and Oleg Gordievsky, *KGB: The Inside Story* (1990), 408, 502-507.

5. Fischer, *Reversal,* 90-93; George P. Shultz, *Turmoil and Triumph: My Years as Secretary of State* (1993), 3-15, 21-23, 117-119.

6. Shultz, *Turmoil,* 165-166.

7. Ibid.

8. Robert McFarlane, *Special Trust* (1994), 295; Shultz, *Turmoil,* 376; Don Oberdorfer, *The Turn: From the Cold War to a New Era* (1991), 71; Fischer, *Reversal,* 139.

9. *Weekly Compilation of Presidential Documents* 20 (1984), 40-45. (Hereafter cited as *WCPD.*)

10. Reagan, *Life,* 595-596.

11. Raymond L. Garthoff, *The Great Transition: American-Soviet Relations and the End of the Cold War* (1994), 178.

12. *New York Times,* September 30, 1984.

13. *New York Times,* January 30, 1984.

14. *National Journal,* October 20, 1984; *New York Times,* September 6, 1984.

15. *Congressional Quarterly,* June 23, 1984, 1482; September 22, 1984, 2291.

16. Neil Rosenbaum, "Chronology of the Comprehensive Test Ban," *Arms Control Today* 20 (November 1990): 35.

17. *AFP: CD 1984* 20 (1986), 226.

18. Oberdorfer, *Turn,* 97; *DD: 1985,* 7-32.

19. NSSD-153: "Overall U.S. Security Strategy—Shultz-Gromyko Meeting," in, Simpson, *National Security Directives,* 439, 469-484.

20. Fischer, *Reversal,* 47; Reagan, *Life,* 13-14.

21. Christopher Mark Davis, "Economic Influences on the Decline of the Soviet Union as a Great Power: Continuity Despite Change," in David Armstrong and Erik Goldstein, eds., *The End of the Cold War* (1990), 90.

22. Shultz, *Turmoil,* 534.

23. Rosenbaum, "Chronology," 34.

24. NSDD-183: "Meeting with Gorbachev in Geneva," in Simpson, *National Security Directives,* 454-455, 579-581.

25. *New York Times,* October 1, 1985.

26. Garthoff, *Great Transition*, 227.
27. Raymond L. Garthoff, "Present at the Transformation: Shultz, Reagan and Gorbachev," *Arms Control Today* 23 (October 1993): 24-26.
28. Strobe Talbott, *Master of the Game: Paul Nitze and the Nuclear Peace* (1990), 243.
29. Raymond L. Garthoff, *Policy versus the Law: The Reinterpretation of the ABM Treaty* (1987), 6-18.
30. *Department of State Bulletin* 85 (December 1985): 33; Garthoff, *Policy versus the Law*, 5, 8-9.
31. U.S. Arms Control and Disarmament Agency, *Facts Concerning Soviet Charges of U.S. Arms Control Noncompliance* (1984), 2; U.S. Department of State, *Soviet Noncompliance with Arms Control Agreements*, Special Report no. 136 (1985), 6.
32. Shultz, *Turmoil*, 581-582.
33. *Washington Times*, February 6, 1987.
34. *Department of State Bulletin* 85 (December 1985):23. U.S. Senate, Subcommittee on Strategic and Theater Nuclear Forces of the Senate Armed Services Committee, Hearing: *Strategic Defense Initiative*, 99th Cong., 1st sess. (1986), 40.
35. *Washington Post*, November 17, 1985; Garthoff, *Policy versus the Law*, 11.
36. Allan Girrier and Catherine Girrier, *American Policy and Alleged Soviet Treaty Violations* (1987), 32-42.
37. Shultz, *Turmoil*, 522-524; Simpson, *National Security Directives*, 988.
38. Girrier and Girrier, *American Policy*, 32, 80-81.
39. Shultz, *Turmoil*, 592-593.
40. *New York Times*, November 1, 2, 4, 7, 8, 1985.
41. Shultz, *Turmoil*, 602.
42. Ibid., 604; *DD: 1985*, 866-871.
43. *DD: 1985*, 878-879.
44. Reagan, *Life*, 660; Garthoff, *Great Transition*, 250.
45. *DD: 1986* (1991), 10-19, 79-80; *New York Times*, February 25, 27, 1986.
46. *DD: 1986* (1991), 260-278; NSDD-232: "Abandonment of the SALT I and SALT II Treaties," in Simpson, *National Security Directives*, 645-646.
47. Matthew Bunn, *Foundation for the Future: The ABM Treaty and National Security* (1990), 171; NSDD-233: "Draft Reply to Gorbachev's Arms-Control Proposals," in Simpson, ed., *National Security Directives*, 646.
48. Shultz, 745-750. Garthoff, *Great Transition*, 283.
49. *New York Times*, October 11, 1986.
50. *New York Times*, October 14, 1986; Garthoff, *Great Transition*, 285-291.
51. *New York Times*, October 14, 16, 1986.
52. *New York Times*, October 14, 1986.
53. *New York Times*, October 14, 16, 17, 1986.
54. Shultz, *Turmoil*, 773; Garthoff, "Present at the Transformation," 24-26.
55. (Cleveland) *Plain Dealer*, October 15, 1986.
56. *New York Times*, October 22, 1986.
57. Kerry L. Hunter, *The Reign of Fantasy: The Political Roots of Reagan's Star Wars Policy* (1997), 49.
58. *WCPD* 22 (1986), 1375-1379, 1387; *Pravda*, October 14, 1986.

59. *Pravda*, October 15, 1986.

60. Sanford Lakoff and Herbert F. York, *A Shield in Space? Technology, Politics, and the Strategic Defense Initiative* (1989), 211; Hunter, 151.

61. George J. Hochbrueckner and Frank McCloskey, "A Sensible Initiative for the SDI Budget," *Arms Control Today* 18 (June 1988): 3-4.

62. Ibid.

63. Ibid.

64. Joseph Romm, "Pseudo-Science and SDI," *Arms Control Today* 19 (October 1989): 18.

65. *Wall Street Journal*, June 20, 1988.

66. Bunn, *Foundation*, 28, 173; NSDD-261: "Consultations on Adoption of the 'Broad' Interpretation of the Anti-Ballistic Missile (ABM) Treaty," in Simpson, 734.

67. Bunn, *Foundation*, 173.

68. Ibid.

69. Ibid.

70. Ibid.

71. Ibid.

72. *New York Times*, February 7, 1987; Bunn, *Foundation*, 60.

73. Jesse James, "Senate Approves Ratification of Historic INF Treaty," *Arms Control Today* 18 (July-August 1988): 22-23.

74. Garthoff, *Great Transition*, 325.

75. Ibid., 305; *WCPD* 23 (1987): 204.

76. Michael J. Sodaro, *Moscow, Germany, and the West: From Khrushchev to Gorbachev* (1990), 349.

77. Ibid., 350.

78. For a text of the INF Treaty, see *Department of State Bulletin* 88 (August 1988): 23-31, 42-45.

79. Jesse James, "Senate Approves Ratification of Historic INF Treaty," *Arms Control Today* 18 (July-August 1988): 22.

80. Talbott, *Master of the Game*, 334.

81. Garthoff, *Great Transition*, 328.

82. *WCPD* 23 (1987): 321. Shultz, *Turmoil*, 1013-1014.

83. Bunn, *Foundation*, 174.

84. Garthoff, *Great Transition*, 329.

85. *Department of State Bulletin* 87 (November 1987): 34-37.

86. *WCPD* 24 (1988): 1579-1580.

87. Charles Van Doren, "Pakistan, Congress, and the Nonproliferation Challenge," *Arms Control Today* 17 (November 1987): 6-8.

88. Ibid.

89. Mitchell Reiss, *Bridled Ambition: Why Countries Constrain Their Nuclear Capabilities* (1995), 187-188.

90. Leonard S. Spector, "Nonproliferation: After the Bomb Has Spread," *Arms Control Today* 18 (December 1988): 9.

91. Michael Klare, *Rogue States and Nuclear Outlaws: America's Search for a New Foreign Policy* (1994): 49-51.

92. Leonard Weiss, "Tighten Up on Nuclear Cheaters," *Bulletin of the Atomic Scientists* (May 1991): 11.

93. Wyn Q. Bowen, "U.S. Policy on Ballistic Missile Proliferation: The MTCR's First Decade (1987-1997)," *Nonproliferation Review* 5 (Fall 1997): 21-39.

94. Ibid., 26; Kathleen C. Bailey, *Doomsday Weapons in the Hands of Many: The Arms Control Challenge of the 90s* (1991): 126-129.

95. Rosenbaum, "Chronology," 34-35.

96. Ibid.

97. Robert Guldin, "CORRTEX: Backbone of U.S. Testing Policy," *Arms Control Today* 18 (June 1988): 22.

98. Rosenbaum, "Chronology," 35.

Chapter 3

1. George Bush and Brent Scowcroft, *A World Transformed* (1998), 12. *Weekly Compilation of Presidential Documents* 25 (1990): 121. (Hereafter cited as WCPD.) Seyom Brown, *The Faces of Power: Constancy and Change in United States Foreign Policy from Truman to Clinton*, 2d ed. (1994), 506.

2. WCPD 25: 699-702; Raymond L. Garthoff, "The Bush Administration's Policy toward the Soviet Union," *Current History* 90 (October 1991): 312.

3. Brown, *Faces of Power*, 509-510.

4. *New York Times*, April 25, 1989; Bush and Scowcroft, *A World Transformed*, 71.

5. Michael Beschloss and Strobe Talbott, *At the Highest Levels: The Inside Story of the End of the Cold War* (1993), 74; Bush and Scowcroft, *A World Transformed*, 81.

6. Martin Olav Sabo, "The Accountant's Budget: Bush and Cheney Fail to Respond to a Changing Era," *Arms Control Today* 19 (June-July 1989): 11-14.

7. Ibid.

8. Hans Kristensen, "Targets of Opportunity," *Bulletin of the Atomic Scientists* 53 (September-October 1997): 22-28.

9. Dunbar Lockwood, "Panel Calls for New War Plan," *Arms Control Today* 22 (January-February 1992): 43; *New York Times*, June 2, 1990.

10. *New York Times*, January 27, 1989.

11. *New York Times*, March 26, 1989; Rebecca Bjork, *The Strategic Defense Initiative: Symbolic Containment of the Nuclear Threat* (1992), 93.

12. Matthew Bunn, "Brilliant Pebbles," *Arms Control Today* 19 (April 1989): 28.

13. Bruce W. MacDonald, "Lost in Space: SDI Struggles through Its Sixth Year," *Arms Control Today* 19 (September 1989): 24.

14. Thomas E. Halverston, "First Bush Defense Budget Reveals Program Cuts, Strategic Decisions," *Arms Control Today* 19 (May 1989): 21.

15. James B. Rubin, "As START Resumes, Bush Pushes Early Verification," *Arms Control Today* 19 (August 1989): 25.

16. *Department of State Bulletin* 89 (December 1989): 20-26.

17. *Congressional Quarterly*, September 30, 1989, 2572-2573.

18. James B. Rubin, "Baker, Shevardnadze Generate Arms Control Progress," *Arms Control Today* 19 (October 1989): 26-27.

19. Matthew Bunn, *Foundation for the Future: The ABM Treaty and National Security* (1990): 177-178.
20. James B. Rubin, "Arms Control in Jackson Hole: Baker/Shevardnadze and Beyond," *Arms Control Today* 19 (October 1989): 13; *Congressional Quarterly*, September 30, 1989, 2572-2573; "Joint Statement Issued by the Governments of the United States and the Soviet Union," U.S. Department of State, *American Foreign Policy: Current Document, 1989*, (thereafter cited as *AFP: CD*) (1990), 369-373.
21. Rubin, "Baker, Shevardnadze," 26-27. *Congressional Quarterly*, September 30, 1989, 2573.
22. *Congressional Quarterly*, September 30, 1989, 2573.
23. Ibid.; Rubin, "Baker, Shevardnadze, and Beyond," 27.
24. Rubin, "Baker, Shevardnadze, and Beyond," 27.
25. Dunbar Lockwood, "Testing Protocols Clear Road for Treaties' Ratification," *Arms Control Today* 20 (June 1990): 34.
26. Ibid.
27. Michael Klare, *Rogue States and Nuclear Outlaws: America's Search for a New Foreign Policy* (1994): 195.
28. Gregory P. Webb, "Unlimited Test Ban Treaty" *Arms Control Today* 20 (April 1990): 30.
29. Neil Rosenbaum, "Chronology of the Comprehensive Test Ban," *Arms Control Today* 20 (November 1990): 35.
30. Raymond Garthoff, "Beyond Containment: The Malta Summit," *Current History* (October 1991): 312.
31. Constantine C. Menges, *The Future of Germany and the Atlantic Alliance* (1991), 62-107.
32. "Malta Summit Makes Waves: Leaders to Seek START, CFE Pacts in 1990," *Arms Control Today* 19 (December 1989-January 1990), 6.   *AFP: CD, 1989* (1990): 385-388.
33. *AFP: CD*, 1989 (1990): 385-388.
34. Dunbar Lockwood, "START Talks Falter, Early Summit Scheduled," *Arms Control Today* 20 (May 1990): 24-25.
35. Ibid.
36. *New York Times*, April 8-9, 1990.
37. Garthoff, *Great Transition*, 416-418, 422-423.
38. *New York Times*, May 20, 1990; Dunbar Lockwood, "Bush, Gorbachev Concur: START to Finish by Year's End," *Arms Control Today* 21 (June 1990): 28-29.
39. Lockwood, "Bush, Gorbachev Concur," 28-29.
40. Ibid. *New York Times*, May 20-21, 1990.
41. Lockwood, "Bush, Gorbachev Concur," 28-29. *New York Times*, June 1-2, 1990.
42. The texts of the Bush-Gorbachev joint statements appear in *Arms Control Today* 21 (June 1990): 22-23.
43. Ibid.
44. *Congressional Quarterly*, May 26, 1990, 1663, 1668.
45. Ibid., 1665, 1668; *New York Times*, May 20, 1990.
46. *Congressional Quarterly*, May 26, 1990, 1663.

47. Ibid.
48. Ibid.
49. Andrew J. Pierre, "The United States and the New Europe," *Current History* 89 (November 1990): 355; Garthoff, *Great Transition*, 427.
50. U.S. Department of State, *Dispatch* 1 (October 10, 1990): 163.
51. For a text of the Kohl-Gorbachev accord, see *Current History* 89 (October 1990): 382.
52. *Dispatch* 1 (October 17, 1990): 199.
53. Dunbar Lockwood, "February START Summit Uncertain As Negotiations Inch toward Finish," *Arms Control Today* 21 (January-February 1991): 23-24.
54. Ibid.
55. Ibid.
56. Dunbar Lockwood, "Moscow Summit, START Signing Postponed," *Arms Control Today* 21 (March 1991): 25, 28.
57. Ibid.
58. Ibid.
59. Matthew Bunn, *Foundation*, 96.
60. John Pike, "The Ballistic Missile Defense Debate," *Current History* (April 1997): 160; *Wall Street Journal*, January 23, 1991.
61. John Conyers Jr., "The Patriot Myth: Caveat Emptor," *Arms Control Today* 22 (November 1992): 3; Pike, "Defense Debate," 160.
62. *Dispatch* 2 (February 4, 1991): 66.
63. Peter Clausen, "Star Warriors Try Again," *Bulletin of the Atomic Scientists* 47 (June 1991): 9-10.
64. Ibid., 9.
65. Bruce W. MacDonald, "Falling Star: SDI's Troubled Seventh Year," *Arms Control Today* 22 (September 1990): 7-11.
66. Matthew Bunn, "Bush Announces New Star Wars Plan to Protect against 'Limited' Strikes," *Arms Control Today* 21 (March 1991): 27.
67. Matthew Bunn, "Attack on ABM Treaty Repelled—For Now," *Arms Control Today* 21 (April 1991): 21.
68. Ibid.
69. Ibid.
70. Jack Mendelsohn, "Why START?" *Arms Control Today* 21 (April 1991): 3-9.
71. Dunbar Lockwood, "START Work Intensifies," *Arms Control Today* 21 (July-August 1991): 22.
72. Dunbar Lockwood, "START: The End Game and SDI," *Arms Control Today* 21 (September 1991): 3-6.
73. Ibid.
74. U.S. Arms Control and Disarmament Agency, *START: Treaty between the United States of America and the Union of Soviet Socialist Republics on the Reduction and Limitation of Strategic Offensive Arms* (1991).
75. Mendelsohn, "Why START?" 63.
76. Matthew Bunn, "Muddying the ABM Waters," *Arms Control Today* 21 (July-August 1991): 24.

77. Spurgeon M. Keeny Jr., "Limited ABM Defense: Dangerous and Unnecessary," *Arms Control Today* 21 (October 1991): 14, 16-18; Michael Krepon, "Limited ABM Defense: A Prudent Step," *Arms Control Today* 21 (October 1991): 15, 19-20; *Congressional Record*, Senate, 102d Cong., 1st sess. (1991), 11431.

78. Keeny, "Limited ABM Defense," 14, 16-18; Krepon, "Limited ABM Defense," 15, 19-20.

Chapter 4

1. Dunbar Lockwood, "Superpowers Downplay `Loose Nukes' Risk," *Arms Control Today* 21 (October 1991): 23.

2. U.S. Senate, Subcommittee on European Affairs of the Committee on Foreign Relations, Hearings, *Loose Nukes, Nuclear Smuggling, and the Fissile-Material Problem in Russia and the NIS*, 104th Cong., 1st sess. (1995), 34.

3. Lockwood, " `Loose Nukes' Risk," 23, 30.

4. Christopher Paine and Thomas B. Cochran, "Kiev Conference: Verified Warhead Controls," *Arms Control Today* 22 (January-February 1992): 16.

5. For the text of Bush's speech, see *Arms Control Today* 21 (October 1991): 3-5.

6. Ibid.

7. For the text of Gorbachev's proposal, see *Arms Control Today* 21 (October 1991): 6.

8. Ibid.

9. Ibid.

10. Ibid.

11. Spurgeon M. Keeny Jr., "Limited ABM Defense: Dangerous and Unnecessary," *Arms Control Today* 21 (October 1991): 14, 16-18.

12. *Arms Control Today* 21 (October 1991): 5; Christopher Paine and Thomas B. Cochran, "So Little Time, So Many Weapons, So Much to Do," *Bulletin of the Atomic Scientists* 48 (January-February 1992): 15.

13. Paine and Cochran, "So Little Time," 15-16.

14. Ibid.

15. Paine and Cochran, Kiev Conference, 15-17.

16. Steven M. Kosiak, *Challenges and Opportunities: U.S. Nonproliferation and Counterproliferation Programs in 1996* (1996), 13.

17. Dunbar Lockwood, "Commonwealth Agrees on Unified Command," *Arms Control Today* 22 (January-February 1992): 39, 50.

18. Ibid., Ashton B. Carter, "Reducing the Nuclear Dangers from the Former Soviet Union," *Arms Control Today* 22 (January-February 1992): 10-14.

19. Dunbar Lockwood, "Kiev Summit Leavers Key Military Issues Unresolved," *Arms Control Today* 22 (April 1992): 23.

20. Ibid.

21. Lawrence Scheinman and David A. V. Fischer, "Managing the Coming Glut of Nuclear Weapon Materials," *Arms Control Today* 22 (March 1992): 11.

22. Dunbar Lockwood, "U.S. Security Aid to the Former Soviet Union," *Arms Control Today* 22 (December 1992): 32.

23. Dunbar Lockwood, "Ukraine to Join START and NPT: All Tactical Nukes

Removed," *Arms Control Today* 22 (May 1992): 16, 22.

24. Robert S. Norris, "The Soviet Nuclear Archipelago," *Arms Control Today* 22 (January-February 1992): 25; Lockwood, "Kiev Summit," 23.

25. Lockwood, "Kiev Summit," 23.

26. Steven E. Miller, "The Former Soviet Union," in Mitchell Reiss and Robert S. Litwak, eds., *Nuclear Proliferation after the Cold War* (1994), 104.

27. Dunbar Lockwood, "Chronology of Commonwealth Security Issues," *Arms Control Today* 22 (May 1992): 28.

28. Lockwood, "Ukraine to Join START and NPT," 22. Dunbar Lockwood, "U.S., Four Commonwealth States Sign START Protocol in Lisbon," *Arms Control Today* 22 (June 1992): 18.

29. Dunbar Lockwood, "Senate Ratifies START Agreement; Sets Groundwork for Deeper Cuts," *Arms Control Today* 22 (October 1992): 30, 38.

30. Mitchell Reiss, *Bridled Ambition: Why Countries Constrain Their Nuclear Capabilities* (1995), 101.

31. Lockwood, "Ukraine to Join START and NPT," 22.

32. Dunbar Lockwood, "U.S. Security Aid to the Former Soviet Union," *Arms Control Today* 22 (December 1992): 32.

33. *Public Papers of the Presidents of the United States, George Bush: 1992-93* (1993), 177-181. (Hereafter cited as *BPP: 1992-93*.)

34. Matthew Bunn, "Bush and Yeltsin Press New Nuclear Cutbacks," *Arms Control Today* 22 (January-February 1992): 38, 48-49.

35. Ibid.

36. Ibid.

37. Ibid.

38. Ibid.

39. Matthew Bunn, "Yeltsin Suggests Joint Missile Defense," *Arms Control Today* 22 (January-February 1992): 38, 48-49.

40. Bunn, "Bush and Yeltsin Press New Nuclear Cutbacks," 49.

41. Dunbar Lockwood, "Baker, Kozyrev Discuss Deep Cuts," *Arms Control Today* 22 (March 1992): 21.

42. James A. Baker III, *The Politics of Diplomacy: Revolution, War, and Peace, 1989-1992* (1995), 669 (italics are Baker's).

43. Ibid.

44. Ibid., 669-670.

45. Yeltsin is quoted in Matthew Bunn, "Bush-Yeltsin Summit Brings Deep New Strategic Arms Cuts," *Arms Control Today* 22 (June 1992): 26.

46. *BPP: 1992-93*, 994-996; Baker, *Politics of Diplomacy*, 671.

47. Baker, *Politics of Diplomacy*, 670-671.

48. Bunn, "Bush-Yeltsin Summit," 17, 26-27.

49. Ibid.

50. Ibid.

51. Ibid.

52. Ibid.; for a text of the START II Treaty, see http://www.acda.gov.

53. Lockwood, "Senate Ratifies START," 30, 38; "START II: New Thinking in an Era of

Nuclear Cooperation," *Arms Control Today* 22 (December 1992): 3-9; Dunbar Lockwood, "Strategic Nuclear Forces Under START II," *Arm Control Today* 22 (December 1992): 10-14.

54. Ibid.

55. David Albright and Mark Hibbs, "Iraq's Bomb: Blueprints and Artifacts," *Bulletin of the Atomic Scientists* 48 (January-February 1992): 31; David Albright and Robert Kelley, "Has Iraq Come Clean at Last?" *Bulletin of the Atomic Scientists* 50 (November-December 1995): 53-63; Khidir Hanza, "Inside Saddam's Secret Nuclear Program," *Bulletin of the Atomic Scientists* 54 (September-October 1998); *New York Times*, August 15, 1998.

56. Jon Wolfsthal, "Nonproliferation Roundup: Two Steps Forward, One Step Back," *Arms Control Today* (July-August 1991): 25-26, 31.

57. Michael Klare, *Rogue States and Nuclear Outlaws: America's Search for a New Foreign Policy* (1994): 173.

58. David Albright and Mark Hibbs, "India's Silent Bomb," *Bulletin of the Atomic Scientists* 48 (September 1992): 27-31.

59. Ashok Kapur, "Western Biases," *Bulletin of the Atomic Scientists* 51 (January-February 1995): 38.

60. Jon B. Wolfsthal, "South Africa Joins NPT, North Korea Stonewalls," *Arms Control Today* 21 (October 1991): 34.

61. Wyn Q. Bowen, "U.S. Policy on Ballistic Missile Proliferation: The MTCR's First Decade (1987-1997), *Nonproliferation Review* 5 (Fall 1997): 26-30.

62. Ibid., 27, 30-36.

63. Ibid.

64. Klare, *Rogue States*, 198.

65. Dunbar Lockwood, "Bush Opposition to Test Ban under Increasing Pressure," *Arms Control Today* 22 (June 1992): 25.

66. Dunbar Lockwood, "Few Changes Actually Planned," *Arms Control Today* 22 (July-August 1992): 26.

66. Ibid.

68. Spurgeon M. Keeny Jr., "The Twilight of Nuclear Testing," *Arms Control Today* 22 (September 1992): 2.

69. *Washington Post*, August 4, 1992.

70. Charles N. Van Doren, "Prognosis for the Fourth NPT Review Conference," *Arms Control Today* 20 (June 1990): 19-21.

71. Tom Zamora Collina, "Nuclear Weapons Take a Dive," *Bulletin of the Atomic Scientists*, 48 (November 1992), 6.

72. Dunbar Lockwood, "Congress OKs $274 Billion Defense Budget 2.4 Percent Off Bush Request," *Arms Control Today* 22 (October 1992): 32-33, 40.

Chapter 5

1. Dunbar Lockwood, "On Clinton's Calendar," *Bulletin of the Atomic Scientists* 49 (January-February 1993): 6-8.

2. Ibid., 7; Jon B. Wolfsthal, "President Clinton Unveils New Non-Proliferation, Export Policies," *Arms Control Today* 23 (November 1993): 22; *Public Papers of the*

Presidents of the United States: William J. Clinton: 1993 (1994), 2: 1612-1618. (Hereafter this work is cited as *CPP*, followed by the year of the volume.)

3. John Deni, "Chronology of U.S.-Soviet-cis Nuclear Relations," *Arms Control Today* 14 (June 1994): 33.

4. Ibid.

5. Craig Cerniello, "Ukraine Completes Final Transfer of Nuclear Warheads to Russia," *Arms Control Today* 24 (May-June 1996): 22.

6. Dunbar Lockwood, "START I Enters into Force, Clears Way for START II Approval," *Arms Control Today* 25 (January-February 1995): 19, 26.

7. John Isaacs, "The Senate's Fits and START," *Bulletin of the Atomic Scientists* 52 (March-April 1996): 13-14.

8. Ibid.

9. John W. R. Lepingwell, "Is START Stalling?" in George Quester, ed., *The Nuclear Challenge in Russia and the New States* (1995), 113.

10. *Washington Post*, March 16, 1998.

11. Lepingwell, "Is START Stalling?" 111-113.

12. *New York Times*, March 20, 1998.

13. *New York Times*, February 5, 1997.

14. A text of the "Founding Act on Mutual Relations, Cooperation, and Security Between NATO and the Russian Federation" appears in Jack Mendelsohn, "The NATO-Russian Founding Act," *Arms Control Today* 27 (May 1997): 19-24; *New York Times*, July 31, 1997.

15. Anatol Lieven, "A New Iron Curtain," *Atlantic Monthly* 277 (January 1996): 20-25.

16. David Raikow, "SDIO Changes Its Letterhead to BMDO," *Arms Control Today* 23 (June 1993): 31; Spurgeon Keeny Jr., "A New Threat to the ABM Treaty: The Administration's TMD Program," *Arms Control Today* 24 (January 1994): 11.

17. U.S. Department of Defense, *Annual Report to the President and the Congress* (1994), 51.

18. Steven M. Kosiak, *Challenges and Opportunities: U.S. Nonproliferation and Counterproliferation Programs in 1996* (1996): 26-27; John Pike and Marcus Corbin, "Taking Aim at the ABM Treaty: THAAD and U.S. Security," *Arms Control Today* 25 (May 1995): 3-8.

19. Pike and Corbin, "Taking Aim," 3.

20. John Pike, "Theater Missile Defense Programs: Status and Prospects," *Arms Control Today* 24 (September 1994): 11-14.

21. Dunbar Lockwood, "Senators Appear Skeptical of ABM Treaty Modifications," *Arms Control Today* 24 (April 1994): 17. For a text of the ABM Treaty, see U.S. Arms Control and Disarmament Agency, *Documents on Disarmament, 1972* (1973), 197-217.

22. Pike and Corbin, "Taking Aim." 5.

23. Lockwood, "Senators Appear Skeptical," 17.

24. Dunbar Lockwood, "Administration Moves Unilaterally to Begin Testing THAAD System," *Arms Control Today* 25 (January-February 1995): 26.

25. Dunbar Lockwood, "U.S. Rejects Moscow's Proposal to Limit ATBM Interceptor

Speeds," *Arms Control Today* 24 (May 1994): 19.

26. Stanley A. Riveles, "The Treaty Is Safe," *Bulletin of the Atomic Scientists* 52 (January-February 1996): 27; Rodney Jones and Nikolai N. Sokov, "After Helsinki, the Hard Work," *Bulletin of the Atomic Scientists* 48 (July-August 1997): 26-27; "Joint Statement Concerning the Antiballistic Missile Treaty," *Arms Control Today* 27 (March 1997): 20.

27. Sarah Walking, "U.S., Russia Near Agreement on Lower-Velocity TMD Systems," *Arms Control Today* 26 (July 1996): 19.

28. Ibid.

29. Ibid.

30. Ibid., 19, 27.

31. Ibid.

32. Craig Cerniello, "U.S., Russia Cancel Signing of TMD `Demarcation' Agreement," *Arms Control Today* 26 (October 1996): 20.

33. "Joint Statement Concerning the Antiballistic Missile Treaty," 20.

34. Jack Mendelsohn and Craig Cerniello, "The Arms Control Agenda at the Helsinki Summit," *Arms Control Today* 27 (March 1997): 18.

35. Ibid, 27.

36. Craig Cerniello, "SCC Parties Clear Final Hurdle for ABM-TMD `Demarcation' Accords," *Arms Control Today* 27 (August 1997): 20.

37. Andrew Koch, "New Year's TMD Troubles," *Weekly Defense Monitor*, February 5, 1998; http://www.cdi.org.

38. Ibid.

39. John Isaacs, "Cold Warriors Target Arms Control," *Arms Control Today* 25 (September 1995): 3.

40. Ibid.

41. Ibid.

42. Joseph Cirincione, "Why the Right Lost the Missile Defense Debate," *Foreign Policy* 106 (Spring 1997): 39-56.

43. Ibid., 39.

44. Craig Cerniello, "Push for National Missile Defense Stalled by CBO Report on Costs," *Arms Control Today* 26 (May-June 1996), 23.

45. Cirincione, "Why the Right Lost," 39.

46. Ibid., 39-42.

47. Ibid., 45.

48. Ibid., 48.

49. Ibid., 49.

50. Ibid., 49-50.

51. Ibid., 52-53; Craig Cerniello, "Clinton BMD Program Reorientation," *Arms Control Today* 26 (March 1996): 22.

52. Ibid.

53. Cirincione, "Why the Right Lost," 44.

54. Ibid., 45.

55. Craig Cerniello, "NMD Debate in Congress Heats Up," *Arms Control Today* 26 (January-February 1997): 21.

56. Craig Cerniello, "Senate Committee Approves NMD Bill," *Arms Control Today* 26 (April 1997): 38.
57. Craig Cerniello, "Panel Criticizes U.S. 'Rush' to Deploy Missile Defense Systems," *Arms Control Today* 28 (March 1998): 20; Andrew Koch, "Dangerous Missile Defense," *Weekly Defense Monitor*, March 26, 1998, http://www.cdi.org.
58. *New York Times*, July 20, 1998; Richard L. Garwin, "What We Did," *Bulletin of the Atomic Scientists* 54 (November-December, 1998). For an executive summary of the Rumsfeld Report, see Federation of American Scientists' Website, http://www.fas.org/irp/threat/bm-threat.htm.
59. Craig Cerniello, "NMD Bill Stalled in Senate," *Arms Control Today*, August-September, 1998.
60. Ibid.
61. *Washington Post*, March 15, 1998.
62. *Washington Post*, March 15, 1998; Sami Fournier, "U.S. Test-Fires 'MIRACL' at Satellite Reigniting ASAT Weapons Debate," *Arms Control Today* 27 (October 1997): 30.
63. Fournier, "U.S. Test Fires," 30.
64. *Washington Post*, March 15, 1998.
65. Ibid; Andrew Koch, "Taking Nuclear Weapons Off Alert," *Weekly Defense Monitor*, January 22, 1998; http://www.cdi.org.
66. *New York Times*, September 2, 1998.
67. Koch, "Taking Nuclear Weapons Off Alert."
68. *Washington Post*, March 16, 1998.
69. Koch, "Taking Nuclear Weapons Off Alert."
70. *Washington Post*, March 15, 1998.
71. *Washington Post*, March 16, 1998.
72. *Washington Post*, March 16, 1998.
73. *Washington Post*, March 16, 1998.
74. *Washington Post*, May 14, 1998.
75. *Washington Post*, May 14, 1998.
76. *Washington Post*, March 16, 1998.
77. *Washington Post*, December 25, 1997; May 14, 1998.
78. *Washington Post*, December 25, 1997.
79. Robert Bell, "Strategic Agreements and the CTB Treaty: Striking the Right Balance," *Arms Control Today* 28 (January-February 1998): 3-10.
80. Spurgeon M. Keeny Jr., "Advancing the Arms Control Agenda: Pitfalls and Possibilities," *Arms Control Today* 28 (January-February 1998): 11-19.
81. Ibid.

Chapter 6

1. Jon B. Wolfsthal, "President Clinton Unveils New Non-Proliferation, Export Policies," *Arms Control Today* 23 (November 1993): 22.
2. Joseph Cirincione, "Third Prep Com Highlights Uncertainties: NPT Showdown Ahead," *Arms Control Today* 24 (December 1994): 3.
3. Wolfgang K. H. Panofsky and George Bunn, "The Doctrine of the Nuclear-

Weapon States and the Future of Non-Proliferation," *Arms Control Today* 24 (July-August 1994): 3.

4. Cirincione, "Third Prep Com Highlights Uncertainties," 3.

5. William Epstein, "Indefinite Extension with Increased Accountability," *Bulletin of the Atomic Scientists* 51 (July-August 1995): 27-29.

6. *New York Times*, January 31, 1995.

7. George Bunn, "Expanding Nuclear Options: Is the U.S. Negating Its Non-Use Pledges? *Arms Control Today* 26 (May-June 1996): 7-10.

8. Robert Bell, "Strategic Agreements and the CTB Treaty: Striking the Right Balance," *Arms Control Today* 28 (January-February 1998): 3-10; George Bunn, "Moving Toward `Legally Binding' Negative Security Assurances," *Arms Control Today* 28 (March 1998): 27.

9. Epstein, "Indefinite Extension," 28-29.

10. William Epstein, "Revolt of the Non-Aligned," *Bulletin of the Atomic Scientists* 52 (March 1996): 39-40.

11. Steve Fetter and Frank Von Hippel, "A Step-By-Step Approach to a Global Fissile Materials Cutoff," *Arms Control Today* 25 (October 1995): 3-8; Oleg Bukharin, "Technical Aspects of Proliferation and Nonproliferation," in George Quester, *The Nuclear Challenge in Russia and the New States of Eurasia* (1995), 51.

12. Dunbar Lockwood, "U.S., Russia Reach Agreement for Plutonium Site Inspections," *Arms Control Today* 24 (April 1994): 22.

13. Fetter and Von Hippel, "Step-by-Step Proposal," 5-8.

14. Tom Zamora Collina, "Cutoff Talks Delayed," *Bulletin of the Atomic Scientists* 51(March 1995): 16-18.

15. Fetter and Von Hippel, "Step-by-Step Proposal," 7-8.

16. "Clinton Removes Fissile Material from Stockpile," *Arms Control Today* 25 (April 1995): 22.

17. Fetter and Von Hippel, "Step-by-Step Proposal," 7-8; Wade Boese, "CD Convenes Committee to Work on Fissile Cutoff," *Arms Control Today* 28 (August-September 1998).

18. Dunbar Lockwood, "Clinton Administration Considers Plan for Resuming Nuclear Tests," *Arms Control Today* 23 (July-August 1993): 20.

19. Frank Von Hippel and Tom Zamora Collina, "Nuclear Junkies: Testing, Testing, 1, 2, 3," *Bulletin of the Atomic Scientists* 49 (July-August 1993): 29.

20. *Public Papers of the Presidents of the United States: William J. Clinton: 1993* (1994), 994-995.

21. "Fifty-one Years of Nuclear Testing:The Final Tally?" *Arms Control Today* 26 (August 1996): 38.

22. Rebecca Johnson, "The In-Comprehensive Test Ban," *Bulletin of the Atomic Scientists* 52 (November-December 1996): 30.

23. Ibid.

24. Frank Von Hippel and Suzanne Jones, "Taking a Hard Look at Subcritical Testing," *Bulletin of the Atomic Scientists* 52 (November-December 1996): 44-45.

25. Ibid.

26. Ibid.
27. Johnson, "In-Comprehensive Test Ban," 30.
28. Ibid.; "The Signing of the Comprehensive Test Ban Treaty," Arms *Control Today* 26 (September 1996): 8-14. For a text of the treaty, see *Arms Control Today* 26 (August 1996): 19-30.
29. *New York Times*, June 2, 1998.
30. "The Issues behind the CTB Treaty Ratification Debate," *Arms Control Today* 27 (October 1997): 6-13.
31. Ibid.; *New York Times*, June 2, 1998.
32. Craig Cerniello, "Clinton Urges Senate to Act on CTB," *Arms Control Today* 28 (January-February 1998): 28, 37.
33. Ibid.
34. Ibid.
35. Michael Klare, *Rogue States and Nuclear Outlaws: America's Search for a New Foreign Policy* (1994), 139-140.
36. *Washington Post*, July 12, 1993; Klare, 126-127.
37. Michael J. Mazarr, *North Korea and the Bomb: A Case Study in Nonproliferation* (1995): 143.
38. Leon V. Sigal, "Who Is Fighting Peace in Korea? An Undiplomatic History," *World Policy Journal* 14 (Summer 1997), 44-58.
39. Ibid.
40. "Agreed Statement between the United States and North Korea," *Arms Control Today* 24 (September 1994): 23.
41. Sigal, "Fighting Peace in Korea," 56-58.
42. Jon B. Wolfthal, "U.S. Korea Nuclear Accord Remains on Track despite Incident," *Arms Control Today* 25 (January-February 1995): 20, 26.
43. *New York Times*, September 23, 1998; January 3, 1999.
44. *New York Times*, September 1, 23, 1998.
45. Evan S. Medeiros, "China, Russia Plan to Go Ahead with Nuclear Reactor Sales to Iran," *Arms Control Today* (May 1995); Gary T. Gardner, *Nuclear Nonproliferation: A Primer* (1994): 101-102.
46. David Albright and Mark Hibbs, "Spotlight Shifts to Iran," *Bulletin of the Atomic Scientists* 48 (March 1992): 10; "Iran, Russia Sign Nuclear Deal Raising Proliferation Concerns," *Arms Control Today* 25 (January-February 1995).
47. Gardner, *Nuclear Nonproliferation*, 102; Andrew Koch and Jeanette Wolf, "Iran's Nuclear Procurement Program: How Close to the Bomb?" *Nonproliferation Review* 5 (Fall 1997): 123-135.
48. Victor Zaborsky, "U.S. Missile Nonproliferation Strategy toward the NIS and China: How Effective?" *Nonproliferation Review* 5 (Fall 1997): 88-94.
49. *Washington Post*, May 29, 1998.
50. Kathleen C. Bailey, *Doomsday Weapons in the Hands of Many: The Arms Control Challenge of the 90s* (1991), 109; *U.S. News and World Report*, February 12, 1996, 42-46.
51. Bailey, *Doomsday Weapons*, 120; Howard Diamond, "U.S. Renews Effort to Bring

China into Missile Control Regime," *Arms Control Today* 28 (March 1998): 22; *Washington Post*, November 11, 1998; Wyn Q. Bowen, "U.S. Policy on Ballistic Missile Proliferation," *Nonproliferation Review* 5 (Fall 1997): 29, 33.

52. Bailey, *Doomsday Weapons*, 109; *Washington Times*, January 22, 1990; Bowen, "Ballistic Missile Proliferation," 33.

53. Howard Diamond, "Russia Issues New Export Decree to Stem Missile Transfers to Iran," *Arms Control Today* 28 (January-February): 31, 34.

54. *Washington Post*, June 17, 1998; *New York Times*, September 1, 23, 1998.

55. *New York Times*, April 27, 1998.

56. *Boston Globe*, June 6, 1998; *U.S. News and World Report*, May 25, 1998, 16-18.

57. Arjun Makhijani, "India's Options," *Bulletin of the Atomic Scientists* 53 (March-April 1997): 51-53; *Washington Post*, May 28, 1998.

58. Praful Bidwai and Achin Vanaik, "After the CTB: India's Intentions," *Bulletin of the Atomic Scientists* 53 (March-April 1997): 49-50; Makhijani, "India's Options," 52.

59. Makhijani, "India's Options," 52.

60. *New York Times*, May 13, 1998; *Bulletin of the Atomic Scientists*, "Current News," May 13, 1998; http://www.bullatomsci.org.

61. *U.S. News & World Report*, May 25, 1998, 16.

62. Gregory van der Vink et al., "False Accusations, Undetected Test and Implications for the CTB Treaty," *Arms Control Today* 28 (May 1998): 4.

63. *Los Angeles Times*, September 25, 1998; *New York Times*, May 28; July 10, 1998.

64. *New York Times*, May 17, 1998.

65. *New York Times*, July 12, 1998; *Washington Post*, June 11, 1998.

66. *New York Times*, September 24-25, 1998; *Los Angeles Times*, September 25, 1998.

67. *New York Times*, September 25, 1998; Van der Vink et al., "False Accusations," 4.

68. *Washington Post*, June 11, 1998.

69. *Washington Post*, October 10, 1998; *New York Times*, August 27, 1998.

70. *New York Times*, August 27, 1998; *Washington Post*, October 12, 1998.

71. *Washington Post*, October 12, 1998.

72. *Washington Post*, December 20, 1998.

73. *Newsweek*, July 12, 1993, 50-51.

74. John Foster, "Nuclear Weapons," *Encyclopedia Americana* 20 (1973), 520-522. U.S. Congress, Subcommittee on European Affairs of the Senate Committee on Foreign Relations, Hearings: *Loose Nukes, Nuclear Smuggling, and the Fissile Material Problem in Russia and the NIS*, 100th Cong., 1st sess. (1995), 100. (Hereafter cited as Hearings: *Loose Nukes*)

75. Phil Williams and Paul N. Woessner, "The Real Threat of Nuclear Smuggling," *Scientific American* 274 (January 1996): 40-44; James E. Doyle, "Improving Nuclear Materials Security in the Former Soviet Union," *Arms Control Today* 28 (March 1998): 12; James Baker, "Coping with the New 'Clear and Present Danger' from Russia," *Arms Control Today* 25 (April 1995): 13-16.

76. William H. Webster, *The Nuclear Black Market: Global Organized Crime Project* (1996).

77. Dale R. Herspring, "Russia's Crumbling Military," *Current History* 97 (October 1998): 325-328.
78. Jack F. Matlock Jr., "Russia's Leaky Nukes," *New York Review of Books*, February 5, 1998, 15; *Washington Post*, March 16, 1998.
79. Evan S. Medeiros, "Senate Hearings Focus Spotlight on `Real' Threat of Nuclear Smuggling," *Arms Control Today* 26 (March 1996): 24; *New York Times*, September 30, 1996.
80. Rensselaer W. Lee III, "Post-Soviet Nuclear Trafficking: Myths, Half-truths, and the Reality," *Current History* 94 (October 1995): 343-348; *New York Times*, September 30, 1998.
81. Webster, *Nuclear Black Market*, 18; Lee, "Post-Soviet Nuclear Trafficking," 345; Rensselaer W. Lee III, "Smuggling Update," *Bulletin of the Atomic Scientists* 53 (May-June 1997): 11-14.
82. Williams and Woessner, "Real Threat," 43.
83. Hearings: *Loose Nukes*, 75.
84. Ibid., 79.
85. *Nuclear Black Market*, 15.
86. Hearings: *Loose Nukes*, 83-84.
87. Ibid., 108.
88. *New York Times*, March 12, 1998.
89. Doyle, "Improving Nuclear Materials Security," 13.
90. *New York Times*, September 2, 1998.
91. Jason D. Ellis and Todd Perry, "Nunn Lugar's Unfinished Agenda," *Arms Control Today* 27 (October 1997): 14-22.
92. Doyle, "Improving Nuclear Materials Security," 12-14, 18.
93. Ibid., 18.
94. Ellis and Perry, "Nunn Lugar," 19.
95. Williams and Woessner, "Real Threat," 44.

Conclusion

1. *Public Papers of the Presidents of the United States: Ronald W. Reagan, 1988-1989* (1991), 1636.
2. Kenneth L. Adelman, "United States and Soviet Relations: Reagan's Real Role in Winning the Cold War," in Eric J. Schmertz, Natalie Datlof, and Alexej Ugrinsky, eds., *President Reagan and the World* (1997), 81-90.
3. George Shultz, *Turmoil and Triumph: My Years as Secretary of State* (1993) 159-162.
4. Forrest Waller, "Strategic Offensive Arms Control," in Jeffrey A. Larsen and Gregory J. Rattray, eds., *Arms Control: Toward the 21st Century* (1996), 110.

Suggested Readings

A valuable collection of public documents (unfortunately discontinued in 1985) is U.S. Arms Control and Disarmament Agency, *Documents on Disarmament*, 1981-1985 (1982-1986). Another important collection of documents is Christopher Simpson, ed., *National Security Directives of the Reagan and Bush Administrations: The Declassified History of U.S. Political and Military Policy, 1981-1991* (1995).

Among the more important memoirs of the Reagan years are Ronald W. Reagan, *An American Life* (1990); Alexander M. Haig Jr., *Caveat: Realism, Reagan, and Foreign Policy* (1984); George Shultz, *Turmoil and Triumph: My Years as Secretary of State* (1990); Robert McFarlane, *Special Trust* (1994); Caspar Weinberger, *Fighting for Peace* (1990); and Martin Anderson, *Revolution* (1988).

Among the best secondary sources dealing with Reagan's military policies is Daniel Wirls, *Buildup: The Politics of Defense in the Reagan Era* (1992).

For the Strategic Defense Initiative, see Donald R. Baucom, *The Origins of* SDI, *1944-1983* (1992); Kerry L. Hunter, *The Reign of Fantasy: The Political Roots of Reagan's Star Wars Policy* (1997); Sanford Lakoff and Herbert F. York, *A Shield in Space? Technology, Politics, and the Strategic Defense Initiative* (1989); Rebecca Bjork, *The Strategic Defense Initiative: Symbolic Containment of the Nuclear Threat* (1992).

For Reagan's efforts to revise the ABM Treaty, see Raymond L. Garthoff, *Policy versus the Law: The Reinterpretation of the* ABM *Treaty* (1987); Matthew Bunn, *Foundation for the Future: The* ABM *Treaty and National Security* (1990). For a related topic, see Allan Girrier and Catherine Girrier, *American Policy and Alleged Soviet Treaty Violations* (1987).

Among the best secondary accounts dealing with nuclear arms control during the Reagan years are Keith L. Shimko, *Images and Arms Control: Perceptions of the Soviet Union in the Reagan Administration* (1991); Michael Mandelbaum and Strobe Talbott, *Reagan and Gorbachev* (1987); Strobe Talbott, *Deadly Gambits: The Reagan Adminis-*

tration and the Stalemate in Nuclear Arms Control (1983); and his *Master of the Game: Paul Nitze and the Nuclear Peace* (1988). See also Jeffrey A. Larsen and Gregory J. Rattray, eds., *Arms Control toward the 21st Century* (1996); Robert Travis Scott, ed., *The Race for Security: Arms and Arms Control in the Reagan Years* (1987); Michael Krepon, *Arms Control in the Reagan Administration* (1989); George L. Rueckert, *Global Double Zero: The* INF *Treaty from Its Origins to Implementation* (1993); Beth A. Fischer, *Reversal: Foreign Policy and the End of the Cold War* (1997); and Seweryn Bialer and Michael Mandelbaum, eds., *Gorbachev's Russia and American Foreign Policy* (1988).

The most important memoirs of the Bush administration to appear so far are George Bush and Brent Scowcroft, *A World Transformed* (1998), and James A. Baker III, *The Politics of Diplomacy* (1995).

A highly readable account of Bush's Soviet diplomacy is Michael R. Beschloss and Strobe Talbott, *At the Highest Levels: The Inside Story of the Cold War* (1993). See also Raymond L. Garthoff, *The Great Transition: American-Soviet Relations and the End of the Cold War* (1994); Joseph G. Whelan, *Soviet Diplomacy and Negotiating Behavior, 1988-90: Gorbachev-Reagan, Bush Meetings at the Summit* (1991).

For Soviet nuclear policy, see George E. Hudson, ed, *Soviet National Security Policy under Perestroika* (1990).

One of the first memoirs to emerge from the Clinton administration is Warren Christopher, *In the Stream of History: Shaping Foreign Policy for a New Era* (1998).

For the Clinton administration's policies, see Stephen Cimbala, ed., *Clinton and Post-Cold War Defense* (1996); Eric Arnett, ed., *Nuclear Weapons after the Comprehensive Test Ban: Implications for Modernization and Proliferation* (1996).

For a recent collection of essays on nuclear weapon doctrine, see T.V. Paul, Richard J. Harknett, and James J. Wirtz, eds., *The Absolute Weapon Revisited: Nuclear Arms and the Emerging International Order* (1998); and Michael J. Mazarr, ed., *Nuclear Weapons in a Transformed World* (1997).

For more specialized topics, see Bruce G. Blair, *The Logic of Accidental Nuclear War* (1993); Bruce G. Blair, *Global Zero Alert for Nuclear Forces* (1995); Scott D. Sagan, *The Limits of Safety: Organizations, Accidents, and Nuclear Weapons* (1993).

For the problem of horizontal nuclear proliferation, see Leonard S. Spector, *The Undeclared Bomb* (1988); Mitchell Reiss and Robert S. Litwak, eds., *Nuclear Proliferation after the Cold War* (1994); Mitchell Reiss, *Bridled Ambition: Why Countries Constrain Their Nuclear Capabilities* (1995); Michael Klare, *Rogue States and Nuclear Outlaws: America's Search for a New Foreign Policy* (1994); and Kathleen C. Bailey, *Doomsday Weapons in the Hands of Many: The Arms Control Challenge of the 90s* (1991).

The problem of securing former Soviet nuclear weapons is discussed in William Webster, *The Nuclear Black Market: Global Organized Crime Project* (1996); George Quester, ed., *The Nuclear Challenge in Russia and the New States* (1995); and Graham T. Allison, Owen R. Coté Jr., Richard A. Falkenrath, and Steven E. Miller, eds., *Avoiding Nuclear Anarchy: Containing the Threat of Loose Russian Nuclear Weapons and Fissile Material* (1998).

For background on the NPT and the nuclear nonproliferation regime, see Jozef Goldblat, *Twenty Years of the Non-Proliferation Treaty: Implementation and Prospects* (1990); Gary T. Gardner, *Nuclear Nonproliferation: A Primer* (1994); Andrew Latham, ed., *Non-Proliferation Agreements, Arrangements, and Responses* (1997); Robert D. Blackwill and Albert Carnesale, eds., *New Nuclear Nations: Consequences for U.S. Policy* (1993); and Steven M. Kosiak, *Nonproliferation-Counterproliferation: Investing for a Safer World?* (1995).

The growing ballistic missile threat is covered in Aaron Karp, *Emerging Ballistic Missile Threat to the United States* (1993); William C. Potter and Harlan W. Jencks, eds., *The International Missile Bazaar* (1994).

Three periodicals dealing with nuclear arms control issues and containing the texts of documents and extensive bibliographies are *Arms Control Today*, the *Bulletin of the Atomic Scientists*, and the *Nonproliferation Review*.

See also William M. Arkin and Robert Norris, *The Internet and the Bomb: A Research Guide to Policy and Information about Nuclear Weapons* (1997).

Index

287

LaVergne, TN USA
02 March 2011
218471LV00002B/25/A